Indian Political Thought

'In our time of globalization, people in the West are increasingly looking beyond the limits of the West for insights and teachings. It is very important and fascinating to find out what is happening today in India in terms of political philosophy. This *Reader* is timely and very much needed as there is simply no comparable text available. The group of texts presented bring together simply the most outstanding and most well known Indian political thinkers today. It is in fact a 'who's who' in contemporary Indian political thought.'

Fred Dallmayr, Notre Dame University, US

'A significant attempt to construct a foundational text for contemporary Indian political thought, this volume meets a deeply felt need. Singh and Mohapatra have put together a first-rate *Reader* that will challenge, educate and provoke. It will serve as an indispensible source of reference to students and teachers alike.'

Shashi Tharoor, former Under-Secretary General of the United Nations

This *Reader* provides a comprehensive introduction to the study of contemporary Indian political theory. Tracing the development of the discipline and offering a clear presentation of the most influential literature in the field, it brings together contributions by outstanding and well-known academics on contemporary Indian political thought. The *Reader* weaves together relevant works from the social sciences – sociology, anthropology, law, history, philosophy, and feminist and postcolonial theory – which shape the nature of political thought in India today. Themes both unique to the Indian political milieu as well as of universal significance are reflected upon, including tradition, secularism, communalism, modernity, feminism, justice and human rights.

Presenting a canon of names and offering a framework for further research within the broad thematic categories, this is a timely and invaluable reference tool, indispensable to both students and scholars.

Aakash Singh is Research Professor at the Center for Ethics and Global Politics, Luiss University, Italy. His scholarly interests range from comparative political philosophy to liberation theology and applied critical theory.

Silika Mohapatra is Research Scholar in the Department of Philosophy at the University of Delhi, India and currently Visiting Researcher at the Department of Philosophy, University of Ottawa, Canada. Her research interests include classical metaphysics, phenomenology, and the ethics of self and society.

Indian Political Thought
A reader

Aakash Singh and Silika Mohapatra

Routledge
Taylor & Francis Group

LONDON AND NEW YORK

First published 2010
by Routledge
2 Park Square, Milton Park, Abingdon, Oxon OX14 4RN

Simultaneously published in the USA and Canada
by Routledge
270 Madison Ave, New York, NY 10016

Routledge is an imprint of the Taylor & Francis Group, an informa business
© 2010 Aakash Singh and Silika Mohapatra

Typeset in TimesNewRoman by Taylor & Francis Books
Printed and bound in Great Britain by T. J. International, Padstow, Cornwall

British Library Cataloguing in Publication Data
A catalogue record for this book is available from the British Library

Library of Congress Cataloging in Publication Data
Indian political thought : a reader / [edited by] Aakash Singh and Silika Mohapatra.
p. cm.
Includes bibliographical references and index.
1. Political science–India–Philosophy. 2. Politics and culture–India. 3. Political customs
and rites–India. 4. India–Politics and government. I. Singh, Aakash. II. Mohapatra,
Silika.
JA84.I4I525 2010
320.0954–dc22
2009039415

ISBN13: 978-0-415-56293-5 (hbk)
ISBN13: 978-0-415-56294-2 (pbk)
ISBN13: 978-0-203-85494-5 (ebk)

Contents

Acknowledgements

The editors must first convey profound gratitude to each of the individual contributors for their cooperation and encouragement. We also would like to gratefully acknowledge their publishers for permission to use the articles that have appeared before. Several of these texts have been modified or abridged, sometimes by the author, sometimes by the editors, sometimes by both – always reluctantly, of course, but with due permission, as noted at the start of each chapter. We would also like to acknowledge Dorothea Schaefter from Routledge for the enthusiasm she showed from the beginning of this project, and the skill she showed till the end.

Aakash Singh would like to thank his colleagues at the Center for Ethics and Global Politics, Luiss University, Rome, who have all been eager to see me finish this book so that I would get back to work. Sebastiano Maffettone deserves to be singled out for his unrelenting support. Also, Daniele, Gaia, Gianfranco, Raf, and Vale for their friendship. As much of this collaborative volume that I may lay some claim to – alas, not much – I dedicate to my wife, Devyani, and our beautiful daughters, Amaya and Shaira.

Silika Mohapatra is indebted to the space–time matrices that made this volume possible. Teachers for leading the muse, spirited conversations, inspiration. Friends for riding thoughts, sincere conviction and endearing moments. It is impossible to imagine this work without their constant support, silent or articulated. To my sister, Rimina, for our innumerable expeditions. To Mom and Papa for all that is and can be. This is for them.

About the editors

Aakash Singh (a.k.a. Aakash Singh Rathore) is Research Professor, Center for Ethics and Global Politics, Luiss University of Rome, Italy. He is author of *Eros Turannos* (2005), editor/translator of a French edition of Maulana Azad's *India Wins Freedom* (2006) and co-editor of a Critical Edition of B. R. Ambedkar's *The Buddha and His Dhamma* (forthcoming). He co-edited *Discoursing the Postsecular: Essays on Habermas's Postsecular Turn* (2010); *From Political Theory to Political Theology* (2010); *Reading Hegel: The Introductions* (2008); and *Buddhism and the Contemporary World – An Ambedkarian Perspective* (2007). His forthcoming books from Routledge include *Wronging Rights? Philosophical Challenges for Human Rights* and *Global Justice: Deparochializing the Debate*.

Silika Mohapatra is Research Scholar at the Department of Philosophy, University of Delhi, India and currently Visiting Researcher at the Department of Philosophy, University of Ottawa, Canada. She studied Philosophy at St Stephen's College, Delhi. Her research interests include classical metaphysics, phenomenology, and ethics of self and society. Her postgraduate dissertation was entitled 'Deconstructing Selfhood'. She is the recipient of the Indian Philosophical Congress Medal (2009), The Sumitomo–St Stephen's College Scholarship (2004–7) among other awards. She was Research Coordinator for 'An Inquiry into the Philosophical Foundation of Gandhi's Notion of Truth and Non-Violence' (2006–7), a joint research project by Posco TJ Park Foundation, Korea and St Stephen's College, Delhi.

Contributors

Akeel Bilgrami is Johnsonian Professor of Philosophy at Columbia University, and the Director of the Heyman Center for the Humanities. He has an abiding interest in issues of political philosophy and moral psychology especially as they surface in politics, history, and culture. He is the author of *Belief and Meaning* (1992), *Self-Knowledge and Resentment* (2006), and *Politics and the Moral Psychology of Identity* (forthcoming).

Amartya Sen is an economist, philosopher, and winner of the 1998 Nobel Prize in Economic Sciences for his contributions to welfare economics. He is currently Lamont University Professor, and Professor of Economics and Philosophy, at Harvard University. From 1998 to 2004 he was Master of Trinity College at Cambridge University. Among his many books are *The Argumentative Indian* (2005), *Inequality Reexamined* (2004) and *Development as Freedom* (1999). His books have been translated into more than 30 languages.

Ashis Nandy is a political psychologist and influential social theorist. He is Senior Fellow at the Centre for the Study of Developing Societies, Delhi. He has been a Woodrow Wilson Fellow at the Wilson Center, Washington DC, a Charles Wallace Fellow at the University of Hull, and a Fellow of the Institute for Advanced Studies in Humanities, University of Edinburgh. Among his numerous writings are *Traditions, Tyranny, and Utopias: Essays in the Politics of Awareness* (1987), *The Illegitimacy of Nationalism: Rabindranath Tagore and the Politics of Self* (1994), *Creating a Nationality: The Ramjanmabhumi Movement and Fear of the Self* (1996).

Bhikhu Parekh is Professor of Political Philosophy at the University of Westminster. His main academic interests include political philosophy, ancient and modern Indian political thought, and the philosophy of ethnic relations. He is author of *Rethinking Multiculturalism: Cultural Diversity and Political Theory* (2000); *Gandhi* (2001); *Colonialism, Tradition and Reform* (1999); and, *Gandhi's Political Philosophy* (1989). He is the recipient of the Sir Isaiah Berlin Prize for lifetime contribution to political philosophy by the Political Studies Association (2002); the Distinguished Global Thinker Award by the India International Centre, Delhi (2006); and in 2007 was awarded the Padma Bhushan.

Dilip M. Menon is Professor of History and Chair in Indian Studies at the University of Witwatersrand, Johannesburg. He works on the social and cultural history of modern India and has published *Caste, Nationalism and Communism in South India, 1900–1948* (1994) and *The Blindness of Insight: Essays on Caste in Modern India*

(2006). He is currently finishing a manuscript titled 'The Uses of History: Historical Imagination and Colonial Cosmopolitanism In South India, 1850–1960'.

Gayatri Chakravorty Spivak is University Professor and the Director of the Institute for Comparative Literature and Society at Columbia University. Her books include *In Other Worlds: Essays in Cultural Politics* (1987), *Selected Subaltern Studies* (ed. 1988), *The Post-Colonial Critic: Interviews, Strategies, Dialogues* (1990), *Thinking Academic Freedom in Gendered Post-Coloniality* (1993). Her translator's introduction to Derrida's *Of Grammatology* has been described as 'setting a new standard for self-reflexivity'. Her significant articles include 'Subaltern Studies: Deconstructing Historiography' (1985), 'Three Women's Texts and a Critique of Imperialism (1985), 'Can the Subaltern Speak? (1988), 'The Politics of Translation' (1992), and 'Righting Wrongs' (2003).

Gyan Prakash is Dayton-Stockton Professor of History at Princeton University. He specializes in the history of colonial India, and his research and teaching interests include the relationship between colonialism and production of knowledge. He is the author of *Bonded Histories: Genealogies of Labor Servitude in Colonial India* (1990), and his publications include the edited volume, *After Colonialism: Imperial Histories and Postcolonial Displacements* (1995). His more recent book, *Another Reason: Science and the Imagination of Modern India* (1999), explores the historical composition and functioning of science's cultural authority in colonial and postcolonial India.

Harjot Oberoi teaches South Asian History at the University of British Columbia. He has a long-standing interest in the formation of religious identities in modern India. For his research work he has been awarded numerous prizes, including the Best First Book Prize by the American Academy of Religion for his book *The Construction of Religious Boundaries*, the Crawford Prize and the Killam Prize.

Homi K. Bhabha is Anne F. Rothenberg Professor of the Humanities, Department of English, Harvard University, and Director of the Humanities Center at Harvard. His book, *Location of Culture,* has recently been reprinted as a Routledge Classic and has been translated into Korean, Spanish, Italian, Slovenian, German, Arabic, and Portuguese. His 1990 book, *Nation and Narration*, has also been formative for postcolonial studies.

Meera Nanda is a philosopher of science with initial training in biology. She has received research fellowships from the American Council of Learned Societies and the John Templeton Foundation, USA. She is a visiting fellow at the Jawaharlal Institute of Advanced Studies, JNU, New Delhi for 2009–10, and author of the award-winning book, *Prophets Facing Backward: Postmodernism, Science and Hindu Nationalism*. Other books include: *The God Market: How Globalization is Making India More Hindu* (2009) and *Tryst with Destiny: Scientific Temper and Secularism in India* (forthcoming).

Mushirul Hasan is former Vice-Chancellor of Jamia Millia Islamia, Delhi. He has previously been Professor of Modern Indian History at JMI; Professorial Fellow at Nehru Memorial Museum and Library, New Delhi; Fellow, Wissenschaftskolleg, Berlin; and Visiting Scholar at the University of Cambridge. He was awarded Padma Shri in 2007. Among his recent publications are *A Moral Reckoning: Muslim*

Intellectuals in Nineteenth Century Delhi (2005) and *From Pluralism to Separatism: Qasbas in Colonial Awadh* (2004).

Neera Chandhoke is Professor of Political Science, and Director of the Developing Countries Research Centre, University of Delhi. Her main teaching and research interests are political theory, comparative politics, and the politics of developing societies with special focus on India. She has authored *The Conceits of Civil Society* (2003), *Beyond Secularism: The Rights of Religious Minorities* (1999), and *State and Civil Society: Explorations in Political Theory* (1995), and has edited *Mapping Histories* (2000), *Grass-Roots Politics and Social Transformation* (1999), and *Understanding The Post-Colonial World* (1995).

Partha Chatterjee is Professor of Political Science at the Centre for Studies in Social Sciences, Kolkata, and a Visiting Professor in Anthropology at Columbia University. He is actively engaged in the collective project of Subaltern Studies. His publications include *Nationalist Thought and the Colonial World* (1986), *The Nation and its Fragments* (1993), *Texts of Power* (1995), *A Possible India* (1997), *The Present History of West Bengal* (1997), *A Princely Impostor? The Strange and Universal History of the Kumar of Bhawal* (2003), and *The Politics of the Governed: Popular Politics in Most of the World* (2004).

Rajeev Bhargava is Senior Fellow at the Centre for the Study of Developing Societies, New Delhi. He was formerly a Professor at the University of Delhi and JNU, Visiting Fellow at Harvard University and the British Academy, a Leverhulme fellow at the University of Bristol, Senior Fellow at the Institute of Advanced Studies at Jerusalem and Distinguished Resident Scholar at Columbia University. His publications include *Individualism in Social Science* (1992); among his edited works are *Secularism and its Critics* (1998), *Multiculturalism, Liberalism and Democracy* (1999), *Transforming India* (2000), and *Politics and Ethics of the Indian Constitution* (2008).

Ramachandra Guha is a well-known historian and columnist with *The Telegraph*. His books include a pioneering environmental history, *The Unquiet Woods*, and an award-winning social history of cricket, *A Corner of a Foreign Field*. His most recent book is *India after Gandhi: The History of the World's Largest Democracy*, which was chosen as the Book of the Year by the *Economist*, the *Washington Post*, the *Wall Street Journal*, the *San Francisco Chronicle*, *Time Out*, and *Outlook*. In May 2008, *Prospect* and *Foreign Policy* magazines nominated Ramachandra Guha as one of the world's 100 most influential intellectuals.

Ratna Kapur is Director, Centre for Feminist Legal Research, New Delhi, and also teaches at the Geneva School of Diplomacy and International Relations. A practising lawyer in India, she has also served as a visiting scholar at Cambridge and Harvard universities, and was recently the Bertha Wilson Visiting Professor in Human Rights at Dalhousie Law School, Halifax, Canada. She is author of *Erotic Justice: Law and the New Politics of Postcolonialism* (2005), co-author of *Subversive Sites: Feminist Engagements with Law* (1996), *Secularism's Last Sigh? Hindutva and the (Mis)Rule of Law* (2001), and editor of *Feminist Terrains in Legal Domains: Interdisciplinary Essays on Women and Law* (1996).

Romila Thapar is Professor Emeritus of History at Jawaharlal Nehru University, New Delhi. She was Distinguished Visiting Professor at Cornell University and Visiting

Professor at the University of California, Berkeley, University of Pennsylvania and University of Beijing. She has written several books, including *Asoka and the Decline of the Mauryas* (1961), *A History of India* (1966), *Cultural Pasts: Essays in Early Indian History* (2003), *Early India: From Origins to AD 1300* (2002), *History and Beyond* (2000), and *India: Another Millennium?* (2000).

Sudipta Kaviraj is Professor, South Asian Politics, at Columbia University. Formerly he was Professor in Politics at the School of Oriental and African Studies at the University of London; Associate Professor of Political Science at JNU, New Delhi; and Visiting Fellow at St. Antony's College, Oxford. He was a founding member of the Subaltern Studies Collective. His publications are *The Unhappy Consciousness: Bankimchandra Chattopadhyay and the Formation of Nationalist Discourse in India* (1993), *Politics in India* (1999) and *Civil Society: History and Possibilities* (2001).

T. N. Madan is Professor (Emeritus) at the Institute of Economic Growth, Delhi, and Distinguished Senior Fellow at the Centre for the Study of Developing Societies, Delhi. Awarded *Docteur Honoris Causa* by the University of Paris (X), he also received the Lifetime Achievement Award of the Indian Sociological Society in 2008. Author and editor of many books, his most recent publications include *India's Religions: Perspectives from History and Sociology* (2004) and *Images of the World: Essays on Religion, Secularism and Culture* (2006).

Upendra Baxi is Professor of Law at the University of Warwick. He has been Vice-Chancellor of the University of Delhi and of South Gujarat University; Research Director of the Indian Law Institute; President of the Indian Society of International Law, and founder-member of the International Commission on Folk Law and Legal Pluralism. He has published extensively; among his more recent works are *Human Rights in a Posthuman World: Critical Essays* (2007) and *The Future of Human Rights* (2002).

Introduction

What is Indian political thought?

Post-independence India has failed to throw up either a major political theorist or significant theoretical works on such subjects as social justice, the specificity of the Indian state, secularism, legitimacy, political obligation, the nature and structure of political argument, the nature of citizenship in a multi-cultural state, the nature and limits of the law, the ideal polity, and the best way to understand and theorize the Indian political reality. There is little attempt even to test the major ideas and categories of Western political theory against the Indian political experience, and to show their ethnocentric biases and limitations. Although some work is beginning to be done in some of these areas, it remains isolated and patchy. Indian political theorists often do not take each others' work seriously enough to comment on it, and the questions raised and the concepts developed by one are not generally taken up by the others. As a result there is no cooperative engagement in a shared form of inquiry, and as yet no sign of the development of an Indian tradition of political theory.

(Parekh 1992: 545; see p. 25 of this volume)

Motivation

Just over 15 years separate the appearance of this volume on *Indian Political Thought* and the publication of Lord Bhikhu Parekh's powerful and provocative essay on 'The Poverty of Indian Political Theory' (Parekh 1992). Has anything changed in the interim? In his essay (see Chapter 1 of this volume), Parekh specifically indicated crucial problems arising out of the nature of the Indian state post independence, and laments that these problems had yet to be adequately theorized. He points to Indian secularism, communalism, and caste-related policy; reflection on what Parekh refers to as 'India's national political philosophy', which is to say, the commitment to modernization and ingraining the scientific temper; interrogation of the application of the modern nation-state model to India, including all the ancillary problems such as sovereignty, power, and state violence; and, finally, queries on legitimacy, law, legal obligation (duty), rights, and disobedience (ibid.: 553; see p. 27 of this volume). Let us leave to one side whether Parekh's judgement is correct[1] that these fundamental political themes had been inadequately treated between 1947 (independence) and 1992 (the appearance of Parekh's essay), and instead turn our attention for a moment to work appearing in these areas in the last 15 years or so.

There is certainly no need to lay out a comprehensive bibliography here, but as a foretaste, we might evoke some names and texts that have begun to set standards; that have begun – to employ Parekh's expression – to signal the development of an Indian tradition of political thought. We present them loosely following the same order in which Parekh enumerates the untreated themes in his article:

- Sudipta Kaviraj's *Politics in India* (1997), while oriented toward political sociology, contains valuable articles on social structure, refigurations of power, caste and class, and state crisis, while his *Civil Society* (2001) takes up the task of – again recycling Parekh's expression – testing 'the major ideas and categories of Western political theory against the Indian political experience, illustrating at times their ethnocentric biases and limitations' (Parekh 1992: 545; see p. 25 of this volume).
- Rajeev Bhargava's titles speak for themselves: *Multiculturalism, Liberalism, and Democracy* (1999); *Civil Society, Public Sphere, and Citizenship* (2005a); *Secularism and its Critics* (2005b); *What is Political Theory and Why Do We Need It?* (2010) – Bhargava's writing, which reflects upon and appraises the work of his colleagues like Ashis Nandy and T. N. Madan, flies in the face of Parekh's remorseful claim that Indian political theorists do not take each others' work seriously enough to comment on it, and that the questions raised or concepts developed by one are not taken up by others.
- Neera Chandhoke has diligently applied herself to theorizing the problem of collective rights (*Beyond Secularism: The Rights of Religious Minorities*, 1999) and the catchphrase 'civil society' (*The Conceits of Civil Society*, 2003), and is currently struggling with a conundrum of post-independence India's politico-constitutional dispensation, *secession*.
- Secularism is now becoming exhaustively treated, apparent from occasional works such as T. N. Srinivasan (*The Future of Secularism*, 2006) through to the prolific writings of Ashis Nandy (e.g., *Creating a Nationality*, 1995), who has also systematically struggled with what Parekh called India's national political philosophy, modernization and the scientific temper, as well as numerous other themes of peculiar relevance to the political climate of post-independence India (*Bonfire of Creeds: The Essential Ashis Nandy*, 2004).
- While a 'coherent and systematic' treatment of caste and theorization of caste politics in contemporary India is still lacking, due to many complicating factors, among which must be included the continued sensitivity of the topic, brilliant sporadic attempts have appeared, such as Dilip M. Menon's *The Blindness of Insight: Essays on Caste in Modern India* (2006), which reflect on and transcend the work of ᵗhe previous generation (captured, e.g., by Andre Beteille and Dipankar Gupta).
- There is also clearly an urgent need for more 'systematic and rigorous' approaches to legal theory and the nexus of legal and political philosophy in India (as Upendra Baxi himself points out in Chapter 17 of this volume). Nevertheless, there certainly are 'patches' of illuminating work related to justice, constitutionalism, human rights, and other similar areas, from Upendra Baxi's own vanguard studies dating back to the 1980s (*The Indian Supreme Court and Politics*, 1980; *The Crisis of the Indian Legal System,* 1982) right up to today (*Human Rights in a Posthuman World*, 2007), and Ratna Kapur's feminist approaches to theorizing law and legitimacy in India and beyond (*Erotic Justice*, 2005), as well as Rajeev Bhargava's recent foray into this field in his edited volume *The Politics and Ethics of the Indian Constitution* (2008).
- Finally, in his 1992 article, Parekh had acknowledged the pioneering historiography of the subaltern studies group, but expressed a doubt on whether they could make the transition from historiography to political theory (ibid.: 547; see

p. 25 of this volume). Partha Chatterjee's *oeuvre* should serve to ameliorate that doubt. The development of his reflection from the early *Nationalist Thought and the Colonial World* (1986) and *The Nation and its Fragments* (1993) through to *A Possible India* (1997) and the more recent *The Politics of the Governed* (2004), illustrates beautifully what Parekh longed for: the development of an Indian tradition of political theory.

These advances, however, appear to have proved altogether insufficient to Parekh, who repeated in 2006 elements of the same 1992 critique. He writes even in 2006 that several political concepts still cry out for a 'rigorous theoretical investigation' in the post-independence context,

> such as the ideas of majority, minority, community, nation, development, tradition, modernity, equality and secularism. Each of them raises difficult questions, contains deep ambiguities, and rests on several muddled assumptions that have distorted our political practice. One would have thought that during the half a century that these concepts have dominated Indian political thought and practice, its political philosophers would have subjected them to a critical scrutiny. They certainly have, but it is somewhat patchy, tentative, either too abstract or patently partisan, often driven by political crises rather than a quest for theoretical clarity, and in general, does not add up to a coherent and comprehensive philosophical articulation of Indian political experiences (Parekh 2005: 454).

Parekh's 1992 assessment is surely more fair and accurate than his 2006 recapitulation, as visible even from the brief list of recent works on topics in political philosophy provided above. The profundity and volume of contemporary writing available on political themes such as community, modernity, or secularism, for example, are far from 'patchy, tentative'; nevertheless, rather than expending energy in attempting to discredit Parekh's judgments, we would suggest that it is far more profitable to try to learn from him.

Therefore, taking the cue from Parekh's critique, the present collection serves to lay a cornerstone for the construction of an authentic, vibrant tradition of Indian political thought, a step that would satisfy even those most difficult to please, such as Bhikhu Parekh himself. For scholars, we aim to establish a reference point, a canon of names and work to serve as a touchstone for deepening research within the broad thematics. But it is intended that this collection should also be useful for students, providing them with a valuable overview of the current state of the art. We are aware of the dozens of Indian Political Theory courses taught throughout Indian universities that lack a primary sourcebook. It is worth mentioning that Parekh sees ostensibly minor shortcomings, such as the paucity of quality sourcebooks in Indian universities, as one of the major causes of the poverty of Indian political theory.

Succinctly stated, we believe that contemporary Indian political thought is not in fact as impoverished as Bhikhu Parekh holds, but rather that there is a sufficient quantity and quality of material to demand the publication of a representative reader. But on the other hand, granting the thrust of Parekh's argument that deeper and more systematic work is urgently required, we believe that taking first steps to carve out a canon could serve to kindle and promote this work in a manner consistent with Parekh's apparent aims.

Clarification

At a certain point in his essay, Bhikhu Parekh notes that India 'still awaits its Bodin and hopefully a Hobbes' (Parekh 1992: 539, n 5; see p. 29 of this volume). By evoking European authors from the sixteenth and seventeenth centuries, Parekh accidentally undermines the explicit problematic of his paper, which is not only to prove that post-independence Indian political theory is impoverished (sections 1 and 2 of his paper), but also to uncover the causes of this neglect (section 3 of his paper) (ibid.: 536–59; see pp. 20–29 of this volume). Parekh provides three main factors responsible for the under-development of Indian political theory: (1) the status of the social sciences in Indian universities post-independence; (2) the hegemony of Nehru's modernization paradigm that serves even now as the indisputable national political philosophy; and, (3) the inscrutability of the contemporary Indian political reality (ibid.: 549–59; see pp. 26–29 of this volume). Obviously, these factors relate to the poverty of *contemporary* Indian political theory and not to Indian political thought *simpliciter*. Thus, Parekh should have restrained his temptation to state that India had never produced a Hobbes, keeping within the historical scope of the paper, which is Indian political theory since 1947; or, otherwise, he should have extended the genealogical reach of his investigation back into the causes of the neglect of political theory in India for centuries preceding independence.[2]

But we mention this complication only to move into a certain clarification of the scope and nature of the present book. Through the title *Indian Political Thought*, we intend for the last term, *Thought*, to convey contemporaneity. We really do mean 'contemporary', not even merely 'post-independence'. For each of the authors represented herein is living; the pieces have all been composed within the last decade or two. This, we believe, allows us to better face up to the provocation of Bhikhu Parekh. That is, we concentrate specifically on the contemporary precisely because it is the contemporary that has received insufficient attention. This is abundantly clear through contrast with the magnitude of writing – monographs, anthologies, and so on – available on 'modern' political thought. There is no shortage of work on Raja Rammohan Roy, M. K. Gandhi, Maulana Azad, B. R. Ambedkar, Jawaharlal Nehru, *et al*. Their writings have been anthologized, serialized, canonized, sacralized. It is the work of their successors in political philosophy that remains dispersed and in need of collation and dissemination.

This book is unique, then, because it prioritizes the current state of the art over the tradition(s) – whether recent modern, or early modern, or further back, medieval, or back further still, ancient – that *in some way* gave rise to it. It presents a snapshot of a continuous process of transmission, where the wisdom of tradition is or may be present, but where it gets freely refracted through innovation and insight, and touches off the possibility of developing a new tradition or traditions of *contemporary* Indian political thought, what we shall later characterize as a 'journey'.

We have now thus briefly addressed the third word of the title of this book – *Indian Political Thought* – by distinguishing the *contemporary* from the modern (the latter being that which primarily receives the academic attention), but with reference nevertheless to tradition. The traditions that have served to give rise ('in some way') to contemporary Indian political thought are distinctively important in clarifying the second term of the title: 'Indian'.

Bhikhu Parekh mentions in his article that by 'Indian political theory' he intends 'works on political theory written by Indian writers irrespective of whether they live in India or outside it, and exclude the works of non-Indian writers on India' (1992: 535;

see p. 19 of this volume). Succinctly put, he is stating that he refers to theory *by* Indians, not theory *about* India. This, however, does not speak to our query; in fact it begs the question. Who, precisely, qualifies as an 'Indian' writer? We do not seek analytic precision here, but only wish to get an overall sense of what we mean by the term.

Following Parekh, living in India does not seem to be an essential criterion for 'Indian' – and thankfully so: only half of the authors represented here reside in India. Indian citizenship seems equally problematic; it would surely not be necessary, although it might, on the other hand, arguably be sufficient. But to speak less at the formal level and more at the substantive level, what seems to especially characterize the *Indianness* of Indian political thought is the way in which it is infused by Indian tradition(s) – whether to accommodate, assimilate, sublimate, or even negate. Wrestling with the tradition(s), evoking the tradition(s), evading the tradition(s), these are all characteristics useful in delimiting the notion of 'Indian' within the context of Indian political thought.

Thus, more than formal considerations of citizenship, residency, or even hollow ethnic considerations, most substantively, contemporary *Indian* political thought carves out a determinate space for itself by means of ascribing value to – evaluating – the relevant literature of the tradition(s) that preceded it. To turn this coin over, we might mention that Western political philosophy can be held in contradistinction to Indian political philosophy by the *general exclusion* of any reflection on material from the Indian tradition(s), whether in the form of a work like the *Arthashastra*, or the life and work of moderns such as Gandhi or Ambedkar and so on. In sum, the bearing, or the burden, of tradition seems to be a necessary element (albeit not a sufficient one) in concretizing the meaning of the term 'Indian' within the phrase 'Indian political thought'. This is why we chose to begin the book with a section specifically illustrating contemporary Indian political philosophers' *evocation* of founders of independent India, like Gandhi, Ambedkar and Tagore.

As for the second term, there is nothing novel or exceptional about our conception of the term 'political', which, as everyone already knows, derives from the ancient Greek *polis*, or city. 'Political' referred originally to anything city-related; that is, referred to dispensations, decisions, organizations, institutions, and other bodies or entities or acts existing by virtue of the existence of the *polis*. Naturally, people were forced to interrogate all these dispensations, institutions and what not, query their origins, their authority, their legitimacy, their status, and even their future(s). These were all, and still remain, essentially political questions.

What would seem to require some explanation, however, is why we have decided to include the work not only of political scientists, or people working in departments of politics, but also the work of anthropologists, historians, sociologists, psychologists, philosophers, and jurists. Firstly, in point of historical fact, *the political* has never really been the exclusive domain of political scientists. If we reflect on the classical Western tradition, the most significant and influential political writings that have appeared – e.g., Plato's *Republic*, Aristotle's *Politics*, Machiavelli's *Prince*, Hobbes' *Leviathan*, and the work of Locke, Rousseau, Hegel, Marx – predate political science as a discrete discipline. Even the salient political theory of the twentieth century – including such notables as Hannah Arendt, Raymond Aron, Carl Schmitt, Leo Strauss, Eric Voegelin, Michel Foucault, Jürgen Habermas, John Rawls – has been articulated in an entirely cross-disciplinary framework, and with no exclusive rights granted to political scientists.

Irrespective of the departmental affiliation of the authors, we have selected the writings of contemporary scholars whose work bears heavily upon, and has consistently impacted, political thought. There are, for example, certain historiographical considerations that cannot be ignored when reflecting upon contemporary political ideas. The same is true for certain juridical, or social, or psychological considerations, provided, of course, they are not over-coded, but articulated in a manner comprehensible to and consistent with the broad horizon of the discourse of political theory or political philosophy.

The phrase just deployed, 'political theory or political philosophy' brings us back around once again to the final term in the title, 'thought'. We frequently interchange 'thought' with the word 'theory' or 'philosophy'. While we would certainly hesitate to equate 'thought', 'theory' and 'philosophy' in all cases (we would hesitate to equate any two of the words, let alone all three), in the specific instance of *political* thought, we do think the occasional synonymization of 'thought' with 'theory' or 'philosophy' is justi-fied – always with the caveat that we intend contemporaneity. As for conflation of the latter two terms (theory and philosophy), the distinction seems to arise only in relation to the academic department involved. That is, the same content or syllabus might be called 'political philosophy' if it is taught in a philosophy department, but called 'political theory' if it is taught in a political science or politics department. The termi-nological difference is in this case external to the substance.

But what, then, do we really mean by *thought* in the title, and how to distinguish this canon of Indian political thinkers from other writers/forms of writing on broadly poli-tical topics? In his book *What Is Political Theory and Why Do We Need It?* (2010), Rajeev Bhargava identifies six essential features of theory, and then goes on to char-acterize political theory in light of these six enumerated requisite features:

> (a) conceptual sensitivity, (b) rational structure, (c) aspiration for a humanly achievable truth and objectivity, (d) generality, (e) an explicit mandate to unearth assumptions and presuppositions, (f) strong non-speculative intent – the need not to bypass results of micro-enquiries into the particular. [Theory] is not identical to any one feature but must possess all six. Thus, a theory must be distinct from ad hoc reflections, speculation, empirical enquiry into the particular, rich insights, imaginative but fictive prose and other related narratives. It must also be dis-tinguished from ideology, world-view and cosmology.
>
> Political theory then is a particular form of word-dependent systematic reflection (with each of the six features mentioned above) on any or all of the following: (a) the general condition of human kind or a particular society, (b) the collective power to take decisions about the good life of a community, (c) the mechanisms by which power is exercised by one group over another, (d) the use of state power to achieve the good of the community or to exercise power by one group over another and finally (e) the values by which the entire human kind or a particular commu-nity governs its life (ibid.).

Without wishing to commit ourselves to Bhargava's exposition in its entirety, we would underline certain criteria related to the distinctiveness of theory that we have abided by, while employing the word *thought*, in the present collection. To wit, *political thought* differs from ideology, although there are of course overlapping elements, and it differs, for basically the same reasons, from cosmology. As Bhargava would argue, ideologies or cosmologies exhibit some of the six features of theory, but not all of them together. The same would hold for ad hoc or aphoristic reflections, nationalistic or ethnicist propaganda, political party platforms, and so on. *Indian Political Thought* provides a set of exemplary writings which entail or at least engage with Bhargava's six criteria, work which is elevated to the status of theory, and – and this is important – *not* work that aspires to be representative of the expansive range of quotidian political positions in contemporary India.

Justification

So far so good. But why precisely *these* texts and not others? That is, granting that all of the works appearing here conform to the determinations we have set out with respect to the terms 'Indian', 'political', and 'thought', the question may still be posed as to the criteria of selection within the admittedly large pool of work that fulfills these requirements.

In the first place, for anyone familiar with contemporary political theory in India, there are a handful of names that naturally come to mind, such as Sen, Bhargava, Nandy, Kaviraj, and others. Then, thinking thematically, if we wish to address the concepts and conundrums listed by Bhikhu Parekh in both his 1992 and 2006 writings on Indian political theory, then, again, we are obliged to select works pertinent to these areas. Putting together the foremost names that come to mind along with the broad thematic areas which we seek to have represented produces the (rather impressive) result to be found in the table of contents of this reader.

It would be disingenuous, however, to deny that there have been arbitrary components active within the decision-making processes. Generalizing from what is visible in the available international literature along similar lines (discussed further below), it would seem to be inevitable. Nevertheless, we beg for some indulgence and a sympathetic reception. After all, we do not aim to close the book on contemporary Indian political thought; *we aim to open it*. Other methods of organization were possible, as were other selections of source material – and indeed, by setting the precedent of trying out one format, we are eager to encourage the appearance of alternatives.

Among the inspirations for the conception of this volume, in addition to Bhikhu Parekh's provocation, are Will Kymlicka's well-known book *Contemporary Political Philosophy: An Introduction* (2005), and Goodin and Pettit's now classic anthology *Contemporary Political Philosophy* (1997). While Kymlicka's masterpiece is organized thematically (with just seven chapters: 1. Introduction, 2. Utilitarianism, 3. Liberal Equality, 4. Libertarianism, 5. Marxism, 6. Communitarianism, and 7. Feminism), Goodin and Pettit's enormous volume consists of some 48 chapters representing a huge array of classical essays, conceptual chapters, and excerpts of technical discussions of fine points within larger theoretical debates. And yet, as encompassing as Goodin and Pettit's volume is, there is a rub: a *total lack* of international representation. For example, French thought receives about five pages of attention (out of a book of some 770 pages) by means of an excerpt from Foucault. Similarly, German thought receives about five pages of attention through an excerpt from Habermas. And, more predictably, the only Indian name to appear is that of Amartya Sen. Everyone else involved, and every other topic (coming to the remaining 755 pages of this 770-page book) is Anglo-American. And yet, the book is entitled simply *Contemporary Political Philosophy* – no reason to bother delimiting the title; apparently there is no world beyond of any relevance to political thought. Kymlicka's title is no more modest, although there is such an element of economy in its table of contents that one would fain rather not to raise the point of its parochialism.

From across the Atlantic, the German volume *Politische Philosophie des 20. Jahrhunderts* (*Political Philosophy of the 20th Century*) (1990) is as exclusive as the Anglo-American ones. French thought appears in about 15 pages (in a book of some 325 pages) through a chapter on Raymond Aron. Ironically – that is, it is ironic when juxtaposed with the Goodin and Pettit volume – Anglo-American political philosophy gets a chapter of only about 20 pages. Needless to add, even Sen does not make an appearance in this one. The remaining 300 pages go to Germans – but neither do they feel compelled to delimit the title of the book in any way, by addition of an adjective like *German* or even *Western*. The situation is precisely the same for a recent French book, *La pensée politique* (*Political Thought*), which features almost exclusively French political philosophers (with a perfunctory tip of the hat to Rawls and Habermas), without any compunction to add the adjective *French* to the title.[3]

Reading these and similar publications from around the world naturally motivate international or comparative political philosophers to take some corrective measures, however insufficient. Moreover, goaded on as we Indian political theorists have been for so long by the likes of Bhikhu Parekh, there seems no choice but to stiffen the upper lip and step forward. We hope that *Indian Political Thought* will serve as a source of inspiration and recognition for the many scholars of Indian political theory/ philosophy who have been trying, against the odds, to inaugurate and cultivate a new tradition of Indian political philosophy in recent years.

Chapterization

We mentioned above that the book begins with a section specifically illustrating the evocation of traditional Indian thinkers – more precisely, it is Part II, *Evocation*, that does this, and it contains essays evoking the thought, work, and activity of M. K. Gandhi, B. R. Ambedkar and R. Tagore (Part I, 'Provocation', presents the touchstone essay of **Bhikhu Parekh**, 'The Poverty of Indian Political Theory, which we have already discussed in some detail). Specifically, in Chapter 2, 'Gandhi's Ambedkar', **Ramachandra Guha** aims to put the Gandhi–Ambedkar debates into a wider historical and simultaneously narrower personal framework, thereby serving to establish the legitimacy of both positions. In not only polemical but even political writings since Independence, scholars – as Guha points out, usually divided along caste lines – have exhibited a partiality for one of these men always at the expense of the other. Guha argues, against this tendency, that in the contemporary political climate, it would seem that these two great founders and pioneers of twentieth-century Indian self-identity may have a *complementary* role: 'Whereas in their lifetime Gandhi and Ambedkar were political rivals, now, decades after their death, it should be possible to see their contributions as complementing one another's' (see p. 38 of this volume).

The subsequent two chapters take up Gandhi and Tagore, respectively.

In Chapter 3, 'The quest for justice: Evoking Gandhi', **Neera Chandhoke** explores the method of Satyagraha as an answer to political deadlocks in plural societies and in tackling the encounter with the 'other' in socio-political space. As Chandhoke points out, a dialogue cannot happen in a vacuum; there are pre-conditions, such as a common space, which create the possibility for dialogue in spite of natural apprehension towards that which is different and unknown. What stands at the core of Gandhian Satyagraha is a very peculiar notion of truth, and this serves as the reference point for dialogue. It derives largely from the Jaina theory of *syadavada*, of the multi-facetedness of truth. An individual's moral journey defines his pursuit of truth and creates a common ground for discourse. Truth, however, remains partial; one can never access it in its entirety. This creates sensitivity towards other perspectives and at the same time allows one to bracket suspicions. An essential element of Satyagraha is non-violence, a spirit which again facilitates communication and inhibits any sense of alienation. Satyagraha is thus a method to create space for discourse, to negotiate disagreements and generate solutions to the problems facing the profound plurality found in Indian democracy.

In the final chapter (4) of Part II, 'Tagore and his India', **Amartya Sen** turns towards Rabindranath Tagore, Gandhi's perhaps most intimate critic. He presents the remarkable contrast between these two leading contemporaries of the twentieth-century political scene. Despite his reverence for 'the Mahatma', Tagore differed with him on critical matters: liberal humanism versus parochial nationalism, industrial innovation versus indigenous economy, pursuit of modern rationality and science versus conservative traditionalism. His 'passion for freedom' went beyond the question of colonial liberation to the desire for the absolute freedom of mind, hence his recurring emphasis on education. Sen ends with the discussion of Tagore's hypothetical appraisal of the present society, a story of the realization of envisioned India or its betrayal.

We had earlier referred to Bhikhu Parekh's claim that several political concepts continue to demand 'rigorous theoretical investigation' in the context of post-independence India: 'minority, community, nation, development, tradition, modernity, equality and secularism' (2006: 454). If Part II can only be said to have obliquely addressed 'tradition', in subsequent sections, notions such as secularism (Part III), community (Part IV), and modernity (Part V) receive 'rigorous theoretical investigation'.

In Chapter 5, **Romila Thapar** asks and answers the question, 'Is secularism alien to Indian civilization?' Thapar avers that pitting secularism against religion, as Hindutva supporters tend to do, restricts the debate on secularism to only a fragment of orthodox Hinduism. This generates a lopsided view because it ignores the richer and more extensive expressions of religion that have been witnessed in India and which would permit us to acknowledge what Thapar calls 'proto-secularism' within popular Indian traditions, such as the Guru-Pir, early Buddhist, Jain, and Islamic practices.

T. N. Madan's 'Secularism revisited: Doctrine of destiny or political ideology?' (Chapter 6) problematizes the notion of secularism, and sets it within the recent historical context – as opposed to Thapar's far wider historical context. Madan argues that through the Indian struggle for independence, secularism was instated as the indispensable condition for a just social order. Yet the peculiar cultural framework of India was not ready to embrace the 'decline of religion in human affairs' (see p. 87 of this volume). The onus was to carve out an indigenous model of secularism and this led to evolution of several uses of the term. One of these was reverence for plurality and inter-religious sympathy. Religious differences, however, continued to create mistrust between communities. It is now necessary to nurture a well defined pluralistic notion of secularity based on principles of dignity, equality, freedom and acceptance in our peculiar socio-cultural landscape.

In Chapter 7, however, **Rajeev Bhargava** – in 'The distinctiveness of Indian secularism' – argues that the Indian conception of secularism is already distinctive and attuned to the exigencies of the Indian context. Through a carefully reasoned presentation of what he calls 'principled distance' and 'contextual secularism', Bhargava suggests that far from being inappropriate or suffering from shortcoming compared to secularism in Western nations, 'a good hard look at Indian secularism could also change the self-understanding of other western secularisms' (see p. 116 of this volume).

With **Dilip M. Menon**'s powerful and provocative Chapter 8, 'The blindness of insight: Why communalism in India is about caste', we transition from secularization (Part Three) to communalization (Part Four) – which Menon sees as intimately related to one another and to caste. Menon suggests that while the hierarchical and inegalitarian aspects of Hinduism are widely acknowledged, academic discourse turns a blind eye to the violence perpetrated against low-or out-caste Hindus. Consequently, he believes that 'what we need to explore is the inner violence within Hinduism as much as the violence directed outwards against Muslims and acknowledge that the former is historically prior. The question needs to be: how has the employment of violence against an internal Other (defined in terms of inherent inequality) i.e. the Dalit, been displaced as one of aggression against an external Other (defined in terms of inherent difference) i.e. the Muslim. *Is communalism a deflection of the central issue of violence and inegalitarianism within the Hindu religion?*' (see p. 123 of this volume).

In Chapter 9, **Mushirul Hasan** – in his essay entitled 'In search of integration and identity: Indian muslims since independence' – documents the tension between the need for communal identity and the lofty ideals of secularism. According to Hasan, in contrast to Bhargava, Nehru's vision of a progressive, democratic and secular framework for post-partition India was largely unsuccessful: a surge of communal forces have drowned attempts at secularization. In weaving the history of Indian Muslims struggling to integrate into the secular Indian fabric, Hasan poignantly illustrates the contradiction of values witnessed by the community: embracing secularism was arduous for a tradition which did not permit one to be aloof from religion and which was entrenched in doctrines of religious fundamentalism. Muslim conservatism insisted on preservation of the religious identity which secularism was portrayed as threatening. The result, as Hasan puts it, was the 'alienation' of a community and its inability to integrate or identify with the mainstream.

Chapter 10, **Harjot Oberoi**'s essay, 'Sikh fundamentalism: Translating history into theory', parallels in many respects the previous chapter. Although Oberoi frames his topic within the purview of fundamentalism, he uses that concept to reflect more broadly upon 'issues of Sikh identity, the crisis of agrarian development, class antagonisms, and the process of state formation in India, including popular resistance to this process' (see p. 151 of this volume). According to Oberoi, it is useful to peg these considerations to the question of fundamentalism, because today when much of the Sikh population query their identity, how they should understand themselves and the world around them, many of the answers emerge from what we would refer to as a 'discourse and ideology of fundamentalism'.

Part V moves from communalization to modernization, another concept which Parekh had – we believe quite mistakenly – referred to as untheorized in contemporary Indian political thought (2006: 454). Beginning with **Akeel Bilgrami** – in 'Gandhi, Newton and the Enlightenment' (Chapter 11) – Part V displays three ways of reflecting on modernity, each distinctively related to Indian thought, tradition, history and practices. Bilgrami attempts to understand Gandhi's critique of modernity in relation to critiques arising in Newton's own time to his idea of matter and nature as 'brute and inert', breaking with earlier conceptions of nature as 'shot through with an inner source of dynamism, which is itself divine' (see p. 165 of this volume). Even during the dawn of the Enlightenment in the seventeenth century there were dissenters who accepted

Newtonian science but protested its underlying metaphysics; thus, the concerns of the 'radical enlightenment' were in a sense recapitulated later by Gandhi. According to Bilgrami, both Gandhi as well as these earlier thinkers argued that in abandoning our ancient, 'spiritually flourishing' sense of nature, we simultaneously abandoned the moral psychology that governs our engagement with the natural, 'including the relations and engagement among ourselves as its inhabitants' (see p. 166 of this volume). This essay, then, is one of Bilgrami's many recent experimental reinterpretative essays, where he innovatively attempts to apply the critical method of analytic philosophy to Gandhi's life and work, albeit in a sympathetic vein (Bilgrami 2002, 2003, forthcoming).

In Chapter 12, **Meera Nanda**'s 'Scientific temper: Arguments for an Indian Enlightenment', the architects of modern India are presented as secular humanists who saw science and modernization as a means not just toward industrial development but for fostering an overall critical rationalism in the face of caste and gender inequalities sanctified by superstition and religion. Nanda presents the 'full cast' of secular humanists, founding fathers of independent India, and argues that they held 'that scientific demystification of fundamental beliefs about the natural order would lead to a genuine change in the normative order of Indian society, or in simpler words, change in mind would lead to a change of heart' (see p. 175 of this volume).

In the final chapter (13) of Part V, **Sudipta Kaviraj**'s 'Outline of a revisionist theory of modernity' offers a *tour-de-force* critique of the dominant conceptions of modernity, and attempts to sketch a revisionist one within which the post-colonial world would not find itself in a time-lag, with its future constituted by the West's past. Indeed, Kaviraj goes a step further, albeit cautiously, when he concludes that, despite the West's military dominance, its 'historically *declining imaginative power* ... makes it unlikely that diverging trajectories of the modern in other parts of the world can be folded back into recognizable Western patterns—that people can be persuaded to force their futures into versions of the Western past' (see p. 197 of this volume, emphasis added).

In Part Six, we move toward a domain of Indian political thought that perhaps moves beyond the horizon of Parekh's notion of political theory, insofar as his conception is entrenched in a sort of self-confessed, albeit minimal, eurocentrism. While entitled *Reconstruction*, it is akin to Kaviraj's *revision*, and could just as well have been called *deconstruction*[4] or something else better serving to indicate its simultaneous immanent critique of eurocentrism and attempt to reconstruct a sort of Indianness apposite to (contemporary) Indian (political) thought that is neither purely savage (in Nandy's terminology), nor romanticized (as Prakash cautions), nor conceived as immaculate or free from hybridity (as Bhabha discusses).

Ashis Nandy's 'Reconstructing childhood: A critique of the ideology of adulthood' (Chapter 14) strikes an atypical chord in the discourse about the ethics of politicization, of the evolution of desirable social ideals, and the simultaneous construction of a value-loaded narrative. Nandy constructs a unique analogy in the form of a parallel discourse where the idea of 'bringing up' children is concurrent with the colonial ambition to 'civilize' the third world. The 'ideology' of adulthood is thus a mirror image of political ideology. The child becomes the locus of the trials of history, being branded, as Nandy puts it, as an 'inferior version of the adult', and consequently, being a victim of adulthood. This victim in turn becomes the icon of a critique that problematizes the very notion of normalcy, and what it is to be 'rational' and 'productive' in modernity. The roots of this ideology permeate even societies originally free from such an approach, creating indigenous adaptation of the Western conception of childhood. Nandy's contention remains that modernity's pretension of a homogenous world must be unveiled in order for the right of the diversity of cultures and of their existing and flourishing as alternative philosophies.

Nandy's chapter strikingly illustrates how political psychology provides a unique insight into the psychopathology of politics. That which is dominant projects itself as an ideal and in doing so defines the *telos* for everybody else: the child must grow up to be an adult, the uncivilized third world must be civilized, the periphery ought to move towards the centre. Thus notions of 'normalcy', 'rationality', 'acceptability', 'productivity', etc. are constructed. It might be fruitful to read Nandy's chapter alongside Parekh's, and see what new light this may shed on the latter's exhortatory appeals and usage of terms like 'poverty' and 'development'.

Chapter 15 – 'Subaltern studies as postcolonial criticism' – is descriptive of a movement of Indian historiography, Subaltern Studies, that has by now spread throughout the 'third world' and has ripened into a profound theme of contemporary post-colonial critical thought. **Gyan Prakash** eloquently charts the origin, development, present and even speculates on the future of Subaltern Studies, and in so doing, clearly illustrates the scope and relevance of this influential and still-radical, critical but ultimately (re)constructive approach to political thought.

In the final chapter of Part VI, **Homi Bhabha** defends 'The commitment to theory' from the 'damaging and self-defeating assumption that theory is necessarily the elite language of the socially and culturally privileged' (see p. 227 of this volume). In the process, Bhabha articulates and illustrates some of his most subversive concepts, most importantly, 'hybridization'. This brilliant, path-breaking essay has now become a classic of post-colonial studies, and serves to round off this section of the volume that demonstrates not only that Indian political thought is far from impoverished, it is rich in innovation, originality, and insights – insights that may lead to a reconstruction or reconception (or who knows, perhaps even recuperation) of Indian thought that supersedes the regnant epistemology/ontology that lies behind Parekh's censure.

In Part VII, 'Emancipation', we find on the one hand indications of picking up the torch where the work of reconstruction from the previous section began (especially through the contributions of Kapur and Spivak) but on the other hand, the persistence of a Parekh-type skepticism toward the actuality of any as-yet distinct or mature Indian political thought (as apparent through Baxi's remarks). In Chapter 17, **Upendra Baxi**'s essay 'The justice of human rights in Indian constitutionalism', challenges Indian political thought for neglecting to thematically address the problematics of justice within constitutional thought and praxis. India has an active (and activist) judicial system which daily adjudicates, pontificates, even legislates – all in the name of justice; and yet, there is no significant Indian political theory critically examining or even attempting to address this justice industry and its (binding) output. Beyond these challenges, at the theoretical level, Baxi asks whether we have any theories regarding the justice of human rights by means of which we could evaluate the justice of constitutional arrangements? Additionally, assuming that we had, how could these theories/conceptions be put to work in relation to judicial praxis in a manner that overcomes what Baxi refers to as the 'foundational'–'reiterative' dichotomy?

If Baxi had posed a challenge to the adequacy of Indian political thought, in 'Emancipatory feminist theory in postcolonial India: Unmasking the ruse of liberal internationalism', feminist legal theorist **Ratna Kapur** (Chapter 18) exposes the false universalism and predatory nature of the liberal internationalist paradigm, through an analysis of the work of Martha Nussbaum. Kapur first faithfully presents Nussbaum's position, highlights its reliance on the work of Amartya Sen, and then attempts to show that Nussbaum's position – and the sort of liberalism it represents – fails to engage with or account for how power actually operates *in situ* vis-à-vis political and legal practice(s), or even in theory, with respect to the formation of liberal values and rights: 'Nussbaum fails to pay attention to the subtle operations of power and how liberal feminism cannot begin to bring about political repair through the application of one simple antidote – inclusion' (see p. 260 of this volume). A second defect Kapur identifies is Nussbaum's failure to engage with postcolonial and subaltern feminist theory, which Kapur spends a great deal of time elucidating and characterizing in order to intimate the subtle and profound ways they bear upon and serve as a critique of and corrective to basic assumptions of liberal internationalism. Kapur then suggests – and here seems to try to extricate Sen from her accusations against Nussbaum – that the presence and resilience of alternative (intellectual) traditions, especially Indian and subcontinental traditions, indicate that there may be different viable options for achieving the desired emancipatory ends that do not suffer the insurmountable (practical and onto-epistemological) defects of liberal internationalism.

Emancipatory talk and practice also receive reflective and critical treatment in Chapter 19, **Gayatri Chakravorty Spivak**'s 'Righting wrongs', an essay quite characteristic of the author's polyphonic technique of simultaneous self-reflexivity and wide-ranging scholarship, deconstruction and activism. Spivak, like Kapur, seeks to lay the ground for more authentic, localist techniques of addressing inequalities – her focus, true to her vocation, is through a radically reconfigured understanding and practice of *pedagogy*.

In the final section, Part VIII, of *Indian Political Thought*, the conclusion reflects or rather refracts the provocation of Part I. **Partha Chatterjee** turns the tables by exposing 'The poverty of Western political theory: Concluding remarks on concepts like "community" East and West'. This is not some knee-jerk tit-for-tat, but rather a well-considered evaluation and exposé of the profound parochialism that inevitably surfaces when any single concept of Western political thought is isolated and interrogated, especially against a non-Western background or context. As an illustration, Chatterjee focuses on the concept 'community' as it was theorized within the debate in Anglo-American academia between liberals and communitarians. Chatterjee remarks, 'one feature of this debate that particularly struck me was the narrow and *impoverished* concept of *community* that was being employed on both sides' (see p. 288 of this volume, emphasis added).

This is not to suggest, however, that the concept received more adequate treatment in the Indian discourse: 'The theoretical terms had been set by the categories of Western social theory; apparently, all that non-Western thinkers could do was fill up those categories with a different cultural content and then play out the same arguments in a different national arena' (see p. 290 of this volume).

Chatterjee, then, in his conclusion teases out of this dialectics of the 'poverty' of *both* Indian and Western political thought, the task that squarely faces Indian political theorists: 'to find an adequate conceptual language to describe the non-Western career of the modern state not as a distortion or lack, which is what inevitably happens in a modernization narrative, but as the history of different modernities shaped by practices and institutions that the universalist claims of Western political theory have failed to encompass' (see p. 291 of this volume).

In this – as should already be clear from the above brief descriptions of the chapters – Chatterjee merely makes general and programmatic what had already been expressed, at times tacitly, other times explicitly, by Chandhoke (Part II), Madan (Part III), Menon (Part IV), Kaviraj (Part V), Nandy and Bhabha (Part VI), and Kapur and Spivak (Part VII) – that is, Chatterjee lays bare what had already been adumbrated throughout the diverse themes (tradition, secularism, communalism, modernity, revision, justice) addressed by authors of every section of this volume. What Chatterjee calls 'the incomplete universalism of modern political theory', or 'the poverty of modern social theory' – which he illustrates by means of 'community' as one example – seems already to have been recognized and problematized by contemporary Indian scholars working across various interrelated themes of political thought.

This is, of course, just another way of saying that the intuition which Bhikhu Parekh had himself had and which he articulated so provocatively, was perhaps far more widely shared than he had ever realized, but that this widely-shared intuition was responded to in less polemical and more subtly (re)constructive ways across the wide spectrum of the emerging contemporary Indian political discourse(s).

With a resonance of Parekh's own aspiration, Chatterjee writes: 'This, I am suggesting, is one of the principal tasks of political theory today: to provide a conceptual map of the emerging practices of the new political societies of the East' (see p. 297 of this volume). Chatterjee, less committed to the *form* of Western political theory than Parekh, however, prefers to describe the charting of that map as a 'journey'; as he concludes his essay: 'In the course of that journey, political theory as we have known it for so long will also get rewritten' (ibid.).

To put it simply, then, our aim in *Indian Political Thought* is not meant just to reveal the error of Parekh's judgment that 'there is no co-operative engagement in a shared form of inquiry, and as yet no sign of the development of an Indian tradition of political theory' (Parekh 1992: 545; see p. 25 of this volume). That is anyway too easy. Rather, more constructively, we seek to provide readers with some of the contours of the emerging conceptual map about which Chatterjee speaks: to document a few of the paths that have already been explored in contemporary Indian political thought along this continuous and certainly arduous journey of rewriting political theory.

Notes

1 More fundamentally, we also put to one side whether Parekh provides any justification at all for the suppositions behind his value-conceptions *in toto*. For, in the first place, it is apparent even from the short passage cited above that Parekh assumes the perfection of the *form* of Western political thought – Indian political theory is not necessarily impoverished in terms of *content*, but in terms of *form*. His recurrent mantra – 'although some work is beginning to be done in some of these areas, it remains isolated and patchy' – reveals that Parekh values not an (isolated) work of extraordinary insight or genius, but a network or system of interrelated (perhaps even mediocre?) texts and treatments. (This dyad, 'isolated and patchy', used to describe thematic work in Indian political theory, elides into others throughout the essay: elsewhere, Parekh uses 'it is patchy and lacks rigour'; then, it is 'unable systematically and rigorously' to address the theme; later, it is not 'coherent and systematic'.) Notice the trope in the opening line cited: 'Post-independence India has failed to throw up either a major political theorist or significant theoretical works'; why did he not write '*a* significant theoretical work' to match his '*a* major political theorist'? Parekh's tacit and unjustified assumption that value lies in a network over a work bleeds into a second-order problematic: that the absent network he bemoans structurally relies upon another network; that of the interrelation of

capitalist ('knowledge') economies and academic research, writing, and publishing. At both orders, Parekh assumes – as we all do from time to time – the modernist, progressive-historical paradigm, which from the time of its inception, through to its grandest formulation in Hegel (and final reformulation in Fukuyama), has always been fuelled by ... *thought*, or better, the *realization* of thought (in Hegel's terms, the concretion of the universal, in Fukuyama, its institutionalization, and in (at least early) Marx, conversely, the *poverty* of thought lies precisely in its lack of concretion/institutionalization, its inability to 'transcend itself'). Thus does Parekh seamlessly resort to the metaphor of 'development' (as in, 'developing countries'): 'Reasons for what I will call the underdevelopment of political theory vary from country to country' (see p. 19 of this volume). The 'underdevelopment' and 'poverty' of India as conceived within the onto-epistemology of current liberalism is then the horizon within which Parekh locates the 'underdevelopment' and 'poverty' of Indian political theory. We can hear the echo of the increase-the-size-of-the-pie development economist's conundrum, How can such a resource-rich (both natural and human) nation remain so underdeveloped and impoverished? in Parekh's 'I intend to concentrate on post independence India, and to explore why ... a rich tradition of philosophical inquiry has not thrown up much original political theory' (ibid). However, Parekh argues, against the presentation in this note, that his notion of political theory 'is not or only minimally open to the charge of ethnocentrism or universalizing its Western form' (see p. 20 of this volume). 'Minimal ethnocentrism', whatever it means, is a fascinating category. But one may like to believe that the space – both ontologically and epistemologically – that separates *not* ethnocentric from *minimally* ethnocentric is not merely situated on a horizontal axis, where the zero-point is 'not ethnocentric', 'minimally ethnocentric' is 1, and then gradations of ethnocentrism stretch on out into infinity.

2 Parekh, it seems, does intend to limit his critique only to post-independence political philosophy, and not to Indian political philosophy *simpliciter*, apparent from passages such as this: 'Indian political theorists have a great opportunity to theorize ... on the rich heritage of political philosophy left behind'. See Parekh (2006: 455).

3 It should be mentioned that this radically parochial approach is more or less unique to Anglo-American (including Australian), German, and French publications. For (counter) example, works on contemporary political philosophy from Italian publishers which treat preponderantly the writings of Italian theorists, would definitely feature the adjective *Italian* in their title.

4 This is true insofar as Derrida refers to deconstruction in terms of 'restoration' (*remonter*) rather than 'demolition'. See Derrida (1985: 4).

References

Ballestrem, Karl and Ottmann, Henning (1990) *Politische Philosophie des 20: Jahrhunderts*, München: R. Oldenbourg.
Baxi, Upendra (1980) *The Indian Supreme Court and Politics*, Lucknow: Eastern Book Co.
—— (1982) *The Crisis of the Indian Legal System*, New Delhi: Vikas.
—— (2007) *Human Rights in a Posthuman World*, New Delhi: Oxford University Press.
Bhargava, Rajeev (1999) *Multiculturalism, Liberalism, and Democracy*, New Delhi: Oxford University Press.
—— (2005a) *Civil Society, Public Sphere, and Citizenship*, New Delhi: Sage Publications.
—— (2005b) *Secularism and its Critics*, New Delhi: Oxford University Press.
—— (2008) *The Politics and Ethics of the Indian Constitution*, New Delhi: Oxford University Press.
—— (2010) *What is Political Theory and Why Do We Need It?*, New Delhi: Oxford University Press.
Bilgrami, Akeel (2002) 'Gandhi's integrity: the philosophy behind the politics', *Postcolonial Studies*, 5(1): 79–93.
—— (2003) 'Gandhi, the philosopher', *Economic and Political Weekly*, September 27.
—— (forthcoming) 'Value, disenchantment, and democracy', *Economic and Political Weekly*.
Chandhoke, Neera (1999) *Beyond Secularism: The Rights of Religious Minorities*, New Delhi: Oxford University Press.

—— (2003) *The Conceits of Civil Society*, New Delhi: Oxford University Press.

Chatterjee, Partha (1986) *Nationalist Thought and the Colonial World*, Minneapolis: University of Minnesota Press.

—— (1993) *The Nation and its Fragments*, Princeton, N.J.: Princeton University Press.

—— (1997) *A Possible India*, New Delhi: Oxford University Press.

—— (2004) *The Politics of the Governed*, New York: Columbia University Press.

Derrida, Jacques (1985) [1983] 'Letter to a Japanese friend', in David C. Wood and Robert Bernasconi (eds) *Derrida and Difference*, Warwick: Parousia Press, pp. 1–5.

Goodin, Robert E. and Pettit, Philip (1997) *Contemporary Political Philosophy: An Anthology*, Cambridge, MA.: Blackwell Publishers.

Kapur, Ratna (2005) *Erotic Justice*, Delhi: Permanent Black.

Kaviraj, Sudipta (1997) *Politics in India*, New Delhi: Oxford University Press.

—— (2001) *Civil Society*, Cambridge: Cambridge University Press.

Kymlicka, Will (2005) *Contemporary Political Philosophy: An Introduction*, Oxford: Oxford University Press.

Menon, Dilip M. (2006) *The Blindness of Insight: Essays on Caste in Modern India*, Pondicherry: Navayana.

Nandy, Ashis (1995) *Creating a Nationality*, New Delhi: Oxford University Press.

—— (2004) *Bonfire of Creeds: The Essential Ashis Nandy*, New Delhi: Oxford University Press.

Parekh, Bhikhu (1992) 'The poverty of Indian political theory', *History of Political Thought*, 13 (3): 545.

—— (2006) 'Limits of the Indian political imagination', in Vrajendra Raj Mehta and Thomas Pantham (eds) *Political Ideas in Modern India: Thematic Explorations*, Thousands Oaks, CA: Sage Publications.

Srinivasan, T. N. (2006) *The Future of Secularism*, New Delhi: Oxford University Press.

Part I
Provocation

1   The poverty of Indian political theory[1]

Bhikhu Parekh

Non-Western societies have frequently and rightly complained that Western political theory is ethnocentric and has a limited explanatory power when applied outside the West. One would have thought that they would therefore produce both a well-considered critique of its central categories and modes of inquiry, and an original body of ideas capable of illuminating their political experiences. Surprising as it may seem, this is not the case. *No* contemporary non-Western society has produced much original political theory. Reasons for what I will call the underdevelopment of political theory vary from country to country. In this chapter I intend to concentrate on post-independence India, and to explore why a free and lively society with a rich tradition of philosophical inquiry has not thrown up much original political theory. The chapter falls into three parts. In the first part I outline some of the fascinating problems thrown up by post-independence India, and in the second I show that they remain poorly theorized. In the final part I explore some of the likely explanations of this neglect.

In order to avoid misunderstanding, some points of clarification are necessary. First, by Indian political theory I mean works on political theory written by Indian writers irrespective of whether they live in India or outside it, and exclude the works of non-Indian writers on India.

Secondly, I am primarily concerned with Indian political theory rather than with Indian political *theorists*. Although political theory is generally practiced by political theorists, it is not their monopoly. Sociologists, historians, economists, philosophers, jurists and others too ask theoretical questions about political life. I will therefore cast my net wider and look at the works of these writers as well. It is my contention that political theory is underdeveloped among not only Indian political theorists but also their cousins in allied disciplines.

Thirdly, I define the term political theory in as culturally neutral a manner as possible. For a variety of reasons too complex to discuss here, political theory has a longer history and is more developed in the West than elsewhere. However it is not absent in most other civilizations. Minimally it is concerned to offer a coherent and systematic understanding of political life, and is three-dimensional. It is conceptual in the sense that it defines, analyses and, distinguishes concepts, and develops a conceptual framework capable of comprehending political life. It is also explanatory in the sense that it seeks to make sense of political life, and to explain why it is constituted and conducted in a particular manner and how its different parts are related. Finally, it is normative in the sense that it either justifies the way a society is currently constituted, or criticizes and offers a well-considered alternative to it. Since political theory understood in these terms is to be found in most major traditions of thought including the Indian, albeit in different forms and degrees, our definition is not or only minimally open to the charge of ethnocentrism or universalizing its Western form (see Parekh 1989).

I

India is the only country in the world to enshrine in its Constitution a fairly extensive programme of positive discrimination in favour of such deprived groups as the ex-untouchables and the tribals. Seats are reserved for them in parliament and in state assemblies; jobs are reserved for them in such public institutions as the civil service and the universities; and admissions are given to them on a preferential basis in professional faculties. After an interesting debate, the Constituent Assembly of India accepted positive discrimination on the grounds that it was necessary to integrate deprived groups into the mainstream of political life, to remove the handicaps resulting from their centuries of neglect and oppression, and to break down the social barriers imposed by caste-conscious Hindus.

The policy of positive discrimination, especially one as extensive as the Indian, obviously raises important questions about the nature of justice, the trade-off between justice and such other equally desirable values as efficiency, social harmony and collective welfare, and the propriety of making social groups bearers of rights and obligations. It also raises questions about the nature and basis of inter-generational obligations, the redistributive role of the state, the nature and extent of the present generation's responsibility for the misdeeds of its predecessors, and the meaning and nature of social oppression. In the traditional Western and even Indian thought, justice is generally defined in terms of what is due to an individual on the basis of his qualifications and efforts. It is an individualist concept and is tied up with the ideas of agency, merit and responsibility. If social groups are to be made subjects of justice-based rights and obligations, the concept of justice must obviously be redefined in non-individualist terms. Agency and responsibility must be conceptualized in social and historical terms, so that we can demonstrate continuity between the past and present oppressors and oppressed. We must also analyze the nature of current deprivation and show that it is a product of past oppression and confers moral claims on the oppressed: These questions become particularly important in India where the idea of positive discrimination has no roots in the indigenous cultural tradition and is much resented.

In the United States where positive discrimination has been introduced on a limited scale considerable work has been done on these and related questions. In India where it is one of the central tools of government policy and an alien import, and where therefore one would expect considerable theoretical literature, the important questions raised by it have received little attention. It is difficult to think of a single legal or political theorist who has produced a major work on the subject either challenging or articulating the theory of justice lying at its basis. Some work has been done by sociologists, but most of them are content to rely on the American literature, without appreciating that the historical relations between caste Hindus and the untouchables and tribals bear little resemblance to those between the American whites and blacks.

The nature of the Indian state is another important area requiring investigation. Since its emergence in sixteenth century Europe, the modem state has been conceived as a homogeneous, sovereign, centralized and territorially bounded association of individuals. It recognizes only the individuals as bearers of political rights and obligations, and enjoys undivided and unlimited authority over all those within its area of jurisdiction: The modern state represented a novel political formation without a parallel either in pre-modern Europe or anywhere else in the world. When the British half-heartedly introduced it in India, it underwent important changes, partly because of the requirements of colonial rule and partly in response to Indian traditions and social structure. While at one level the colonial state subtly restructured the long-established communities to suit its interests, at another level it 'accepted' their laws and practices and superimposed on them a minimal body of mainly criminal laws. It did not, indeed dared not, transform the wider society along the modernist lines as its counterpart had done in Europe. Unlike its European counterpart, it permitted a plurality of legal systems, shared its 'sovereignty' with largely self-governing communities, and remained both socially segmentary and transcendental.

Post-independence India only partially rationalized the colonial state and remains a complex political formation. It has a uniform body of criminal but not civil laws. Muslims continue to be governed by their own personal laws, which the state enforces but with which it does not interfere. The tribals too are governed by their separate laws, and the state has committed itself to making no changes in the practices and laws of the Christians without their explicit consent and approval. The Parsis are subject to the same civil laws as the rest of non-Muslim Indians, but the interpretation and application of the laws is in some cases left to their *panchayats* or community councils. Thus the ordinary civil courts will hear a Parsi divorce case, but leave it to the Parsi *panchayat* to decide on the machinery of reconciliation and the amount of alimony. The Indian state is thus both an association of individuals and a community of communities, recognizing both individuals and communities as bearers of rights. The criminal law recognizes only the individuals, whereas the civil law recognizes most minority communities as distinct legal subjects. This makes India a liberal democracy of a very peculiar kind.

It is tempting to say, as many Indian and foreign commentators have said, that the Indian state is too 'deeply embedded' in society and too 'plural' and 'chaotic' to be considered a properly constituted state, and that it is not a state in the 'true' sense of the word. But such a view is obviously too superficial and ethnocentric to be satisfactory. There is no reason why we should accept that the modern Western manner of constituting the state is the only true or proper one, and deny India and other non-Western societies the right to indigenize the imported institution of the state and even to evolve their own alternative political formations. Rather than insist that the state *must* be autonomous and separate from society, and then set about finding ways of restoring it to the people, we might argue that it should not be separated from society in the first instance. Rather than insist that a state *must* have a uniform legal system, we might argue that it should be free to allow its constituent communities to retain their different laws and practices, so long as these conform to clearly laid down and widely accepted principles of justice and fairness. Thus the law might require that a divorced wife must be provided for, and leave it to different communities to decide whether the husband, his family or his community as a whole should arrange for her maintenance, so long as the arrangements are foolproof and not open to abuse or arbitrary alteration.

Again, there is no obvious reason why a federal state may not ignore the principle of abstract equality, and grant one or more of its constituent units a privileged status if the latter's history or the considerations of national interest so require. Nor is it necessary that the state *must* enjoy sovereign and undivided power over its subjects. If its historical circumstances so require, it might leave all or some of its constituent communities alone to run their affairs themselves provided that they do not transgress certain limits.[2] It is at least arguable that once we reject the idea that the state must be constituted in a particular manner, and allow different states to develop their distinct modes of internal organization, we might be better able to deal with ethnic conflicts and secessionist movements that the dominant model of the state finds so threatening. In the ultimate analysis the state is an institution for creating an orderly and peaceful collective life. It is not impossible that in a multi-communal or multi-national society, the modern state, uncompromisingly committed to the ideas of uniform laws, individualism, abstract equality and undivided legal sovereignty, might alienate minorities and *provoke* conflicts and secessionist movements. Instead of being an agent of *order*, it might become an unwitting instrument of avoidable *disorder*.

Whether or not one accepts the view that the modern state can be constituted in different ways, the fact remains that the Indian state does not conform to the Western model. One might consider it defective and seek to modernize it, or one might welcome it as a tentative but imaginative attempt to indigenize the Western model and to adopt it to the country's distinct needs. In either case it raises important questions, and challenges some of the basic categories of Western political thought. It is striking that hardly any Indian political theorist has wrestled with these questions and theorized the specificity of the Indian state. J. P. Narain and other political activists have thrown up interesting ideas on the best ways of reconstituting the Indian state (Narain 1959), but these remain utopian and poorly worked out and have not received critical examination at the hands of political theorists.

Since the Indian state is multi-religious and was born out of the trauma of partition on religious lines, its founding fathers concluded that it must remain secular. But they remained unclear about the meaning, implications and basis of secularism. For Jawaharlal Nehru, its first Prime Minister, religion was a private matter for individual citizens and had no public or political significance. The state was to 'transcend' and cultivate studied indifference to religion. He discouraged his ministers and party colleagues from attending religious functions, and was deeply offended when the President of India attended a function to mark the restoration of the Somanth temple whose destruction had for centuries been seen by the Hindus as a symbol of Muslim atrocity. Since Nehru's brand of secularism was impossible in a deeply religious society, it was hardly surprising that his government found it impossible to live up to its demands. Furthermore, for obvious political reasons he had no choice but to accept the autonomy of the Muslim personal law. This not only privileged Muslims, but also gave their religion a legal and political status. He was forced to grant a similar status to other minorities. His government gave public money to religious schools, especially Muslim, which was hardly a secular policy by his own definition. Again, Nehru rightly insisted on reforming the oppressive and discriminatory Hindu personal law. Since he was himself a Hindu, and since his government mainly consisted of the Hindus, they thought that they would not be accused of 'interfering' with Hindu social practices. Neither he nor his colleagues fully appreciated that in reforming the Hindu law in the teeth of considerable conservative opposition, the state was acting as the reformist arm of the Hindus and was not being neutral and fully secular.

Although Nehru and his successors defined secularism as indifference to religion, the cultural reality of India quietly continued to assert itself in these and other ways. Nehru's model was abandoned during his daughter's period of office, and secularism came to be defined not as equal indifference to but as equal respect for all religions. The new definition was as vague and incoherent as the old. No one was clear about what 'respecting' religion meant and involved, and whether it implied taking account of religious views and practices. The idea of 'equal' respect for all religions in a state whose population and leadership were predominantly Hindu continued to pose the kinds of problems raised during the Nehru period. In effect the new definition was a skillful way of allowing government leaders including the Prime Minister to indulge their religious sensibilities with a clear conscience, and for all practical purposes India became a multi-religious rather than an areligious state. Over time it became legitimate to play the 'religious card' during the elections, the state became an arena for and indeed a party to religious conflicts, and secularism was all but abandoned.

No government since independence has fully explained why India should be a secular state in its current sense, and such arguments as they have offered are unimaginative, based on fear, and derived from Western history. Most leaders have argued that secularism is necessary to ensure religious tolerance and harmony. But the argument is false. A secular state is not necessarily tolerant, for example the Soviet Union during the Communist rule or France after the French Revolution. Conversely a religious state is not necessarily intolerant of or discriminatory against minority religions, for example traditional Hindu kingdoms in India, and Muslim kingdoms in the Middle East and most of the time even in India. It could also be argued that by denying religion public identity and expression, a secular state might *provoke* religious conflicts. The Sikh separatists, for example, have often maintained, among other things, that the secular Indian state emasculates their religious identity and denies them collective self-expression, and that they can only preserve their identity in an independent Sikh state. The argument is unconvincing but it makes an important point. Since different religions are differently structured and come to terms with the secular world in different ways and degrees, secularism inescapably impinges on them differently and cannot be wholly impartial between them. It is of course true that in a multi-religious society the state cannot afford to be identified with a particular religion. It is also true that the state is primarily concerned with the material interests of its citizens rather than with the salvation of their souls. For these and other reasons the relation between the state and religion raises acute problems in India, but they cannot be solved by importing an alien and much-misunderstood secularist model from the West developed in a very different culture during its aggressively rationalist phase.

It is striking that with such notable exceptions as T. N. Madan (1987) and Ashis Nandy (1989), hardly any Indian social or political theorist has seriously grappled with the question of secularism (see also Chatterji 1984). There are very few books analyzing the term, distinguishing its various senses, elucidating the ways in which its meaning and practice have changed since independence, explaining when and how it entered the political vocabulary of India, and what model of it best suits the country. Only a few have asked if the term itself makes sense in the Indian context where the majority religion is unorganized and doctrinally eclectic, and whether it has conceptual equivalents in the vernacular languages in which ordinary Indians think about the subject. Hardly anyone has examined if Western states are secular in the sense in which Nehru and the modernists used the term, and how religion impinges on their public life, both as a cultural force and in the shape of Christian democratic parties. Since Indian civilization has a deep religious core, many secular-minded Indians have felt that they cannot be truly secular unless they reject their past, and that they must choose between their past and their future. Hardly anyone has cared to show that the dilemma is unnecessary and arises from a falsely defined model of secularism.

The legitimacy of the Indian state and the grounds of political obligation too raise difficult questions. When India became independent, the new state drew upon two theories of legitimacy: It was legitimate because it was run by Indians and based on their consent, as expressed in the Constitution which they had freely given themselves and in the post-independence elections. It was legitimate also because it was committed to leading the country along the 'historically inevitable' path modernization initiated but later blocked by the colonial rulers. The consensual and historicist theories of legitimacy generated different perceptions and expectations of the state, and their tension has informed much post-independence political debate. For the advocates of the consensual theory, a duly elected government has a right to the obedience of its subjects; for the champions of the historicist theory, only a government modernizing the country and promoting collective well-being has such a right. For the former, the rule of law and respect for the citizens' rights and liberties are the central concerns of the government. For the historicists the modernization of the country takes precedence, and if its 'imperative' so require, citizens' rights and the rule of law may be infringed. The tension between the two was evident even during Nehru's period of office, but it became acute in the early 1970s when his daughter skillfully used it to legitimize the Emergency.

The question of political obligation is closely connected with that of legitimacy. If the Indian state is unable to protect the basic rights and guarantee the physical security of a large body of its citizens, the question arises whether they have a moral obligation to obey it. At a different level a similar difficulty arises in the case of the wretched slum-dwellers, for whom the state not only does little but to whose oppression it is at best a passive spectator and at worst an active accomplice. Such familiar grounds of political obligation as explicit or tacit consent, political participation, collective welfare, fairness and gratitude make little sense in their case. The historicist theory upon which most politicians rely, namely that poverty and wretchedness are the inevitable price of modernization, is more plausible, but it too runs into obvious difficulties. The burdens of modernization must be shared by all, not just the poor, and they must be shared equitably, if the moral obligation to obey the law is to apply to all Indians equally. One needs to show too that alternative models of modernization entailing less heavy or unequal burdens are not available to the country, and that the poverty and wretchedness of the millions does really promote the long-term collective interests of all rather than those of the rich and powerful alone.

The functions and limits of the law too raise large questions, important both in themselves and because of their implications for political obligation. The question becomes particularly acute in such a multi-cultural and multi-religious society as India. The law is not and can never be morally neutral. It enjoins one class of actions and prohibits another, and needs guiding principles. If it derives these principles from one culture or religion, it discriminates against the others. If it derives them from outside the constituent cultures and religions, which is what secularism entails, they might not accept the authority of that source or prefer to define it differently. Even the so-called secular or worldly interests, which are supposed to be shared by all, are defined and graded differently by different religions. The difficulty is avoided only when the principles on which the law acts are shown to be common to all the constituent religions and cultures. But such principles are rare and the state based on them is obviously not secular in the currently dominant sense. It is hardly surprising that the question of the sources of legal morality remains unresolved in India and is evaded by all manner of subterfuges, including appeals to the loosely defined national interest the allegedly universal but essentially liberal moral principles.

There are also several other important questions thrown up by the Indian political experience. They include such questions as the ways in which Western ideas and institutions are appropriated and filtered through their indigenous analogues, the languages of political discourse, the deep differences between the way political discourse is conducted in English and in the regional languages, the emerging distinction between private and public in a society which refuses to separate the two, and the concept of the political in a society which has long seen it as an inseparable dimension of the social. At a different level the Indian political experience raises questions about the kinds of concepts and methods of inquiry needed to capture the authenticity of the Indian political reality, and the merits and limitations of different methodological approaches. It also raises questions about what is likely to happen when a society, which is not structured around the state and does not consider political power and authority autonomous, decides to reorganize itself on statist lines.

II

I offered above a brief and tentative list of the kinds of questions, thrown up by post-independence India. Surprising as it may seem, Indian political theorists have taken only a limited interest in them.

Post-independence India has failed to throw up either a major political theorist or significant theoretical works on such subjects as social justice, the specificity of the Indian state, secularism, legitimacy, political obligation, the nature and structure of political argument, the nature of citizenship in a multi-cultural state, the nature and limits of the law, the ideal polity, and the best way to understand and theorize the Indian political reality. There is little attempt even to test the major ideas and categories of Western political theory against the Indian political experience, and to show their ethnocentric biases and limitations. Although some work is beginning to be done in some of these areas, it remains isolated and patchy. Indian political theorists often do not take each other's work seriously enough to comment on it, and the questions raised and the concepts developed by one are not generally taken up by the others. As a result there is no cooperative engagement in a shared form of inquiry; and as yet no sign of the development of an Indian tradition of political theory.

Since most Indian political theorists are not theorizing their political reality, we might ask what they are doing. Broadly speaking most of their work falls into three categories. First, considerable work, some fascinating but much of it repetitive, has been and is being done on specific nationalist leaders, or on the development and structure of nationalist thought in general.[3] Second, some work, mostly derivative, is being done on such contemporary Western writers as Habermas, Foucault, Gramsci and the deconstructionists, or on such movements as positivism, behaviourism and post-modernism.[4] It is striking that such mainstream Western political theorists as Oakeshott, Rawls, Arendt, Leo Strauss, Macpherson and Nozick are almost entirely ignored. Finally, some work, much of it tentative and exploratory, is being done on the philosophy of the social sciences, historiography and relativism. During the colonial rule the British insisted that Western forms of life and thought were universally valid and superior to their Indian counterparts. Most Indians resented such a claim then, and continue to do so today. Their response took and continues to take the form of *both* demonstrating the ethnocentricity of Western forms of thought and life and insisting on the possibility of an East-West dialogue as a means to mutual enrichment. Such a critical relativism is very popular in India. *Relativism* deflates Western pretensions and affirms the autonomy and integrity of Indian forms of thought and life. *Critical* relativism enables Indians *both* to borrow from the West with a clear conscience and to claim that they also have something to offer it in return. Since it establishes a partnership of equals, critical relativism has considerable following and is a subject of much discussion. There is as yet no major work in this area, but enough spadework has been done for one to emerge before long.[5]

Of the three categories of writings, the first constitutes the greatest bulk. It is not too difficult to see why this is so. The ideas of nationalist writers are still deeply inscribed in Indian political reality and offer clues to its nature and dynamics. Such work is also easier to undertake in a country where library facilities are poor, the knowledge of the classical and medieval past is limited, and where intellectual self-confidence, thanks to years of Western domination, is too low to permit bold and creative theorizing. Ancestral piety is an important virtue in India and it too plays a role. Although there are only limited pointers in this direction, it seems that the preoccupation with the recent past is beginning to generate interest both in the pre-modern past and in the general methodological problems raised by the study of the past.

III

I argued in the previous section that Indian political theorists have taken limited interest in addressing and reflecting on the large questions raised by their unique political experiences, and that they have produced little creative political theory. This calls for an explanation. As we saw there is no shortage of material. There is no shortage of talent either, as is evident in such limited work as has been done. There is also a great need and demand for political theory to help clarify the complex and frightening nature of Indian political reality. Although political theory of the analytical and argumentative kind is relatively new to India, the country has a long tradition of writing moral and political treatises, and it has now been exposed to Western political theory for at least two centuries. In the light of all this the puzzle about the causes for the underdevelopment of political theory deepens. Without pretending to offer a conclusive or even a complete explanation, I suggest that three interrelated factors might throw some light on the subject. They are the way political theory is taught in Indian universities, the domination of the unofficially official political philosophy to which India committed itself at independence, and the complex nature of Indian political reality and the political theorist's inescapably ambiguous attitude to it.

Teaching political theory

The institutional context in which the teaching of political theory takes place in India leaves a great deal to be desired. As one would expect in a poor country the social sciences do not generally attract the ablest students, who tend to gravitate towards the professional faculties and the civil service. Furthermore, as a recently published report based on a survey of politics teaching in 70 out of the country's 150 universities points out, a large body of politics students have an inadequate command of English.[6] They have difficulty coping with books written in English by Indian authors; as for those published abroad, they are simply 'not … intelligible to the bulk of our students'. Most students rely on literature written in regional languages, which is generally so poor that it 'cannot be recommended or recommended only at [our] peril' (ibid.: 776–77). Many a teacher of politics is recruited from such mediocre students.

Talented Indians do, of course produce first-rate works. But they are subject to all kinds of temptation which only a few manage to resist. Thanks to the frustrating and bureaucratic academic climate, and to the widely noticed sense of colonial inferiority, Indian scholars tend to look to the West for recognition and approval, and they can obviously secure it only by writing on themes acceptable to the Western intellectual establishment. There is a rarely articulated but nonetheless unmistakable Western view of what 'serious' Third World scholars should think and write about, how they should study Western or their own societies, along what lines they may criticize either, and so on. The view is propagated through familiar channels, and well-tuned Indian scholars quickly pick up the message.

While Indian political thought remains a poor cousin, all politics departments teach Western political thought at the undergraduate: level, but it too is centred around mainly modem and somewhat badly-selected individual thinkers.[7] The situation is better at the postgraduate level where important concepts and problems are explored. But they are often highly general, have little relevance to India, and ignore many of the questions relating to the nature of the Indian state, political obligation, social justice, positive discrimination, violence, and the languages of Indian political discourse that were mentioned earlier.

India's national political philosophy

On becoming India's first prime minister, Nehru declared his total commitment to comprehensive modernization; he called it India's new 'national philosophy' or 'national ideology', which was 'settled once and for all' and to which the country was 'irrevocably' committed. In his view it was India's 'only hope' and 'last chance' to turn the corner, and any form of tampering with it was bound to prove 'disastrous'. For Nehru modernization involved the seven more-or-less clearly defined 'national goals' of parliamentary democracy, national unity, large-scale industrialization, socialism, secularism, nonalignment, and the development of the scientific temper. For 17 long years he threw his great personal and political authority behind the 'national philosophy', used his three election victories as evidence of popular commitment to it, ridiculed, abused and attacked those daring to challenge it, and created in the country a deep fear of disintegration should it ever waver in its commitment.

Since independence, then, India has had an unofficially official political philosophy. It has become so deeply embedded in national self-consciousness that even those feeling uneasy about some aspects of it rarely express their doubts, or do so in muted and hesitant tones. Since they often share the modernist analysis of the causes of Indian decline, they feel deeply worried lest they should unwittingly send the country back to its now notorious historical slumber or strengthen its regressive tendencies. The national political philosophy has also so profoundly structured the political discourse that its critics lack an adequate vocabulary in which to articulate their doubts and criticisms, let alone develop coherent alternatives. If someone is against secularism, he must be for Hindu *raj*; if against socialism, he must be for unbridled capitalism; if against the scientific temper, he must be for religious obscurantism and so on. As a result there is little conceptual and psychological space for a critical political philosophy to grow. Unless they feel intellectually and morally confident enough to deconstruct the national political philosophy and the mode of discourse generated by it even if only to put it together in more or less its present form, they cannot produce serious political philosophy.

Indian political reality

Another factor that may partly explain the underdevelopment of Indian political theory has to do with the enormous complexity and fluidity of the Indian political reality and the political theorist's deeply ambiguous relation to it.

Tradition and modernity are locked in Indian society in a fascinating relationship of partnership and combat, sometimes reinforcing, sometimes correcting and modifying, and sometimes fighting and defeating each other, and in the process redefining themselves and their relationship. Nothing has a clear and recognizable shape; nothing stands still long enough to permit careful and patient investigation; and nothing is distinct and separate enough to be studied in its own terms and without getting confused with something else. When everything is on the way to becoming something else, one is not entirely clear what concepts to use, what questions to ask, and how to go about answering them.

The Indian political reality, further, is a product of different historical influences. There is the old Hindu India, itself a product of several different influences, still full of life, and increasingly being rediscovered by a society that had for centuries lost intimate contact with its past. The Muslim rule made a deep impact on the Hindu India, and so did the British. Thanks to these and other influences, felt differently in different parts of the country and in different areas of life, India lives in different historical times and contains several undigested and unassimilated chunks of different civilizations. One cannot make sense of it, let alone theorize it, unless one is reasonably familiar with the sources of the influences that have shaped it and still contain clues to its current profile.

Unlike Western societies today, which have relatively stable structures and can at least up to a point be understood atemporally and in their own terms, India can only be understood in terms of its history. Time is a far greater political reality in India than in the West, requiring an Indian political theorist to master the history not only of his own society but also of those who shaped it. Thanks to colonialism and the 'modernist' educational policy of post-independence India, very few political theorists have had classical education or know Sanskrit. Unlike such Western theorists as Bodin, Hobbes and Locke who theorized the emerging European state, Indian political theorists have no direct access to their history and its idioms.

As if these demands were not onerous enough, the Indian political theorist must also be a keen student of Western political theory. Political theory in the West has had a continuous history and is better developed than anywhere else. Although the Indian political theorist sometimes pretends otherwise, his traditional theoretical resources are exiguous and of limited relevance to the kinds of questions he needs to ask and answer today. He cannot learn the craft of political theory and acquire the necessary skills and sensibilities without mastering the tools of Western political thought. But having done so he must return to his own society, master its forms of thought, and readjust the tools to suit its distinct character. The West can help him understand *what it is to do political theory*: his own society can help him decide *what kind of political theory to do*. To master one tradition is difficult enough; to acquire an adequate command of two is beyond the reach of most. The Indian political theorist needs to go West *in order to* get back to the East. This is a long way back home, but it is the only way.

IV

In the previous section I discussed three factors responsible for the under-development of Indian political theory. There are also many others, which for reasons of space I have not examined. These include such things as the colonial rupture in Indian thought, the cognitive alienation of intellectuals from their society, the great difficulty of theorizing in English a reality lived and constituted partly in vernaculars and partly in a mixture of them and English, and the practical, even utilitarian, orientation of much of the traditional Indian concept of theory. The three factors I selected above are some of the most important, and both work through and provide the nodal points for most of the rest. The three are closely related and support each other. For long, Indians were more-or-less convinced that their national political philosophy was wisely chosen and that it was the only one available to them. Since most political theorists shared that view they neither subjected it to a critical examination nor explored an alternative to it. Some of those who were unhappy with the national political philosophy were put of by the daunting task of theorizing their complex reality afresh. Most of those who tried found it difficult to develop realistic and coherent perspectives. All this affected the way they taught and continue to teach political theory. In the absence of the original and creative theorizing of contemporary reality, teaching and research in political theory became unimaginative and centred largely around the history of nationalist political thought and fashionable Western writers. Such teaching and research in turn produced generations of students lacking the courage and the ability to engage in creative theorizing. In this and other related ways the three factors reinforced each other.

If our explanation of the underdevelopment of Indian political theory is correct, it has a wider message. Political theory does not develop in a vacuum. It requires bold and talented minds and a love of theoretical understanding for its own sake. It also requires challenging material, intellectual self-confidence, a climate of tolerance and fearlessness, a relatively firm political reality, the theorist's ability to get a critical purchase on it, and his stable moral and emotional relationship to his environment.[8] In the absence of all or most of these conditions, such a politically sensitive and existentially based form of inquiry as political theory cannot flourish. This may perhaps explain why political theory has not developed in many a Third World country, as also why it has developed in some Western countries and not others and only during certain historical periods.

Notes

1 This is an abridged version of the article that appeared in *History of Political Thought*, 13 (3), 1992.

2 The Indian experience has shown up the limitations of the traditional notion of sovereignty. It still awaits its Bodin and hopefully a Hobbes.

3 Partha Chatterjee and the subaltern school in general have done some good work in this area. V. R. Mehta and V. P. Varma have also done interesting work, especially on Gandhi and Aurobindo, but it remains largely expository. Sudipta Kaviraj's book (1995) on Bankim breaks new grounds.

4 Thomas Pantham, Upendra Baxi and Sudipta Kaviraj have done interesting work in this area.

5 V. R. Mehta, Thomas Pantham, Sudipta Kaviraj, Frank Thakurdas, Partha Chatterjee, V. P. Verma and others have all written in this area. For the attraction of comparative philosophy in India, see Halbfass (1990: 307ff., 548 ff.).

6 *Report on the Curriculum Development Centre in Political Science* (Delhi, 1991). I thank Professor A. P. Rana for sending me a copy.

7 In most universities they include Rawls, Habermas, Foucault, Derrida and Gramsci.

8 Rajni Kothari not only shares my view of the poverty of Indian political thought but presents an even darker picture. However he offers no coherent explanation of it. See Kothari (1986: Chapter l).

References

Baxi, U. and Parekh, B. C. (1995) *Crisis and Change in Contemporary India*, New Delhi: Sage Publications/The Book Review Literary Trust.

Chatterjee, P. (1987) *Nationalist Thought: A Derivative Discourse*, London: Zed.

Chatterji, P. C. (1984) *Secular Values for a Secular India*, Delhi: Lola Chatterji.

Ghoshal, U. N. (1959) *A History of Indian Political Ideas*, London: Oxford University Press.

Halbfass, W. (1990) *India and Europe*, Delhi: Motilal Banarsidass.

Kaviraj, Sudipta (1995) *The Unhappy Consciousness: Bankimchandra Chattopadhyay and the Formation of Nationalist Discourse in India*, Delhi: Oxford University Press.

Kothari R. (1974) *Footsteps into the Future*, Delhi: Orient Longman.

—— (1988) *State Against Democracy*, Delhi: Ajanta.

—— (1986) *A Survey of Research in Political Science, Vol. 4: Political Thought*, Delhi: Indian Council of Social Science Research.

Madan, T. N. (1987) 'Secularism in its Place', *The Journal of Asian Studies,* 4.

Mehta, V. R. (1987) 'Political science in India: in search of an identity', *Government & Opposition,* 22(3).

—— (2005) *Foundations of Indian Political Thought: An Interpretation: From Manu to the Present Day*, New Delhi: Manohar Publishers & Distributors.

Mehta, V. R. and Pantham, Thomas (eds) (2006) *Political Ideas in Modern India: Thematic Explorations*, New Delhi: Sage Publications.

Nandy, A. (1989) 'An anti-secular manifesto', in J. Hick and L. Hempel (eds) *Gandhi's Significance for Today*, London: Palgrave Macmillan.

Narain, J. P. (1959) *A Plea for Reconstruction of the Indian Polity*, Delhi: Akhil Bharat Sarva Seva Sangh Prakashan.

Parekh, B. (1989) *Colonialism, Tradition and Reform*, Delhi: Sage Publications.

—— (1989) *Gandhi's Political Philosophy*, London: University of Notre Dame Press.

—— (1991) 'Nehru and the national philosophy of India', in *Economic and Political Weekly*, January.

Parekh, Bhikhu and Pantham, Thomas (eds) (1987) *Political Discourse: Explorations in Indian and Western Political Thought*, New Delhi: Sage Publications.

Thakurdas, F. (1980) *Perspectives in Political Theory*, New Delhi: Radiant Publishers.

—— (1982) *Essays in Political Theory*, New Delhi: Gitanjali Publishing House.

Varma, V. P. (1954) *Studies in Hindu Political Thought and its Metaphysical Foundation*, Delhi: Motilal Banarsidass.

—— (1979) *Philosophical Humanism and Contemporary India*, Delhi: Motilal Banarsidass.

Part II
Evocation

2 Gandhi's Ambedkar[1]

Ramachandra Guha

I

Mahatma Gandhi was not so much the Father of the Nation as the mother of all debates regarding its future. All his life he fought in a friendly spirit with compatriots whose views on this or that topic diverged sharply from his. He disagreed with Communists and the *bhadralok* on the efficacy and morality of violence as a political strategy. He fought with radical Muslims on the one side and with radical Hindus on the other, both of whom sought to build a state on theological principles. He argued with Nehru and other scientists on whether economic development in a free India should centre on the village or the factory. And with that other giant, Rabindranath Tagore, he disputed the merits of such varied affiliations as the English language, nationalism, and the spinning wheel.

In some ways the most intense, interesting and long-running of these debates was between Gandhi and Ambedkar. Gandhi wished to save Hinduism by abolishing untouchability, whereas Ambedkar saw a solution for his people outside the fold of the dominant religion of the Indian people. Gandhi was a rural romantic, who wished to make the self-governing village the bedrock of free India; Ambedkar an admirer of city life and modern technology who dismissed the Indian village as a den of iniquity. Gandhi was a crypto-anarchist who favoured non-violent protest while being suspicious of the state; Ambedkar a steadfast constitutionalist, who worked within the state and sought solutions to social problems with the aid of the state.

Perhaps the most telling difference was in the choice of political instrument. For Gandhi, the Congress represented all of India, the Dalits too. Had he not made their cause their own from the time of his first ashram in South Africa? Ambedkar however made a clear distinction between freedom and power. The Congress wanted the British to transfer power to them, but to obtain freedom the Dalits had to organize themselves as a separate bloc, to form a separate party, so as to more effectively articulate their interests in the crucible of electoral politics. It was thus that in his lifetime, and for long afterwards, Ambedkar came to represent a dangerously subversive threat to the authoritative, and sometimes authoritarian, equation: Gandhi = Congress = Nation.

Here then is the stuff of epic drama, the argument between the Hindu who did most to reform caste and the ex-Hindu who did most to do away with caste altogether. Recent accounts represent it as a fight between a hero and a villain, the writer's caste position generally determining who gets cast as hero, who as villain. In truth both figures should be seen as heroes, albeit tragic ones.

The tragedy, from Gandhi's point of view, was that his colleagues in the national movement either did not understand his concern with untouchability or even actively deplored it. Priests and motley *shankaracharyas* thought he was going too fast in his challenge to caste – and why did he not first take their permission? Communists wondered why he wanted everyone to clean their own latrines when he could be speaking of class struggle. And Congressmen in general thought Harijan work came in the way of an all-out effort for national freedom. Thus Stanley Reid, a former editor of the *Times of India*, quotes an Indian patriot who complained in the late 1930s that 'Gandhi is wrapped up in the Harijan movement. He does not care a jot whether we live or die; whether we are bound or free.'

The opposition that he faced from his fellow Hindus meant that Gandhi had perforce to move slowly, and in stages. He started by accepting that untouchability was bad, but added a cautionary caveat – that inter-dining and inter-marriage were also bad. He moved on to accepting inter-mingling and inter-dining (hence the movement for temple entry), and to arguing that all men and all *varnas* were equal. The last and most far-reaching step, taken only in 1946, was to challenge caste directly by accepting and sanctioning inter-marriage itself.

The tragedy, from Ambedkar's point of view, was that to fight for his people he had to make common cause with the British. In his book, *Worshipping False Gods*, Arun Shourie (2004) has made much of this. Shourie takes all of 600 pages to make two points: (*i*) that Ambedkar was a political opponent of both Gandhi and the Congress, and generally preferred the British to either; (*ii*) that Ambedkar cannot be called the 'Father of the Constitution' as that implies sole authorship, whereas several other people, such as K. M. Munshi and B. N. Rau, also contributed significantly to the wording of the document. Reading *Worshipping False Gods*, one might likewise conclude that it has been mistakenly advertised as being the work of one hand. Entire chapters are based entirely on one or other volume of the *Transfer of Power*, the collection of official papers put out some years ago by Her Majesty's Stationery Office. The editor of that series, Nicholas Mansergh (1970), might with reason claim co-authorship of Shourie's book. In a just world he would be granted a share of the royalties too.

Practised in the arts of over-kill and over-quote, Shourie is a pamphleteer parading as a historian. He speaks of Gandhi only as 'Gandhiji' and of the national movement only as the 'National Movement', indicating that he has judged the case beforehand. For to use the suffix and the capitals is to simultaneously elevate and intimidate, to set up the man and his movement as the ideal, above and beyond criticism. But the Congress' claim to represent all of India was always under challenge. The Communists said it was the party of landlords and capitalists. The Muslim League said it was a party of the Hindus. Ambedkar then appended a devastating caveat, saying that the party did not even represent all Hindus, but only the upper castes.

Shourie would deny that these critics had any valid arguments whatsoever. He is in the business of awarding, and more often withholding, certificates of patriotism. The opponents of the Congress are thus all suspect to him, simply because they dared point out that the National Movement was not always as national as it set out to be, or that the Freedom Struggle promised unfreedom for some. But how did these men outside the Congress come to enjoy such a wide following? This is a question Shourie does not pause to answer, partly because he has made up his mind in advance, but also because he is woefully ill-informed. Consider now some key facts erased or ignored by him.

That Ambedkar preferred the British to the Congress is entirely defensible. Relevant here is a remark of the eighteenth century English writer Samuel Johnson (1913). When the American colonists asked for independence from Britain, Johnson said: 'How is it that we hear the greatest yelps for liberty among the drivers of Negroes?' Untouchability was to the Indian freedom movement what slavery had been to the American struggle, the basic contradiction it sought to paper over. Before Ambedkar another outstanding leader of the lower castes, Jotiba Phule, also distrusted the Congress, in his time a party dominated by Poona Brahmins. He too preferred the British, in whose armies and factories low castes could find opportunities denied them in the past. The opening up of the economy and the growth of the colonial cities also helped many untouchables escape the tyranny of the village. The British might have been unwitting agents of change; nonetheless, under their rule life for the lower castes was less unpleasant by far than it had been under the Peshwas.

Shourie also seems unaware of work by worthy historians on low-caste movements in other parts of India. Mark Juergensmeyer has documented the struggles of untouchables in Punjab, which, under its remarkable leader Mangoo Ram, rejected the Congress and the Arya Samaj to form a new sect, Adi-Dharm, which was opposed to both. Sekhar Bandyopadhyay has written of the Namasudras in Bengal, who, like Ambedkar and his Mahars, were not convinced that a future Congress government would be sympathetic to their interests. And countless scholars have documented the rise of the Dravidian movement in South India that took as its point of departure Brahmin domination of the Congress in Madras: the movement's founder, E. V. Ramaswami 'Periyar', also fought bitterly with Gandhi.

The leaders of these movements, and the millions who followed them, worked outside the Congress and often in opposition to it. Enough reason perhaps for Shourie to dismiss them all as anti-national. Indeed, Shourie's attitude is comparable to that of white Americans who question the patriotism of those blacks who dare speak out against racism. For asking blacks to stand up for their rights, men of such stature as W. E. B. Du Bois and Paul Robeson were called all kinds of names, of which 'anti-American' was much the politest. Later, the great Martin Luther King was persecuted by the most powerful of American agencies, the Federal Bureau of Investigation, whose director, J. Edgar Hoover, equated patriotism with acquiescence to white domination.

Much of the time, Shourie writes as if there is a singular truth, with him as its repository and guarantor. Time and again he equates Ambedkar with Jinnah as an 'accomplice of Imperial politics'. He dismisses all that Ambedkar wrote about Hinduism as 'caricature' and 'calumnies'. Not once does he acknowledge that there was much truth to the criticisms. There is not one admission here of the horrendous and continuing sufferings of Dalits at the hands of caste Hindus that might explain and justify Ambedkar's rhetoric and political choices. For Shourie, the fact that Ambedkar disagreed long and often with Gandhi is proof enough that he was anti-national. He even insinuates that Ambedkar 'pushed Gandhi to the edge of death' by not interfering with the Mahatma's decision to fast in captivity. Of the same fast other historians have written, in my view more plausibly, that by threatening to die, Gandhi blackmailed Ambedkar into signing a pact with him.

Somewhere in the middle of *Worshipping False Gods*, the author complains that Ambedkar's 'statues, dressed in garish blue, holding a copy of the Constitution – have been put up in city after city'. However, this aesthetic distaste seems rather pointless. For the background to the statues and the reverence they command lies in the continuing social practices of the religion to which Shourie and I belong. If caste lives, so will the memory of the man who fought to annihilate it. The remarkable thing is that 50 years after independence, the only politician, dead or alive, who has a truly pan-Indian appeal is B. R. Ambedkar. Where Gandhi is forgotten in his native Gujarat, and Nehru vilified in his native Kashmir, Ambedkar is worshipped in hamlets all across the land. For Dalits everywhere he is the symbol of their struggle, the scholar, theoretician and activist whose own life represented a stirring triumph over the barriers of caste.

Shourie's attacks on Dalits and their hero follow in quick succession the books he has published attacking Communists, Christians, and Muslims. Truth be told, the only category of Indians he has not attacked – and going by his present political persuasion will not attack – are high-caste Hindus. Oddly enough, this bilious polemicist and baiter of the minorities was once an anti-religious leftist who excoriated Hinduism. To see Shourie's career in its totality is to recall these words of Isaac Deutscher (1977), on the communist turned anticommunist:

> He brings to his job the lack of scruple, the narrow-mindedness, the disregard of truth, and the intense hatred with which Stalinism has imbued him. He remains sectarian. He is an inverted Stalinist. He continues to see the world in black and white, but now the colours are differently distributed. ... The ex-communist ... is haunted by a vague sense that he has betrayed either his former ideals or the ideals of bourgeois society. ... He then tries to suppress the guilt and uncertainty, or to camouflage it by a show of extraordinary certitude and frantic aggressiveness. He insists that the world should recognize his uneasy conscience as the clearest conscience of all. He may no longer be concerned with any cause except one – self-justification.

II

Ambedkar is a figure who commands great respect from one end of the social spectrum. But he is also, among some non-Dalits, an object of great resentment, chiefly for his decision to carve out a political career independent of and sometimes in opposition to Gandhi's Congress. That is of course the burden of Shourie's critique but curiously, the very week his book was published, at a political rally in Lucknow the Samajvadi Party's Beni Prasad Verma likewise dismissed Ambedkar as one who 'did nothing else except create trouble for Gandhiji'. This line, that Ambedkar had no business to criticize, challenge or argue with Gandhi, was of course made with much vigour and malice during the national movement as well.

I think, however, that for Ambedkar to stand up to the uncrowned king and anointed Mahatma of the Indian people required extraordinary courage and will-power. Gandhi thought so too. Speaking at a meeting in Oxford in October 1931, Gandhi said he had 'the highest regard for Dr Ambedkar. He has every right to be bitter. That he does not break our heads is an act of self-restraint on his part.' Writing to an English friend two years later, he said he found 'nothing unnatural' in Ambedkar's hostility to the Congress and its supporters. 'He has not only witnessed the inhuman wrongs done to the social pariahs of Hinduism', reflected this Hindu, 'but in spite of all his culture, all the honours that he has received, he has, when he is in India, still to suffer many insults to which untouchables are exposed'. In June 1936 Gandhi pointed out once again that Dr Ambedkar 'has had to suffer humiliations and insults which should make any one of us bitter and resentful'. 'Had I been in his place', he remarked, 'I would have been as angry'.

Gandhi's latter-day admirers might question Ambedkar's patriotism and probity, but the Mahatma had no such suspicions himself. Addressing a bunch of Karachi students in June 1934, he told them that 'the magnitude of [Dr Ambedkar's] sacrifice is great. He is absorbed in his own work. He leads a simple life. He is capable of earning one to two thousand rupees a month. He is also in a position to settle down in Europe if he so desires. But he doesn't want to stay there. He is only concerned about the welfare of the Harijans'.

To Gandhi, Ambedkar's protest held out a lesson to the upper castes. In March 1936 he said that if Ambedkar and his followers were to embrace another religion, 'We deserve such treatment and our task [now] is to wake up to the situation and purify ourselves'. Not many heeded the warning, for towards the end of his life Gandhi spoke with some bitterness about the indifference to Harijan work among his fellow Hindus: 'The tragedy is that those who should have especially devoted themselves to the work of [caste] reform did not put their hearts into it. What wonder that Harijan brethren feel suspicious, and show opposition and bitterness'.

The words quoted in the preceding paragraphs have been taken from that reliable and easily accessible source: the *Collected Works of Mahatma Gandhi* (2000). The 100 volumes of that set rest lightly on my shelves as, going by other evidence, they rest on the shelves of the man who compiled *Worshipping False Gods*. Perhaps the most perverse aspect of an altogether perverse book is that Shourie does not once tell us what Gandhi said or wrote about his great adversary. A curious thing or, on reflection, a not-so-curious thing: for if that scholarly courtesy was resorted to, the case that Ambedkar was an anti-national careerist would be blown sky-high.

One of the few Gandhians who understood the cogency of the Dalit critique of the Congress was C. Rajagopalachari. In the second half of 1932, Rajaji became involved in the campaign to allow the so-called untouchables to enter the Guruvayoor temple in Kerala. The campaign was led by that doughty fighter for the rights of the dispossessed, K. Kelappan Nair. In a speech at Guruvayoor on 20 December 1932, Rajaji told the high castes that

> it would certainly help us in the fight for Swaraj if we open the doors of the temple [to Harijans]. One of the many causes that keeps Swaraj away from us is that we are divided among ourselves. Mahatmaji received many wounds in London [during the Second Round Table Conference of 1931]. *But Dr Ambedkar's darts were the worst. Mahatmaji did not quake before the Churchills of England. But as representing the nation he had to plead guilty to Dr Ambedkar's charges.*

As it was, the managers of temples across the land could count upon the support of many among their clientele, the *suvarna* Hindus who agreed with the shankaracharyas that the Gandhians were dangerous revolutionaries who had to be kept out at the gate. Unhappily, while upper caste Hindus thought that Gandhi moved too fast, Dalits today feel he was much too slow. The Dalit politician Mayawati has, more than once, spoken of the Mahatma as a shallow paternalist who sought only to smooth the path for more effective long-term domination by the *suvarna*. Likewise, in his book *Why I am Not a Hindu* Kancha Illiah (2002) writes of Gandhi as wanting to 'build a modern consent system for the continued maintenance of brahminical hegemony' – a judgement as unfair as Shourie's on Ambedkar.

Whereas in their lifetime Gandhi and Ambedkar were political rivals, now, decades after their death, it should be possible to see their contributions as complementing one another's. The Kannada critic D. R. Nagaraj once noted that in the narratives of Indian nationalism the 'heroic stature of the caste-Hindu reformer', Gandhi, 'further dwarfed the Harijan personality' of Ambedkar. In the Ramayana there is only one hero but, as Nagaraj points out, Ambedkar was too proud, intelligent and self-respecting a man to settle for the role of Hanuman or Sugreeva. By the same token, Dalit hagiographers and pamphleteers generally seek to elevate Ambedkar by diminishing Gandhi. For the scriptwriter and the mythmaker there can only be one hero. But the historian is bound by no such constraint. The history of Dalit emancipation is unfinished, and for the most part unwritten. It should, and will, find space for many heroes. Ambedkar and Gandhi will do nicely for a start.

Note

1 This article was originally published in Ramachandra Guha, *An Anthropologist among the Marxists and Other Essays* (Delhi: Permanent Black, 2001).

References

Deutscher, Isaac (1977) 'The conscience of the ex-communist', in M. A. Sperber (ed.) *Arthur Koestler: A Collection of Critical Essays*, Englewood Cliffs, NJ: Prentice-Hall.

Gandhi, M. K. (2000) *The Collected Works of Mahatma Gandhi*, New Delhi: Publications Division, Ministry of Information and Broadcasting, Government of India.

Guha, R. (2007) *India after Gandhi: The History of the World's Largest Democracy*, New York: Ecco.

Ilaiah, K. (2002) *Why I am not a Hindu: A Sudra Critique of Hindutva, Philosophy, Culture, and Political Economy*, Calcutta: Mandira Sen for Samya.

Johnson, Samuel (1913) 'Taxation no tyranny: an answer to the resolutions and address of the American Congress', in *The Works of Samuel Johnson*, vol. 14, Troy, NY: Pafraets & Company, pp. 93–144.

Mansergh, N., Lumby, E. W. R. and Moon, P. (1970) *The Transfer of Power 1942–7*, London: HMSO.

Shourie, A. (2004) *Worshipping False Gods: Ambedkar and the Facts Which Have been Erased*, New Delhi: Rupa & Co.

3 The quest for justice

Evoking Gandhi[1]

Neera Chandhoke

I

Identifying the problem

That members of a given plural society are likely to disagree not only on what the precise nature of substantive justice is, but also on what the governing norms which can arbitrate between competing notions of substantive justice are, is by now well known. It is also realized that these two issues pose a rather intractable problem for political theory, simply because they defy aspirations that a political community will be able to balance diversity of conceptions of justice with allegiance to shared norms such as a master concept of justice. Now that the assumption that the public sphere is neutral towards competing notions of the good has been exposed as one of the vanities of political modernity in society after society, the carefully constructed, but the rather precarious boundary between the public and the private has become even more unstable, even prone to collapse. Along with this debacle, the belief that people can fashion and pursue their projects according to their notions of the good, *provided* these projects conform to certain shared norms in the public sphere, has taken a hard knock. For these reasons, plural societies are more often than not deeply divided societies, divided not only over issues of substantive justice, but also on the moral norms that can referee competing conceptions of justice. Yet the first tension between different conceptions of justice can be resolved. The resolution might well consume time, and extract patience, energy, imagination, and political innovation, but it can be done. The second issue is considerably more inflexible, and resists resolution, simply because the status of the norm, as one that is morally binding, comes under dispute.

In India three issues that regularly bedevil public debate over what is just, might serve to illustrate the point I am trying to make. Whereas the Indian Constitution codes secularism as one of the main pillars of constitutionalism in the Preamble, what secularism actually means has become a matter of contentious debates. Is secularism about constructing a 'wall of separation' between the state and religion? Or is secularism about treating different religions equally, making religion thereby a matter of state policy? Which of these policies can possibly deliver justice in a multi-religious society? Can we combine both these interpretations, and evoke thereby a fuller concept of secularism in and for a religious society? Still, these debates over differing interpretations of secularism are not that deep or stubborn, because the moral status of secularism as an intrinsic principle of justice for a religiously plural society is uncontested. But when groups belonging to the Hindu right dismiss secularism out of hand: by rejecting the principle of equality of all religions, as well as the principle that the state should not adopt a particular religion which thereby becomes the state religion, the moral status of secularism is in some trouble. Also in trouble is the commitment to justice for all religious groups. The pogrom of the Muslim minority in the state of Gujarat, by cadres of the Hindu Right in 2002, exemplifies the contempt with which these cadres treat secularism. Dismissing the axiom that secularism is a way of ensuring justice to all religious groups, they also write off the proposition that no one religious group has the right to stamp the country with its ethos *even* if it is in a majority, and that no religious group can be discriminated against *even* if it is in a minority.

The second tension that continuously bedevils political debate in India is the one between universal conceptions of gender justice, and personal laws of minority religions. This was more than evident in the famous Shah Bano case. On 23 April 1985, a Supreme Court Bench under Chief Justice Chandrachud ruled that article 125 of the Criminal Procedure Code, which regulates the payment of maintenance to divorced women, overrides all personal laws, and that it is uniformly applicable to all women. The Bench also called upon the Government of India to enact a Uniform Civil Code under article 44 of the Constitution. Expectedly patriarchal sections of the Muslim community opposed the judgement on the ground that it disregarded and downgraded the personal laws of the Muslim community which are based on the *Shariat*. The argument was that the *Shariat* is divinely sanctioned; therefore, it can neither be tampered with, nor interpreted by the Court. The controversy snowballed into a major political problem as thousands of Muslim citizens took to the street to demonstrate against the judgement. What norm of gender justice can we appeal to in order to resolve this dilemma? The problem is deeper. Is it possible to extract women from their constitutive attachments and construct them as universal and abstract units of justice? Conversely how do norms of justice deal with personal laws which are highly subversive of gender justice?

The third tension-ridden issue in India is that of protective discrimination for the dalits/scheduled castes. These castes have been throughout history doubly disprivileged because they are socially discriminated against, as well as economically marginalized. For these reasons, it is generally agreed that these groups are entitled to compensation for historical wrongs. The debate around protective discrimination is essentially one between norms of formal equality and that of egalitarianism, which takes into consideration background inequalities. In theory both conceptions of equality are reconcilable, *provided* we subscribe to a substantive notion of equality. In practice however, affirmative action policies, particularly reservation of seats in educational institutions and in public jobs for the scheduled castes as well as for the scheduled tribes has led to repeated confrontations, standoffs, the construction of demeaning imageries, and perverse stereotyping, all of which feeds into the alienation of one group from another. Students and job seekers belonging to the 'upper castes' ask for how long they are expected to pay for the sins of their forbears? How long do those who have benefited from history have to compensate the victims of history? In any case, is not protective discrimination on such a scale an infringement of article 15 of the fundamental rights chapter in the Constitution, which codifies the right not to be discriminated against? At stake in these angry confrontations, is the very status of the norm of substantive equality as a component of justice.

Often acerbic disagreements over these three principles of justice: secularism, gender justice, and protective discrimination, pose some of the most difficult problems for

Indian democracy. Should the state treat the claims of all religious groups equally? Or should it privilege the demand of the majority group that it is entitled to monopolize political power by virtue of numbers? Should the state enact codes of gender justice according to procedures that honour universal and abstract concepts of justice? Or should procedures for delivering justice to women take as their referral the personal codes of minority religious groups? Should the state enact laws which recognize the claims of all groups that position themselves as historically disprivileged? Or should the state balance these demands against those of other groups? It is not surprising that disputes over the status of morally binding principle of justice, as well as over the norms and procedures that regulate conflicts between rival claims, lead to repeated deadlocks, and resultant breaks in inter-group communication.

The only politically viable way in which these obdurate tensions can be addressed is to institutionalize procedures which enable dialogue among different groups on specific policies, as well as on the appropriate normative structures that should regulate a good society.

Arguably, dialogue, appears particularly appropriate for plural societies, which are marked not only by a variety of perspectives, belief systems, and values, but also stamped by deep disagreements on the basic norms of a polity. But there is a rather inflexible problem that we can locate precisely here. Theorists tend to assume the following preconditions for dialogue: equality, freedom, open-ness, publicity, readiness to give and accept reasonable arguments, and an equal willingness to modify original positions through debate and deliberation. But plural societies tend to be deeply divided and fractious. For this very reason the assertion and counter-assertion of truth claims are regarded by other groups as representing partisan points of view, and as self-regarding. This closes off the very possibility of dialogue, foments the politics of distrust, leads to constructions of 'otherness', fragments civil society, proclaims an end to inter-group solidarity, and gives to the state immense freedom to manoeuvre between competing claims. None of these consequences are particularly favourable for the augmentation of the status of justice as a supreme norm, which is morally and politically binding, and which can be regarded as the chief governing principle of the body politic.

The question that, therefore, confronts us at this stage of the argument is simply this: how do 'we' (those of us who are committed to dialogue) go about establishing the preconditions for debate and deliberation among participants who see each other as either the 'unknown', perhaps the 'unknowable', or worse as the 'polluting', as the 'inferior', as the 'adversary'; in short as the 'other' with whom there can be neither truck nor transaction? Other troubled questions follow. What are the moral perspectives which agents divided along the axis of religion, caste, and ethnicity, bring to the discursive arena? How do agents who wish to put forth a particular point of view establish their credibility: that their reflection and their proposed courses of action are in the public interest, and not in the pursuit of some selfish private gain, in such societies? How can communication among agents be enabled at all insofar as these agents can be persuaded to modify or moderate their original position in and through the process of dialogue?

I suggest that the Gandhian philosophy of satyagraha provides us with some answers to these vexing questions. Consider, for instance, that Gandhi managed to accomplish precisely the onerous task identified above – that of instituting dialogue – in India in the early years of the twentieth century, against great odds. In the 1920s Gandhi set out to forge a mass movement in the country against British imperialism, and proceeded to transform the Indian National Congress from an elitist to a popular organization. But by the time Gandhi embarked on this venture, colonial policies of enumeration and separate electorates, and the politics of religious organizations which had appeared on the political horizon to push their own separatist agendas, had propelled and consolidated divisive tendencies among the people. If on the one hand communal riots among Hindus and Muslims had scarred the body politic with particularly vicious modes of violence, on the other, caste discrimination proscribed the 'coming together' of members of the Hindu and other communities in any shared struggle. Undeterred by these somewhat formidable impediments to dialogue, Gandhi set about forging massive coalitions of religious groups, castes, and classes, and thereby instituting dialogue. For the foremost prerequisite of coalition politics is that constituent groups begin to speak with each other, transact with each other, deliberate with each other, and, in short, engage each other in a dialogue.

Gandhi did not succeed completely in this endeavour because the country *was* partitioned on religious grounds in 1947. Yet he did not fail either, because millions of people, across caste, creeds, and class did 'come together' in and through the struggle against colonialism. What *is* significant is that in the process, Gandhi gave to us a philosophy, which can perchance help to institutionalize conditions that support dialogue in contentious and fragmented societies. The philosophy is that of satyagraha. Satyagraha, in Gandhian thought, provides the philosophical foundation for practices of civil disobedience against the state, and against undesirable practices within the community. Satyagraha also yields the epistemological foundations for a theory of non-violence which informs these practices, and which is indeed a necessary prerequisite of these practices.

In Gandhian philosophy, satyagraha combines as well as transcends two concepts: *satya* which means truth, and a*graha* which means to grasp, to seize, to hold, or to grapple with. Gandhi defined the concept of satyagraha as literally holding on the truth, and therefore, as 'Truth-Force'. 'Truth is soul or spirit. It is, therefore, known as soul-force' wrote Gandhi (1966b: 466). Distinguishing satyagraha from passive resistance and other forms of civil disobedience, Gandhi suggested that the philosophy is not a weapon of the weak (ibid.). On the other hand, it demands tremendous moral strength and fortitude, because satyagraha involves a relentless *search* for truth with steadfastness, commitment, fearlessness, and willingness to accept punishment (ibid.). The philosophy of satyagraha enlightens the mind, but more importantly gives to us a theory of action. In other words, if satyagraha gives us a theory of knowledge, it also guides us towards the right path. For Gandhi knowledge is action, and action should mirror knowledge.

Admittedly the Gandhian philosophy of satyagraha is historically contextual insofar as it was forged as a political weapon against a deeply unjust colonial state. Satyagraha is also theoretically contextual inasmuch as the concept is grounded in precepts taken from the spiritual traditions of at least four major religions: Hinduism, Buddhism, Jainism, and Christianity. Yet the Gandhian philosophy of satyagraha, and the overlapping theories of civil disobedience and non-violence, has proved highly relevant for struggles against injustice in other parts of the world, and inspired towering figures such as Martin Luther King, Nelson Mandela, and Aung San Suu Kyi. It is perhaps time we begin to explore other rich resources of the philosophy in order to negotiate problems which are endemic to divided societies. Conceivably the philosophy of satyagraha can aid the establishment of dialogue among people who disagree violently on what the truth is, and what justice can be. If justice is the foundational norm of a society, then justice has to be grounded in some notion of the truth, which may possibly constitute a shared referral for political allegiance. Therefore, for Gandhi, the concept of justice was inseparable from that of truth.

II

Satyagraha as dialogue

Take the first problem that confronts divided societies. Considering that dialogue in plural societies is more often than not hampered by the politics of mutual suspicion, how do agents go about establishing their moral credentials? How do they demonstrate to the political public that the issue that they seek to foreground in the discursive community, as one that demands reflection and action, is in the public interest, and not in the pursuit of some private benefit? Gandhi's advice to agents who wish to initiate a dialogue on the nature of justice is the following: prepare yourself for the original struggle; that of convincing other agents that the agenda of action you want to set forth has been arrived at through processes that are indisputably moral. The launch of satyagraha accordingly demands adherence to rather stringent requirements: agents must engage in processes of moral reasoning and moral judgment that allow them to single out an issue as a moral one, assess the issue in light of several competing moral considerations, and identify it as one that demands collective action. For Gandhi these processes are infinitely facilitated, *if* satyagrahi's subject themselves to rigorous codes of self-discipline. For instance, any satyagrahi who embarks upon civil disobedience must practice fasting, refrain from the pursuit of material interests, and adopt celibacy.

Agents have to undergo this rigorous training in self discipline because both the body and the mind have to be completely at rest, and this is only possible if the agent is detached from worldly consideration. Detachment is an indispensable precondition of selfless action, inner strength, and the capacity to bear suffering. More significantly, self-discipline helps to purify the mind of negative thoughts, haste, hatred, and ill will to others. For Gandhi, these sentiments not only cloud perception, and thus thwart the making of choices that are indisputably moral, they are indicative of a tendency to violence. And violence is the greatest betrayer of dialogue, because it subverts the very possibility of a shared search for truth. After all we can hardly enter into a debate with those who we regard as not quite human, or those who we regard with distaste and animosity.

Processes of moral reasoning, moral judgment, and self-discipline might well contribute to the prospect of establishing and reproducing the conditions of dialogue. This is because these processes help to establish the credentials of the agents who invite other moral agents to a dialogue as (a) selfless beings who are committed to the search for truth, in the public interest, and in a non-violent manner, (b) that the cause for which satyagraha has been initiated is a moral one, (c) that agents have undertaken satyagraha in full consciousness of what the penalties are, and (d) that they are willing to bear the costs. And it is possible to establish this, because not only dialogue, but the *preconditions* of dialogue have to be both public and transparent. Gandhi, suggest the Rudolph's, transgresses what are for Habermas 'foundational dichotomies', or the division between the private and the public. Gandhi's ashrams were public places, accessible to all, because these provided the sites for training in satyagraha (Rudolph and Rudolph 2006: 153). In other words, the moment the agent begins the preparation for satyagraha through moral reasoning, moral judgment, and self-discipline, these processes should be as transparent and accessible as the process of dialogue. This by itself contributes much to the moral standing of the agent. Even if we emancipate the moral agent from the somewhat rigorous codes of self discipline, the preconditions that Gandhi lays down hold important lessons for theories of dialogue.

Secondly, the conceptual referral of satyagraha: the nature of Gandhi's truth, enables the process of dialogue immeasurably. Theorists of dialogue tell us that participants must be ready to listen to, respect, and accept other points of view as equally valid. Gandhi articulates compelling reasons *why* participants should be ready to respect the truth claims of others, and why they should be willing to modify their own claims to truth. Satyagrahi's cannot assert that their claims are based upon the discovery of absolute truths and are, therefore, non-negotiable, simply because, for Gandhi, no one can discover the full truth. We can only strive towards the attainment of this truth. This carries the process of dialogue further, because the conviction that we are capable of knowing but the *partial* truth, serves to discipline the self, teaches us to be modest about our own pretensions, and compels us to be accommodative about the claims of others.

Thirdly, the nature of Gandhi's truth pre-empts the use of violence in any form in the dialogical space. Violence for Gandhi symbolizes arrogance; or the conviction that since we know better than others what the truth is, our views should be given pre-cedence in the dialogical sphere. Such a stance kills the very possibility of any mean-ingful exchange of arguments, because it admits of no other version of the truth but ours. Further, to impose our truth upon others is to do violence to their truths. But for Gandhi, since human beings are not capable of knowing the absolute truth, they do not have the competence to punish other people through violent words, deeds, or even thoughts (1966b: 466).

Fourthly, the nature of Gandhi's truth establishes equality in the dialogical space. The readiness to accept that our truth can be modified by the truth claims of others, and that their truth can further be mediated by yet others, and so on, does much to establish that there is no one privileged truth which can arbitrate between other notions, and which puts the owner of this truth in a privileged position. All known truths are partial; therefore, all truths are equally valid and deserving of respect. In sum, the partial nature of known truth acts as a powerful moral imperative to regard other participants as equal.

Therefore, fifthly, the possibility of dialogue is greatly improved, because other par-ties are not constructed as the adversary, as the enemy, or as the 'other', but as partners in a shared search for the truth. This contributes much to validate the standing of other people, as beings who have something worthwhile to contribute to the elaboration of an idea or a worldview. In other words, when we invite others to share in the quest for truth, or justice, on the basis of equal respect, we recognize the other person as some-one who matters. This institutionalizes mutual respect, prohibits the construction of 'otherness', and neutralizes conflict which arises out of non-recognition in divided societies.

Sixthly, Gandhi's notion of satyagraha is grounded in the certainty that the quest for truth has to be a shared venture. Contrary to the popular belief in Hindu and Buddhist spiritual thought, that truth can be found only when the searcher seeking refuge from all distractions – as Gautam Buddha did – retreats to the forest or to the cave, for Gandhi, truth cannot be comprehended in and through the processes of solitary reflection or meditation. The real location of his truth is found in the plurality and the unity of life. 'If I could persuade myself that I should find Him [God] in a Himalayan cave', writes Gandhi, 'I would proceed there immediately. But I know I cannot find Him apart from humanity' (Gandhi 1976: 240). This conviction provides the philosophical underpinnings of theories of dialogue – such as the Habermasian or Gadamerian – that emphasize the interconnectedness of human beings.

The sixth conviction of Gandhi contributes much to the reproduction of the dialo- gical process over time. For Gandhi, substantive rules of justice cannot be produced once and for all. Democratic politics is not a matter of reproducing that which has already been produced. There is, in Gandhian thought, as in theories of dialogue, no notion of an original Hobbesian social contract which binds citizens in perpetuity. The terms of the contract have to be constantly renegotiated, even as new insights on what justice is, and what truth is, emerge onto political horizons. Because we can never know that what we have grasped through intuition, reasoning, and self discipline is the ulti- mate truth, dialogue never reaches stasis.

Finally, for Gandhi, as for philosophers of dialogue, the quest for truth is more sig- nificant than a final arrival, or the discovery of the ultimate truth. It is more important that people continue to speak to each other, rather than proclaim a closure on dialogue because they have arrived at a definitive truth. Dialogue does not have a whit of a chance to succeed if even one participant believes that he or she should have the last word. It may sound paradoxical but truth is always subject to re-negotiation. This is particularly relevant for plural societies, simply because one urgent political task that confronts these societies is the establishment of processes which at least bring agents together, encourage them to speak to each other, and keep the conversation going. And this by itself might contribute to the ironing out of senseless conflicts that arise out of the lack of communication in such societies.

These seven components of satyagraha can possibly enable the institutionalization of and the reproduction of a discursive community, in and through a dialogical quest for what is true, and therefore just, in plural/deeply divided societies. At the centre of the philosophy is the nature of Gandhi's truth, which provides a referral for dialogue.

III

Gandhi's truth

Gandhi's stipulation that the satyagrahi should engage in processes of moral reasoning and judgment *before* he or she initiates a shared quest for the truth, is not entirely unproblematic. Processes of moral reasoning and moral judgment presume the exis- tence of certain truths that constitute pressing considerations on what we consider moral. The proposition is, however, a difficult one, simply because it begs the existence of moral truths. It also begs the question of what the procedures, which help us in arriving at the truth, are. Even if we assume there are some moral truths, what, some sceptic can legitimate ask, makes these truths so true or so moral that they constitute a critical referral when we seek to identify 'this' or 'that' problem as a moral one, arbi- trate between competing considerations when we decide whether this problem needs to be negotiated or not, and reason out how to act? How do we give an account of our moral reasoning in light of truth conditions of moral statements which we can never be sure of?

Gandhi's answer to these troubling questions lies in between moral absolutism and moral relativism or scepticism. He does not deny the existence of truth which for him is absolute and transcendental. But human beings cannot possibly know what the absolute truth is. Gandhi cites a story in the Gospel in which a judge wants to know what the truth is, but gets no answer. The question posed by that judge, suggests Gandhi, has not been answered. For the truth espoused by King Harishchandra who renounced everything he possessed for the sake of the truth, is not the same as the truth of Hussain, who sacrificed his life for the truth. These two truths are equally true, but they may or may not be *our* truth. 'Beyond these limited truths, however, there is one absolute Truth which is total and all-embracing. But it is indescribable' (Gandhi 1991: 223–24).

Gandhi, in effect, tells us that the one ultimate truth is manifested in the shape of many truths, but each of these truths is but an incomplete version of the ultimate truth. Using the metaphor of the seven blind men and the elephant, Gandhi suggests that we are as blind as the seven in the story. 'We must therefore be content with believing the truth as it appears to us' (1969: 111). The ultimate truth is eternal and transcendental, known truth is a fraction of what is eternal and transcendental, but it is only that latter that falls within the competence of human beings.

But where do we begin to look for this truth? Any search must lead somewhere, in some direction, towards some end; for even if we never reach the end, at least the path to that end should be clear. Gandhi, it is well known, was deeply religious, and originally he identified truth with the Supreme Being or God. Rather 'say', he enjoined, 'that God is Truth' (1976: 224). There is some logic here, because the word *satya* comes from *sat*, which means to be, or to exist through time. And only God is the same through all time (ibid.: 225). But Gandhi was not religious in the conventional, or in the doctrinal sense. To understand this aspect of Gandhian thought, we have to understand what religion meant to him. Rather than be unthinkingly bound by religious doctrines, or worse be confined to certain scriptural understandings, Gandhi preferred that religion be viewed as a source of valuable insights into the human condition; as part of a common human heritage (Parekh 1999: Chapter 1). In effect, religion for Gandhi meant pretty much what culture means for the communitarians: as a set of resources which helps us make sense of the world. Therefore the belief that human beings are religiously/culturally constituted by no means implies that they cannot make moral choices. These choices are not made in abstraction from the values bequeathed by the community, but neither are these choices completely determined by the culture. Similarly for Gandhi, religion can only give us the moral context within which we can make intelligible choices. 'God' writes Gandhi, 'is conscience. He is even the atheism of the atheist. ... He is the greatest democrat the world knows, for He leaves us unfettered to make our own choice between evil and good' (Gandhi 1967: 224–25).

In the Gandhian worldview as in the worldview of communitarian philosophers, human beings possess the capacity to tread a careful path between historically handed down understandings, and their own judgment about what is morally right. The intersection of cultural contexts and moral judgment constitutes the context in which we make moral choices. It is because Gandhi trod this particular path that he could criticize with all the passion at his command the practice of untouchability in the Hindu caste system, and seek to turn the caste system upside down by referring to the former untouchables as the children of God – Harijan. Therefore, Gandhi refused to be swayed by any specific religious codes. Belief in the Hindu scriptures did not require him, wrote Gandhi, to accept every word and every verse as divinely inspired. 'I decline to be bound by any interpretation, however learned it may be, if it is repugnant to reason or moral sense' (Gandhi 1966: 246).

If human beings do not follow the beaten track set by particular religious inter-pretations, if they rather concentrate on finding out what is the right path, and if they focus on fearlessly following this path when they embark upon their quest for truth, it follows that it is ethics that is more valuable than formalized codes of religion in helping us realize our objective. Despite his religiosity, Gandhi believed that it was not particularly important that we should be religious in order to discern the truth. For him, God is but a manifestation of the profound inner ethics that morally stimulates persons, even if they are not religious. It is one's duty to obey the laws of ethics whether or not one is religious (1986: 51). Therefore, in his later life, Gandhi could easily replace his proposition that 'God is Truth' with the reverse formulation: 'Truth is God'. In his own words: 'I used to say that "God is Truth". But some men deny God. So now I say "Truth is God". ... It has taken me fifty years of persevering meditation to prefer this way of putting it to the others' (cited in Hardiman 2003: 51).

In sum, even if persons cannot know what the ultimate truth is, they have access to cultural resources as well as their own moral judgment to figure out what is true. Cor-respondingly, all individuals, irrespective of the religion they belong to, or even if they do not belong to a religion and follow the path of atheism, are capable of overcoming their self-interest and approaching the truth through their moral projects. For this very reason persons should take their moral projects seriously, even if they know that the fulfilment of these projects remains elusive. Gandhi would deny that the inability to know the entire truth leads to moral relativism. All that he expects people to do is to judge and reach moral conclusions about the world they encounter (Terchek 1973: 36).

The proposition that human beings can but partially grasp the nature of the ultimate truth, and all that they can do is to pursue the Holy Grail with steadfast commitment yields the following political postulates. Firstly, the nature of Gandhi's truth enjoins all moral beings to seek to discover the truth along with others, in and through dialogical interaction. Dialogue is inbuilt into the philosophy of satyagraha, for satyagraha means nothing less than a shared search for the truth.

The second political postulate generated by the philosophy of satyagraha is that of toleration. The moment persons realize that not just their religion, but all religions yield principles of morality, they also realize that all religions are equally valid. Truth can be found in great religions because each of these religions shares the same moral core: respecting the dignity of persons, and understanding the best life as one that moves beyond hatred or necessity and aims at non violence and morality. The 'rules of morality laid down in the world's greatest religions' writes Gandhi, 'are largely the same ... if morality is destroyed, religion which is built on it comes crashing down' (1986: 62). It follows that all the principal religions are equally valid and deserving of respect (Gandhi 1974: 353). This particular recognition was to define the proposition of *sarva dharma sambhava* or the equality of all religions, which was the unique Gandhian contribution to the concept of secularism in India.

The argument for toleration is deceptively simple. If persons have the moral capacity to know the truth, but not the entire truth, then no one person or group can claim superiority over another on the ground that their truth is the ultimate truth, and that other truths are false or travesties of the real thing. On the contrary we should realize that just as our truth is dear to us, others' truths are bound to be dear to them. There is, therefore, neither any point in comparing religions or in grading them:

> If we had attained the full vision of the Truth' he was to write, 'we would no longer be mere seekers, but become one with God, for Truth is God. But being only seekers, we prosecute our quest and are conscious of our imperfection. And if we are imperfect ourselves, religion as conceived by us must also be imperfect ... [and] is subject to a process of evolution and reinterpretation. ... And if all faiths outlined by men are imperfect, the question of comparative merit does not arise (Gandhi 1932: 55).

This realization leads slowly but surely towards respect for plurality of beliefs and *toleration*. In sum, Gandhi's theory of toleration is anchored in his theory of knowledge. It is of some interest to note that Gandhi's theory of knowledge provides the conceptual basis for his theory of toleration, exactly in the same way as John Locke's theory of knowledge inexorably leads to his theory of toleration. The parallel is not surprising when we recollect that Gandhi's theory of knowledge was fashioned exactly in the same context as the one in which John Locke wrote his famous essay on toleration: that of immense religious strife. Parekh suggests that Gandhi's notion of non-violence is conceptually located in a 'novel epistemological argument' that violence rests on false epistemological foundations (1999: 173). But before Gandhi, Locke had arrived at exactly the same conclusion, through different modes of reasoning. We do not know whether Gandhi read Locke's *Essay on Toleration*, though he was perfectly familiar with all variants of western thought – liberal, romantic, anarchic, and anti-modern – but there are certainly strong overlaps between the two theories, perhaps because the political contexts of these theories were similar. Notably, many of the enduring and authoritative arguments for toleration in seventeenth century Europe arose in the middle of religious strife, the adoption of one religion by states as the state religion, suppression of minority religious groups, and forcible conversions.

Gandhi's theory of toleration and proscription of violence is based on roughly the same context: violence between religious communities that had become the norm during the second decade of the twentieth century. Gandhi wished to negate this violence for three reasons – one was pragmatic, and the other two embedded in his philosophy.

One, conflict between religious communities made the task of forging a mass movement impossible; a way out of this pointless violence had to be found. This he found in the precept of the equality of all religions. Secondly, the employment of violence in the pursuit of goals dictated by 'this' or 'that' religion went against his felt conviction that no religion can ever provide a reason for or legitimate violence. Thirdly, toleration is inbuilt into Gandhi's philosophy of satyagraha in general, and the nature of knowledge in particular.

But notably toleration in Gandhian theory is not passive; it does not amount to the proposition that you remain content with your version of the truth, and I remain content with mine. In this sense Gandhi goes further than Locke, simply because he decrees that uncertainty about knowledge of truth should propel a shared search for the truth. And it is precisely this shared quest that establishes connections in and through processes of dialogue, and through action. The final expression of Gandhi's truth is not knowledge for the sake of knowledge, but knowledge for the sake of moral action.

Satyagraha can therefore be conceptualized as a form of political dialogue in which agents seek to discover truth in and through processes of political engagement with other moral persons. It is difficult to know whose version of the truth is more valid, but it is certainly easier to know which version is more untrue than others. This can only be realized in and through dialogue, through giving of reasons which have been morally arrived at for our considered convictions, a willingness to accept other belief systems as valid, and an equal willingness to move forward with others in the search for truth. This is possible only when participants recognize that it is not their reputation as persons of integrity, or as possessors of truth, which is at stake. *At stake is the conception of truth itself.* Therefore even though we enter the discursive arena of politics with considered convictions, and acquire thereby a certain moral standing, and proceed to engage with others on the nature of these convictions and on the nature of other such convictions, we do so in full comprehension of the limits of our own knowledge. To claim a comprehensive knowledge of the truth is to enforce and apply a truth that no fragment can bestow.

Thirdly, if the acceptance that our convictions cannot be completely true introduces moral restraint on our conduct with others, teaches us the virtue of toleration, and of the need to be receptive to others' notions of the truth, this also instils in us non-violence. For, unthinking and uncritical acceptance of certain norms as being absolutely true, the belief that we are completely right and our opponent is completely wrong, and construction of the 'other' with whom one can share nothing, lead to violence. But when we begin to reflect on the moral status of the norms that we espouse with such political passion in the public sphere, we realize that these norms are but partial realizations of the truth. The search for truth along with others, in concert with others, not only leads to political engagement but also results in the transformation of the self, and transformation of other agents.

Conclusion

If I have identified the problem in and for plural societies correctly, that the very prospect of dialogue in such societies tends to dissolve in a haze of suspicion, and mistrust of each other, then Gandhi's theory of satyagraha might provide a way out of this political impasse for three reasons. One, attention to the *preconditions* of dialogue contributes much to the establishment of moral standing of participants. Secondly, knowledge that our grasp over the truth is but partial inculcates self-restraint on the one hand, and provides a powerful imperative to embark on a shared search for the truth, on the other. Thirdly, commitment to non-violence dissipates feelings of alienation and otherness, and makes persons more receptive to other opinions. All three components of satyagraha encourage a spirit of dialogue. And as anyone who is familiar with the dynamics of plural and divided societies knows, getting people to speak to others, and persuading them that a readiness to compromise does not negate their moral standing, is an achievement in itself. Gandhi has a lot to teach us when it comes to compromise, for compromise is not the opposite of truth: 'all my life ... the very insistence on truth has taught me to appreciate the beauty of compromise. I saw in later life that this spirit was an essential part of satyagraha' (cited in Hardiman 2003: 52).

It is this spirit of compromise, borne through attention to the ideas of others, which allows us to reach understanding on shared norms, which we consider to be morally binding *even* if our own understanding on these norms is modified somewhat in the process.

One troublesome question remains: if in divided societies, the pursuit of separatist agenda's proves more profitable than the forging of a common dialogical space, or a shared search for truth and justice, why should agents opt for the latter rather than the former? Think of leaders of secessionist movements in much of South Asia, who would rather concentrate on what divides the community they seek to represent from others, than on what this community has in common with others. Whereas there are no easy answers to this question, I think that Gandhi gives us one such answer. It is the satya-grahi who has to take up the responsibility of creating and recreating a dialogical space, even if he or she has to undergo 'suffering' in the pursuance of this objective. In that sense the satyagrahi is, as Bilgrami suggests in a different context, a 'moral exem-plar'. 'That is the role of the satyagrahi. To lead exemplary lives, to set examples to everyone by their actions' (Bilgrami 2006: 257). The burden of establishing the pre-conditions, the production and the reproduction of the dialogical process rests some-what disproportionately on the shoulders of moral giants. But perhaps this has always been the case in societies across the world.

Note

1 This is an abridged version of the article that appeared as 'The Quest for Justice: The Gandhian Perspective', *Economic and Political Weekly*, 43(18), 2008.

References

Bilgrami, A. (2006) 'Gandhi's integrity: the philosophy behind the politics', in A. Raghuramaraju (ed.) *Debating Gandhi*, New Delhi: Oxford University Press, pp. 248–68.

Chandhoke, N. (1999) *Beyond Secularism: The Rights of Religious Minorities*, New Delhi: Oxford University Press, pp. 96–101.

Gandhi, M. K (1966a) 'Hinduism', in *The Collected Works of Mahatma Gandhi* [*CWMG*], New Delhi: Government of India, Publications Division, Vol. XXI, pp. 245–50.

—— (1966b) 'Satyagraha, civil disobedience, passive resistance, non-co-operation', in *CWMG*, Vol. XIX, pp. 465–67.

—— (1967) 'God and Congress', in *CWMG,* Vol. XXVI, pp. 222–25.

—— (1969) 'Letter to Mrs R. Armstrong and Mrs P. R. Howard', in *CWMG*, 111.

—— (1976) 'A discussion with Maurice Frydman', in *CWMG,* Vol. LXIII, pp. 240–41.

—— (1986) 'Ethical religions', in Raghavan Iyer (ed.) *The Moral and Political Writings of Mahatma Gandhi,* Vol. II, Oxford: Clarendon Press, pp. 50–69.

—— (1991) 'The vow of truth', in Raghavan Iyer (ed.) *The Essential Writings of Mahatma Gandhi*, New Delhi: Oxford University Press, pp. 223–26.

—— (1932) *From Yeravada Mandir*, Ahmedabad: Navjivan Press.

—— (1974) 'Notes: how do you pray?' *CWMG*, Vol. LVII, pp. 353–54.

Hardiman, D. (2003) *Gandhi: In His Time And Ours*, New Delhi: Permanent Black.

Jacobsohn, G. J. (2003) *The Wheel Of Law: India's Secularism in Comparative Constitutional Context*, Delhi: Oxford University Press.

Locke, J. (1968) *A Letter on Toleration* [Latin Text, *Epistola de Tolerentia*], ed. Raymond Kli-bansky, trans. J. W. Gough, Oxford: Clarendon Press.

Nehru, Jawaharlal (1980) *Jawaharlal Nehru: An Anthology*, ed. S. Gopal, New Delhi: Oxford University Press.

Parekh, B. (1999) *Colonialism, Tradition, and Reform: An Analysis of Gandhi's Political Dis-course*, New Delhi: Sage Publications.

Rudolph, L. I. and Rudolph, S. H. (2006) 'The coffee house and the ashram revisited: how Gandhi democratised Habermas's public space', in Lloyd I. Rudolph and Susanne H. Rudolph (eds) *Postmodern Gandhi and Other Essays*, New Delhi: Oxford University Press, pp. 140–76.

Terchek, R. (1973) *Gandhi: Struggling for Autonomy*, New Delhi: Vistaar.

4 Tagore and his India[1]

Amartya Sen

Voice of Bengal

Rabindranath Tagore, who died in 1941 at the age of eighty, is a towering figure in the millennium-old literature of Bengal. Anyone who becomes familiar with this large and flourishing tradition will be impressed by the power of Tagore's presence in Bangladesh and in India. His poetry as well as his novels, short stories, and essays are very widely read, and the songs he composed reverberate around the eastern part of India and throughout Bangladesh.

In contrast, in the rest of the world, especially in Europe and America, the excitement that Tagore's writings created in the early years of the twentieth century has largely vanished. The enthusiasm with which his work was once greeted was quite remarkable. *Gitanjali,* a selection of his poetry for which he was awarded the Nobel Prize in Literature in 1913, was published in English translation in London in March of that year, and had been reprinted ten times by November, when the award was announced. But he is not much read now in the West, and already by 1937, Graham Greene was able to say: 'As for Rabindranath Tagore, I cannot believe that anyone but Mr. Yeats can still take his poems very seriously'.

The mystic

The contrast between Tagore's commanding presence in Bengali literature and culture, and his near-total eclipse in the rest of the world, is perhaps less interesting than the distinction between the view of Tagore as a deeply relevant and many-sided contemporary thinker in Bangladesh and India, and his image in the West as a repetitive and remote spiritualist. Graham Greene had, in fact, gone on to explain that he associated Tagore 'with what Chesterton calls "the bright pebbly eyes" of the Theosophists'. Certainly, an air of mysticism played some part in the 'selling' of Rabindranath Tagore to the West by Yeats, Ezra Pound, and his other early champions. Even Anna Akhmatova, one of Tagore's few later admirers (who translated his poems into Russian in the mid-1960s), talks of 'that mighty flow of poetry which takes its strength from Hinduism as from the Ganges, and is called Rabindranath Tagore'.

Confluence of cultures

Rabindranath did come from a Hindu family – one of the landed gentry who owned estates mostly in what is now Bangladesh. But whatever wisdom there might be in Akhmatova's invoking of Hinduism and the Ganges, it did not prevent the largely

Muslim citizens of Bangladesh from having a deep sense of identity with Tagore and his ideas. Nor did it stop the newly independent Bangladesh from choosing one of Tagore's songs – the 'Amar Sonar Bangla' which means 'my golden Bengal' – as its national anthem. This must be very confusing to those who see the contemporary world as a 'clash of civilizations' – with 'the Muslim civilization', 'the Hindu civilization', and 'the Western civilization', each forcefully confronting the others. They would also be confused by Rabindranath Tagore's own description of his Bengali family as the product of 'a confluence of three cultures: Hindu, Mohammedan, and British' (Tagore 1961: 105).[2]

Rabindranath's grandfather, Dwarkanath, was well known for his command of Arabic and Persian, and Rabindranath grew up in a family atmosphere in which a deep knowledge of Sanskrit and ancient Hindu texts was combined with an understanding of Islamic traditions as well as Persian literature. It is not so much that Rabindranath tried to produce – or had an interest in producing – a 'synthesis' of the different religions (as the great Moghul emperor Akbar tried hard to achieve) as that his outlook was persistently non-sectarian, and his writings – some two hundred books – show the influence of different parts of the Indian cultural background as well as of the rest of the world.[3]

Abode of peace

Most of his work was written at Santiniketan (Abode of Peace), the small town that grew around the school he founded in Bengal in 1901, and he not only conceived there an imaginative and innovative system of education, but through his writings and his influence on students and teachers, he was able to use the school as a base from which he could take a major part in India's social, political, and cultural movements.

The profoundly original writer, whose elegant prose and magical poetry Bengali readers know well, is not the sermonizing spiritual guru admired – and then rejected – in London. Tagore was not only an immensely versatile poet; he was also a great short story writer, novelist, playwright, essayist, and composer of songs, as well as a talented painter whose pictures, with their mixture of representation and abstraction, are only now beginning to receive the acclaim that they have long deserved. His essays, moreover, ranged over literature, politics, culture, social change, religious beliefs, philosophical analysis, international relations, and much else. The coincidence of the fiftieth anniversary of Indian independence with the publication of a selection of Tagore's letters by Cambridge University Press (Dutta and Robinson 1997a),[4] brought Tagore's ideas and reflections to the fore, which makes it important to examine what kind of leadership in thought and understanding he provided in the Indian subcontinent in the first half of this century.

Gandhi and Tagore

Since Rabindranath Tagore and Mohandas Gandhi were two leading Indian thinkers in the twentieth century, many commentators have tried to compare their ideas. On learning of Rabindranath's death, Jawaharlal Nehru, then incarcerated in a British jail in India, wrote in his prison diary for August 7, 1941:

> Gandhi and Tagore. Two types entirely different from each other, and yet both of them typical of India, both in the long line of India's great men ... It is not so

much because of any single virtue but because of the *tout ensemble,* that I felt that among the world's great men today Gandhi and Tagore were supreme as human beings. What good fortune for me to have come into close contact with them.

Romain Rolland was fascinated by the contrast between them, and when he completed his book on Gandhi, he wrote to an Indian academic, in March 1923: 'I have finished my *Gandhi,* in which I pay tribute to your two great river-like souls, overflowing with divine spirit, Tagore and Gandhi'. The following month, he recorded in his diary an account of some of the differences between Gandhi and Tagore written by Reverend C.F. Andrews, the English clergyman and public activist who was a close friend of both men (and whose important role in Gandhi's life in South Africa as well as India is well portrayed in Richard Attenborough's film Gandhi [1982]). Andrews described to Rolland a discussion between Tagore and Gandhi, at which he was present, on subjects that divided them:

> The first subject of discussion was idols; Gandhi defended them, believing the masses incapable of raising themselves immediately to abstract ideas. Tagore cannot bear to see the people eternally treated as a child. Gandhi quoted the great things achieved in Europe by the flag as an idol; Tagore found it easy to object, but Gandhi held his ground, contrasting European flags bearing eagles, etc., with his own, on which he has put a spinning wheel. The second point of discussion was nationalism, which Gandhi defended. He said that one must go through nationalism to reach internationalism, in the same way that one must go through war to reach peace (Francis 1976: 12–13).

Tagore greatly admired Gandhi but he had many disagreements with him on a variety of subjects, including nationalism, patriotism, the importance of cultural exchange, the role of rationality and of science, and the nature of economic and social development. These differences, I shall argue, have a clear and consistent pattern, with Tagore pressing for more room for reasoning, and for a less traditionalist view, a greater interest in the rest of the world, and more respect for science and for objectivity generally.

Rabindranath knew that he could not have given India the political leadership that Gandhi provided, and he was never stingy in his praise for what Gandhi did for the nation (it was, in fact, Tagore who popularized the term 'Mahatma' – great soul – as a description of Gandhi). And yet each remained deeply critical of many things that the other stood for. That Mahatma Gandhi has received incomparably more attention outside India and also within much of India itself makes it important to understand 'Tagore's side' of the Gandhi-Tagore debates.

In his prison diary, Nehru wrote: 'Perhaps it is as well that [Tagore] died now and did not see the many horrors that are likely to descend in increasing measure on the world and on India. He had seen enough and he was infinitely sad and unhappy'. Toward the end of his life, Tagore was indeed becoming discouraged about the state of India, especially as its normal burden of problems, such as hunger and poverty, was being supplemented by politically organized incitement to 'communal' violence between Hindus and Muslims. This conflict would lead in 1947, six years after Tagore's death, to the widespread killing that took place during partition; but there was much gore already during his declining days. In December 1939, he wrote to his friend Leonard Elmhirst, the English philanthropist and social reformer who had worked closely with him on rural reconstruction in India (and who had gone on to found the Dartington Hall Trust in England and a progressive school at Dartington that explicitly invoked Rabindranath's educational ideals) (Young 1982):

> It does not need a defeatist to feel deeply anxious about the future of millions who, with all their innate culture and their peaceful traditions are being simultaneously subjected to hunger, disease, exploitations foreign and indigenous, and the seething discontents of communalism.

How would Tagore have viewed the India of today? Would he see progress there, or wasted opportunity, perhaps even a betrayal of its promise and conviction? And, on a wider subject, how would he react to the spread of cultural separatism in the contemporary world?

East and West

Given the vast range of his creative achievements, perhaps the most astonishing aspect of the image of Tagore in the West is its narrowness; he is recurrently viewed as 'the great mystic from the East', an image with a putative message for the West, which some would welcome, others dislike, and still others find deeply boring. To a great extent this Tagore was the West's own creation, part of its tradition of message-seeking from the East, particularly from India, which – as Hegel put it – had 'existed for millennia in the imagination of the Europeans'.[5] Friedrich Schlegel, Schelling, Herder, and Schopenhauer were only a few of the thinkers who followed the same pattern. They theorized, at first, that India was the source of superior wisdom. Schopenhauer at one stage even argued that the New Testament 'must somehow be of Indian origin: this is attested by its completely Indian ethics, which transforms morals into asceticism, its pessimism, and its avatar', in 'the person of Christ'. But then they rejected their own theories with great vehemence, sometimes blaming India for not living up to their unfounded expectations.

We can imagine that Rabindranath's physical appearance – handsome, bearded, dressed in non-Western clothes – may, to some extent, have encouraged his being seen as a carrier of exotic wisdom. Yasunari Kawabata, the first Japanese Nobel Laureate in Literature, treasured memories from his middle-school days of 'this sage-like poet':

> His white hair flowed softly down both sides of his forehead; the tufts of hair under the temples also were long like two beards, and linking up with the hair on his cheeks, continued into his beard, so that he gave an impression, to the boy I was then, of some ancient Oriental wizard (Kawabata 1969: 56–57).

That appearance would have been well-suited to the selling of Tagore in the West as a quintessentially mystical poet, and it could have made it somewhat easier to pigeonhole him. Commenting on Rabindranath's appearance, Frances Cornford told William Rothenstein, 'I can now imagine a powerful and gentle Christ, which I never could before'. Beatrice Webb, who did not like Tagore and resented what she took to be his 'quite obvious dislike of all that the Webbs stand for' (there is, in fact, little evidence that Tagore had given much thought to this subject), said that he was 'beautiful to look at' and that 'his speech has the perfect intonation and slow chant-like moderation of the dramatic saint'. Ezra Pound and W. B. Yeats, among others, first led the chorus of adoration in the Western appreciation of Tagore, and then soon moved to neglect and even shrill criticism. The contrast between Yeats's praise of his work in 1912 ('These lyrics … display in their thought a world I have dreamed of all my life long', 'the work of a supreme culture') and his denunciation in 1935 ('Damn Tagore') arose partly from the inability of Tagore's many-sided writings to fit into the narrow box in which Yeats wanted to place – and keep – him. Certainly, Tagore did write a huge amount, and published ceaselessly, even in English (sometimes in indifferent English translation), but Yeats was also bothered, it is clear, by the difficulty of fitting Tagore's later writings into the image Yeats had presented to the West. Tagore, he had said, was the product of 'a whole people, a whole civilization, immeasurably strange to us', and yet 'we have met our own image … or heard, perhaps for the first time in literature, our voice as in a dream' (Yeats 1913).

Yeats did not totally reject his early admiration (as Ezra Pound and several others did), and he included some of Tagore's early poems in *The Oxford Book of Modern Verse,* which he edited in 1936. Yeats also had some favorable things to say about Tagore's prose writings. His censure of Tagore's later poems was reinforced by his dislike of Tagore's own English translations of his work ('Tagore does not know English, no Indian knows English', Yeats explained), unlike the English version of *Gitanjali* which Yeats had himself helped to prepare. Poetry is, of course, notoriously difficult to translate, and anyone who knows Tagore's poems in their original Bengali cannot feel satisfied with any of the translations (made with or without Yeats's help). Even the translations of his prose works suffer, to some extent, from distortion. E.M. Forster noted, in a review of a translation of one of Tagore's great Bengali novels, *The Home and the World,* in 1919: 'The theme is so beautiful', but the charms have 'vanished in translation', or perhaps 'in an experiment that has not quite come off'.[6]

Tagore himself played a somewhat bemused part in the boom and bust of his English reputation. He accepted the extravagant praise with much surprise as well as pleasure, and then received denunciations with even greater surprise, and barely concealed pain. Tagore was sensitive to criticism, and was hurt by even the most far-fetched accusations, such as the charge that he was getting credit for the work of Yeats, who had 'rewritten' Gitanjali. (This charge was made by a correspondent for *The Times*, Sir Valentine Chirol, whom E. M. Forster once described as 'an old Anglo-Indian reactionary hack.') From time to time Tagore also protested the crudity of some of his overexcited advocates. He wrote to C. F. Andrews in 1920: 'These people … are like drunkards who are afraid of their lucid intervals'.

God and others

Yeats was not wrong to see a large religious element in Tagore's writings. He certainly had interesting and arresting things to say about life and death. Susan Owen, the mother of Wilfred Owen, wrote to Rabindranath in 1920, describing her last conversations with her son before he left for the war which would take his life. Wilfred said goodbye with 'those wonderful words of yours – beginning at "When I go from hence, let this be my parting word"'. 'When Wilfred's pocket notebook was returned to his mother, she found 'these words written in his dear writing – with your name beneath'.

The idea of a direct, joyful, and totally fearless relationship with God can be found in many of Tagore's religious writings, including the poems of *Gitanjali*. From India's diverse religious traditions he drew many ideas, both from ancient texts and from popular poetry. But 'the bright pebbly eyes of the Theosophists' do not stare out of his verses. Despite the archaic language of the original translation of *Gitanjali,* which did not, I believe, help to preserve the simplicity of the original, its elementary humanity comes through more clearly than any complex and intense spirituality:

> Leave this chanting and singing and telling of beads! Whom dost thou worship in this lonely dark corner of a temple with doors all shut?
>
> Open thine eyes and see thy God is not before thee!
>
> He is there where the tiller is tilling the hard ground and where the pathmaker is breaking stones.
>
> He is with them in sun and in shower, and his garment is covered with dust.

An ambiguity about religious experience is central to many of Tagore's devotional poems, and makes them appeal to readers irrespective of their beliefs; but excessively detailed interpretation can ruinously strip away that ambiguity.[7] This applies particularly to his many poems which combine images of human love and those of pious devotion. Tagore writes:

> I have no sleep to-night. Ever and again I open my door and look out on the darkness, my friend!
>
> I can see nothing before me. I wonder where lies thy path!
>
> By what dim shore of the ink-black river, by what far edge of the frowning forest, through what mazy depth of gloom, art thou threading thy course to come to see me, my friend?

I suppose it could be helpful to be told, as Yeats hastens to explain, that 'the servant or the bride awaiting the master's home-coming in the empty house' is 'among the images of the heart turning to God'. But in Yeats's considerate attempt to make sure that the reader does not miss the 'main point', something of the enigmatic beauty of the Bengali poem is lost – even what had survived the antiquated language of the English translation. Tagore certainly had strongly held religious beliefs (of an unusually non-denominational kind), but he was interested in a great many other things as well and had many different things to say about them.

Some of the ideas he tried to present were directly political, and they figure rather prominently in his letters and lectures. He had practical, plainly expressed views about nationalism, war and peace, cross-cultural education, freedom of the mind, the importance of rational criticism, the need for openness, and so on. His admirers in the West, however, were tuned to the more otherworldly themes which had been emphasized by his first Western patrons. People came to his public lectures in Europe and America, expecting ruminations on grand, transcendental themes; when they heard instead his views on the way public leaders should behave, there was some resentment, particularly (as E. P. Thompson reports) when he delivered political criticism 'at $700 a scold'.

Reasoning in freedom

For Tagore it was of the highest importance that people be able to live, and reason, in freedom. His attitudes toward politics and culture, nationalism and internationalism, tradition and modernity, can all be seen in the light of this belief (Ray in Robinson 1989). Nothing, perhaps, expresses his values as clearly as a poem in *Gitanjali:*

> Where the mind is without fear
> and the head is held high;
> Where knowledge is free;
> Where the world has not been
> broken up into fragments
> by narrow domestic walls;
> Where the clear stream of reason
> has not lost its way into the
> dreary desert sand of dead habit;
> Into that heaven of freedom,
> my Father, let my country awake.

Rabindranath's qualified support for nationalist movements – and his opposition to the unfreedom of alien rule – came from this commitment. So did his reservations about patriotism, which, he argued, can limit both the freedom to engage ideas from outside 'narrow domestic walls' and the freedom also to support the causes of people in other countries. Rabindranath's passion for freedom underlies his firm opposition to unreasoned traditionalism, which makes one a prisoner of the past (lost, as he put it, in 'the dreary desert sand of dead habit').

Tagore illustrates the tyranny of the past in his amusing yet deeply serious parable 'Kartar Bhoot' ('The Ghost of the Leader'). As the respected leader of an imaginary land is about to die, his panic-stricken followers request him to stay on after his death to instruct them on what to do. He consents. But his followers find their lives are full of rituals and constraints on everyday behavior and are not responsive to the world around them. Ultimately, they request the ghost of the leader to relieve them of his domination, when he informs them that he exists only in their minds.

Tagore's deep aversion to any commitment to the past that could not be modified by contemporary reason extended even to the alleged virtue of invariably keeping past promises. On one occasion when Mahatma Gandhi visited Tagore's school at Santiniketan, a young woman got him to sign her autograph book. Gandhi wrote: 'Never make a promise in haste. Having once made it fulfill it at the cost of your life'. When he saw this entry, Tagore became agitated. He wrote in the same book a short poem in Bengali to the effect that no one can be made 'a prisoner forever with a chain of clay'. He went on to conclude in English, possibly so that Gandhi could read it too, 'Fling away your promise if it is found to be wrong' (Amita Sen 1996: 132).

Tagore had the greatest admiration for Mahatma Gandhi as a person and as a political leader, but he was also highly skeptical of Gandhi's form of nationalism and his conservative instincts regarding the country's past traditions. He never criticized Gandhi personally. In the 1938 essay, 'Gandhi the Man', he wrote:

Great as he is as a politician, as an organizer, as a leader of men, as a moral reformer, he is greater than all these as a man, because none of these aspects and activities limits his humanity. They are rather inspired and sustained by it.

And yet there is a deep division between the two men. Tagore was explicit about his disagreement:

We who often glorify our tendency to ignore reason, installing in its place blind faith, valuing it as spiritual, are ever paying for its cost with the obscuration of our mind and destiny. I blamed Mahatmaji for exploiting this irrational force of credulity in our people, which might have had a quick result [in creating] a superstructure, while sapping the foundation. Thus began my estimate of Mahatmaji, as the guide of our nation, and it is fortunate for me that it did not end there.

But while it 'did not end there', that difference of vision was a powerful divider. Tagore, for example, remained unconvinced of the merit of Gandhi's forceful advocacy that everyone should spin at home with the 'charka', the primitive spinning wheel. For Gandhi this practice was an important part of India's self-realization. 'The spinning-wheel gradually became', as his biographer B. R. Nanda writes, 'the center of rural uplift in the Gandhian scheme of Indian economics' (Nanda 1958: 149). Tagore found the alleged economic rationale for this scheme quite unrealistic. As Romain Rolland noted, Rabindranath 'never tires of criticizing the charka'. In this economic judgment, Tagore was probably right. Except for the rather small specialized market for high-quality spun cloth, it is hard to make economic sense of hand-spinning, even with wheels less primitive than Gandhi's charka. Hand-spinning as a widespread activity can survive only with the help of heavy government subsidies (Amartya Sen 1960: Appendix D).

However, Gandhi's advocacy of the charka was not based only on economics. He wanted everyone to spin for 'thirty minutes every day as a sacrifice', seeing this as a way for people who are better off to identify themselves with the less fortunate. He was impatient with Tagore's refusal to grasp this point:

The poet lives for the morrow, and would have us do likewise. ... 'Why should I, who have no need to work for food, spin?' may be the question asked. Because I am eating what does not belong to me. I am living on the spoliation of my countrymen. Trace the source of every coin that finds its way into your pocket, and you will realise the truth of what I write. Every one must spin. Let Tagore spin like the others. Let him burn his foreign clothes; that is the duty today. God will take care of the morrow (Mohandas Gandhi quoted in Kripalani 1961: 171–72).

If Tagore had missed something in Gandhi's argument, so did Gandhi miss the point of Tagore's main criticism. It was not only that the charka made little economic sense, but also, Tagore thought, that it was not the way to make people reflect on anything: 'The charka does not require anyone to think; one simply turns the wheel of the antiquated invention endlessly, using the minimum of judgment and stamina'.

Celibacy and personal life

Tagore and Gandhi's attitudes toward personal life were also quite different. Gandhi was keen on the virtues of celibacy, theorized about it, and, after some years of conjugal life, made a private commitment – publicly announced – to refrain from sleeping with his wife. Rabindranath's own attitude on this subject was very different, but he was gentle about their disagreements:

> [Gandhiji] condemns sexual life as inconsistent with the moral progress of man, and has a horror of sex as great as that of the author of *The Kreutzer Sonata,* but, unlike Tolstoy, he betrays no abhorrence of the sex that tempts his kind. In fact, his tenderness for women is one of the noblest and most consistent traits of his character, and he counts among the women of his country some of his best and truest comrades in the great movement he is leading.

Tagore's personal life was, in many ways, an unhappy one. He married in 1883, lost his wife in 1902, and never remarried. He sought close companionship, which he did not always get (perhaps even during his married life – he wrote to his wife, Mrinalini: 'If you and I could be comrades in all our work and in all our thoughts it would be splendid, but we cannot attain all that we desire'). He maintained a warm friendship with, and a strong Platonic attachment to, the literature-loving wife, Kadambari, of his elder brother, Jyotirindranath. He dedicated some poems to her before his marriage, and several books afterward, some after her death (she committed suicide, for reasons that are not fully understood, at the age of twenty-five, four months after Rabindranath's wedding). Much later in life, during his tour of Argentina in 1924–25, Rabindranath came to know the talented and beautiful Victoria Ocampo, who later became the publisher of the literary magazine *Sur*. They became close friends, but it appears that Rabindranath deflected the possibility of a passionate relationship into a confined intellectual one.[8] His friend Leonard Elmhirst, who accompanied Rabindranath on his Argentine tour, wrote:

> Besides having a keen intellectual understanding of his books, she was in love with him – but instead of being content to build a friendship on the basis of intellect, she was in a hurry to establish that kind of proprietary right over him which he absolutely would not brook.

Ocampo and Elmhirst, while remaining friendly, were both quite rude in what they wrote about each other. Ocampo's book on Tagore (of which a Bengali translation was made from the Spanish by the distinguished poet and critic Shankha Ghosh) is primarily concerned with Tagore's writings but also discusses the pleasures and difficulties of their relationship, giving quite a different account from Elmhirst's, and never suggesting any sort of proprietary intentions.

Victoria Ocampo, however, makes it clear that she very much wanted to get physically closer to Rabindranath: 'Little by little he [Tagore] partially tamed the young animal, by turns wild and docile, who did not sleep, dog-like, on the floor outside his door, simply because it was not done' (quoted in Radhakrishnan 1961). Rabindranath, too, was clearly very much attracted to her. He called her 'Vijaya' (the Sanskrit equivalent of Victoria), dedicated a book of poems to her, Purabi – an 'evening melody', and expressed great admiration for her mind ('like a star that was distant'). In a letter to her he wrote, as if to explain his own reticence:

When we were together, we mostly played with words and tried to laugh away our best opportunities to see each other clearly ... Whenever there is the least sign of the nest becoming a jealous rival of the sky [,] my mind, like a migrant bird, tries to take ... flight to a distant shore.

Five years later, during Tagore's European tour in 1930, he sent her a cable: 'Will you not come and see me'. She did. But their relationship did not seem to go much beyond conversation, and their somewhat ambiguous correspondence continued over the years. Written in 1940, a year before his death at eighty, one of the poems in Sesh Lekha ('Last Writings'), seems to be about her: 'How I wish I could once again find my way to that foreign land where waits for me the message of love! / ... Her language I knew not, but what her eyes said will forever remain eloquent in its anguish' (Kripalani 1961: 185). However indecisive, or confused, or awkward Rabindranath may have been, he certainly did not share Mahatma Gandhi's censorious views of sex. In fact, when it came to social policy, he advocated contraception and family planning while Gandhi preferred abstinence.

Science and the people

Gandhi and Tagore severely clashed over their totally different attitudes toward science. In January 1934, Bihar was struck by a devastating earthquake, which killed thousands of people. Gandhi, who was then deeply involved in the fight against untouchability (the barbaric system inherited from India's divisive past, in which 'lowly people' were kept at a physical distance), extracted a positive lesson from the tragic event. 'A man like me', Gandhi argued, 'cannot but believe this earthquake is a divine chastisement sent by God for our sins' – in particular the sins of untouchability. 'For me there is a vital connection between the Bihar calamity and the untouchability campaign'.

Tagore, who equally abhorred untouchability and had joined Gandhi in the movements against it, protested against this interpretation of an event that had caused suffering and death to so many innocent people, including children and babies. He also hated the epistemology implicit in seeing an earthquake as caused by ethical failure. 'It is', he wrote, 'all the more unfortunate because this kind of unscientific view of [natural] phenomena is too readily accepted by a large section of our countrymen'.

The two remained deeply divided over their attitudes toward science. However, while Tagore believed that modern science was essential to the understanding of physical phenomena, his views on epistemology were interestingly heterodox. He did not take the simple 'realist' position often associated with modern science. The report of his conversation with Einstein, published in the *New York Times* in 1930, shows how insistent Tagore was on interpreting truth through observation and reflective concepts. To assert that something is true or untrue in the absence of anyone to observe or perceive its truth, or to form a conception of what it is, appeared to Tagore to be deeply questionable. When Einstein remarked, 'If there were no human beings any more, the Apollo Belvedere no longer would be beautiful?' Tagore simply replied, 'No'. Going further – and into much more interesting territory – Einstein said, 'I agree with regard to this conception of beauty, but not with regard to truth'. Tagore's response was: 'Why not? Truth is realized through men' (Marianoff 1930; Dutta and Robinson 1997b).

Tagore's epistemology, which he never pursued systematically, would seem to be searching for a line of reasoning that would later be elegantly developed by Hilary

Putnam, who has argued: 'Truth depends on conceptual schemes and it is nonetheless "real truth"' (Putnam 1987; also see Nagel 1986). Tagore himself said little to explain his convictions, but it is important to take account of his heterodoxy, not only because his speculations were invariably interesting, but also because they illustrate how his support for any position, including his strong interest in science, was accompanied by critical scrutiny.

Nationalism and colonialism

Tagore was predictably hostile to communal sectarianism (such as a Hindu orthodoxy that was antagonistic to Islamic, Christian, or Sikh perspectives). But even nationalism seemed to him to be suspect. Isaiah Berlin summarizes well Tagore's complex position on Indian nationalism:

> Tagore stood fast on the narrow causeway, and did not betray his vision of the difficult truth. He condemned romantic overattachment to the past, what he called the tying of India to the past 'like a sacrificial goat tethered to a post', and he accused men who displayed it – they seemed to him reactionary – of not knowing what true political freedom was, pointing out that it is from English thinkers and English books that the very notion of political liberty was derived. But against cosmopolitanism he maintained that the English stood on their own feet, and so must Indians. In 1917 he once more denounced the danger of 'leaving everything to the unalterable will of the Master,' be he brahmin or Englishman (Berlin 1997: 265).

The duality Berlin points to is well reflected also in Tagore's attitude toward cultural diversity. He wanted Indians to learn what is going on elsewhere, how others lived, what they valued, and so on, while remaining interested and involved in their own culture and heritage. Indeed, in his educational writings the need for synthesis is strongly stressed. It can also be found in his advice to Indian students abroad. In 1907 he wrote to his son-in-law Nagendranath Gangulee, who had gone to America to study agriculture:

> To get on familiar terms with the local people is a part of your education. To know only agriculture is not enough; you must know America too. Of course if, in the process of knowing America, one begins to lose one's identity and falls into the trap of becoming an Americanised person contemptuous of everything Indian, it is preferable to stay in a locked room.

Tagore was strongly involved in protest against the Raj on a number of occasions, most notably in the movement to resist the 1905 British proposal to split in two the province of Bengal, a plan that was eventually withdrawn following popular resistance. He was forthright in denouncing the brutality of British rule in India, never more so than after the Amritsar massacre of April 13, 1919, when 379 unarmed people at a peaceful meeting were gunned down by the army, and 2,000 more were wounded. Between April 23 and 26, Rabindranath wrote five agitated letters to C. F. Andrews, who himself was extremely disturbed, especially after he was told by a British civil servant in India that thanks to this show of strength, the 'moral prestige' of the Raj had 'never been higher'.

A month after the massacre, Tagore wrote to the Viceroy of India, asking to be relieved of the knighthood he had accepted four years earlier:

> The disproportionate severity of the punishments inflicted upon the unfortunate people and the methods of carrying them out, we are convinced, are without parallel in the history of civilized governments, barring some conspicuous exceptions, recent and remote. Considering that such treatment has been meted out to a population, disarmed and resourceless, by a power which has the most terribly efficient organisation for destruction of human lives, we must strongly assert that it can claim no political expediency, far less moral justification. ... The universal agony of indignation roused in the hearts of our people has been ignored by our rulers – possibly congratulating themselves for imparting what they imagine as salutary lessons. ... I for my part want to stand, shorn of all special distinctions, by the side of those of my countrymen who for their so-called insignificance are liable to suffer a degradation not fit for human beings.

Both Gandhi and Nehru expressed their appreciation of the important part Tagore took in the national struggle. It is fitting that after independence, India chose a song of Tagore ('Jana Gana Mana Adhinayaka', which can be roughly translated as 'the leader of people's minds') as its national anthem. Since Bangladesh would later choose another song of Tagore ('Amar Sonar Bangla') as its national anthem, he may be the only one ever to have authored the national anthems of two different countries.

Tagore's criticism of the British administration of India was consistently strong and grew more intense over the years. This point is often missed, since he made a special effort to dissociate his criticism of the Raj from any denigration of British – or Western – people and culture. Mahatma Gandhi's well-known quip in reply to a question, asked in England, on what he thought of Western civilization ('It would be a good idea') could not have come from Tagore's lips. He would understand the provocations to which Gandhi was responding – involving cultural conceit as well as imperial tyranny. D. H. Lawrence supplied a fine example of the former: 'I become more and more surprised to see how far higher, in reality, our European civilization stands than the East, Indian and Persian, ever dreamed of. ... This fraud of looking up to them – this wretched worship-of-Tagore attitude is disgusting'. But, unlike Gandhi, Tagore could not, even in jest, be dismissive of Western civilization.

Even in his powerful indictment of British rule in India in 1941, in a lecture which he gave on his last birthday, and which was later published as a pamphlet under the title *Crisis in Civilization,* he strains hard to maintain the distinction between opposing Western imperialism and rejecting Western civilization. While he saw India as having been 'smothered under the dead weight of British administration' (adding 'another great and ancient civilization for whose recent tragic history the British cannot disclaim responsibility is China'), Tagore recalls what India has gained from 'discussions centred upon Shakespeare's drama and Byron's poetry and above all ... the large-hearted liberalism of nineteenth-century English politics'. The tragedy, as Tagore saw it, came from the fact that what 'was truly best in their own civilization, the upholding of dignity of human relationships, has no place in the British administration of this country'. 'If in its place they have established, baton in hand, a reign of "law and order", or in other words a policeman's rule, such a mockery of civilization can claim no respect from us'.

Critique of patriotism

Rabindranath rebelled against the strongly nationalist form that the independence movement often took, and this made him refrain from taking a particularly active part in contemporary politics. He wanted to assert India's right to be independent without denying the importance of what India could learn – freely and profitably – from abroad. He was afraid that a rejection of the West in favor of an indigenous Indian tradition was not only limiting in itself; it could easily turn into hostility to other influences from abroad, including Christianity, which came to parts of India by the fourth century; Judaism, which came through Jewish immigration shortly after the fall of Jerusalem, as did Zoroastrianism through Parsi immigration later on (mainly in the eighth century), and, of course – and most importantly – Islam, which has had a very strong presence in India since the tenth century.

Tagore's criticism of patriotism is a persistent theme in his writings. As early as 1908, he put his position succinctly in a letter replying to the criticism of Abala Bose, the wife of a great Indian scientist, Jagadish Chandra Bose: 'Patriotism cannot be our final spiritual shelter; my refuge is humanity. I will not buy glass for the price of diamonds, and I will never allow patriotism to triumph over humanity as long as I live'. His novel *Ghare Baire* (The Home and the World) has much to say about this theme. In the novel, Nikhil, who is keen on social reform, including women's liberation, but cool toward nationalism, gradually loses the esteem of his spirited wife, Bimala, because of his failure to be enthusiastic about anti-British agitations, which she sees as a lack of patriotic commitment. Bimala becomes fascinated with Nikhil's nationalist friend Sandip, who speaks brilliantly and acts with patriotic militancy, and she falls in love with him. Nikhil refuses to change his views: 'I am willing to serve my country; but my worship I reserve for Right which is far greater than my country. To worship my country as a god is to bring a curse upon it' (Nussbaum et al. 1996: 3–4).

As the story unfolds, Sandip becomes angry with some of his countrymen for their failure to join the struggle as readily as he thinks they should ('Some Mohamedan traders are still obdurate'). He arranges to deal with the recalcitrants by burning their meager trading stocks and physically attacking them. Bimala has to acknowledge the connection between Sandip's rousing nationalistic sentiments and his sectarian – and ultimately violent-actions. The dramatic events that follow (Nikhil attempts to help the victims, risking his life) include the end of Bimala's political romance.

This is a difficult subject, and Satyajit Ray's beautiful film of *The Home and the World* brilliantly brings out the novel's tensions, along with the human affections and disaffections of the story. Not surprisingly, the story has had many detractors, not just among dedicated nationalists in India. Georg Lukács found Tagore's novel to be 'a petit bourgeois yarn of the shoddiest kind', 'at the intellectual service of the British police', and 'a contemptible caricature of Gandhi'. It would, of course, be absurd to think of Sandip as Gandhi, but the novel gives a 'strong and gentle' warning, as Bertolt Brecht noted in his diary, of the corruptibility of nationalism, since it is not even-handed. Hatred of one group can lead to hatred of others, no matter how far such feeling may be from the minds of large-hearted nationalist leaders like Mahatma Gandhi.

Admiration and criticism of Japan

Tagore's reaction to nationalism in Japan is particularly telling. As in the case of India, he saw the need to build the self-confidence of a defeated and humiliated people, of people left behind by developments elsewhere, as was the case in Japan before its emergence during the nineteenth century. At the beginning of one of his lectures in Japan in 1916 ('Nationalism in Japan'), he observed that 'the worst form of bondage is the bondage of dejection, which keeps men hopelessly chained in loss of faith in themselves'. Tagore shared the admiration for Japan widespread in Asia for demonstrating the ability of an Asian nation to rival the West in industrial development and economic progress. He noted with great satisfaction that Japan had 'in giant strides left centuries of inaction behind, overtaking the present time in its foremost achievement'. For other nations outside the West, he said, Japan 'has broken the spell under which we lay in torpor for ages, taking it to be the normal condition of certain races living in certain geographical limits'.

But then Tagore went on to criticize the rise of a strong nationalism in Japan, and its emergence as an imperialist nation. Tagore's outspoken criticisms did not please Japanese audiences and, as E. P. Thompson wrote, 'the welcome given to him on his first arrival soon cooled' (1991: 10). Twenty-two years later, in 1937, during the Japanese war on China, Tagore received a letter from Rash Behari Bose, an anti-British Indian revolutionary then living in Japan, who sought Tagore's approval for his efforts there on behalf of Indian independence, in which he had the support of the Japanese government. Tagore replied:

> Your cable has caused me many restless hours, for it hurts me very much to have to ignore your appeal. I wish you had asked for my cooperation in a cause against which my spirit did not protest. I know, in making this appeal, you counted on my great regard for the Japanese for I, along with the rest of Asia, did once admire and look up to Japan and did once fondly hope that in Japan Asia had at last discovered its challenge to the West, that Japan's new strength would be consecrated in safeguarding the culture of the East against alien interests. But Japan has not taken long to betray that rising hope and repudiate all that seemed significant in her wonderful, and, to us symbolic, awakening, and has now become itself a worse menace to the defenceless peoples of the East.

How to view Japan's position in the Second World War was a divisive issue in India. After the war, when Japanese political leaders were tried for war crimes, the sole dissenting voice among the judges came from the Indian judge, Radhabinod Pal, a distinguished jurist. Pal dissented on various grounds, among them that no fair trial was possible in view of the asymmetry of power between the victor and the defeated. Ambivalent feelings in India toward the Japanese military aggression, given the unacceptable nature of British imperialism, possibly had a part in predisposing Pal to consider a perspective different from that of the other judges.

More tellingly, Subhas Chandra Bose (no relation of Rash Behari Bose), a leading nationalist, made his way to Japan during the war via Italy and Germany after escaping from a British prison; he helped the Japanese to form units of Indian soldiers, who had earlier surrendered to the advancing Japanese army, to fight on the Japanese side as the 'Indian National Army'. Rabindranath had formerly entertained great admiration for Subhas Bose as a dedicated nonsectarian fighter for Indian independence.[9] But their ways would have parted when Bose's political activities took this turn, although Tagore was dead by the time Bose reached Japan.

Tagore saw Japanese militarism as illustrating the way nationalism can mislead even a nation of great achievement and promise. In 1938 Yone Noguchi, the distinguished poet and friend of Tagore (as well as of Yeats and Pound), wrote to Tagore, pleading with him to change his mind about Japan. Rabindranath's reply, written on September 12, 1938, was altogether uncompromising:

> It seems to me that it is futile for either of us to try to convince the other, since your faith in the infallible right of Japan to bully other Asiatic nations into line with your Government's policy is not shared by me. ... Believe me, it is sorrow and shame, not anger, that prompt me to write to you. I suffer intensely not only because the reports of Chinese suffering batter against my heart, but because I can no longer point out with pride the example of a great Japan.

He would have been much happier with the postwar emergence of Japan as a peaceful power. Then, too, since he was not free of egotism, he would also have been pleased by the attention paid to his ideas by the novelist Yasunari Kawabata and others.[10]

International concerns

Tagore was not invariably well-informed about international politics. He allowed himself to be entertained by Mussolini in a short visit to Italy in May-June 1926, a visit arranged by Carlo Formichi, professor of Sanskrit at the University of Rome. When he asked to meet Benedetto Croce, Formichi said, 'Impossible! Impossible!' Mussolini told him that Croce was 'not in Rome'. When Tagore said he would go 'wherever he is', Mussolini assured him that Croce's whereabouts were unknown.

Such incidents, as well as warnings from Romain Rolland and other friends, should have ended Tagore's flirtation with Mussolini more quickly than it did. But only after he received graphic accounts of the brutality of Italian fascism from two exiles, Gaetano Salvemini and Gaetano Salvadori, and learned more of what was happening in Italy, did he publicly denounce the regime, publishing a letter to the *Manchester Guardian* in August. The next month, Popolo d'Italia, the magazine edited by Benito Mussolini's brother, replied: 'Who cares? Italy laughs at Tagore and those who brought this unctuous and insupportable fellow in our midst'.

With his high expectations of Britain, Tagore continued to be surprised by what he took to be a lack of official sympathy for international victims of aggression. He returned to this theme in the lecture he gave on his last birthday, in 1941:

> While Japan was quietly devouring North China, her act of wanton aggression was ignored as a minor incident by the veterans of British diplomacy. We have also witnessed from this distance how actively the British statesmen acquiesced in the destruction of the Spanish Republic.

But distinguishing between the British government and the British people, Rabindranath went on to note 'with admiration how a band of valiant Englishmen laid down their lives for Spain'.

Tagore's view of the Soviet Union has been a subject of much discussion. He was widely read in Russia. In 1917 several Russian translations of *Gitanjali* (one edited by Ivan Bunin, later the first Russian Nobel Laureate in Literature) were available, and by the late 1920s many of the English versions of his work had been rendered into Russian by several distinguished translators. Russian versions of his work continued to appear: Boris Pasternak translated him in the 1950s and 1960s.

When Tagore visited Russia in 1930, he was much impressed by its development efforts and by what he saw as a real commitment to eliminate poverty and economic inequality. But what impressed him most was the expansion of basic education across the old Russian empire. In Letters from Russia, written in Bengali and published in 1931, he unfavorably compares the acceptance of widespread illiteracy in India by the British administration with Russian efforts to expand education:

> In stepping on the soil of Russia, the first thing that caught my eye was that in education, at any rate, the peasant and the working classes have made such enormous progress in these few years that nothing comparable has happened even to our highest classes in the course of the last hundred and fifty years. ... The people here are not at all afraid of giving complete education even to Turcomans of distant Asia; on the contrary, they are utterly in earnest about it (Tagore 1960: 108).

When parts of the book were translated into English in 1934, the under-secretary for India stated in Parliament that it was 'calculated by distortion of the facts to bring the British Administration in India into contempt and disrepute', and the book was then promptly banned. The English version would not be published until after independence.

Education and freedom

The British Indian administrators were not, however, alone in trying to suppress Tagore's reflections on Russia. They were joined by Soviet officials. In an interview with *Izvestia* in 1930, Tagore sharply criticized the lack of freedom that he observed in Russia:

> I must ask you: Are you doing your ideal a service by arousing in the minds of those under your training anger, class-hatred, and revengefulness against those whom you consider to be your enemies? ... Freedom of mind is needed for the reception of truth; terror hopelessly kills it. ... For the sake of humanity I hope you may never create a vicious force of violence, which will go on weaving an interminable chain of violence and cruelty. ... You have tried to destroy many of the other evils of [the czarist] period. Why not try to destroy this one also?

The interview was not published in *Izvestia* until 1988 – nearly sixty years later (Dutta and Robinson 1995: 297). Tagore's reaction to the Russia of 1930 arose from two of his strongest commitments: his uncompromising belief in the importance of 'freedom of mind' (the source of his criticism of the Soviet Union), and his conviction that the expansion of basic education is central to social progress (the source of his praise, particularly in contrast to British-run India). He identified the lack of basic education as the fundamental cause of many of India's social and economic afflictions:

> In my view the imposing tower of misery which today rests on the heart of India has its sole foundation in the absence of education. Caste divisions, religious

conflicts, aversion to work, precarious economic conditions – all centre on this single factor.

It was on education (and on the reflection, dialogue, and communication that are associated with it), rather than on, say, spinning 'as a sacrifice' ('the charka does not require anyone to think'), that the future of India would depend.

Tagore was concerned not only that there be wider opportunities for education across the country (especially in rural areas where schools were few), but also that the schools themselves be more lively and enjoyable. He himself had dropped out of school early, largely out of boredom, and had never bothered to earn a diploma. He wrote extensively on how schools should be made more attractive to boys and girls and thus more productive. His own co-educational school at Santiniketan had many progressive features. The emphasis here was on self-motivation rather than on discipline, and on fostering intellectual curiosity rather than competitive excellence.

Much of Rabindranath's life was spent in developing the school at Santiniketan. The school never had much money, since the fees were very low. His lecture honoraria, '$700 a scold', went to support it, as well as most of his Nobel Prize money. The school received no support from the government, but did get help from private citizens – even Mahatma Gandhi raised money for it.

The dispute with Mahatma Gandhi on the Bihar earthquake touched on a subject that was very important to Tagore: the need for education in science as well as in literature and the humanities. At Santiniketan, there were strong 'local' elements in its emphasis on Indian traditions, including the classics, and in the use of Bengali rather than English as the language of instruction. At the same time there were courses on a great variety of cultures, and study programs devoted to China, Japan, and the Middle East. Many foreigners came to Santiniketan to study or teach, and the fusion of studies seemed to work.

I am partial to seeing Tagore as an educator, having myself been educated at Santiniketan. The school was unusual in many different ways, such as the oddity that classes, excepting those requiring a laboratory, were held outdoors (whenever the weather permitted). No matter what we thought of Rabindranath's belief that one gains from being in a natural setting while learning (some of us argued about this theory), we typically found the experience of outdoor schooling extremely attractive and pleasant. Academically, our school was not particularly exacting (often we did not have any examinations at all), and it could not, by the usual academic standards, compete with some of the better schools in Calcutta. But there was something remarkable about the ease with which class discussions could move from Indian traditional literature to contemporary as well as classical Western thought, and then to the culture of China or Japan or elsewhere. The school's celebration of variety was also in sharp contrast with the cultural conservatism and separatism that has tended to grip India from time to time.

The cultural give and take of Tagore's vision of the contemporary world has close parallels with the vision of Satyajit Ray, also an alumnus of Santiniketan who made several films based on Tagore's stories (Ray 1993; also see Amartya Sen 1996a). Ray's words about Santiniketan in 1991 would have greatly pleased Rabindranath:

I consider the three years I spent in Santiniketan as the most fruitful of my life. ... Santiniketan opened my eyes for the first time to the splendours of Indian and Far

Eastern art. Until then I was completely under the sway of Western art, music and literature. Santiniketan made me the combined product of East and West that I am.

India today

At the fiftieth anniversary of Indian independence, the reckoning of what India had or had not achieved in this half century was a subject of considerable interest: 'What has been the story of those first fifty years?' (as Shashi Tharoor asked in his balanced, informative, and highly readable account of *India: From Midnight to the Millennium* [1997]). If Tagore were to see the India of today, more than half a century after independence, nothing perhaps would shock him so much as the continued illiteracy of the masses. He would see this as a total betrayal of what the nationalist leaders had promised during the struggle for independence – a promise that had figured even in Nehru's rousing speech on the eve of independence in August 1947 (on India's 'tryst with destiny').

In view of his interest in childhood education, Tagore would not be consoled by the extraordinary expansion of university education, in which India sends to its universities six times as many people per unit of population as does China. Rather, he would be stunned that, in contrast to East and Southeast Asia, including China, half the adult population and two thirds of Indian women remain unable to read or write. Statistically reliable surveys indicate that even in the late 1980s, nearly half of the rural girls between the ages of twelve and fourteen did not attend any school for a single day of their lives (Drèze and Sen 1996a: Chapter 6; 1996b).

This state of affairs is the result of the continuation of British imperial neglect of mass education, which has been reinforced by India's traditional elitism, as well as upper-class-dominated contemporary politics (except in parts of India such as Kerala, where anti-upper-caste movements have tended to concentrate on education as a great leveller). Tagore would see illiteracy and the neglect of education not only as the main source of India's continued social backwardness, but also as a great constraint that restricts the possibility and reach of economic development in India (as his writings on rural development forcefully make clear). Tagore would also have strongly felt the need for a greater commitment – and a greater sense of urgency – in removing endemic poverty.

At the same time, Tagore would undoubtedly find some satisfaction in the survival of democracy in India, in its relatively free press, and in general from the 'freedom of mind' that post-independence Indian politics has, on the whole, managed to maintain. He would also be pleased by the fact noted by the historian E. P. Thompson (whose father Edward Thompson had written one of the first major biographies of Tagore (Thompson 1926)):

> All the convergent influences of the world run through this society: Hindu, Moslem, Christian, secular; Stalinist, liberal, Maoist, democratic socialist, Gandhian. There is not a thought that is being thought in the West or East that is not active in some Indian mind (quoted in Tharoor 1997).

Tagore would have been happy also to see that the one governmental attempt to dispense generally with basic liberties and political and civil rights in India, in the 1970s, when Prime Minister Indira Gandhi (ironically, herself a former student at

Santiniketan) declared an 'emergency', was overwhelmingly rejected by the Indian voters, leading to the precipitate fall of her government.

Rabindranath would also see that the changes in policy that have eliminated famine since independence had much to do with the freedom to be heard in a democratic India. In Tagore's play *Raja O Rani* ('The King and the Queen'), the sympathetic Queen eventually rebels against the callousness of state policy toward the hungry. She begins by inquiring about the ugly sounds outside the palace, only to be told that the noise is coming from 'the coarse, clamorous crowd who howl unashamedly for food and disturb the sweet peace of the palace'. The Viceregal office in India could have taken a similarly callous view of Indian famines, right up to the easily preventable Bengal famine of 1943, just before independence, which killed between two and three million people. But a government in a multi-party democracy, with elections and free newspapers, cannot any longer dismiss the noise from 'the coarse, clamorous crowd' (see Amartya Sen 1984: Chapter 19, 1995).

Unlike Gandhi, Rabindranath would not resent the development of modern industries in India, or the acceleration of technical progress, since he did not want India to be shackled to the turning of 'the wheel of an antiquated invention'. Tagore was concerned that people not be dominated by machines, but he was not opposed to making good use of modern technology. 'The mastery over the machine', he wrote in *Crisis in Civilization,* 'by which the British have consolidated their sovereignty over their vast empire, has been kept a sealed book, to which due access has been denied to this helpless country'. Rabindranath had a deep interest in the environment – he was particularly concerned about deforestation and initiated a 'festival of tree-planting' (vriksharopana) as early as 1928. He would want increased private and government commitments to environmentalism; but he would not derive from this position a general case against modern industry and technology.

On cultural separation

Rabindranath would be shocked by the growth of cultural separatism in India, as elsewhere. The 'openness' that he valued so much is certainly under great strain right now – in many countries. Religious fundamentalism still has a relatively small following in India; but various factions seem to be doing their best to increase their numbers. Certainly religious sectarianism has had much success in some parts of India (particularly in the west and the north). Tagore would see the expansion of religious sectarianism as being closely associated with an artificially separatist view of culture.

He would have strongly resisted defining India in specifically Hindu terms, rather than as a 'confluence' of many cultures. Even after the partition of 1947, India is still the third-largest Muslim country in the world, with more Muslims than in Bangladesh, and nearly as many as in Pakistan. Only Indonesia has substantially more followers of Islam. Indeed, by pointing to the immense heterogeneousness of India's cultural background and its richly diverse history, Tagore had argued that the 'idea of India' itself militated against a culturally separatist view – 'against the intense consciousness of the separateness of one's own people from others'.

Tagore would also oppose the cultural nationalism that has recently been gaining some ground in India, along with an exaggerated fear of the influence of the West. He was uncompromising in his belief that human beings could absorb quite different cultures in constructive ways:

Whatever we understand and enjoy in human products instantly becomes ours, wherever they might have their origin. I am proud of my humanity when I can acknowledge the poets and artists of other countries as my own. Let me feel with unalloyed gladness that all the great glories of man are mine. Therefore it hurts me deeply when the cry of rejection rings loud against the West in my country with the clamour that Western education can only injure us.

In this context, it is important to emphasize that Rabindranath was not short of pride in India's own heritage, and often spoke about it. He lectured at Oxford, with evident satisfaction, on the importance of India's religious ideas – quoting both from ancient texts and from popular poetry (such as the verses of the sixteenth-century Muslim poet Kabir). In 1940, when he was given an honorary doctorate by Oxford University, in a ceremony arranged at his own educational establishment in Santiniketan ('In Gangem Defluit Isis', Oxford helpfully explained), to the predictable 'volley of Latin' Tagore responded 'by a volley of Sanskrit', as Marjorie Sykes, a Quaker friend of Rabindranath, reports. Her cheerful summary of the match, 'India held its own', was not out of line with Tagore's pride in Indian culture. His welcoming attitude to Western civilization was reinforced by this confidence: he did not see India's culture as fragile and in need of 'protection' from Western influence.

In India, he wrote, 'circumstances almost compel us to learn English, and this lucky accident has given us the opportunity of access into the richest of all poetical literatures of the world'. There seems to me much force in Rabindranath's argument for clearly distinguishing between the injustice of a serious asymmetry of power (colonialism being a prime example of this) and the importance nevertheless of appraising Western culture in an open-minded way, in colonial and postcolonial territories, in order to see what uses could be made of it.

Rabindranath insisted on open debate on every issue, and distrusted conclusions based on a mechanical formula, no matter how attractive that formula might seem in isolation (such as 'This was forced on us by our colonial masters – we must reject it', 'This is our tradition – we must follow it', 'We have promised to do this – we must fulfill that promise', and so on). The question he persistently asks is whether we have reason enough to want what is being proposed, taking everything into account. Important as history is, reasoning has to go beyond the past. It is in – the sovereignty of reasoning – fearless reasoning in freedom – that we can find Rabindranath Tagore's lasting voice.[11]

Notes

1 This article was originally published in *The New York Review of Books*, 44: 55–63, 26 June 1997. A version of the article was also later published as a chapter in *The Argumentative Indian: Writings on Indian History, Culture and Identity* (London: Penguin, 2006).

2 The extensive interactions between Hindu and Muslim parts of Indian culture (in religious beliefs, civic codes, painting, sculpture, literature, music, and astronomy) have been discussed by K. Sen (1949, 1961).

3 Rabindranath's father Debendranath had in fact, joined the reformist religious group, the Brahmo Samaj, which rejected many contemporary Hindu practices as aberrations from the ancient Hindu texts.

4 For important background material on Rabindranath Tagore and his reception in the West, see also Dutta and Robinson (1995, 1997a).

5 I have tried to analyze these 'exotic' approaches to India (along with other Western approaches) (A. Sen 1993, 1997).

6 Tagore himself vacillated over the years about the merits of his own translations. He told his friend Sir William Rothenstein, the artist: 'I am sure you remember with what reluctant hesitation I gave up to your hand my manuscript of *Gitanjali,* feeling sure that my English was of that amorphous kind for whose syntax a school-boy could be reprimanded'. These – and related – issues are discussed by N. Sen (1966, 1985).

7 The importance of ambiguity and incomplete description in Tagore's poetry provides some insight into the striking thesis of William Radice (one of the major English translators of Tagore) that 'his blend of poetry and prose is all the more truthful for being incomplete' (Radice 1991).

8 For fuller accounts of the events, see Dutta and Robinson (1995: Chapter 25) and Dyson (1988).

9 For a lucid and informative analysis of the role of Subhas Chandra Bose and his brother Sarat in Indian politics, see Gordon (1990).

10 Kawabata made considerable use of Tagore's ideas, and even built on Tagore's thesis that it 'is easier for a stranger to know what it is in [Japan] which is truly valuable for all mankind' (1969: 55–58).

11 For helpful discussions I am most grateful to Akeel Bilgrami, Sissela Bok (Harvard Professor; the daughter of Gunnar Myrdal, recipient of The Bank of Sweden Prize in Economic Sciences in Memory of Alfred Nobel 1974, and Alva Myrdal, who was awarded The Nobel Peace Prize in 1982), Sugata Bose, Supratik Bose, Krishna Dutta, Rounaq Jahan, Salim Jahan, Marufi Khan, Andrew Robinson, Nandana Sen, Gayatri Chakravorty Spivak, and Shashi Tharoor.

References

Berlin, Isaiah (1997) 'Rabindranath Tagore and the consciousness of nationality', in *The Sense of Reality: Studies in Ideas and Their History*, New York: Farrar, Straus and Giroux.

Drèze, Jean and Sen, Amartya (1996a) *India: Economic Development and Social Opportunity*, Delhi: Clarendon Press/Oxford University Press.

—— (ed.) (1996b) *Indian Development: Selected Regional Perspectives*, Delhi: Clarendon Press/ Oxford University Press.

Dutta, K. and Robinson, A. (1995) 'Rabindranath Tagore, the myriad-minded man', *The New York Times Book Review*, 28.

—— (1997a) *Selected Letters of Rabindranath Tagore*, Cambridge: Cambridge University Press.

—— (1997b) *Rabindranath Tagore: An Anthology*, London: Picador.

Dyson, Ketaki Kushari (1988) *In Your Blossoming Flower-Garden: Rabindranath Tagore and Victoria Ocampo*, New Delhi: Sahitya Akademi.

Francis, R. A. (1976) *Romain Rolland and Gandhi Correspondence: Letters, Diary Extracts, Articles, etc.*, New Delhi: Publications Division, Ministry of Information and Broadcasting, Govt. of India.

Gordon, Leonard A. (1990) *Brothers against the Raj: A Biography of Indian Nationalists Sarat and Subhas Chandra Bose*, Columbia: Columbia University Press.

Kawabata, Yasunari (1969) *The Existence and Discovery of Beauty,* trans. V. H. Viglielmo, Tokyo: The Mainichi Newspapers.

Kripalani, Krishna (1961) *Tagore: A Life*, New Delhi: Orient Longman.

Marianoff, Dmitri (1930) 'Einstein and Tagore plumb the truth', *The New York Times Magazine*, 10 August.

Nagel, Thomas (1986) *The View from Nowhere*, New York: Oxford University Press.

Nanda, B. R. (1958) *Mahatma Gandhi*, Delhi: Oxford University Press.

Nussbaum, Martha (1996) 'The home and the world', in Martha Nussbaum and Joshua Cohen (eds) *For Love of Country*, Boston: Beacon Press.

Putnam, Hilary (1987) *The Many Faces of Realism*, La Salle, Ill.: Open Court.

Radice, William (1991) 'Introduction' in *Rabindranath Tagore: Selected Short Stories,* London: Penguin.

Radhakrishnan, S. (1961) *Rabindranath Tagore: A Centenary Volume, 1861–1961*, New Delhi: Sahitya Akademi.

Ray, Satyajit (1989) 'Foreword', in Andrew Robinson, *The Art of Rabindranath Tagore*, London: André Deutsch.

—— (1991) *The Guardian*, 1 August.

—— (1993) *Our Films, Their Films*, Calcutta: Disha Book/Orient Longman.

Sen, Amartya (1960) *Choice of Techniques*, Oxford: Blackwell.

—— (1984) *Resources, Values and Development*, Cambridge: Harvard University Press.

—— (1993) 'India and the West', *The New Republic,* June 7.

—— (1995) 'Rationality and Social Choice', *American Economic Review*, 85.

—— (1996a) *Anando Sharbokaje* (in Bengali), Calcutta: Tagore Research Institute.

—— (1996b) 'Our culture, their culture', *New York: The New Republic*, 1 April.

—— (1997) 'Indian traditions and the western imagination', *Daedalus* (Spring).

—— (2006) *The Argumentative Indian: Writings on Indian History, Culture and Identity*, London: Penguin.

Sen, Kshiti Mohan (1949) *Bharate Hindu Mushalmaner Jukto Sadhana* (in Bengali), Calcutta: Visva-Bharati.

—— (1961) *Hinduism*, London: Penguin.

Sen, Nabaneeta Dev (1966) 'The "foreign reincarnation" of Rabindranath Tagore', *Journal of Asian Studies,* 25.

—— (1985) *Counterpoints: Essays in Comparative Literature*, Calcutta: Prajna.

Tagore, Rabindranath (1960) *Letters from Russia,* trans. from Bengali by Sasadhar Sinha, Calcutta: Visva-Bharati.

—— (1961) *The Religion of Man*, 2nd edn, London: Allen and Unwin.

Tharoor, Shashi (1997) *India: from Midnight to the Millennium and Beyond*, New York: Arcade Publishing.

Thompson, Edward (1926) *Rabindranath Tagore: Poet and Dramatist*, London: Oxford University Press.

Thompson, E. P. (1991) 'Introduction', in *Tagore's Nationalism*, London: Macmillan.

Yeats, W.B. (1913) 'Introduction', in Rabindranath Tagore, *Gitanjali*, London: Macmillan.

Young, M. D. (1982) *The Elmhirsts of Dartington: The Creation of a Utopian Community*, London: Routledge & Kegan Paul.

Part III
Secularization

5 Is secularism alien to Indian civilization?[1]

Romila Thapar

Secularism and (Indian) religion

In choosing to write on this subject it is my intention to try and question the statement that secularism is alien to Indian civilization and that it therefore follows that the secularization of Indian society has no place in contemporary Indian values. This has become the slogan of supporters of Hindutva who project secularism as antithetical to Hinduism. My concern is not with this kind of rhetoric of political mobilization. I would like to address the proposition of secularism being alien to Indian civilization as has been put forward by some scholars in a more thoughtful manner (Madan 1987, 1997; Nandy 1998). My primary concern is with regard to the fact that when secularism is posited as opposed to religion in India, the discussion is generally limited to only a segment of Hinduism, namely Vedic Brahmanism and Puranic Hinduism, and the more extensive articulation of religion in India is not included.

This chapter therefore focuses on extending the meaning of Indian religion to include the religious identity of not just the few, but of the larger population that would be involved in the secularizing of Indian society. Defining religious traditions requires recognizing differences in such traditions from higher to lower castes and from *dvijas* (the twice-born), to *mlechchhas* (those outside the social pale).

In the nineteenth century, civilizations were defined by geography/territory, religion and language. Indian civilization was located in the Indian sub-continent, the dominant religion was said to be Hinduism and the language of the civilization was therefore Sanskrit. Such a definition has many historical fault lines, but since it is the accepted form even now, we may continue to use it, although pointing out these fault lines. Among the fault lines was the way Indian religion was projected. The reference was largely to the religion of the elite and the tendency was to highlight the group of religions that were selected and placed within the rubric of 'Hinduism'. Others, like Buddhism and Jainism, were marginalized.

What is actually included within the rubric of Hinduism are a vast number of sectarian identities – Vaishnava, Shaiva, Lingayat, Shakta, Natha and so on. An overarching label to include all these various religious sects was not used until recent centuries. But the religious identity and praxis that was more closely adhered to was frequently that of the caste. Given the link between caste and religion in India there is multiple religious articulation across a spectrum of belief and social organization. The secularization of Indian society has therefore also to consider the nature of change in caste society. This substantially alters the picture from that of a single, clearly contoured religion.

Protest against caste inequities was common in religious movements that stemmed from the non-orthodox, heterodox traditions. *Jati*s have their own mythologies and rituals and the variations can sometimes be quite specific. A ritual specialist could in the past, through observing the ritual of a *jati*, have been able to identify its *varna* or ritual status, particularly where the code of the *dharmashastras* and *dharmasutras* was also being observed. Interestingly, until recently, *jati* identities continued to be evident even when a *jati*, or part of one, converted to Islam or Christianity, and many conversions were of this kind. What this means is that secularism in India cannot ignore *jati* identities that are differentiated social identities with some sectarian religious forms specific to the *jati*. Because the practice of religion is so closely tied to caste, the nature of religion is not similar to that of Europe, and in the Indian context the secularist dialogue has to include a discussion of the degree of acceptance or rejection of caste, which again makes it different from the European experience.

Extending the meaning of 'Indian' religion

Indian civilization has registered multiple religions as parallel strands with some becoming more dominant in certain times and some emerging as independent religions. There have been degrees of continuity in some cases and some fundamental differences in others. Religions with recognizable characteristics and influential in many parts of the sub-continent, can be listed chronologically as Vedic Brahmanism, Buddhism, Jainism, Puranic Hinduism, Bhakti, Shakta, Islam, and what I would like to call the religion of the Guru-Pir tradition. To this may be added the input of Christianity and Zoroastrianism going back to around the mid-first millennium AD but with a more limited spread until recently. The evolution of religion in India is frequently seen only through textual sources with a predisposition to privileging the brahmanical sources and socio-legal codes like the *dharmashastras*. But other religions and religious sects projected other ideas. Nevertheless there is a tendency to juxtapose all the sources and view them as manifestations of a single religion, barring the Semitic religions. However, when seen as independent religious articulations, their variations become apparent and point towards a complexity that is often overlooked.

There were therefore strong parallel traditions challenging orthodoxy in all the religions of India and these tended to give greater weight to social ethics rather than to prescriptive texts regulating religious observances. The most powerful exposition of this comes from Buddhism. Although Buddhism later nurtured its own orthodoxy, the early emphasis on social ethics remained constant and was in turn to influence the form of many other popular religious sects through the centuries. I would therefore like to refer to the early teachings of the Buddha at greater length. The context to these teachings was the unease that many thinkers of the time had with the ideas of Vedic Brahmanism.

Vedic Brahmanism, in the first millennium BC, was the religion of the ritual of sacrifice and therefore the ritual specialist – the *brahmana* – was its key propagator. Its social beginnings are linked to the functioning of oligarchies and chiefdoms as pre-state societies and it drew its political authority from the patronage of clan chiefs requiring rituals of validation with claims of divine sanction. In the process of chiefdoms being transmuted into kingdoms and chiefs evolving into kings, the rituals of validation continued and became the rituals of kingship with a heavier dependence on divine sanction and more so in the centuries AD when monarchies became the normal pattern.

But Vedic Brahmanism had to compete with other religious sects and was gradually reduced to symbolic importance, except among its twice-born practitioners.

Buddhism and Jainism and a variety of heterodox sects were among those that questioned Vedic Brahmanism, and Buddhism was a recognized alternative. These sects reflect the historical changes that began in the mid-first millennium BC with the coming of the state and of urbanization. Their influential patronage came from the non-monarchical clans of the middle Ganges valley and from some royal courts, but equally from the trading communities scattered all over the sub-continent. It is often forgotten that Buddhism had a widespread appeal as well as royal support for a millennium after it was first established, and in eastern India this continued for still longer, commanding the patronage of many communities in various regions. Buddhism and associated religions were collectively referred to as the Shramana religions. Buddhism cannot be dismissed as merely one of the many manifestations of Hinduism since it has been fundamentally different in belief and practice. The catalytic role of Buddhism can be seen not only in the emergence of later schools of philosophy – some confrontational and some supportive – but also in the evolution of aspects of Puranic Hinduism. Even as late as the eleventh century Al-Biruni describing the religions of India, highlights the differences between the Brahmans and the Shamaniyya (Shramanas) (Sachau 1964: 21).

Yet it is largely the texts of Vedic Brahmanism and Puranic Hinduism that are quoted in discussions on the possible antecedents to secular concerns in pre-modern India. Because these texts either show no interest in what are today regarded as secular norms, or else are read to deny these norms, it is held that secularism is altogether alien to Indian culture. My contention is that if one is less selective in choosing the texts from early periods, then it is apparent that there were discussions among various groups on issues that do relate, sometimes directly and sometimes obliquely, to what we regard as significant themes in secular thinking.

The hallmark of Buddhism in the early period was the centrality of social ethics. Buddhism emphasized the relationship between the individual and society rather than ritual and belief in the supernatural. The Buddha was therefore treated in some brahmanical texts as a *nastika* and a *charvaka* – an atheist and a materialist. That the confrontation was recognized is evident from his rejection of the theist view.[2]

It is in the initial Buddhist ideas that one could search for seminal notions that might be conducive to a secularizing of Indian society. There has been a debate as to whether what was taught by the Buddha can be called a religion since he does not postulate a belief in a deity. However, even though deities are incorporated a few centuries subsequent to his death, the centrality of social ethics remains a constant factor. It may be said that his contention was that a belief in human relations was more central than a belief in deity. The questioning of deity was not limited to the Buddha. Various groups of Lokayata and Charvaka teachers were even more vehement in regarding deities as unnecessary and religion as a foolish aberration. Such views persisted as parallel schools of thought to Brahmanic and Shramanic ideas well into the second millennium AD (Radhakrishnan 1948: 277*ff.*; Chattopadhyaya 1955). Ethics without religion was an established tradition among many strands of materialist and Shramanic sects and the ethical basis of laws was widely discussed. The Buddha suggested that the existence of a deity was irrelevant, and rejected the traditional significance of Hindu deities. Eternity was embedded not in deity but in notions of *dharma/dhamma* (the teaching) and *nirvana/nibbana* (the individual's liberation from rebirth).

The kernel of his teaching was in the *dhamma-cakkappavattana-sutta*, the teaching on the 'turning of the wheel of law'.[3] This encapsulates the four 'noble truths', *ariyasacca*, and the eightfold path of 'the middle way', *majjhima pattipada*.[4] The basis of the four noble truths is the idea of dependent origination, *paticca samuppada,* a theory of cause and effect that becomes foundational to this ethics.[5] The argument is that suffering is caused by actions motivated by desire and the cessation of this leads to the extinction of suffering and a condition of *nirvana*, which liberates the person from rebirth and future suffering. Understanding the nature of causation is therefore of importance to understanding the human condition and the explanation is not to be found in divine revelation.[6] Liberation can be achieved by observing the middle way of moderation in actions and ambitions. Essential to this idea is the rationality of the argument linking critical thinking to causality.

His discussion of the middle way as the way of social and moral action is at the core of what can be called his social ethics. The centrality of the householder, *gahapati,* was the lynch-pin in this.[7] The ethic, based on insight through knowledge, was encapsulated in conduct towards parents, friends, teachers and servants. The householder was not an enlightened being and had to be helped along by explanations of the moral code. Even the attaining of *nirvana* required such help and the Buddha used the analogy of the raft – those that had crossed to the other shore and been liberated by using the raft of enlightenment should leave the raft for the use of others.[8]

Dhamma was the universal ethic of family and community propelled by *ahimsa* – non-violence, tolerance and respect for rights as embodied in codes of behaviour. As a code of behaviour it assumes the equality of all and the rules apply equally to all. The context to this is the story of the *mahasammata*, the great elected one, with whom the state began.[9] After a long, utopian existence in the remote past, human society gradually began to develop conflicts and contradictions eventually requiring the establishing of rules of family organization and of private property. When even this failed to prevent conflict, it was decided to elect one person to maintain order, to enforce the laws and to ensure the well being of all. The elected one was paid a wage that was a percentage of the produce. There is no divine intervention in this narrative as there was in the Vedic myths of the origin of government, an intervention that continued to be referred to even as late as in the *Arthashastra*.[10] In the Buddhist texts the matter was settled by contract among equals in order to end the disruption of an earlier utopian condition caused by subsequent social disharmony and intolerance. The state was neither a natural institution nor a divine imposition but a necessity required when the actions of a society cause its disruption. Therefore the state has obligations to prevent the disruption of society which it can do by instituting social ethics. The social ethic is so central that the Buddha opposed caste hierarchy because it creates inequality and this in turn encourages disruption.[11] The social ethic was to be taught in the *kutuhalashalas,* the parks on the outskirts of cities and through the preaching of monks.

By way of contrast, the *Mahabharata* also speaks of a social contract in an extract that dates to a period probably contemporary with the recording of the Buddhist texts. In the story of the first ruler Prithu and the establishing of a state there is recourse to a contract. But this is not among the people, probably because they were not regarded as being of equal status. It is a contract in which the *brahmanas* are involved since they control social laws and the making of society and state, all of which derive from the gods.[12] It is intended to prevent the condition of anarchy – *matsyanyaya* – that follows in the absence of a state. The term encapsulates a condition of drought when the big fish in a pool eat the little fish. The mutual interdependence of temporal and spiritual power, represented by the king and the priest and central to the *Vedas*, is rejected by the Buddhist tradition. The *rajan* in the *gana-sanghas* (chiefdoms) functioned for a long period without dependence on the *brahmana*.

The upholding of *dhamma* in the Buddhist texts was said to be the most important duty of the king.[13] An attempt was made towards the inculcation of these ideas during the reign of Ashoka Maurya. He developed on the Buddhist doctrine and made a point of calling upon the *brahmanas* and the *shramanas* (the Buddhist, Jainas and other Orders of monks) and members of religious sects generally, to be tolerant towards each other's teachings. All relationships should be based on mutual concern and consideration including those involving parents and children, employers and employees and communities, professions and sects (Bloch 1950: 96–97). He called upon the gods to manifest themselves so as to persuade people of the righteousness of this teaching (ibid.: 98–99; 146–47), but he too did not attribute the teaching to deities. In the Buddhist tradition he became a pious Buddhist king, but his piety was expressed in a concern for social ethics and the welfare of people and not in performing rituals directed at deities.

A significant difference between Brahmanical and Buddhist texts also lies in the concept of the *chakravartin* (the universal monarch). The Buddhist *chakkavatti* was the *dhammika-dhammaraja* (the king of righteousness or the righteous king), aware of the advantage of a society governed by dhamma. His claim to be regarded as a chakkavatti was because he turned the wheel of law/dhamma.[14] This was unlike most *kshatriya* heroes in Brahmanical texts who were *chakravartin*s because their campaigns brought them victories over their enemies. The latter were also expected to promote the law but this was law pronounced by *brahmanas* with the claim that it was sanctioned by deities: it was specific to caste and was conditioned by social hierarchy. The Buddhist understanding of law did not incorporate hierarchical differences and had universal application. The Buddhist concept of the *cakkavatti* does not detract from the recognition of power and sovereignty. Both of these require that the state ensure what we in modern parlance would call democratic functioning and concern for the welfare of its constituents. The highpoint of these functions were openness of thought and speech, observance of laws, insistence on frequent assembly to discuss matters of state and the equality of all. The need for frequent assemblies was because the authority to rule was derived from those who constitute society, as is evident from the story of the *mahasammata*. What might have been a corollary to equality was the reference to wealth being acquired through labour, effort and righteous means.[15] Wealth should not be spent on useless rituals or on campaigns, but should go towards supporting livestock, agriculture, trade and administration.[16] It is repeatedly stated that the *chakkavatti* has to provide sustenance for the poor apart from ensuring good administration and general prosperity.[17] Stealing and violence arise from poverty; therefore, in order to prevent poverty, the king must punish those who break the law.[18]

It is significant that Buddhism and Jainism were among the early religions to acknowledge the right of a woman to choose to become a renouncer and join an Order of nuns. This was not absolute freedom but at least it permitted an alternate way of life to the conventional one. That this was appreciated by women is evident from the sentiments expressed in the *Theri-gatha* compositions of Buddhist nuns. Religious sects influenced by Buddhism accorded the same freedom to women who were also among their more respected practitioners.

By the mid-second millennium, Vedic Brahmanism was being superseded by Puranic Hinduism as the popular religion which competed with Buddhism and Jainism. There were attempts to appropriate the more attractive aspects of Buddhism, particularly when Buddhists themselves turned from treating deity as irrelevant to deifying a spectrum of beings. It is debatable whether the centrality of *karma* and *samsara,* with the individual being responsible for his/her liberation from rebirth through his/her actions in this birth, was first popularized through Buddhism or through Puranic Hinduism.

The Bhakti tradition as part of Puranic Hinduism focused on particular deities, pre-eminently Vishnu and Shiva. Although some threads of Puranic Hinduism endorsed aspects of Vedic Brahmanism, the sheer diversity of the former led to differences from the latter in various significant ways: in the evolving of individual deities worshipped as icons; in forms of worship embodied in the rituals of *puja* as distinct from the *yajna;* in the emergence of temples as permanent places of worship; and in belief especially in *samsara* and *karma* (actions and rebirth of the soul). Liberation from rebirth was the responsibility of the individual, but unlike Buddhism, Puranic Hinduism made liberation dependent on devotion to the deity. That the change from Vedic Brahmanism was substantial is indicated by the currency of new texts such as the *Puranas* and *Agamas* written to explain the mythology, ritual and worship of emerging deities and added to from time to time (Chakravarti 2001).

Formal ritual was however by-passed by many teachers, hymn singers, preachers, 'holy' men and women, who emphasized a personalized worship. This coincided with a particular emphasis on social ethics, although the deity dominated the ethic. Bhakti was a personalized devotion to a deity or the personification of the divine, and the worshipper could choose whom to worship and how to worship. This flexibility allowed religious boundaries to be relatively fluid. The initial following was from among non-elite groups with an overlay of local forms of worship, but there was a gradual filtration upwards. Those who created the Bhakti movements in various parts of the sub-continent for over a millennium belonged to castes ranging from *brahmana* to Dalit (Lorenzen 1995, 2004).

Scholars have tended to sift the various strands of Bhakti according to deity, language and emphasis on ecstatic devotion. But there is also the question of certain sects articulating a greater concern for social issues. This is apparent in their insisting on equality, not only in the eyes of the deity but also among worshippers, and setting aside or opposing caste norms in favour of a universal social ethic, as evident in the compositions of Dadu, Raidas, Kabir and Nanak, among others. The Virashaiva movement of the twelfth century is an example of a sect that opposed caste hierarchy and gender disabilities and even questioned political sources of power. As such it was both a movement for religious reform as well as social protest. Similar to other such movements it had a large enough following to enable it to evolve into a major caste itself – the Lingayat. Opting out of caste inequality even within the sect strengthened the aspiration towards a universal ethic. They shared no common body of doctrine across sects, were frequently opposed to brahmanical doctrine, but were firm in their commitment to the ethics of social equality. That caste inequality continued should not be seen as the failure of these movements, since a major part of society conformed to their views. The filtration upwards tended to encourage new forms and objects of worship, but the message of social protest was set aside by the dominant castes. The acquiescence of the lower castes in this mutation has yet to be examined.

The Bhakti religious articulation had regional manifestations and used the regional languages. There is a tendency to collapse all variations of Bhakti into one movement, but the manifestations differ to a greater or lesser degree even within regions, and this diversity should be recognized apart from the two broad divisions of Nirguna and Saguna. There were mystics but there were also those who protested against the inequities of social functioning.

After the arrival of Islam, the choice of teacher and deity widened and ranged across Hindu and Muslim articulations of the divine. In this the Sufi teachers were a focus, merging with local society in some instances, and using the local idiom. The dialogue with some Bhakti sects, such as the Kabirpanthis, nurtured much innovative thought. Worshippers were seen as equal in the eyes of the deity and of the devotees, and to that extent there was a negation of social hierarchies. But the negation was not sufficiently universalized. The contribution of the Sufis in parenting to some extent the popular religions of the second millennium AD has been written about but needs further exploration. The tension between formal Islam as reflected in the *shari'a* and that as practiced and preached in the institutions of various communities encouraged by the more liberal Sufis, provides many insights into relations of power, formal and informal religion, and the life of communities (Alam 2004: 81*ff.*; Eaton 1978).

The Shakta religion overlapped with some of the Bhakti teachers as also with the Sufi sects (Bhattacharya 1996, 1992). The latter gave religious sustenance to the *pirs* and *faqirs* who held a similar status to that of the *gurus* and *sants,* and gradually the two mingled. *Guru*s and *pir*s included those that had been brought up as Hindus and Muslims but had forsaken the formal boundaries of these religions to follow the more fluid teachings and practices of the Shaktas, the Bhakti *sants* and the Sufis and sometimes to move beyond even these teachings. As late as the nineteenth century the Meos of Rajasthan for instance were not clearly identified as either Hindus or Muslims but followed the teachings and rituals of the *darvesh, jogi, jangam* and *samnayasi*. A century later there were substantial attempts by the Arya Samaj and the Tablighi Jama't to convert them to a brahmanized Hinduism or to formal Islam (Mayaram 2004).

Among the many striking expressions of worship among both Hindus and Muslims was the widespread following of Satya Pir in Bengal (Roy 1983). This pattern can be seen in many parts of the sub-continent. Recognizable characteristics are the absence of formal religious boundaries and the premise of social equality.

In discussions on Indian secularism and religion, the impact of Islam is, with rare exceptions, either ignored or else it is confined to the Islam of the royal courts and a few elite groups. Confrontations between the latter and the more popular sects are generally disregarded.

Those not in the upper levels of society expressed their religious needs through what I would like to call the Guru-Pir religion. This has been the religion – in all its varied manifestations – of the majority of Indians, for at least the last five centuries, or even earlier, with an inheritance in some of the earlier heterodox forms. It was a religion frequently propagated by renouncers. They spoke of personal devotion to any deity with a spirituality that underlined social ethics, expressed in a message not only of tolerance but also of social equality and a concern for the human condition. Equality was not limited to an underlying principle of the relationship among those who supported this kind of religion but was extended to all men and women. The good society was central to their concerns with a committed advocating of its principles in however generalized a form. These were not incidental sects but were the mainstream religion at the broadest level of functioning in most social communities. Religious institutions claiming legitimacy from these ideas did exist, but their role was far more marginal than the institutions of the formal religions patronized by the elite.

The role of the renouncer in Indian society, as a figure of moral authority reaching beyond a single religious identity also has a bearing on social ethics (Thapar 2002a, 2002b). Some renouncers opted out of social obligations, others who were not identified with a particular religion, emerged as preceptors to communities and preached an ethic of social responsibility. Mysticism apart, many more renouncers were concerned with the mainsprings of society and how these could be directed towards the welfare of its constituents at all levels. It is as well to remember that this moral authority lay in not only challenging deity – as in the multiple myths of gods fearing the power accumulated by *rishis* through asceticism – but also in legitimating political and social protest. Gandhi's adoption of the symbols of asceticism was not an individual quirk or a Hindu identification but was the continuation of a long tradition of linking moral authority, as distinct from religious authority, to protest.

The colonial state recognized only the formal religions of what it called Hinduism and Islam and put everyone in either one or the other slot. It is ironic that colonial ethnography is now among the sources of information on the Guru-Pir religious articulation during recent periods, as are the Gazetteers and Censuses; yet, the distinctive religious identity of such groups was not recognized when these data were being compiled. This was despite the powerful oral tradition through which this articulation was, and is, preached and practiced. The followers of these teachings were the lesser of the lesser breeds without the law, and therefore almost socially invisible except to evoke a certain curiosity. The rhetoric of the colonial interpretation of Indian society as constituted of two monolithic communities was all pervading. The socio-religious reform movements of the nineteenth century, where they were responding to these colonial interpretations, were circumscribed middle-class movements and tended to marginalize the religion/s of the majority of Indians. Nor did nationalism give recognition to these, despite Gandhi's appeal to mass audiences (as distinct from political parties), being couched in terms that echoed the Guru-Pir tradition. The religious nationalisms that are dominant today have no place for religious articulations that cannot be firmly located in one of the two major religions viewed as monolithic. The battle over places of worship and the insistence on converting them from one religion to the other is a case in point. This battle occurs in places where earlier adherents of all kinds of religious sects would have worshiped together.

Religious sects of the Guru-Pir tradition have often been described as the middle ground between Hinduism and Islam. My argument however is that this is not the middle ground but the continuation of a religious tradition which modern scholars have relegated to a substratum status (Thapar 2002d). In going through the sources of pre-modern times, such religious articulations tended to be set aside in favour of the more accessible religious expression of elite groups with their easily accessible texts. Interestingly, the popular religious sects tended more easily to discard the norms of the *dharmashastras* and the *shari'a* and emphasized ameliorating the human condition with an ethic that went above and beyond established religion, and the applicability of which preferably was to be universal.

Discussion of the interface between religion and secularism or of the consciousness of ideas related to secularizing Indian society has to address itself to these articulations as well. This is all the more so since these religious articulations have been consistently and continually concerned about not just the centrality of social ethics but also about actualizing such an ethic. Such an actualizing in the present day involves the relationship between caste, religions, the state and civil society. It is significant that at the level of *jati* there is also an acceptance of the idea of equality within the *jati*.

The close integration between religious and caste identity also raises the question of law and the state. *Dharma* in the sense of law was specified for each *varna* in the *dharmashastra*s and although these were not codes of law, they encapsulated ideal norms of social functioning. But what was not captured in the *dharmashastra*s was that each *jati/varna* observed customary laws (*achara*), which did on occasion contradict the rules of the *dharmashastra*s.[19] This was not peculiar to Hinduism, as there were the same discrepancies between the *shari'a* and the customary law observed by castes that had converted to Islam, as is evident from the differences in the customary law of, for example, the Meos of Rajasthan and the Mappilas of Kerala, both formally Muslim communities. Such customary law was often a continuation of the earlier *jati* practices or resulted from intermarriage between immigrants and local communities. Distance from the norms, if not a refutation of these, may well have been more common than is supposed. Flexibility in law is also reflected in statements that where there was conflict, the king had the right to interpret the law, indicating perhaps a priority for custom over the code.[20]

Much has been written about the religious tolerance of Hinduism. The link between caste and religion could be one explanation for the relatively greater accommodation of alternate religions in South Asian history as compared to Europe. A religious sect when it attained a critical mass could be converted into a caste or a cluster of castes and be accommodated with a variety of other dissenting groups. The sting of protest was removed by allowing them their own custom and ritual within the boundaries of their identity. The hierarchical placement of social statuses follows some religious identities but since the status has its own social boundaries the religious identities could be more flexible. However, even where religious differences were relatively fluid, social hierarchies were less so. Protestors were not easily accommodated and if possible were relegated to lower caste status. Where religious sanctions prevailed in the form for instance, of the purity-pollution nexus, the status of the untouchable being inherited, was immutable, and was at the receiving end of a fierce intolerance, in many ways worse than religious intolerance. The freedom to choose and practice a religion is not alien to south Asian tradition but caste identity could curtail this freedom; therefore, religious sects seeking a wider following tended to oppose caste hierarchies.

Religions with established institutions such as monasteries, temples, *mathas*, *khanqahs*, mosques and churches sought the patronage of the local king and there was a competition for this patronage. The larger amount of this patronage came from royalty, but Buddhist and Jain institutions in particular also received extensive patronage from the communities of financiers, traders and artisan guilds, and from small-scale landowners (Miller 1992). Whereas communities were more selective in their patronage, in part perhaps because of more limited funds, royalty in India in all periods gave grants and donations to a range of religious sects. Such patronage was not neutral and the range of sects as recipients is striking. The basis for the selection was doubtless conditioned by the politics of these religious sects apart from the personal devotion or assessment of the patron. This is a contrast with European patrons confining patronage to a single sect. A medieval European king making a grant for the building of a mosque in Europe would be relatively unknown, yet this was done by non-Muslim rulers in western India. There were occasions when for example, a Shaiva Solanki king annulled the grants to Jain institutions made by his predecessor,[21] but generally Indian royalty seemed to have been aware of the political usefulness of patronizing a number of different sects. This may again have had links with caste and regional interests. The Sultans and the Mughal rulers displayed the same catholicity and in most cases of patronage to non-Islamic sects the intentions would have been varied.

Incidents of religious intolerance often involved competition for patronage. The tensions were not only between the Buddhists and the Shaivas but also between the Shaivas and the Jains, and to a lesser extent between the Vaishnavas and the Shaivas (Thapar 2000: 7–24). At one level, some degree of distribution of royal patyronage has been taken as an expression of the co-existence of all religions or even of the neutrality of the state towards religion, but this would not invariably be a tenable argument. The reason for this patronage was the need to juxtapose patronage in a context where the state was expected to be a patron of religion. Religious networks could also be viewed as potential catchment areas of support and loyalty. Quite apart from the personal religious predilections of a ruler, there was clearly an understanding of the function of religious institutions in a political and social context and the balancing of a number of such institutions. In some cases there may have been a policy of playing off one against the other, or in other cases the state indicating its power over the religious institutions. The pattern of patronage, because it was extended to groups that were thought to be politically and socially important or were intended to be made so, extended largely to the elite, whereas those representing larger but disorganized numbers, were generally ignored by the elite. These groups found their patronage among the lesser members of society whose support they claimed.

From proto-secularism to contemporary secularism

An interesting case of state patronage towards building a temple was raised immediately after Independence, when in 1951 a Minister of the Central Government, K. M. Munshi, asserted that the Government of India was financing the rebuilding of the famous temple at Somanatha, raided by Mahmud of Ghazni in 1026, which by now had become an icon of Hindu-Muslim antagonism in the politics of religious nationalism (Thapar 2004: 197–201). Nehru categorically denied the assertion and stated that as a secular government, the Government of India would not finance the building of the temple. A private Trust was therefore established for the purpose. This was a departure from the earlier tradition and to that extent underlines a difference between the policies of pre-modern states and those of a modern, secular state.

Contemporary secularism has to involve itself with contending the politics of religious institutions and religious organizations playing a political role. The dialogue is not about belief and faith but about institutions and politics and about the control of religious institutions and those that administer them over aspects of civil society. Secularism adopts a code of social ethics that challenges the acceptance of inequalities where these are proposed by religious ideologies. Rights have to be sought after and established through codes and practice, and they have to be backed by a philosophy that endorses these rights and which does not require recourse to divine intervention or formal religious institutions.

As the previous section has shown, there is an element of what might be called proto-secularism available from earlier traditions, should contemporary Indians wish to draw on it. But this is at best an ambience and not an actuality for contemporary secularism, since the values associated with human rights and democratic functioning are of the contemporary world and not of the past. However, drawing from the past has the potential of assisting in the secularizing of society without creating a complete disjuncture with what is believed to be tradition.

In referring to proto-secularism, I am not suggesting that there was an attempt at establishing a secular society in India in c. 400 BC or even later. That this was not secularism is evident from the fact that whereas the appeal was to the individual to adopt a code of behaviour that was derived from values that we would today regard as conducive to secularizing society, there was no requirement that the state should endorse this code or even establish and maintain institutions that would do so. In a secular society the onus is on the state and civil society to establish codes and institutions that would support secular values. The state recognizes the existence of religion but restricts the unquestioned activities of the latter preferably to matters of personal belief. Politics should not function on the basis of religious communities, for the primary identity is the identity of citizens of a nation and not members of a religious community. This space will be contested and has to be won by those in support of secularizing society. But the contest does not concern religion alone and has to extend to all those institutions and structures that are involved with the rights of the citizen.

Secularism as an ideology cannot be imposed, but when the structures that support the status quo are changed, then a secular society may begin to emerge. To that extent the ideology of secularism supports a particular kind of social change. This may be aided if there is a realization that there are antecedents in the cultures of present-day communities that are sympathetic to secular values.

Religious nationalisms have a tendency to appropriate cultural nationalism. Discussions on cultural nationalism need to define the cultures they incorporate. Existing definitions have veered towards the upper caste cultures and religions. The cultures and religious identities of others are set aside. Yet there are other traditions that might even have a larger popular appeal such as those that I have referred to. It is important to the definition and the future of the secularizing of South Asian societies that we explore the wider range of cultural traditions when we search for ancestral elements. Resort to a single religious identity is in any case self-defeating in a multi-religious society. Secularism is not just the confrontation between religion and the state. It requires new initiatives by the state and by the citizens in relation to the essentials of a secularized society. If citizenship is to be the primary identity, it will have to place other identities of caste, class, religion, gender and language, in their appropriate places and will have to define the identities that go into the making of citizenship.

Notes

1 This is an abridged version of the article that appeared in T. N. Srinivasan (ed.) *The Future of Secularism* (New Delhi: Oxford University Press, 2007).
2 *Digha Nikaya*, I. 32, 46 Brahmajala-sutta.
3 *Samyutta Nikaya*, I. 191; *Vinaya*, Mahavagga 1.6.17–26.
4 *Majjhima Nikaya*, I. 167 ff. Ariyapariyesana-sutta; III. 71–78 Mahachattarisaka-sutta; *Samyutta Nikaya*, 3. 94–99 Parileyya; II. 12.1 ff.
5 *Vinaya*, Mahavagga, I. 1. 1–7; *Digha Nikaya*, II 30 ff.
6 *Majjhima Nikaya*, I. p. 160 ff. Ariyapariyesana-sutta.
7 *Digha Nikaya*, III. 180 ff. Sigalovada-sutta.

8 *Majjhima Nikaya,* I. 134–35 Alagaddupama-sutta.
9 *Digha Nikaya,* III. 84–96 Agganna-sutta.
10 *Arthashastra* I. 13. 5–12.
11 *Digha Nikaya,* I. 92 ff. Ambattha-sutta; *Samyutta Nikaya,* 4. 398.
12 Shantiparvan, 59. 12–29; 94–119.
13 *Digha Nikaya,* III. 59 ff Cakkavatti-sihanada sutta; III. 72 ff. Parinibbana sutta.
14 *Digha Nikaya,* I. 59 ff; 88–89; *Majjhima Nikaya,* III. 172 ff; III. 65.
15 *Anguttara Nikaya,* II, 69–70.
16 *Digha Nikaya,* II. 127 ff. Kutadanta-sutta.
17 *Digha Nikaya,* II, 139 ff; III. 60 ff.
18 *Digha Nikaya,* III. 93 ff. Agganna-sutta.
19 Such deviations from the norms are sometimes even mentioned in the texts, as for example, the practice of cross-cousin marriage. There is a debate on the acceptability of custom versus code. *Baudhayana Dharmasutra,* I.2.3.; *Gautama Dharmasutra,* 11.20.
20 *Narada-smriti,* I. 10–14.
21 Merutunga, *Prabandhacintamani,* 4.9.175.

References

Alam, M. (2004) *The Languages of Political Islam in India,* Delhi: Permanent Black.
Bhargava, R. (ed.) (1998) *Secularism and its Critics,* Delhi: Oxford University Press.
Bhattacharya, N. N. (1992) *History of Tantric Religion,* Delhi: Manohar.
—— (1996) *History of Sakta Religion,* Delhi: Munshiram Manoharlal.
Bloch, Jules (1950) *Les Inscriptions d'Asoka,* Paris: Les Belle Lettres.
Chakravarti, K. (2001) *Religious Process, The Puranas and the Making of a Regional Tradition,* Delhi: Oxford University Press.
Chattopadhyaya, D. P. (1955) *Lokayata,* Delhi: People's Publishing House.
Eaton, R. (1978) *The Sufis of Bijapur,* Princeton: Princeton University Press.
Lorenzen, D. N. (ed.) (1995) *Bhakti Religion in North India: Community, Identity and Political Action,* Albany: State University of New York Press.
—— (2004) *Religious Movements in South Asia,* Delhi: Oxford University Press.
Madan, T. N. (1987) 'Secularism in its place', *Journal of Asian Studies,* 46(4): 747–59.
—— (1997) *Modern Myths and Locked Minds,* Delhi: Oxford University Press.
Mayaram, S. (2004) 'Hindu and Islamic transnational religious movements', *Economic and Political Weekly,* 3 January, pp. 80–88.
Nandy, A. (1998) 'The politics of secularism and the recovery of religious toleration', in R. Bhargava (ed.) *Secularism and its Critics,* Delhi: Oxford University Press, pp. 297–344.
Radhakrishnan, S. (1948) *Indian Philosophy,* vol. I, London: Allen & Unwin.
Roy, Asim (1983) *The Islamic Syncretistic Tradition in Bengal,* Princeton: Princeton University Press.
Sachau, E.C. (ed.) (1964 rpt) *Alberuni's India,* Delhi: Rupa & Co.
Stoler Miller, B. (ed.) (1992) *The Powers of Art,* Delhi: Oxford University Press.
Thapar, R (2000) 'Cultural transaction and early India', *History and Beyond,* Delhi: Oxford University Press.
—— (2002a) 'The householder and renouncer in Brahmana and Buddhist texts', *Cultural Pasts,* Delhi: Oxford University Press, pp. 914–45.
—— (2002b) 'Renunciation: the making of a counter-culture?' *Cultural Pasts,* Delhi: Oxford University Press, pp. 876–913.
—— (2002c) 'Syndicated hinduism', *Cultural Pasts,* Delhi: Oxford University Press, pp. 1025–54.
—— (2002d) 'The tyranny of labels', *Cultural Pasts,* Delhi: Oxford University Press, pp. 990–1014.
—— (2004e) *Somanatha: The Many Voices of a History,* Delhi: Penguin.
Vanaik, A. (1997) *The Furies of Indian Communalism,* London: Verso.

6 Secularism revisited

Doctrine of destiny or political ideology?[1]

T. N. Madan

[Feuerbach's] work consists in the dissolution of the religious world into its secular basis. He overlooks the fact that after completing this work, the chief thing still remains to be done. For the fact that the secular foundation detaches itself from itself and establishes itself in the clouds as an independent realm is really to be explained by the self-cleavage and self-contradictoriness of this secular basis.

Karl Marx, 'Theses on Feuerbach'

The historical modus vivendi of secularism, while seeking to chasten religious dogmatism, embodies unacknowledged elements of immodesty in itself. The very intensity of the struggle it wages against religious intolerance may induce blind spots with respect to itself.

William Connolly, *Why I am not a Secularist*

I

Alongside democracy, federalism, and socialism, secularism was one of the foundational principles on which the leaders of the new state of independent India set out in the middle of the twentieth century to create an economically developed and socially just society. Democracy was of course the legacy of the freedom movement and the animating spirit of the Constitution adopted in 1949; it found prominent mention in its Preamble. The federal structure of the state – an imperative in view of the large size and huge population of the country and its regional diversities – was also laid out in great detail in the Constitution. Socialism and secularism did not find direct mention despite the efforts of many members to have them written into it. B. R. Ambedkar, the presiding deity as it were of the drafting committee, considered it unwise to constitutionally bind the future generations to a socio-economic agenda that may have to be changed with the passage of time (see Madan 2006: 84–85, 106).

As for secularism, the liberty of 'belief, faith and worship', inscribed in the Preamble and spelled out in a number of clauses in the chapter on fundamental rights (see Madan 2006: Chapter 2), was obviously considered adequate enough for the word secularism also to be mentioned in the Constitution. Fearful of the mutual hostility of religious communities (which had led to the partition of the subcontinent) though India's leaders were, and committed to a modern rational outlook on national life, secularism in its original sense of the ideology of those committed to bringing about the decline of religion in human affairs (see Madan 1997: Chapter 1), obviously was considered inappropriate in the Indian cultural setting. Widely respected and influential intellectuals actually said so. [...] Radhakrishnan's view (see Madan 2006: Chapter 4) [was] that [...] India needed [...] to evolve its own concept of secularism. The effort to do so began straightaway and we do indeed now have our own definition of the term, although the same is not followed consistently; nor has it yet entered into sociological literature generally or such widely consulted dictionaries as the *Concise Oxford English Dictionary*, which now abounds with Indian words.

Indian secularism has come to have both a focused meaning and also a wider connotation. Interestingly, Jawaharlal Nehru brought them together in an early statement. In a letter to the chief ministers in 1952, he observed that the word 'secular' meant more than the 'free play of religions': it also conveyed 'the idea of social and political equality'. Thus, he did not consider 'a caste ridden society ... properly secular'. He concluded: 'we must always keep the ideal of the unity of India and of the political and social equality of her people, to whatever group, religion or province they might belong' (see Austin 1999: 557–58). As is well known, Nehru was not happy about caste-based reservations in civil services and legislatures. It is indeed ironical that today's 'secular forces' (so called) are headed by, among others, mutually antagonistic caste leaders for whom secularism and casteism are not at all contradictory as Nehru correctly perceived them to be. The 'wretched national agonizing about secularism' about which Shashi Tharoor (2003: 3) has written simply does not go away.

II

There are two bodies of reflection and writing on Indian secularism understood as the freedom of conscience (or religion) of the individual, and as the commitment of the state to protect this freedom and to ensure that religious identity in no way interferes with citizenship rights. There is a multi-vocal public discourse carried on by politicians, journalists, and lawyers and judges; and there is an academic discourse. In my reading of these two discourses, the former is, of course, much older and therefore the original discourse; the latter is generally reactive and hesitant to break new ground. Of late it has begun to seem even insular, somewhat cut off from discussions on secularization and secularism (actually the former term is used to refer to both the *process* and to the *thesis* that the process is linear and universal, and the latter term is not equally in vogue) among political and social theorists in the West.

In the public or political discourse, the secularist position (or what could be called so) first made its appearance as nationalist rhetoric towards the end of the nineteenth century. Its precise context was the efforts of the leaders of the newly founded Indian National Congress to secure participation of the Muslims in its activities and programmes. As I have already pointed out elsewhere (Madan 1997: 267*ff.*), a Muslim leader from Bombay, Badruddin Tyabji, in his presidential address to the Congress in 1887, hoped that there was nothing in the mutual relations of the various religious communities that would make anyone of them refrain from joining the others to obtain from the British 'general' administrative reforms and civic rights 'for the common benefit' of all people. The principal opponent of this point of view was Sayyid Ahmad Khan, one of the most prominent public figures of north India and an energetic promoter of modern education among the Muslims. Through an exchange of letters in 1888, these two distinguished Muslims may be said to have opened the secularism debate of modern India, although they did not use the term 'secularism'. Tyabji argued that community and national interests were both equally legitimate and they were non-antagonistic; Khan insisted on the priority of the former and questioned the validity of the latter in India where the Hindus outnumbered Muslims three to one. In Tyabji's judgement, Muslim interests would be best served by linking them to general interests, and not by pursuing a separatist strategy.

From the nationalist Muslim point of view, secularism (read nationalism) could be an encompassing or a residual concept: general interests could be so stated as to include community interests; or community interests even when granted primacy still would leave a residual space for common interests. Muhammad Ali Jinnah, a follower of Tyabji and a Congressman who later also became Muslim League leader, put the secularist position succinctly when he famously rebuked one of his protégés (and clients), the Raja of Mahumdabad, who showed increasing consciousness of his Muslim identity, that he was 'an Indian first and then a Muslim' (Wolpert 1985: 79). Actually, as far as I have been able to find out, Jinnah was one of the first public figures of modem India to speak of the 'affairs of our common secular existence'. He did this in his presidential address to the Indian Muslim League in 1916, when he was also one of the leading lights of the Congress.

It is not my intention here to undertake a survey of usages: I only want to draw attention to three noteworthy conceptions of secularism discernible in the public discourse during the years of the national movement. The first has been noted above. The second we owe to Mahatma Gandhi. His support in 1920 to the Khilafat movement in India, which campaigned for the grant of sufficient temporal powers to the defeated Sultan of Turkey, so that he might discharge his duties as the *Khalifa* of the Muslims (that included notably the protection of the major holy places of Islam worldwide), appeared to be paradoxical from a nationalist (secular) point of view. He defended his decision in terms of his moral obligation (dharma) to forge bonds of 'friendship' between Hindus and Muslims and thereby promote 'internal peace' in the country (see Brown 1992: 142). He placed the burden of winning Muslim participation in national affairs on the shoulders of Hindus, the majority community. For him, this too was an issue of moral obligation; his critics considered it a policy of appeasement. But he firmly denied that there was any element of bargaining in his politics (see Nanda 1989: 223–24). If secularism in the context of the 1920s was the cultivation of common interests, even when these interests were apparently not secular, like the Muslim demand for the protection of the *Khalifa* and the Hindu demand for the protection of the cow, then the Gandhian version of it was a morally grounded social contract of mutual benefit, which also served higher national interests through a reconciliation of the two communities. But Gandhi was not a secularist; he was very much a religious person. Given his absolute stand that good ends do not justify bad means, his approach cannot really be considered (as some critics have done) a compromise with communalism for the furtherance of national goals. That his actions contributed to the communalization of politics can only be called 'an unintended consequence'.

The third conception of secularism was characteristic of the thinking of Jawaharlal Nehru (discussed in Madan 2006: Chapters 3 and 4). It came closest to the Western conception of secularism as agnosticism and rationalism. Nehru was actually more concerned with exposing the economic foundations of Muslim separatism and the negative ideology of communalism than with the elaboration of a positive ideology of secularism. The word (or its cognates) do not occur in either his autobiography (Nehru

1936) or *The Discovery of India* (Nehru 1946). He did, however, write about the secular state in *Glimpses of World History* (Nehru 1942: 706) in the specific context of Kemalist Turkey.

These formulations, made in the context of the movement for independence rooted in the ideology of nationalism, are now of no more than historical interest. As already noted, Jinnah eventually promoted the thesis of incompatibility of cultural values and secular interests of the two major 'nations' of the subcontinent (Hindus and Muslims) that became the basis for partition, and swept away Gandhi's politico-moral endeavour to build a social contract between the religious communities. Nehru's modernist thesis about the primacy of secular interests, and the irrelevance (if not unreal character) of the religious factor in public life, to which he adhered until the very last years of the freedom movement, also fell by the way.

After independence, the focus shifted to the making of the state, and secularism, so called, derived from Western sources, but not wholly faithful to them, was presented as its ideology. The limited appeal of the liberal or Marxist notions of secularism among the people generally convinced Nehru and other leaders that in India, 'a religious country' (as he called it) (see Madan 2006: 81) secularism would have to mean, at least in the foreseeable future, that the state would honour all faiths without discrimination (*sarva dharma samabhava*), and that it would provide equal opportunities to all citizens. This position was, of course, in consonance with Gandhi's pluralist perspective on inter-religious understanding. It is this which has become the state ideology, and has now been for quite a while the basis of virtually all discussions of Indian secularism, whether in the public arena or the academe.

In the post-Nehruvian period, the characterization of the current pluralist ideology as 'pseudo-secularism' by the intellectuals of the Hindu right, because of its emphasis on minority rights, allegedly denies Hindus the advantage of numbers that an unqualified policy of equal treatment would give them, is a clever political ploy to further the agenda of majoritarianism. Hence, they bring forward the charge of appeasement of the minorities, which does, however, stick on some political parties. Untrustworthy minorities are a creation of diffident and mistrusting minds that pick up aberrant cases of espionage, sabotage, terrorism, etc., as evidence of a general malaise.

III

[...] The 1950s and early 1960s, up to Nehru's passing in 1964, were the years of high hope, and even heady enthusiasm, for the votaries of the ideologies of secularism and socialism. When anxieties began to emerge, and later in the 1970s to thicken, these concerned the slow pace of secularization and the recurrence of communal conflict rather than the suitability or viability of received ideas and institutions. A widely discussed public document, voicing serious concern about 'the accelerating pace of retreat from reason' and 'the decay of rationality', was 'A statement on scientific temper', issued in 1981 by a galaxy of intellectuals (see Bhaduri et al. 1981). It called for the fostering of 'scientific temper' (the phrase was attributed to Jawaharlal Nehru) and the recognition of science and technology as 'viable instruments of social transformation'. It drew a spirited retort from the cultural psychologist Ashis Nandy in the form of a 'Counter-statement on humanistic temper' (1981), in which he focused attention on the role of science in 'the institutionalization of suffering' and promotion of modern 'superstitions' and 'authoritarianism'.

Subsequently, Nandy published a radical critique of ideological secularism, under the provocative title of an 'An anti-secularist manifesto' (1985), pointing out that the Indian national movement had stressed that religious tolerance may be derived from an attitude of respectfulness toward all religions, and did not have to depend upon the devaluation of religion. If secularism 'is not to become a reformist sect within modernity, [it] must respect and build upon the faiths and visions that have refused to adapt to the modern worldview' (ibid.: 2). It is not people of faith, Nandy added, but religious zealots and secularists who are respectively against religious tolerance and religion itself. He argued that religious violence becomes unmanageable when its foundation is secular logic and political calculation rather than orthodox religious passion. An increase in the 'pathologies of religion' was, however, only a part of the full story. There was also a turning back to traditional ('non-secular') ideas of religious tolerance (Nandy 2001: 161–88).

Nandy's assertations did not come as a surprise to those Indian scholars familiar with Western sociological literature on secularization; unfortunately not many are, even now. After all, the high noon of the secularization thesis was in the 1970s (see Glasner 1977), and the thesis about its 'self-limiting' nature was being increasingly argued in the 1980s: the process of secularization generates its own reversal through religious revival. The Iranian Revolution of 1978–79 was the best known example of this phenomenon. Nandy's polemical style and occasional carelessness (for example, the opening sentence of his 1985 article – 'Gandhi said once in a while that he was secular' [sic] – evoked hostile reactions that have been frenetic and have expanded their scope to excoriate the work of several other scholars who engaged in serious examination of the infirmities of the concept of secularism.

In [...] [a] recent essay, Nandy writes that the twilight of the certitudes of dogmatic secularism may already be upon us, that the 'concept' [ideology] 'has begun to deliver less and less' (2003: 67). He reiterates his well-known earlier position that tradition had its own ways of dealing effectively with bigotry and communal conflict, which in any case never flared into the kind of large scale riots that defaced the Indian landscape in the twentieth century. But these ways have been eroded by an aggressive secularism just as traditional systems of medicine have been displaced by modern (allopathic) medicine. Nandy thinks that secularism survives today because it serves the 'interests of the hegemonic state (cherished equally by self-styled secularists as well as those they call communalists, by the Congress no less than by the Bharatiya Janata Party) and of those who serve this state' (ibid.: 70–75). In spite of its sweeping character there is much weight in this argument.

I have followed, over the years, Nandy's writings on the theme of religious tolerance, and am in sympathy with the main thrust of his arguments. I agree that, paradoxical though it may seem, religion itself can perhaps still be a resource in the fight against religious bigotry. I also agree that modernity (including secularism), being hegemonic in character, narrows rather than enlarges the domain of significant choice-making, but it surely is not all bad. I do not also agree with all the claims Nandy makes on behalf of abstract religion as against historical religions. He tends to idealize tradition, and does not recognize the enormous philosophical doubts and practical difficulties that will attend any serious attempt at the recovery of religious tolerance in a measure that proves adequate in today's circumstances. It is not only the place of religion in public life that has been challenged, so much else also has changed, including the scale and technology of violence. Our times are not of the local riot of the *lathi* and the knife, they are of the terror symbolized by 9/11.

Let me hasten to add, I am not against such critiques of modernity by intellectuals and civil society groups, and indeed support them. I only want to stress that the cultivation of the pluralist attitude, and of religious tolerance in particular, is not going to be easy. Considering, for instance, the lack of success of the three-language formula, because most Indians are reluctant to seriously learn a second Indian language, what are the chances of religious-minded people in this country taking a genuine interest in faiths other than their own? Is religious tolerance possible unless it is based on engagement and dialogue rather than indifference or avoidance? And what about the secularists? Moreover, historical memories of the pasts of India as shaped by, among other things, the century-old debate about secular and religious nationalisms, have tended to be divisive rather than cohesive.

IV

Starting off from a different point of departure than Nandy's, I have presented a critique of ideological secularism in several essays, some of which have been collected in [...] a book (Madan 1997). One of the early such writings was an address (Madan 1987, 2006: Chapter 3) in which I emphasized, first, the origin of secularism in the dialectic of Protestant Christianity and the Enlightenment and, second, its incompatibility with India's major religious traditions. Consequently, I expressed scepticism about an easy passage of the Western ideology of secularism to India, and stressed the importance of taking religion seriously. The intention was to warn against complacency in both thought and action, to sound a wakeup call. Such is the zeal of the missionaries of secularism that my essay was promptly judged to be heretical and I, along with Nandy, was called 'anti-secularist', a term that he had of course used to describe himself (Nandy 2001: 67). Thanks to the furore, [this essay, entitled] 'Secularism in its place', has enjoyed a long life!

The critiques have been wide-ranging, but unfortunately – with only a few exceptions – have missed the mark in various ways. Generally, the strategy of critics has been (*i*) partial or out of context quotation, (*ii*) disregard of such of my arguments as clearly contradict the critics' assertions, (*iii*) insertion of words into my text that are not there, and (*iv*) attribution of motives. I have responded to some of these in previous works, attempting to clear up the misconceptions (Madan 1994 and 2003a). [...]

Not long after Nandy's and my early essays, Partha Chatterjee, a political theorist, also sought to clear the conceptual confusion and carry the discussion forward. Ignoring significant differences in the scope and style of these interventions, the uncritical critics slapped the label of anti-secularists on us to reiterate their own dogmatic positions. I must briefly recall here Chatterjee's seminal contribution to the debate on secularism (1998).

V

Partha Chatterjee's point of departure was 'the political challenge of Hindu majoritarianism', particularly I presume in the wake of the Ramjanmabhumi agitation of the late 1980s and the subsequent demolition of the Babri Masjid at Ayodhya in 1992. 'The majoritarianism of the Hindu right', he wrote perceptively, 'is perfectly at peace with the institutional procedures of the "western" or "modern state"' (Chatterjee 1998: 346). The question that arose therefore was, 'Is the defence of secularism an appropriate ground for meeting the challenge of the Hindu right? Or should it be fought where the attack is being made, i.e. should the response be a defense of the duty of the democratic state to ensure policies of religious toleration' (ibid.: 348)? The short history of the secular state in India, which derived its basic principles of liberty, equality, and neutrality from the West had revealed the anomalies into which it had run in the Indian historical and cultural setting.

The crucial issue that had emerged from the muddling was the articulation of the best means of protecting the right of a minority to live as a minority. Chatterjee's carefully argued answer was 'toleration ... premised on autonomy and respect for persons' was the reasonable course to follow in the Indian situation, so that the minorities can 'resist homogenization from outside and push for democratization from inside' (ibid.: 375, 378). Chatterjee's constructive intervention in the debate did indeed seek to move 'beyond secularism' after pointing out the difficulties in which the secular state in India had become enmeshed. But almost as he had expected, Chatterjee too had to face resistance, but the wall had surely begun to show some cracks.

Writing about the same time as Chatterjee, economist Amartya Sen (1998) drew attention to a new 'intellectual scepticism', underscored the 'incompleteness of secularism, and the need to go beyond', and regretted the 'reluctance' of 'secularist intellectuals in India' to address the issues that had been presented by critics such as Varshney (1993), Nandy and myself, and later others. In a well organized but rapid review of the various critiques, he concluded that in an 'integrally pluralist society' secularism as the 'symmetric political treatment of different religious communities' (ibid.: 484) was an imperative. In fact, the pluralist social structure of the country had long had the cultural backdrop of toleration (ibid.: 478). That, such open mindedness notwithstanding, Sen chooses to call himself an 'unreformed secularist' is, I believe, a matter of personal preference. The important thing is that he emphasized the need for discussion, which is what I also have stressed all along.

Another political theorist, Rajeev Bhargava, presented a defence of secularism which included a significant clarification of the concept and a constructive critique of 'the Madan–Nandy thesis' (Bhargava 1994, 1998). I accept his contention that 'Secularism in its place' suffers from a certain conflation of two distinct notions of secularism (the ethical and the political, as he calls them). My essay did mention the Enlightenment and Indian versions of secularism, the one calling for the privatization of religion and the other advocating the state policy of acknowledgement of the presence (even legitimacy) of religion in public life and the symmetric treatment of their followers. My criticism of the former was read by many critics as my rejection of the latter. Actually, this misunderstanding should not have occurred (Bhargava did not get me right on this point) because I had explicitly written that in South Asia we need to take both religion and secularism seriously. It should hardly be necessary in our time to have to say that, as many scholars, including Durkheim and Weber among the sociologists (see Madan 2006: Chapter 1), have long acknowledged, religion and science do not pertain to the same areas of human life and, therefore, there is no essential conflict between them.

Bhargava's thesis of two secularisms is an important contribution and should be pursued seriously. According to him:

> Ethical Secularism ... seeks the separation of religion from politics by virtue of the contribution it makes to the realization of some ultimate ideal. The second type of secularism, I shall call, Political Secularism because, rather than contribute to the

realization of some external comprehensive set of ultimate ideals, the separation of religion from polities, on this view, merely makes for a more livable polity (Bhargava 1998: 492).

It is clear that, although narrower in scope, political secularism is no less important than ethical secularism. In its absence the larger enterprise of providing space for the pursuit of ethical secularism itself may be jeopardized. Political secularism does not challenge the legitimacy of ultimate goals, whether these be said to flow from religion or ethical secularism; it only excludes them from the political arena and the larger public sphere, or neutralizes them by treating different religions and ethical traditions symmetrically (the celebratory *sarva dharma samabhava* of India).

The problem that remains is how to render a society 'guided by principles of political secularism … in the long run … a viable community' (ibid.: 508). Obviously, Bhargava holds the view (and I agree with it) that societies do not live on stratagems alone, even though politics maybe a matter of, in F. G. Bailey's (1969) famous phrase, 'stratagems and spoils'. Politics do not constitute human life in its entirety as (to borrow Weber's deeply insightful words of almost a century ago) 'every one of us who is not spiritually dead must realize'. It follows that 'an ethic of ultimate ends and an ethic of responsibility are not absolute contrasts but rather supplements' (Weber 1948: 127). Considerations of ethical secularism, or of religion, may be postponed, they must not be shelved.

As for the relationship of ethical secularism and religion, Bhargava detects the existence of 'quite irreconcilable conflict', although he says in an aside that this may not be true of all versions of ethical secularism (1998: 495). This is a complex issue with definitional and substantive dimensions, and calls for a fuller and more nuanced discussion than he provides. One would have to convincingly argue that the principle of ethical secularism (or secular humanism), such as respect for human life, liberty, and dignity, is necessarily absent from religious ethics. I am sure Bhargava does not want to take such a position, for he agrees with Nandy and me that 'the resources of religious tolerance', derived from the religious traditions (I presume), must be deployed to confront bigotry and social conservatism. Indeed, he considers such deployment, alongside 'a strong defence of minority rights' and the consolidation of 'whatever space of the common good [that] already exists' (ibid.: 542), as a kind of minimum definition of Indian secularism. I find this agreeable. I do think, however, that the issue of the determination of the minority status of community is not addressed adequately by him.

I again agree with Bhargava, political secularism is more than 'a good fallback strategy', it may be 'the only available way to prevent a community from falling apart' (ibid.: 511). And if that political community happens to be multi-religious like the Indian, the secular state may have to intervene in the areas of life of the citizenry that are seen by them to belong to the domain of religion, so long as this is done in a non-discriminatory (which does not necessarily mean identical) manner. In the language of the Indian Constitution, for example, 'The state shall endeavour to secure for the citizens a uniform [not *common*] civil code throughout the territory of India' (Article 44). Moreover, the state shall have to ensure 'a strong defence of minority rights' (Bhargava 1998: 542), the justification for which I have argued earlier, juxtaposing 'Hindu insensitivity to the feelings of those who consider themselves non-Hindu' with the valid 'anxieties and sensitivities of the minorities' (see Madan 2006: 92, 103).

I have discussed at some length and to historical perspective the majority-minority conundrum (ibid.: Chapter 4). It lies at the very core of the contemporary debate on Indian secularism. In *Beyond Secularism*, Neera Chandhoke (1999), [...] another political theorist, argues rigorously for the rights of religious minorities. She writes that formal equality is the justificatory principle of Indian secularism and the foundation of the secular state's policy of non-discrimination. But formal equality in a setting of demographic and socio-economic inequalities is a recipe for the perpetuation of inequalities. The policy of *sarva dharma samabhava*, unexceptionable in itself, is of little use if minorities are victims of systematic neglect on the part of the state, and unable to mobilize the necessary resources to hold their own against the assertiveness of the majority. What is called for, therefore, Chandhoke maintains, is a corrective policy based on the notion of substantive equality, so that the minorities may be compensated for the conditions of political and economic deprivation that cannot reasonably be said to be their own creation, and enabled to preserve their cultural heritage. The state should therefore be required to put in place 'supportive structures', which are exclusive to the minorities, to enable them to survive without loss of cultural identity and prosper like anybody else.

'The idea of shifting ground from secularism to equality', Chandhoke observes, 'is not meant to devalue the concept', but to strengthen it and, indeed, to help it to realize the goal of equality. 'Secularism alone cannot do this; for in its present form, it has simply exhausted its potential. We will have to go beyond secularism to look for ways in which relationships between communities can be arranged in a just and fair manner' (ibid.: 95–96). The notion of tolerance too is inadequate: she develops at length a holistic framework for achieving the stated goal on the basis of interwoven patterns of democracy, equality, and rights. The last category is in some ways the most crucial and also complex as there is inherent in it a tension arising from the fact that the rights of the individual do not always coincide with that of the community. Chandhoke comes out on the side of the individual characterizing the rights of the community as 'conditional'.

The supportive structures that Chandhoke mentions were in principle written into the Constitution as, for instance, when, under Articles 29 and 30, the minorities were given the fundamental (inalienable) right to establish their own educational institutions. But more can be done as, for instance, in promoting minority languages and literatures and other artistic and creative activities. She goes quite far in developing this argument, and runs the risk of being criticized for making recommendations that would perpetuate communal identities and also not be quite workable. Thus, how could the state prevent the Parsis from dying out through intermarriage, or a tribal community from disappearing through gradual absorption into the surrounding caste-based Hindu society or willing conversion to Christianity? [...]

VI

In the debate on secularism the 'academic field' reflects, I think, the 'power field', which may be characterized in terms of different sets of relations. One such characterization hinges on the interplay of demography, geography, history, and ideology.

The four-fifths majority of the Hindus (80.5 per cent) in the population of the country, and the considerable share at 13.4 per cent of the Muslims in it (between themselves the two religious 'communities' account for 94 per cent of the total, with

Christians and Sikhs accounting for a little over 4 per cent in about equal measure), creates a severe lack of balance which generates fears of majoritarianism that are not wholly unrealistic. I might add in passing that among those counted at the 2001 census, less than 1 per cent were silent on the question of their religious identity. This is not merely a demographic datum; it is a sociological fact of immense political significance.

The geographical distribution of the Muslims, with only two states out of 35 having an absolute majority (Lakshadweep 95 per cent and Jammu and Kashmir 67 per cent) and three others having about one-fourth share in the population (Assam 31 per cent, West Bengal and Kerala 25 per cent each), reveals extreme spatial unevenness. Moreover, at the district and lower levels, there are many pockets of Muslim concentration (old or new) generating a sense of security among the residents, but renewed fears of Muslim separatism among the others. Parochial programmes of traditional (madrasa) education, resistance to social reform, exclusivist claims to historical monuments, etc., aggravate the situation.

History speaks in multiple voices. Hindu and Muslim readings of the past are often not the same. The demand for parity for the two communities, or for weightage, in employment and political representation in the years leading up to partition in disregard of the population statistics, but in recognition of the historical role of Muslims during the 'medieval' period, on the one hand, and negative readings of the same period by some Hindu historians and their empathetic readers, on the other, went a long way in creating both deep cleavage and distrust. Eventually the partition came to be seen on both sides as the result of a community consensus among the Muslims rather than the handiwork of a party (Muslim League) or its top leadership (see Shaikh 1989). As such, it was and is generally regarded as an achievement by Pakistani and Bangladeshi Muslims, and as the betrayal of Muslim interests by Indian Muslims (see Hasan 1997), and of larger national interests by many others. One might have thought all these differences now belonged to the past, but the unfortunate course of events that ultimately led to the demolition of the Babri Masjid and the Gujarat pogrom, from which the country has not yet recovered, revealed that this is not so. The situation has been complicated by the emergence of a militant separatist movement among Kashmiri Muslims in the late 1980s (see Madan 2006: Chapters 6 and 7), some of whom claim to be the third nation of the subcontinent, and international terrorism, and by the upsurge of Hindutva.

Finally, the ideological ambiguities of Indian secularism, which I have discussed above, have generated more heat than light. The facts of demographic and geographic distribution are virtually unalterable. But multiple readings of history and construction of accommodative, forward-looking, ideologies of nationhood and pluralism provide immense scope for human agency. Some years ago, as the movement for the European Union gathered support, one of France's leading intellectuals, Paul Ricoeur, and others like him, gave the call for overcoming the bitter legacies of the past through such means as the 'exchange of memories', 'promotion of plural readings of founding events', 'narrative hospitality', and above all, 'forgiveness' (Ricoeur 1992). If the West, which we like to call materialist, can think in such terms (Ricoeur writes of 'spiritual density'), maybe Indian intellectuals also can do the same. And maybe secularism can yet be reworked as an ideology of participatory pluralism based on the values of dignity (equality of rights) and freedom of conscience, attentive to new situational exigencies and open to radical ways of conceptualizing and coping with them. The foregoing values (and others like them), it must be remembered, can become imperatives only within the normative frameworks of particular configurations of cultural life, and the social practices of particular communities.

As for the state, its policy, as I have argued in more than one place [...], should have the twin objectives of, first, protecting everybody's freedom of conscience (as provided for in the Constitution) and, secondly, contrary to present practice, denying without exception financial assistance for the practice of religion. Let me recall, once again, Gandhi's admonition that a religion that depends on state support for its existence does not deserve to exist. Thus would the policy of uniform treatment of all religious communities (*sarva dharma samabhava*) be truly implemented.

Notes

1 This is an abridged version of the article that appeared in T. N. Madan, *Images of the World: Essays on Religion, Secularism, and Culture* (New Delhi: Oxford University Press, 2006).

References

Austin, Granville (1999) *Working a Democratic Constitution: The Indian Experience*, New Delhi: Oxford University Press.

Bailey, F. G. (1969) *Stratagems and Spoils: A Social Anthropology of Politics*, Oxford: Basil Blackwell.

Bhaduri, Amit et al. (1981) 'A statement on scientific temper', *Mainstream*, 25 July.

Bhargava, Rajeev (1994) 'Giving secularism its due', *Economic and Political Weekly*, 9 July.

—— (1998) 'What is secularism for?' in Rajeev Bhargava (ed.) *Secularism and its Critics*, New Delhi: Oxford University Press.

Brown, Judith (1992) *Gandhi: Prisoner of Hope*, New Haven: Yale University Press.

Chandhoke, Neera (1999) *Beyond Secularism: The Rights of Religious Minorities*, New Delhi: Oxford University Press.

Chatterjee, Partha (1998) [1994] 'Secularism and toleration', in Rajeev Bhargava (ed.) *Secularism and its Critics*, New Delhi: Oxford University Press.

Chatterjee, P. C. (1995) *Secular Values and Secular India*, New Delhi: Manohar.

Connolly, William (1999) *Why I am not a Secularist*, Minneapolis: University of Minnesota Press.

Glasner, Peter (1977) *The Sociology of Secularization: A Critique of a Concept*, London: Routledge and Kegan Paul.

Hasan, Mushirul (1997) *Legacy of a Divided Nation: India's Muslims since Independence*, New Delhi: Oxford University Press.

Madan, T. N. (1987) 'Secularism in its place', *Journal of Asian Studies*, 46(4): 747–59.

—— (1993) 'Whither secularism in India?', *Modern Asian Studies*, 27(3): 667–97.

—— (1994) 'Secularism and the intellectuals', *Economic and Political Weekly*, 19: 1995–96.

—— (1997) *Modern Myths, Locked Minds: Secularism and Fundamentalism in India*, New Delhi: Oxford University Press.

—— (1999) 'Perspectives on pluralism', *Seminar* 484: 18–23.

—— (2003a) 'Introduction', *Modern Myths, Locked Minds: Secularism and Fundamentalism in India*, 4th impression, New Delhi: Oxford University Press.

—— (2003b) 'On secularism and religion: The case of India', *Daedalus*, 132(3): 62–66.

—— (2005) 'Participatory pluralism', *The Telegraph* (Calcutta), 9 February.

—— (2006) *Images of the World: Essays on Religion, Secularism, and Culture*, New Delhi: Oxford University Press.

Nanda, B. R. (1989) *Gandhi, Pan-Islamism, Imperialism and Nationalism*, New Delhi: Oxford University Press.

Nandy, Ashis (1981) 'Counter statement on humanistic temper', *Mainstream*, 10: 16–18.
—— (1985) 'An anti-secularist manifesto', *Seminar*, October, 314: 1–12.
—— (2001) 'The politics of secularism and the recovery of religious tolerance', in *Time Warps: The Insistent Politics of Silent and Evasive Pasts*, New Delhi: Permanent Black.
—— (2003) 'The twilight of certitudes: secularism, Hindu nationalism and other masks of deculturation', in *The Romance of the State and the Fate of Dissent in the Tropics*, New Delhi: Oxford University Press.
Nehru, Jawaharlal (1942) [1933] *Glimpses of World History*, New York: John Day.
—— (1936) *An Autobiography*, London: John Lane.
—— (1946) *The Discovery of India*, Calcutta: Signet Press.
Radhakrishnan, S. (1956) 'Foreword in Abid Hassain', *The National Culture of India*, Bombay: Jaico.
Ricoeur, Paul (1992) 'Quel ethos nouveau pour l'Europe', in Peter Koslowski (ed.) *Imaginer l'Europe*, Paris: Editions de Cerf.
Sen, Amartya (1998) [1993] 'Secularism and its discontents', in Rajeev Bhargava (ed.) *Secularism and its Critics*, New Delhi: Oxford University Press.
Shaikh, Farzana (1989) *Community and Consensus in Islam: Muslim representation in colonial India*, Cambridge: Cambridge University Press.
Tharoor, Shashi (2003) 'Interrogating Indianness', *The Hindu Magazine* (New Delhi), 16 February, 3.
Varshney, Ashutosh (1993) 'Contested meanings: Indian national unity and the politics of anxiety', *Daedalus*, 122.
Weber, Max (1948) 'Politics as vocation', in H. H. Gerth and C.W. Mills (trans. and ed.) *From Max Weber: Essays in Sociology*, London: Routledge and Kegan Paul.
Wolpert, Stanley (1985) *Jinnah of Pakistan*, New Delhi: Oxford University Press.

7　The distinctiveness of Indian secularism[1]

Rajeev Bhargava

Though the election of a Congress-led coalition has opened up new opportunities for secular space, only someone with a blinkered vision would assert that the growth of militant Hindu nationalism has been stalled and deny that secularism in India continues to be in crisis. However, an ambiguity lying at the very heart of this claim has not altogether been dispelled: is the crisis due primarily to external factors as when a good thing is undermined by forces always inimical to it, when it falls into incapable or wrong hands, when it is practised badly? Or, is it rather that the blemished practice is itself an effect of a deeper conceptual flaw, a bad case of a wrong footed ideal? Madan, Nandy and Chatterjee have all argued that the external threat to secularism is only a symptom of a deeper internal crisis. Secularism in their view has long faced an internal threat in the sense that the conceptual and normative structure of secularism is itself terribly flawed. In different ways, each argues that secularism is linked to a flawed modernization, to a mistaken view of rationality, to an impractical demand that religion be eliminated from public life, to an insufficient appreciation of the importance of communities in the life of people and a wholly exaggerated sense of the positive character of the modern state. In what follows, I try to argue against this view. I do not dispute their claims about modernity, rationality and the importance of religion and community. But I do disagree on their understanding of secularism and with their view that it is necessarily tied to a flawed modernist project. In particular, I contend that these critics fail to see that India developed a distinctively Indian and differently modern variant of secularism. Ideals are rarely if ever and never simply transplanted from one cultural context to another. They invariably adapt, sometimes so creatively to suit their new habitat that they seem unrecognizable. This is exactly what happened to secularism in India. Indian critics of secularism neither fully grasp the general conceptual structure of secularism nor properly understand its distinctive Indian variant. Indian secularism did not erect a strict wall of separation, but proposed instead a 'principled distance' between religion and state. Moreover, by balancing the claims of individuals and religious communities, it never intended a bludgeoning privatization of religion. It also embodies a model of contextual moral reasoning. All these features that combine to form what I call contextual secularism remain screened off from the understanding of these critics.

Though I do not agree with these critics that secularism is conceptually flawed, I do agree that it faces an internal threat. However, I have a different understanding of the nature of this threat. Isaiah Berlin has reminded us that the history of ideas is replete with great liberating ideas slowly turning into suffocating straightjackets. One reason for this is that we forget that they need continual interpretation: no idea can flourish without its defenders finding better and better ways of articulating and formulating them. An idea faces an internal threat when its supporters, out of akrasia, willful or unwitting neglect, ignorance, confusion or delusion cease to care for it, or when its own proponents mistakenly turn against it. I have no reason to doubt secularism is threatened by forces fiercely opposed to it. But my focus in this chapter is on the internal threats to secularism. The principal contention of my chapter is that one such internal threat is the failure of secularists to properly defend it largely because they see it as a mere replication of one of the Western variant rather than as embodying an alternative modern ideal with real trans-cultural potential.

Three preliminary points

I cannot proceed further without making three preliminary points. The term 'distinctive' in the title of the chapter may lead someone to expect that I will unravel something startlingly uncommon about Indian secularism. If I believed so, I would have used the term 'unique'. I have not. This is because of my belief that, by now, the elementary formal constituents of secularism are the same throughout the world. Broadly speaking, secularism, anywhere in the world, means a separation of organized religion from organized political power inspired by a specific set of values. Just as without separation there is no secularism, just so a value-less separation does not add up to secularism. In this sense, secularism is a universal normative doctrine. But it does not follow that these elements are interpreted or related to each other in any one particular way or that there is a single ideal way in which they should be interpreted or related to one another. Many ways exist of interpreting these elements as do different ways of relating them. Each conception of secularism may unpack the metaphor of separation differently or select different elements from the stock of values that give separation its point. It may also place different weights on the same values. So when I talk about the distinctiveness of Indian secularism, I do not imply that it has a unique conceptual structure. I only mean that embedded in it is a specific and interestingly different way of interpreting and relating the basic constituents of secularism. Indeed this is why the distinctive character of Indian secularism does not make it non-universalizable. Indian secularism has trans-cultural potential.

My *second* point concerns a mistake not uncommon among those who write and think about contemporary secularism. They unwittingly assume that it is a doctrine with a fixed content. It is also believed to be timeless, as if it has always existed in the same form. But all living doctrines evolve and therefore have a history. Secularism too has a history made at one time largely by Europeans, then a little later by North Americans and much later by non-Western countries. Non-Western societies inherited from their Western counterparts specific versions of secularism but they did not always preserve them in the form in which they were received. They often added something of enduring value to them and, therefore, developed the idea further. Western theorists of secularism do not always recognize this non-Western contribution. It may have once been adequate for Western scholars to focus exclusively on that part of the history of secularism which was made in and by the West. But today it would be a gross mistake to identify Western variants of secularism with the entire doctrine, if the part was viewed as the whole. For a rich, complex and complete understanding of secularism, one must examine how the secular idea has developed over time trans-nationally.

There are other reasons why we must attend to the histories of secularism. The current crisis of secularism must compel one to ask why we need it at all. After all, one rarely mourns the loss of a useless thing. But it breaks one's heart to see a valuable thing decay. In such transitional moments, when a thing is born, is dying or in crisis, evaluative judgments become especially urgent and it is crucial to get them right. However, when a thing is in good health, when it is working well and effectively, such judgments appear to be redundant. In these periods of the stability and well-being of an entity, we bother little about its value and purpose. As it is taken for granted, its purpose, as Charles Taylor has reminded us, frequently recedes into the background. Over time, its underlying point may even be forgotten. This may happen with material things as well as with institutions, ideas and doctrines. Now, something like this appears to have happened also to secularism. When it was working well, no one took the trouble to foreground its purpose, taking it for granted and eventually forgetting it. This forgetting was not troublesome or threatening as long as the secularism remained challenged. But when increasingly questioned, this forgetfulness becomes a terrible handicap. To reduce a rich and complex idea to a dead and monotonously repeated formula is bad enough but to know that an ideal is valuable and yet not know what precisely its value consists in is worse. The only option in such situations is to bring the idea back to life, to remember and retrieve its value-content.

But why must this be done with the help of a historical account? I believe this necessity arises because at some remote point in the past, say at the time of its birth, the idea had to prove its worth to its potential beneficiaries. To make place for itself in a climate of fierce competition it had to marshal all forms of argumentative resources. It could not have survived without being explicit about its normative structure. In short, it could not be in the state of inarticulacy in which it currently happens to be. This is why its retrieval from the background involves going back in time. We can no longer do without its history.

It is not a coincidence that the external threat to Indian secularism has intensified precisely at a time of its degeneration into a meaningless formula (Perhaps the real crisis of Indian secularism began when the real meaning of secularism was forgotten and ritualistically, the word 'secular' was introduced in the Indian constitution) or when it is viewed purely as a procedural doctrine that mechanically separates religion from the state and is foolishly innocent of its ties with substantive values. Critics of secularism are quick to point out its links with all kinds of things they dislike: the nation state, instrumental rationality, the hegemony of science, mindless industrialization and realist state-craft. But both its critics and its defenders appear to have forgotten its constitutive relation with substantive values. Undoubtedly, because of a history that it shares with the West, Indian secularism is at least partly Western. But this Western history can also be told as a history of important values. The distancing of religion from the state became necessary, both in India and the West, to protect individual citizens from their own oppressive religiously sanctioned social customs. Hence the connection of secularism with individualistically conceived liberty and equality. Unfortunately, Indian critics of secularism have developed an amnesia about these values. They also seem not to recall that 'separation' in the early constitutional history of India was never understood to mean the blanket exclusion of religion from the state.

Thus, it is important that we go back in time and retrieve the complex purposes underlying it, to examine how Indian secularism was originally conceived and identify the distinctiveness of Indian secularism. However, this is not always easy. To answer why brings me to my *third* point. In India, everything has begun to be seen in terms of an irritatingly dichotomous grid that divides the social world into two groups, the

Western modern and the indigenous traditional. Those who accept this grid are ineluctably inducted into a certain pattern of thinking. If secularism is modern, they believe, then it must be Western. The whole of Western secularism is then identified with one's preferred variant, usually that which is currently dominant. For example, the currently dominant Western stereotype has it that secularism entails a strict separation of religion and the state for the sake of religious liberty and individual autonomy. This stereotype is uncritically also accepted in India by its defenders as well as its opponents. Thus those who defend secularism in India proclaim unstinting support for this Western stereotype. Similarly, secularism is opposed in India because critics have good reason to be unhappy with this Western stereotype. Since they also accept the view that to be Indian, a thing or an idea must be rooted wholly in home-grown traditions uncontaminated by the West, they seek to replace secularism by ideas of toleration available within indigenous religious traditions. Much of the debate on secularism in India has been framed by this interpretative framework. But I wonder how useful it is to hold on to it, for it misses out on the simple point that something can be at once Indian and modern, that something that started out as Western can over time be transformed, and in responding to specific Indian problems and by being nurtured in an Indian context, can become distinctively Indian; different from both its Western counterpart and from anything found within indigenous traditions. Unless those who defend secularism grasp this point, they will continue to defend a version that has little validity in the Indian context. Since they are seen to support a doctrine that can be legitimately criticized, the popular legitimacy of every version of secularism is bound to be eroded in the long run. Critics of secularism too fail to realize that a persistent attack on the very idea of secularism has grave practical consequence. In a context in which secularism is anyhow under threat from Hindu extremists, the mistaken occlusion of the distinctiveness of Indian secularism only ends up granting intellectual legitimacy to the larger political attack on the secular idea.

In these preliminary remarks, I hope to have drawn attention to the importance of grasping that Indian secularism provides an alternative to mainstream, Western conceptions. In what follows I must try to demonstrate this to be so. I argue that Indian secularism is distinguished from other versions because of the full-blooded self-recognition of its multi-value character. It is also distinctive because it rejects the claim that separation must mean strict exclusion or neutrality and espouses what I call principled distance. In my view, this particular feature of Indian secularism is unique to it.

The conceptual structure of secularism

Theocracy, establishment, multiple establishment

To identity the conceptual structure of secularism, it is best to begin with some ideal-typical distinctions, the first of which is between a state that establishes religion and a theocratic state. A theocratic state is governed by divine laws directly administered by a priestly order claiming a divine commission. The Islamic republic of Iran run by Ayatullahs is an obvious example. On the other hand, a state that establishes religion grants it official, legal recognition. Here, religion benefits from a formal alliance with government. The sacerdotal order does not govern a state where religion is established.

Establishment of religion takes two forms. On the classical European view, it means that 'a *single* Church or religion enjoys formal, legal, official monopolistic privilege through a union with the government of the state' (Levy 1997: 7). The phrase 'establishment' has been used for centuries to describe the established Protestant Churches of England, Scotland and Germany, and the Catholic Churches in Italy and Spain. Thus, if, in preference to all other religions, the state recognizes a particular religion as the official religion, compels individuals to congregate for only one religion, punishes them for failing to profess a particular set of religious beliefs, levies taxes in support of one particular religion or makes instruction in one religion mandatory in educational institutions or in the media, then it is known as the establishment of religion. Where a particular religion is established, equality among religions is non-existent, and while members of the established religion may enjoy a modicum of religious liberty, those belonging to religions that have not been established are unlikely to enjoy any liberty. If the number of such persons is large, then such a multi-religious society may be wrecked by inter-religious wars. If the number is small, then religious minorities may not only fail to enjoy full religious liberty but may not even be tolerated. They are likely to face persistent religious persecution.

This classical European view of establishment is to be distinguished from one where the state respects more than one religion, recognizes and perhaps nurtures all religions without preferring one over the other. This might be termed 'multiple establishment' or 'establishment without a name' (Levy 1997: 12). Such a state may levy a religious tax on everyone and yet grant the freedom to remit the tax money to a Church or religious organization of their choice. It may financially aid schools run by religious institutions but on a non-discriminatory basis. It may punish people for disavowing or disrespecting religion, though not compel them to profess the beliefs of a particular religion. A state that respects multiple establishment treats all religion non-preferentially. It gives liberty to each group to conduct its religious affairs but is indifferent to the freedom of members within the group. The state of New York in the middle of the 17th century that allowed every Church of the Protestant faith to be established furnishes perhaps the earliest example of 'multiple establishment'. The colonies of Massachusetts, Connecticut and New Hampshire show a similar pattern (Levy 1997: 11). Related examples abound in India, for example the 14th century Vijayanagar kingdom that granted official recognition to the Shaivites, the Vaishnavites and perhaps even the Jains. Arguably, the British empire gave de facto legitimacy to multiple establishments.

States with multiple establishments are better than states with singular establishments. For example, such states are likely to be relatively peaceful. Members of each religious group are likely to tolerate one another. There may even be inter-religious equality; the state may treat all religions equally and grant each religious group considerable autonomy in its own affairs. But states with multiple establishments have their limitations. For a start, they may persecute atheists. Second, they are indifferent to the liberty of individuals within each religious group. Even the slightest internal dissent may not be tolerated. Third, they may not allow an individual to exit his religious community and embrace another religion or remain unattached to any religion whatsoever. Fourth, such states give recognition to particular religious identities but fail to recognize what may be called non-particularized identities, i.e. identities that simultaneously refer to several particular identities or transcend all of them. Fifth, such states are unconcerned with the non-religious liberties of individuals or groups. Finally, such states are entirely indifferent to citizenship rights.

A secular state is to be distinguished not only from theocracy but also from a state where religion is established. A non-theocratic state is not automatically secular because it is entirely consistent for a state not to be run by priests inspired by 'divine laws', but to have a formal alliance with one or more religions. A secular state on the other hand refuses to establish religion or has disestablished it. Therefore, it follows what can be called the principle of non-establishment. The non-establishment of religion means that the state is separated not merely from one but from all religions (I shall call it feature-a). No religious community in such a state can say that the state belongs to it. A secular state is not anti-religious but exists and survives only when religion is no longer hegemonic. It admits a more general equality between believers and unbelievers. It allows freedom for all religions but also freedom from religion itself. Thus, in a secular state, a formal or legal union between state and religion is impermissible. Official status is not given to religion. Persons are as free to disavow religion as they are to profess one. No one is compelled to pay tax for religious purposes or to receive religious instruction. No automatic grants to religious institutions are available.

Values of a secular state

This brings me to more explicitly articulate the connection of a secular state with several important and substantive values. The first of these is peace or rather the prevention of a society from its regression into barbarism, not an uncommon tendency where there exist two or more incompatible visions of the good life. The second is toleration, i.e. the state does not persecute anyone on grounds of religion. I may here mention an auxiliary point. We must eschew the tendency within Western modernist discourse to conceive of civil strife as a result purely of a clash of interests. The development of secularism in the West and elsewhere cannot be properly understood without fully comprehending the fear of cruelty and disorder that marks the conflict of ultimate ideals. This is equally true of the American and the French experience as it is of India. Consider the United States. One might say that the first amendment, the pivot of American secularism is a product of the widespread feeling of vulnerability experienced in different religious denomination such as the Anglicans, the Presbyterians and the Quakers, each dominant in one particular area but vulnerable in others and each viewing the other as fanatical, or at least as extremely odd (McConnell 1993: 497–510).

Third, a secular state is constitutively tied to the value of religious liberty that has three dimensions. The first refers to the liberty of members of any one religious group (feature-b). It is a brute fact that in most religious communities, one or two interpretations of its core beliefs and practices come to dominate. Given this dominance, it is important that every individual or sect within the group be given the right to criticize, revise or challenge these dominant interpretations. The second aspect of this important liberty in a secular state (feature-c) is that it is granted non-preferentially to all members of every religious community. It is entirely possible that non-preferential treatment by the state of groups that accord religious liberty to its members is also found in states respecting multiple establishment. But religious liberty is not part of the core principles of multiple establishment. However, it is a constitutive feature of the secular state. The third dimension of religious liberty (feature-d), unthinkable in states with multiple establishment, is that individuals are free not only to criticize the religion into which they are born, but at the very extreme, to reject it and further, given ideal conditions of deliberation, to freely embrace another religion or to remain without one.

Religious liberty, when understood broadly, is one important value of a secular state. To understand another crucial ingredient, it is necessary to grasp the point that liberty and equality in the religious sphere are all of a piece with liberty and equality in other spheres. It is not a coincidence that the disestablishment clause in the first amendment to the American constitution institutes not only religious freedom but also the more general freedom of speech, of peaceful assembly and political dissent. It is entirely possible that a state respecting multiple establishment permits *religious* liberty and equality but forbids other forms of freedom and equality. For instance, a person may challenge the authority of the religious head of his own denomination but not be free to challenge the authority of the state. This is impossible in a secular state which is committed to a more general freedom and equality. Thus, the second value to which a secular state is constitutively linked is the equality of free citizenship.

The value of equal citizenship has two dimensions, one active, the other passive. It is a feature of democratic polities that these two roles of citizens coincide and therefore a democratic government must be continuously justifiable from both points of views (Beitz 1989: Chapter 5). To be a passive citizen is to be entitled to physical security, a minimum of material well-being and a sphere of one's own in which others ought not to interfere. Although a part of this idea of passive citizenship goes back to ancient Rome, the radical emphasis on material well-being and on privacy is a result of a profound trans-valuation of values that has taken place under conditions of modernity (Taylor 1989). This lies at the root of the idea of the right to life, liberty, material welfare and perhaps, education – crucial elements if ordinary people are to lead their ordinary life with dignity. Any citizen of the state must be entitled to these benefits. This is partly an extension of the point implicit in the defence of religious liberty but in part it adds something substantial of its own. The benefits of citizenship – resources that enable a dignified ordinary life – must be available to everyone and there is no room here for discrimination on grounds of religion (feature-e). This equal treatment is entailed by equal (passive) citizenship. State agencies and the entire system of law must not work in favour of one religious group. If the state works to protect the security and well-being of some individuals or groups but fails to secure these meagre but important benefits to others then the principle of equal (passive) citizenship is violated. Likewise, since citizenship is conditional upon education, no one must be denied admission to educational institutions, solely on grounds of religion (feature-f).

The active dimension of citizenship involves the recognition of citizens as equal participants in the public domain. Such active citizenship rights can be denied in two ways. Either when they are brutally excluded from the political domain (they are politically dead) (Beitz 1989: 109), or when their recognition in the public domain betrays the social acceptance of a belief in the intrinsic superiority of one group as when there is communally weighed voting or efforts to dilute the votes of religious minorities through the use of gerrymandering techniques (Beitz 1989: 110). Groups singled out as less worthy are demeaned and insulted, encouraged to feel that patterns of disrespect existing in society at large enjoy official sanction. In contrast to this, equality of citizenship to which secularism is tied conveys a community wide acknowledgement of equal respect for everyone in the political domain (feature-g).

A simple comparison between different types of state-religion political orders shows that at least in multi-religious society and relative to theocracies and states with established religion, a secular state gives maximum liberty and equality, conceived individualistically or non-individualistically to all its citizens.

Indian secularism

The state in the Indian constitution appears to possess all the features (feature-a to-g) of a secular state. Feature-a is specified in Article 27 which rules out the public funding of religion and Article 28(1) under which 'no religious instruction is to be provided in any educational institution wholly maintained out of state funds'.

Articles 25, 27 and 28 guarantee religious liberty and meet the conditions specified by features-b, c and d. Under Article 25(1), 'all persons are equally entitled to freedom of conscience and the right freely to profess, practice and propagate religion' (feature-b and -c). The phrase 'freedom of conscience' is meant to cover the liberty of persons without a religion (feature-d). Under Article 27, 'no person is compelled to pay any taxes, the proceeds of which are specifically appropriated in payment of expenses for the promotion or maintenance of any particular religion or religious denomination.' Finally, under Article 28(3), 'no person attending any educational institution ... shall be required to take part in any religious instruction or to attend any religious worship that may be conducted in such institution'.

Equality of citizenship is guaranteed by Articles 14, 15(1) and 29(2) of the Indian constitution. Article 15(1) states that the state shall not discriminate against any citizen on grounds only of religion, race, caste, sex, place of birth or any of them (feature-e). Article 29(2) declares that no citizen shall be denied admission into any educational institution maintained by the state on grounds only of religion, race etc. (feature-f). Article 16(1) and (2) of Indian constitution affirm an equal opportunity for all citizens in matters relating to employment or appointment of any office under the state. It further affirms that no citizen, on grounds of religion or race be eligible for or discriminate against in respect of any employment or office under the state. The clause on universal franchise as well as Article 325 that declares a general electoral roll for all constituencies and states that no one shall be ineligible for inclusion in this roll or claim to be included in it on grounds only of religion, etc. embody the value of equal active citizenship. Thus feature-g is specified in the Articles on equality of active citizenship.

The implications of accepting that the state in the Indian constitution is meant to possess features-a to -g are not always spelt out. First, the constitution rules out theocracy and the establishment of religion. The term 'secular state' is usually contrasted simply with theocracy. This is misleading, if not false, because the absence of theocracy is compatible with the establishment of religion. The secular credentials of the state cannot be derived from the mere absence of theocracy.[2] Second, the Indian state is not meant to be merely tolerant (in the sense specified above). Indian secularism must not be confused with a generally professed Hindu tolerance. It is frequently claimed that Indians have a natural, traditional affinity with secularism. In view of our traditional obsession with subtle and not so subtle hierarchies, this claim must be taken with a pinch of salt if not pepper. Of course, this should not detract from the important point that tolerance, even within a hierarchical framework, forms an important background condition for the development of modern secularism. Elements of this important background condition can certainly be found within India. Third, the secularism of the Indian constitution is neither a simple-minded single-value idea nor over-inflated and hyper-substantive. Rather, it is a complex, multi-value doctrine.

A further point to note concerns the precise form of secularism to be found in the constitution. Broadly, secularism is taken to be the view that religion must be separated from the state for the sake of extensive religious liberty and equality of citizenship. This view can be differently interpreted. For Donald Smith, the secular state involves three distinct but interrelated relations concerning the state, religion and the individual (Smith 1963: 3–8). The first relation concerns individuals and their religion, from which the state is excluded. Individuals are thereby free to decide the merits of the respective claims of different religions without any coercive interference by the state – the libertarian ingredient in secularism. The second concerns the relation between individuals and the state, from which religion is excluded. Thus, the rights and duties of citizens are not affected by the religious beliefs held by individuals – the egalitarian component in secularism. Finally, for Smith, the integrity of both these relations is dependent on the third relation, between the state and different religions. Here he argues that secularism entails the mutual exclusion of state and religion. Just as political power is outside the scope of religion's legitimate objectives, just so it is not the function of the state to promote, regulate, direct or interfere in religion. This interpretation is in line with the dominant American interpretation of secularism as erecting 'a wall of separation' between religion and state. On the classical American view of disestablishment, there can be no support for religion even on a non-preferential basis. Even partial aid to educational institutions run by religious organizations will constitute some form of establishment. Moreover, a state that disestablishes all religions is one that has no power to interfere in the affairs of religious institutions. For better or for worse, the state is powerless to bring about changes in religion. So, for Smith, secularism means the strict exclusion of religion from the state for the sake of the religious liberty and equal citizenship of individuals. This is also the dominant understanding of Western secularism.

Departures from mainstream Western secularism

Does Indian secularism erect a similar 'wall of separation' for the sake of individualistically construed values? Is it a Western idea on Indian soil? Articles 15, 16, 25, 29(2) and 325 support this interpretation. Though there is no direct reference to disestablishment, Articles 27 and 28(1) imply strict separation. By giving the President of the Republic the option of not taking an oath in the name of God, Article 60 confirms the strictly neutral character of the Indian constitution. From the discussion so far, it appears that the state in India is constitutionally bound to follow Smith's model of Western secularism. However, further examination of the constitution reveals this impression to be mistaken. To begin with, Article 30(1) recognizes the rights of religious minorities and therefore, unlike other Articles applicable to citizens qua individuals, it is a community-based right. Indeed, another community-specific right granting political representation to religious minorities was almost granted and was removed from the constitution only at the last minute. Second, Article 30(2) commits the state to give aid to educational institutions established and administered by religious communities. Also permitted is religious instruction in educational institutions that are partly funded by the state. These are significant departures from the 'wall of separation' view of the secular state. Even more significant are Articles 17 and 25(2) that require the state to intervene in religious affairs. Article 25(2)(b) states that 'nothing in Article 25 (1) prevents the state from making a law providing for social welfare and reform or the throwing open of Hindu religious institutions of a public character to all classes and sections of Hindus.' Article 17 is an uninhibited, robust attack on the caste system, arguably the central feature of Hinduism, by abolishing untouchability and by making the enforcement of any disability arising out of it an offence punishable by law. Both appear to take away the individual freedom of religion granted under Section 1 of Article 25 and to contravene Article 26.

These features of the Indian constitution depart from the stereotypical Western model in two ways. First, unlike the strict separation view that renders the state powerless in religious matters, they enjoin the state to interfere in religion. Second, more importantly, by giving powers to the state in the affairs of one religion, they necessitate a departure from strict neutrality or equidistance. This power of interference may be interpreted to undermine or promote Hinduism. Either way it appears to strike a powerful blow to the idea of non-preferential treatment.

In short, some Articles in the Indian constitution support an individualist interpretation and others a non-individualist one. Some conceive separation as exclusion, others as non-preferential treatment and, finally, some depart altogether from separation understood as exclusion or neutrality. At the end of the day, a confusing, somewhat contradictory picture on secularism emerges from a reading of the constitution. Critics could hardly fail to notice this and for many of them, Articles 17, 25(2) and 30 (1 and 2) comprise the secularity of the Indian state. For Donald Smith, any intervention in Hinduism – for example the legal ban on the prohibition of Dalit entry into temples or any protection of the rights of communities – seriously compromises secularism. For others, like Chatterjee, the presence of these features in the Indian constitution shows why the Indian state cannot be really secular. The Indian constitution does not give an unambiguous criteria for maintaining the secularity of the state and, quite simply, given Indian conditions, it could never have.

By accepting community-based rights for religious minorities and endorsing state-intervention in religion, did the constitution depart from secular principles? I do not think it did. Rather, it developed its own modern variant. This distinctiveness of the Indian secularism can be understood only when the cultural background and social context in India is properly grasped. At least four such features of this socio-cultural context call for attention. First, there exists the mind boggling diversity of religious communities in India. Such diversity may coexist harmoniously but it invariably generates conflicts, the most intractable of which, I believe, are deep conflicts over values. Second, within Hinduism in particular and in South Asian religions more generally, a greater emphasis is placed on practice rather than belief. A person's religious identity and affiliation are defined more by what she or he does with and in relation to others, than by the content of beliefs individually held by them. Since practices are intrinsically social, any significance placed on them brings about a concomitant valorization of communities. Together, these two features entail inter-community conflicts which are further exacerbated if fuelled by competing conceptions of democracy and nationalism. Third, many religiously sanctioned social practices are oppressive by virtue of their illiberal and inegalitarian character, and deny a life of dignity and self-respect. Therefore, from a liberal and egalitarian standpoint, they desperately need to be reformed. Such practices frequently have a life of their own, independent of consciously held beliefs, and possess a causal efficacy that remains unaffected by the presence of conscious beliefs. Furthermore, a tendency to fortify and insulate themselves from reflective critique makes them resistant to easy change and reform. It follows that an institution vested with enormous social power is needed to transform their character. Fourth, in Hinduism, the absence of an organized institution such as the Church has meant that the impetus for effective reform cannot come exclusively from within. Reform within Hinduism can hardly be initiated without help from powerful external institutions such as the state.

In such a context, India needed a coherent set of intellectual resources to tackle inter-religious conflict, and to struggle against oppressive communities not by dis-aggregating them into a collection of individuals or by de-recognizing them (and therefore, not by privatizing religion) but by somehow making them more liberal and egalitarian. A political movement for a united, liberal, democratic India had to struggle against hierarchical and communal conceptions of community but without abandoning a reasonable communitarianism. Besides, the state had an important contribution to make in the transformation of these communities; for this reason, a perennial dilemma was imposed on it. The state in India walked a tight rope between the requirement of religious liberty that frequently entails non-interference in the affairs of religious communities, and the demand for equality and justice which necessitates intervention in religiously sanctioned social customs. Secularism in India simply had to be different from the Western liberal model that does not recognize communities, and dictates strict separation between religious and political institutions.

If we abandon the view, such as Donald Smith's, that political secularism entails a unique set of state policies valid under all conditions which provide the yardstick by which the secularity of any state is to be judged, then we can better understand why despite 'deviation' from the ideal, the state in India continues to embody a model of *secularism*.[3] This can be shown even if we stick to Smith's working definition of secularism as consisting of three relations. Smith's first relation embodies the principle of religious liberty construed individualistically, i.e., pertaining to the religious beliefs of individuals. However, it is possible to make a non-individualistic construal of religious liberty by speaking not of the beliefs of individual but rather of the practices of groups. Here religious liberty would mean distancing the state from the practices of religious groups. The first principle of secularism can then be seen to also grant the right to a religious community to its own practices. Smith's second relation embodies the value of equal citizenship. But this entails – and I cannot substantiate my claim – that we tolerate the attempt of radically differing groups to determine the nature and direction of society as they best see it. In this view, then, the public presence of the religious practices of groups is guaranteed and entailed by the recognition of community-differentiated citizenship rights. Smith's version of secularism entails a charter of uniform rights. But it is clear that the commitment of secularism to equal citizenship can dictate community-based rights and therefore differentiated citizenship. In principle, this could easily accommodate a reasonable demand for community-specific political rights. In India, for reasons outlined above, it meant community-specific social rights, such as the right to administer and maintain educational institutions. Smith's third principle pertains to non-establishment and therefore to a strict separation of religion from state, under which religion and the state both have the freedom to develop without interfering with each other. Separation, however, need not mean strict non-interference, mutual exclusion or equidistance, as in Smith's view. Instead, it could be a policy of principled distance, which entails a flexible approach on the question of intervention or abstention, combining both, dependent on the context, nature or current state of relevant religions. This theoretical interpretation of separation sits much better with its own best practice but perhaps also with the practice of other Western secular states, something that is never properly recognized by Western theories of secularism. But what is this idea of principled distance?

Principled distance

Principled distance is one particular way of unpacking the metaphor of separation. In conventional Western secularism, separation of state and religion means either mutual exclusion or neutrality. Let me elaborate. Clearly, the demand for separation comes in the wake of some undesirable pre-existing unity, in this case, a complete intermeshing of religion and state. Against the view that religion and state possess an identical overall agenda, a common, indistinguishable project, the separationists argue for a parting of ways. This much is uncontroversial. But from here, a bifurcation occurs. One avenue leads to total exclusion; separation here means the meticulous refusal of any contact whatsoever between religion and the state. The two must keep off one another. This stand-offishness may be robust or mild. When robust, it generates mutual hostility. For example, the secular state, on this view, must be anti-religious. This anti-religiosity may be interventionist or non-interventionist. In its interventionist form the state actively discourages religion. In its non-interventionist incarnation it typifies a hysterical brahminical attitude: Religion is untouchable, so any contact with it contaminates secularist purity. Secularism here becomes a doctrine of political taboo; it prohibits contact with certain kinds of activities. The milder variety of exclusion of religion from politics proposes that religious and political institutions live as indifferent strangers to each other. At best, this mutual incomprehension leads to some perplexity. But no further curiosity is possible. The second view on separation does not demand total exclusion. Some contact is possible but also some distance. But the terms of engagement and disengagement are antecedently fixed. This is central to the notion of strict neutrality. Those who interpret separation as neutrality demand that a secular state be neutral with respect to all religions. It may help or hinder all religions to an equal degree. If it intervenes in one religion, it must also do so in others.

Principled distance must be distinguished from both strict mutual and equally strict neutrality. This complex notion builds upon two ideas, at least one of which derives from a distinction explicitly drawn by the American philosopher, Ronald Dworkin between equal treatment and treating everyone as an equal (Dworkin 1978: 125). The principle of equal treatment, in the relevant political sense, requires that the state treat all its citizens equally in relevant respect, for example in the distribution of a resource of opportunity. The principle of treating people as equals entails that every person is treated with equal concern and respect. This second principle may sometimes require equal treatment, say equal distribution of resources but it may also occasionally dictate unequal treatment. Treating people as equals is entirely consistent with differential treatment. This idea is the second ingredient in what I have called principled distance. To say that a state keeps principled distance from religion is to claim that it intervenes or refrains from interfering in religion, depending entirely upon whether or not some values are protected or advanced. Moreover, it is to admit that a state may interfere in one religion more than in others, depending once again on the historical and social condition of all relevant religions. For the promotion of a particular value constitutive of secularism, some religion, relative to other religions, may require more interference from the state. For example, suppose that the value to be advanced is social equality. This requires in part undermining caste hierarchies. If this is the aim of the state, then it may be required of the state that it interferes in caste-ridden Hinduism much more than say Islam or Christianity. However, if a diversity-driven religious liberty is the value to be advanced by the state, then it may have to intervene in Christianity and Islam more than in Hinduism. If this is so, the state can neither strictly exclude considerations emanating from religion nor keep strict neutrality with respect to religion. It cannot antecedently decide that it will always refrain from interfering in religions or that it will interfere in each equally. Indeed, it may not relate to every religion in society in exactly the same way or intervene in each religion to the same degree or in the same manner. To want to do so would be plainly absurd. All it must ensure is that the relationship between the state and religions is guided by non-sectarian motives consistent with the values and principles mentioned above.

Consider those laws that interfere with Hinduism. The relevant consideration in their evaluation is not whether they immediately encompass all groups but whether or not they are just and consistent with the values undergirding secularism. Three reasons exist for why all social groups need not be covered by these laws. First, they may be relevant only to Hindus. Take the abolition of child marriage and devadasi dedication or the introduction of the right to divorce. Here, before deciding whether it was necessary to enact a special provision for Hindus, the legislature took into account their social customs and beliefs. Similar laws for Muslims were simply redundant. Second, laws in liberal democracies require legitimacy; the consent of at least the representatives of communities is vital. If consent has indeed been obtained from the representatives of only one community, it is sometimes prudent to enact community-specific laws. It is wise to apply the general principle in stages, rather than not have it at all. Finally, 'it is perfectly within the competence of the legislature to take account of the degree of evil which is prevalent under various circumstances and the legislature is not bound to legislate for all evils at the same time. Therefore, an act passed by the legislature cannot be attacked merely because it tackles only some of the evils in society and does not tackle other evils of the same or worse kind which may be prevalent.' Thus, if the legislature acting on these considerations, wanted to enact a special provision in regard to, say, bigamous marriages among Hindus, it cannot be said that the legislature was discriminating against Hindus only on the ground of religion (AIR 1952). The Indian courts have frequently followed this line of reasoning. They have defended a policy if they found that its purpose is the eradication of a social evil traceable to religious practices, even if the policy was targetted at specific communities. It has argued that so long as the state has taken gradual steps towards social welfare and reform and has not introduced distinctions or classifications that are unreasonable or oppressive, equality before law is not breached. A state interfering in one religion more than in others does not automatically depart from secularism. Indian secularism rejects the assumption that one size fits all. Thus, secularism requires principled distance, not exclusion or equidistance.

Contextual secularism

A context-sensitive secularism, one based on the idea of principled distance, is what I have elsewhere called contextual secularism. Contextual secularism is contextual not only because it captures the idea that the precise form and content of secularism will vary from context to context and from place to place but also that it embodies a certain model of contextual moral reasoning. This it must do because of its character as a multi-value doctrine. Let me explain this point by introducing a distinction between types of situations and types of moral doctrines. Some conflict-ridden human situations are such that their morally defensible resolution is dictated by single-value doctrines, i.e., those which give priority to a value held to be supreme. For example, bodily integrity may be viewed as such an important value that nothing can justify its violation. I may be prevented from torturing someone no matter what my reasons for doing so: neither self-interest nor pursuit of truth can justify it. Other human situations are different because they genuinely involve a value conflict and the resolution of this conflict cannot be read off the values themselves. Single-value doctrines do not suffice here because they always dictate a unique outcome antecedently favourable to the protection of one value. In these situations multi-value doctrines are more appropriate. They take on board these conflicts and admit that no general a priori procedure can antecedently arbitrate between competing value claims. Rather, whether a value will outweigh others or which, if at all, will override others will be decided entirely by the context. Frequently, such situations necessitate a trade-off or compromise albeit one that is morally defensible.

By explicitly accepting that secularism is a multi-value doctrine, we recognize that its constitutive values do not always sit easily with one another. On the contrary, they are frequently in conflict. Some degree of internal discord and therefore a fair amount of instability is an integral part of secularism. For this reason, it forever requires fresh interpretations, contextual judgments and attempts at reconciliation and compromise. No general a priori rule of resolving these conflicts exist; no easy lexical order, no pre-existing hierarchy among values or laws that enables us to decide that, no matter what the context, a particular value must override everything else. Everything then is a matter of situational thinking and contextual reasoning. Whether one value overrides or is reconciled with another cannot be decided before hand. Each time the matter presents itself differently and will be differently resolved. If this is true, then the practice of secularism requires a different model of moral reasoning than the one that straight-jackets our moral understanding in the form of well delineated, explicitly stated rules (Taylor 1994: 16–43). This contextual secularism recognizes that the conflict between individual rights and group rights or between claims of equality and liberty or between claims of liberty and the satisfaction of basic needs cannot always be adjudicated by a recourse to some general and abstract principle. Rather they can only be settled case by case and may require a fine balancing of competing claims. The eventual outcome may not be wholly satisfactory to either but will still be reasonably satisfactory to both. Multi-value doctrines such as secularism encourage accommodation – not the giving up of one value for the sake of another but rather their reconciliation and possible harmonization, i.e., to make each work without changing the basic content of apparently incompatible concepts and values.

This accommodation may be accomplished in a number of ways. First, by placing values at different levels (see Austin 1962). Second, by seeing them as belonging not to water-tight compartments but as sufficiently separate so that an attempt is made to make a value work within its own sphere without frontally conflicting with another value operating in a different sphere. This endeavour to make concepts, view-points and values work simultaneously does not amount to a morally objectionable compromise. This is so because nothing of importance is being given up for the sake of a less significant thing, one without value or even with negative value. Rather, what is pursued is a mutually agreed middle way that combines elements from two or more equally valuable entities. The roots of such attempts at reconciliation and accommodation lie in a lack of dogmatism, in a willingness to experiment, to think at different levels and in separate spheres and in a readiness to take decisions on a provisional basis. It captures a way of thinking characterized by the following dictum: 'why look at things in terms of this or that, why not try to have both this and that.' In this way of thinking, it is recognized that though we may currently be unable to secure the best of both values and therefore be forced to settle for a watered-down version of each, we must continue to have an abiding commitment to search for a transcendence of this second best condition. Such contextual reasoning was not atypical of the deliberations of the Constituent Assembly in which great value was placed on arriving at decisions by consensus. Yet, the procedure of majority vote was not given up altogether. On issues that everyone judged to be less significant, a majoritarian procedure was adopted. It is by virtue of this kind of reasoning that the Indian constitution appears at once federal and unitary, and why it favours both individual and group-specific rights. It is frequently argued against Indian secularism that it is contradictory because it tries to bring together individual and community rights, and that articles in the Indian Constitution such as 25 and 26(b) that have a bearing on the secular nature of the Indian state are deeply conflictual and at best ambiguous. This is to misrecognize a virtue as a vice. In my view, this attempt to bring together seemingly incompatible values is a great strength of Indian secularism. Secularism in India is not understood to be a mechanical doctrine with a uniform, technical application. Therefore, the demand that the relevant articles in the Indian constitution give us unambiguous criteria for evaluating separation or the complaint that the best of Indian secularists have an inconsistent understanding of the relationship between state and religion remains wide off the target and altogether fails to grasp the conceptual structure of secularism in India. If secularism embodies contextual reasoning, it must be understood that this is not private-moral reasoning applied to politics but rather public-political reasoning infused with a moral character.

Back to preliminaries

This is an appropriate point at which to briefly elaborate two points I made at the very beginning. First, that it is inadequate if not mistaken to focus on current formulations of Western secularism. To grasp the rich and complicated structure of secularism, it is extremely important to examine the history of the secular ideal. An idea begins to have a life much before its clear formulation and before human beings bring it to self-consciousness. Often what is taken to be the birth of an idea is partly a discovery, a re-articulation of older ideas and only in part an invention. And, as Hegel reminded us, we grasp this point only when that idea achieves a distinct and clear self-consciousness. This is certainly true of secularism. The complex set of values that coalesce around what later came to be called secularism began to live much earlier. For example, in a religiously diverse society, organized political power simply had to maintain some distance from the dominant religious group for the sake of stability and peace. The same motivation lay behind a partial acceptance and therefore the toleration of the less dominant religious groups and the half-hearted recognition of particular religious identities. States that promoted peace and toleration can certainly not be called secular but there is no doubt that they are historically connected to modern secular states and can be said to constitute the latter's pre-history. At best they may be seen to embody a local, customary or traditional secularism.

This traditional secularism is found in different societies and cultures. This is why the development of modern secularism cannot be understood as growing out of the relationship between the Church and the state. The Church-state model is one variant of traditional secularism. The presence in background cultural conditions of other variants such as the religious strife model is equally conducive to the growth of modern secularism. I have elsewhere written in detail about these two models (see Bhargava 1997, 1998). Suffice here to say that it is sufficient for the Church-state model to be operating within a non-pluralist Christian society. However, a religious strife model necessarily operates within a society in which there exist diverse and radically differing religions or religious denominations. The Church-state model is operative in societies in which separation is an internal feature of the dominant religion. The religious strife model of secularism, on the other hand, develops even if separation within some religions is not internally permissible but purely out of the contextual necessity in a situation of contending religions. In short, in the first model, the state wrenches away from one religion whereas in the other model, it must distance itself from all religions at once. And, as I mentioned, this distancing is dictated by the vulnerabilities experienced by every single religious group. Each one fears persecution from the other as well as the disorder resulting from religious conflict.

Secular states really began to exist when, apart from securing peace and toleration, they protected the religious liberties of individuals, in particular by providing secure conditions in which individuals could lead a decent life even when they dissented from the orthodoxy or orthopraxy of their own respective religions. Secularism advanced further when many aspects of an individual's well-being began to be regulated not simply by a regime of toleration but rather by a formal and legal regime of rights, so that it became possible for individuals to make formal claims of entitlement against each other or against the state: to the protection of their life, or to a private sphere in which they were free to do what they want and were secure that any interference by the state in the life or private world of the individual could proceed only according to due process of law. Thus, a secular state comes into its own when it does not discriminate on grounds of religion in the distribution of passive citizenship rights.

It would be wrong however to identify secularism simply with the view for which the state must be separated from organized religion for the sake of peace, toleration, religious liberty and equality of passive citizenship rights. For over time at least two values have gradually become integral to the secular idea. First, that a state must not discriminate on grounds of religion in the distribution of active citizenship rights. For example, a state must not debar members of minority religious groups from standing for public office. Second, in keeping with the spirit of inter-religious equality as well as equality of citizenship, a fully secular state extends rights to minority religious groups qua groups. In short, it grants community-based rights to religious minorities.

One can now see that over time the secular idea has both transcended already existing values and/or added to them. For example, after the advent of nationalism and democracy, the value of treating everyone as equal and therefore not discriminating in the distribution of active citizenship rights was added to existing conceptions of secularism. Similarly, there is a sense in which a regime of rights better articulates the point behind toleration. A rights-based secularism supersedes toleration because it incorporates all values served by toleration and adds something more and valuable to it. Yet, it would be wrong to think that a secular state has no need at all for a regime of toleration. The regime of rights to which it is attached cannot reach every social space and in such not-so-easily approachable spaces, the ones not covered by legal rights, there still remains a need for decent relations governed by the value of toleration.

This brings me to the second point. Western theories of secularism have tended to see it as a single-value doctrine. For them, the state is to be separated from organized religion for the sake of the fullest possible liberties of individuals including their religious liberty. More recently, this separation is seen to serve individual autonomy. However, a history of the secular idea shows secularism to be a multi-value doctrine, as tied to several important values. The Indian variant of secularism more explicitly recognizes it to be a multi-value doctrine. Furthermore, Western theories of secularism, quite in contrast to the internally variegated practice of Western states, have tended to unpack the metaphor of separation to mean either exclusion or neutrality. To my mind, this has been a very limiting interpretation of what is meant by separation.

Thus, a proper study of Indian secularism shows not only that it shares a past with the West but also that it has its own distinctive past. Indian and Western secularisms have their own distinctive pre-histories as well as a common history. But apart from and beyond these histories, the Indian version has taken forward the idea of secularism because, from the very beginning, by virtue of an integral link with nationalism and democracy, it has had to be explicitly tied to citizenship rights, including to the rights of religious minorities. By doing so, it has never tried to completely annul particular religious identities. To discover its own rich and complex structure, Western secularism can either look backward, to its own past or else look sideways, at Indian secularism that mirrors not only the past of secularism, but in a way, also its future. Doing so will certainly benefit the secularisms of many Western societies. For example, French secularism needs to look beyond its own conceptions of laicite in order to take into account its own multi-cultural and multi-religious reality. It cannot continue to take refuge in claims of exceptionalism (Bauberot 1998: 94–136). In theory, the early French model of laicite introduced a strict separation between church and state. However, strict separation was not interpreted as mutual exclusion or neutrality but rather as one-sided exclusion. In another words, while religion was excluded from the affairs of the state, the state had the power to intervene in religion in order to control and subordinate it. The social sentiment of anti-clericism was frequently made into state policy. By 1905, however, this one-sided exclusion gave way to mutual exclusion. Anti-clericism declined. Indeed, mutual exclusion gave way to neutrality which in some aspects permitted contact with and recognition to religion as much as in other aspects it disallowed it. In 'normal' periods, when Islamic identity was not unusually assertive, this policy of neutrality was useful in handling the demands of France's Muslim population. However, the moment some controversial issues such as the wearing of the head scarf entered public life, the French state fell back sometimes on the idea of mutual exclusion and at other times on one-sided exclusion. Either way neutrality gave way to strict separation between church and state. Likewise, the more accommodative flirtation with multiple values was set aside in favour of a commitment to equal citizenship rights, even when it conflicted with the value of religious freedom of Muslims. The controlling authority of the state over religion was re-asserted. The idea that a religious group may have some limited right to express itself in public spaces such as schools was decisively abandoned. In short, the moment a deeper religious diversity began to question the theoretical model of laicite, its more accommodating interpretation, one that would have made it resemble the Indian model, was quickly abandoned. To my mind, this is unfortunate. It is myopic not to let the idea of laicite theoretically grow, particularly in response to the needs of a changing, now increasingly multi-religious society. Clearly, the French can benefit from the lessons implicit in the Indian conception of secularism. I feel that a good hard look at Indian secularism could also change the self-understanding of American liberal secularism.

Ironically, this need to attend to the distinctiveness of Indian secularism is as pressing in India as it is in the West. Several critics of Indian secularism have identified it with one or the other Western versions and have ignored its special character. This has been a source of gross misinterpretation and several problems. For example, it is frequently argued that secularism is purely a Christian, Western doctrine and therefore, cannot adapt itself easily to the cultural conditions of India, infused as they are by religions that grew in the soil of the sub-continent. This necessary link between secularism and Christianity is exaggerated, if not mistaken. It is true that traditional secularism is derived almost wholly from Christianity. The idea that to achieve religious integrity, peace or toleration, the state must be strictly separated from religion is part of Christianity and its internal history. But as I have argued, the mutual exclusion of religion and the state is not the defining feature of secularism. The idea of separation can be interpreted differently. Nor are religious integrity, peace and toleration uniquely Christian values. Most non-Christian civilizations have given significant space to each. Therefore, none of them are exclusively Christian. It follows that, even though it is in Christian writings that we find the clearest and most systematic articulation of this doctrine, even traditional secularism is not exclusively Christian. More importantly, traditional secularism must not be confused with its modern counterpart. Traditional secularism is a sufficient but not necessary part of the background condition of modern secularism. Modern secularism may be helped by the presence of traditional secularism but it can also be nourished by other traditions of peace and toleration.

All right, one might say, secularism is not just a Christian doctrine, but is it not Western? I have argued above that the answer to this question is both yes and no. Up to a point, it is certainly Western. More specifically, as a clearly articulated doctrine, it has distinct Western origins. Although elements that constitute secularism assume different cultural forms and are found in several civilizations, one cannot deny that the idea of the secular first achieved self-consciousness and was properly theorized in the West. One might then say that the middle history of secularism is almost entirely dominated by Western societies. However, the same cannot be said of its later history. Nationalism and democracy arrived in the West after the settlement of religious conflicts, in primarily religiously homogenous societies. The absence of deep religious diversity and conflict meant that issues of citizenship could be addressed almost entirely disregarding religious context; the important issue of community specific rights to religious groups could be wholly ignored. This could not be done in India. Both national and democratic agendas in India had to face issues raised by deep religious difference and diversity. In India, nationalism had to choose between the religious and the secular. Similarly, the distribution of active citizenship rights could not be conceived or accomplished by ignoring religion. It could be done either by actively disregarding religion or by developing a complex attitude to it. It also had to balance claims of individual autonomy with those of community obligations. In addressing these complex issues, the very idea of the secular was taken further than had been evolved in the West. In the course of doing so, it also began to embody a form of contextual moral reasoning with which the notion of principled distance is associated. This distinguishes it from other variants of modern secularism that are grounded in more abstract, theoreticist and context-insensitive conceptions of rationality. There is nothing particularly Western about these ideas. On the contrary, most conceptions of Western secularisms have taken little note of them and therefore are struggling to deal with post-colonial religious diversity of their societies. The later history of secularism is more Indian than Western.[4]

It may still be argued that the Indianness of Indian secularism is derived entirely from its strong link with home-grown traditions and that therefore India had worked out its own conception of secularism that is neither Christian nor Western. For example, secularism for many means 'sarva dharma sambhava': (a) religious coexistence or (b) inter-religious tolerance or finally (c) equal respect for all religions. Each of these interpretations of 'sarva dharma sambhava' point to a crucial ingredient of secularism but not only fails to capture its full richness and complexity but entirely ignores its relationship with extremely significant, internally constitutive values of secularism. I take religious co-existence to be equivalent to peace but to identify the secular state with a state that maintains peace between religions, that allows different religions to co-exist does little justice to the rich history and conceptual structure of secularism as a multi-value doctrine. Much the same is true of the interpretation of Indian secularism as inter-religious toleration. There are many good reasons why these two ideals should not be conflated but I shall mention only one. The mainstream idea of toleration is that it enjoins us to refrain from interfering in the affairs of others, even when one has the power to do so and additionally, even when one finds the beliefs and practices of others morally repugnant. In this sense, toleration is entirely consistent with a total refusal to respect the religion of others. It is also compatible with gross inequality and hierarchy. One may tolerate the religion of another person even as one treats him as inferior. Secularism, on the other hand, is grounded in notions of equality – equal concern and respect – and therefore goes far beyond the notion of inter-religious tolerance.

It is equally inappropriate to identify secularism with equal respect for all religions. Now it must be conceded that there is something valuable in this interpretation and something Indian about this idea. The internal plurality of Hinduism has the potential for a space where equal respect can indeed be accorded to all religions. Besides, a respect for other religions is entirely consistent with the development of their critique and the identification of local faults within them. Respecting other religions as equals does not entail their blind acceptance or endorsement. Indeed, it is precisely because respect is consistent with difference and critique that the idea of equal respect for all religions is closely linked with the proposal for an inter-faith dialogue. Yet, even an important ingredient of secularism cannot become the whole of it. Indeed, to equate the two is to do gross injustice to secularism. This equation implies that one ignores the non-religious part of human existence that all modern states must confront and which are also an integral part of modern secularism. Let me take an example. The idea of equal respect for all religions is entirely consistent with the equal unavailability of active citizenship rights to all members of society. It is also consistent with a total indifference to the freedom of individuals within each religious group. A fruitful dialogue on equal footing is entirely possible between religious groups that sanction gender and caste-related injustices or remain indifferent to them. But sensitivity to such issues is the hallmark of modern secularism. If so, it would be a terrible mistake to identify secularism with equal respect for all religions or modern Indian secularism with 'sarva dharma sambhava'. As political attitude and practice, 'Sarva dharma sambhava' is more in tune with states that establish multiple religions than it does with states that are secular.

I have argued that it is wrong to identify Indian secularism with Western secularism or with notions of inter-religious tolerance. No doubt, Indian secularism has some relationship with both but it is not one of identity. At the heart of such identification is a failure to notice that we developed a version of secularism that was at once modern and Indian. Those who identify Indian secularism entirely with home-grown traditional conceptions are able to grasp the pre-history of Indian secularism (even though they do not see it as such, as pre-history), but they entirely bypass its connection with a larger common trans-national history as well as with its later history towards which Indians contributed significantly. On the other hand, those who identify the Indian variant with Western conceptions fail to notice both the pre-history and the later history of secularism. As I mentioned above, like Western theorists, they focus only on the middle history of secularism, one developed almost exclusively by Western societies. This limited vision is shared by both advocates and opponents of secularism. For example, Indian critics of Indian secularism claim that it has privatized religion. Nothing could be further from the truth. Indian religion has a public presence that is ratified by the Indian constitution. The constitution gives official recognition to religious communities to maintain their own educational institutions. Such institutions foster particular religious identities and are sometimes even funded by the state. There could not be a more suitable illustration of the point that far from privatizing religion, the Indian constitution continues to support its publicization.

I have focused in this chapter on internal threats to secularism. I have argued that a continuous failure to recognize the distinctiveness of Indian secularism strengthens this threat. I believe this problem afflicts the self-understanding of secularism in both India and several Western countries. Western states need to improve the understanding of their own secular practices just as Western secularism needs a better theoretical self-understanding. Rather than get stuck on a model they developed at a particular time in their history, they would do well to learn from the original Indian variant. Equally, both the self-proclaimed supporters of secularism and some of its misguided opponents could learn from examining the original Indian variant. Indeed it is my conviction that many critics of Indian secularism will embrace it once they better understand its nature and point.

Notes

1 This article was originally published in T. N. Srinivasan (ed.) *The Future of Secularism* (New Delhi: Oxford University Press, 2006).
2 Partha Chatterjee's piece on secularism exemplifies this error. Thus he mistakenly concludes that since the Hindu right does not want the laws of the state to be in conformity with the general spirit of the Dharmasastra, it is at peace with the institutional procedures of modern

Western secularism (see Chatterjee 1998: 345–79). Arguably, the Hindu Right may wish the de facto, somewhat disguised establishment of its own variant of Hinduism.

3 For an interesting critique of Smith's interpretation of Indian secularism as derived from the American model with an 'extra dose of separation', see Galanter (1998: 234–67).

4 And by implication, the history of secularism must include the history of other non-western societies that have sought to install and maintain secular states.

References

AIR (1952) Bom.84, *The State of Bombay vs. Narasu Appa.*

Austin, Granville (1962) *The Indian Constitution: Cornerstone of a Nation*, New Delhi: Oxford University Press.

Baubérot, Jean (1998) The two thresholds of laicization, in Rajeev Bhargava (ed.) *Secularism and its Critics,* New Delhi: Oxford University Press.

Beitz, Charles R. (1989) *Political Equality*, Princeton NJ: Princeton University Press.

Bhargava, Rajeev (1997) Review of T. N. Madan's *Modern Myths, Locked Minds, Book Review*, 21(8), August, pp. 11–13.

—— (1998) 'What is secularism for?', in Rajeev Bhargava, (ed.) *Secularism and its Critics*, New Delhi: Oxford University Press.

Chatterjee, Partha (1998) 'Secularism and tolerance', in Rajeev Bhargava, (ed.) *Secularism and its Critics*, New Delhi: Oxford University Press.

Dworkin, Ronald (1978) 'Liberalism', in Stuart Hampshire (ed.) *Public and Private Morality*, Cambridge: Cambridge University Press.

Galanter, Marc (1998) 'Secularism, east and west', in Rajeev Bhargava, (ed.) *Secularism and its Critics*, New Delhi: Oxford University Press.

Levy, Leonard W. (1994) *The Establishment Clause*, Chapel Hill: The University of North Carolina Press.

McConnell, Michael (1993) 'Taking religious freedom seriously', in Terry East Land (ed.) *Religious Liberty in the Supreme Court,* Michigan and Cambridge: William B. Eerdamans Publishing Company.

Smith, Donald (1963) *India as a Secular State*, Bombay: Oxford University Press.

Taylor, Charles (1989) *Sources of the Self*, Cambridge: Cambridge University Press.

—— (1994) 'Justice after virtue' in John Horton and Susan Mendus (ed.) *After MacIntyre*, Cambridge: Polity Press.

Part IV

Communalization

8 The blindness of insight

Why communalism in India is about caste[1]

Dilip M. Menon

[A] large part of our intellectual discourse has in fact been an autobiography of the secular (read: upper-caste) self, its origin, its conflict with tradition, its desire to be modern. The intimate ... connection between the biography of the nation-state and the autobiography of the secular self structures, in ways that we have barely begun to understand, our relationship to caste (Dhareshwar 1992).

Caste is the central fault line of modern India, yet Indian social science has a tendency to study it as a displacement of what are seen as more fundamental identities such as class or ethnicity. This is despite the fact that the public spaces of modern India are inflected by violence against lower castes and its domestic spaces structured by strict prohibitions against caste miscegenation. Post-colonial scholarship has written the history of our modernity in terms of a deeply desirable transition to a notion of the Indian citizen unmarked by affinities other than to a national identity. This has had the effect of obscuring fundamental inequities that make some Indians more equal than others. And among the threats to the emergence of a modern India, 'communalism' or the political organization of religious community has come to be seen as the central agent of violence in India. Hindu-Muslim violence has become emblematic of the question of an as yet unresolved modernity in India. The construction of a secular citizen is the exigent national project.

There has been a reluctance to engage with what is arguably an intimate relation between the discourses of caste, secularism and communalism (see Varshney 2002 for a typical example of such blindness). That Hinduism, as religion, social system or way of life is a hierarchical, inegalitarian structure is largely accepted, but unacknowledged in academic discourse is both the casual brutality as well as the organized violence that it practices towards its subordinate sections. What we need to explore is the inner violence within Hinduism as much as the violence directed outwards against Muslims and acknowledge that the former is historically prior. The question needs to be: how has the employment of violence against an internal Other (defined in terms of inherent inequality) i.e. the Dalit, been displaced as one of aggression against an external Other (defined in terms of inherent difference) i.e. the Muslim. *Is communalism a deflection of the central issue of violence and inegalitarianism within the Hindu religion?* This is the point of departure for this chapter.

In this historical conversion of an earlier, involuted violence, how do we explain the persistent, nagging, fact of the involvement of Dalit and tribal groups in the killings of Muslims whether in the late nineteenth century, the Partition riots of 1947–48, or in

Gujarat in 2002? How have lower castes come to be suborned as the 'foot soldiers' of a militant Hindu identity for over a century? This requires us to offer a more historically textured and nuanced explanation than the mere fact of the operations of the brute power of upper castes in coercing participation, or the somewhat condescending assumption that material inducements are the major factor in ensuring participation. What might be the subjective reasons on the part of Dalits who participate in violence against those Muslims, very often sharing the same spaces as they do, and often engaged in similar occupations?[2]

Dhareshwar poses the puzzle of 'the solipsism of the secular self with regard to caste' (1992: 115). He argues that the desire of the Indian post-colonial elite to be modern has worked within the progressive narrative of liberal humanism. Self-fashioning is seen as the result of a jettisoning of ethnic, linguistic, caste and other markers to attain the abstract identity of the individual-citizen. To this end, the post-colonial elite in India have used English, both as language as much as a 'semiotic system symbolizing modernity', to impose their secular categories on the social world. This modern subjectivity, framed in English, has allowed caste to be approached only at one remove, as something restricted to the private domain suffused with the vernacular. English has acted as a 'meta-language' with reference to caste and other 'traditional' practices and those who appropriate English claim a subject position which is free from caste and religious markings. The public sphere is narrowly constructed as the sphere governed by secular categories. Witness for example, the censoring of the word 'Muslim' in the national English press and the use of the persistent, pernicious euphemism: 'the minority community' (of a piece with the official description of the demolished mosque, the Babri Masjid, as the 'disputed structure'). As also the seemingly trivial, but semiotically significant fact that signs enjoining public hygiene in Indian cities are nearly always in English, which are observed more in the breach by the 'not-yet-modern' occupiers of public space (Chakrabarty 1991; Kaviraj 1996). What follows from this is the claim by the upper caste secular self that s/he does not practice caste, using as s/he does impeccably unmarked categories in public discourse, while Dalits and others are casteist since they deploy the language of caste in the public sphere. As Dhareshwar points out, there is often a 'certain slippage that equates caste exclusively with lower-caste and that this slippage is systematic rather than accidental' (1992: 121, 118–20). This also leads us to the question so poignantly posed by the political scientist Gopal Guru, 'Can the Dalit articulate a universal position?'

This occlusion of caste in the public sphere is paralleled by the recognition of the need to eliminate public expressions of religion as part of the requirement of secularism, though this remains a vexed question. So here again, we are faced with the piquant situation that while *periodic* violence against Muslims invites outrage in the national press by public intellectuals, the *quotidian* violence against lower castes goes largely unremarked upon and occupies the space of unremarkable journalistic reportage.[3] Of course, sociologists and anthropologists study caste in villages, but where caste is not seen as an element of an irreducible Indian essence, it is represented as part of a transactional system where statuses are contextual, contingent and negotiated. The fact that being a Dalit may represent the zero-degree of subalternity is masked by appeals to historical change as much as the idea of performativity of self. That Dalit performance of self operates within a severely circumscribed range as also the fact that it runs the risk of attracting a disciplining violence needs to be remembered. When the question of violence does surface it is generally rendered as the preserve of the state (epistemic, developmental and national security) and as arising from the imperatives of governmentality. Little if any attention is paid to the bloodshed arising from the everyday preservation of hierarchy. Gyanendra Pandey points to the normalization of governmentality through a rendering of the very idea of violence as 'exceptional'. More pertinent for our argument is his astute observation that, 'It is the denial of violence "in our midst", the attribution of harmony *within* and the consignment of violence to the *outside* that establishes community' (Pandey 2001: 188; cf. Das 1995; Das and Kleinman 2000).

So how do we look at communalism through the problematic of caste and violence that is *endemic* to Hinduism itself? To put forward my argument briefly, in the period from 1850–1947, communal violence has always followed periods of lower caste mobility and assertion. As structures of coercion were challenged in the villages, the increasing difficulty of exercising violence against subordinate castes in the face of their self-assertion resulted in a closing of ranks within Hinduism both around symbols of unity such as the cow in the nineteenth century and through a deflection of violence onto Muslims. I would argue that the sequentiality of Mandal (the anti-reservation riots) and Masjid (the anti-Muslim riots) in the early 1990s was part of a longer historical pattern. We need to revisit the history of the colonial period from the conjuncture of the 1990s which was arguably the defining moment of post-Independence India. Thomas Hansen has argued that the rise of the Hindu right can be seen as a 'conservative revolution', against forces both from within (the growing assertiveness of backward and lower castes) as well as from without i.e. the threat of liberalization and the incorporation into a global mass culture. He suggests that post-colonial India had been built on a distinction between proper 'society' (what Dhareshwar would term the English, secular public sphere) and the world of the 'masses' (the realm of the vernacular private) (Hansen 1999). The turmoil of the 1990s threw the separation of these two worlds into crisis and made evident the disarticulation of what had appeared to be a seamless transition to an independent India under the leadership of a hegemonic elite. I shall now turn to two themes: the emergence of a public sphere under colonialism, and the production of a discourse of communalism to argue that the trajectory of politics in north and south India has diverged on the issue of the resolution of caste. This may have been central to the politics of religious violence in colonial north India.

The public sphere under colonialism

Eighteenth century north India had seen the emergence of an incipient urban public sphere, premised on collective activities in a public realm and characterized by debates around issues of religion, community and identity. This carried forward traditions of state negotiation with communities through the administrative structures of the Mughals, informal networks of association around pilgrimage centres, performative congregations around the Ramlila, as also formal debates between *maulavis* and *pandits* in centres such as Benares and Agra (Bayly 1998, 1996; Hansen 1992; Lutgendorf 1991). Central to this array of thick, social interaction were notions both of conceptualization of urban space enabling 'public' activities to take place as also the notion that some literary and speech forms were more amenable to articulating 'public' concerns of 'general interest' (see Freitag 1991). The decline of Mughal authority meant the slow deterioration of structures of compromise and negotiation within and between communities. The early Company state had been more amenable to negotiation within an existing social and sacral realm to the extent of 'playing nursemaid to

Vishnoo' as a later missionary critique put it. However, the entry of Christian missionaries after the passing of the Charter act of 1833 introduced a new element within the discussions animating the public realm. Earlier gentler forms of cultural interchange like the Muslim–Christian dialogues of the *munazara* tradition were superseded by the framework of a new harsher polemics of Evangelical Christianity that questioned the foundations of both Islam and Hinduism (Powell 1993). This in turn was to generate the heated polemical exchanges in public initiated by the Arya Samaj in the late nineteenth century.

The emerging British structures of governance in the nineteenth century were premised, particularly after the experience of 1857, both on a strict nonintervention in matters construed as 'religious' as also the attempt at creating a denatured public realm freed from the influence of religion. Religion was to be a private, community matter and its public manifestations were transferred to a discourse of law and order. Public religious identity and 'communal' identity became synonymous in the eyes of the state (see Pandey 1990; Freitag 1989). The colonial state neglected to integrate an emergent alternative realm: an arena of what Sandria Freitag terms 'localized, familial and fictive kin-based activities, frequently articulated in terms with religious and kinship resonances' (1991). Inevitably, the political arena of colonialism was a limited, morally empty space. Freitag argues that the colonial state, working on the assumption that distinctions between 'private' and 'public' were easily made, identified itself as the protector for 'general' and 'public' interests, relegating 'private' or 'particular' interests to an increasingly reified notion of community. This was premised on two related assumptions: that the state's institutions could accommodate all 'political' issues and that issues relating to religion, kinship and so on were apolitical. The removal of the state from what it perceived as private issues allowed Indians to 'experiment and contest freely the status and ideological constructs they expressed in public' (Freitag 1996).

Missionary effort, both in education as well as the creation of a vernacular press created a parallel reaction in which Hindu organizations began to 'project a novel version of a public, all-India Hinduism under attack from Western interference' (Bayly 1994). In north India, there were two kinds of response to a muscular articulation of Christianity. The first was the revivalist tendency which attempted to recreate traditional religion in the image of its challenger. Textual exegesis, a return to essentials, and a distancing from popular forms of religion marked both Hindu and Islamic revivalism. The *pandits* of Calcutta fighting a rearguard action through the revival of a Sanskritic apologetics as much as the Deoband enterprise of Nanautawi and Gangohi in the late nineteenth century seeking to guide Muslims in a new faithless world were bound by the need to streamline religion in the face of the modern (Metcalf 1982, 1992; Young 1981). Aggressive counter attacks whether through debate or through war characterized the second approach. The characterization of colonial India as a *dar-ul-harb* provided the rationale for such diverse nineteenth century Islamic movements such as Barelwi's attempts to set up an alternate state authority in the north-west and Titu Mir's in the east to mount an armed challenge to colonial rule. The Arya Samaj, founded in the late nineteenth century by Dayananda Saraswati, combined revivalism (a return to the Vedas) with aggressive public debates against Christian and Muslim preachers. The nineteenth century cannot be understood except within the crucible of a three-cornered polemic between Hindu, Christian and Muslim (Jones, 1976, 1989; Jordens 1978).

However, in the heat of conflict, unity, rather than internal difference and inequality, was the main issue. Among the Muslims there was a consolidation of an upper class *ashraf* identity premised on pure, textual practice and a move away from spaces of shared practices with a popular realm. Sir Syed Ahmad Khan's attempt to create a Muslim elite educated in an Oxbridge style environment at Aligarh at the Anglo-Mohammedan Oriental College, was but the most deliberate of such measures (Lelyveld 1975). The emergent public sphere in northern India was upper class and male in character and in the case of the Hindus, upper caste as well. Vasudha Dalmia in her magisterial work on the Hindi poet Bharatendu Harischandra and the emergence of a public sphere in nineteenth century north India shows how the discursive sphere of Hindi literature and periodicals reaffirmed Hinduism and its hierarchical order. In the face of colonial interventions in Hinduism (as in the case of anti-*sati* legislation) as well as Christian polemic, public defences of Hinduism began to lay stress on its timeless character: a *sanatana dharma* beyond caste, creed and of course, history (Dalmia 1997). Religion was seen as the one factor that bound the Hindus together, for ruling dynasties had come and gone, while Hindu *dharma* went on for ever. Thus, the Christian polemic against the inegalitarianism of Hinduism led to a closing of ranks around a revivified, all-inclusive high Hinduism forgetful of hierarchy. As Francesca Orsini puts it, 'The ideal Indian society, the *varna* system, seemed ... to ward off the mirage of equality, the dangers of class conflict, and the evil of materialism ... to reassert India's claims to superiority'. While there were occasional dissident voices that raised the issue of caste oppression, there were no untouchable interlocutors in the nineteenth century public sphere in north India. In the face of the upper caste reconstitution of Hinduism in its own image, no counter-historiography emerged (Orsini 2002). As we shall see later, the clean lower castes moved towards adoption of a militant Hinduism while untouchables initially adopted a principled distance from being Hindu through the adoption of radical *bhakti* that stressed devotion to their caste *gurus* (see Gooptu 2001).

In south India, Christianity afforded an interface with modernity for lower castes. And it was Christianity that allowed for their entry into a public sphere generated by inter-religious discussions. Unlike north India, the lowest castes were party to the expansion of the sphere of public debate through the missionary led proliferation of print and the appearance of textbooks, journals and magazines (Sam 1988; see Menon 2004). The missionary journals democratized access to a literate sphere of debate and knowledge, and also provided an alternative sphere of reflection on self and society. It was not only at an intellectual level that lower castes entered the new public sphere of debate. In colonial Madras, Paraya converts had been agitating since the early nine-teenth century over a whole range of secular concerns, including protests against the delimiting of their neighbourhoods or *paraceris* by colonial authorities, as well as agi-tating to get their caste headmen appointed as leaders of Christian convert commu-nities (see Balachandran 1999; Raman 1999).

The publication of Bishop Caldwell's study of the Dravidian language in the mid-nineteenth century helped popularize the idea that the Brahmins were not indigenous to south India. This was to have further ramifications in the idea that a traditional casteless culture had been stunted by the invasion of Brahmins from the north. Resur-gent histories were the norm in south India; whether in the discovery of a glorious age of Tamil civilization, or the reconstruction of an egalitarian Buddhist past in the works of Dalit intellectuals like Iyothee Thass (see Geetha and Rajadurai 1998; Ramaswamy 1997). The question of caste hierarchy was central to these discussions and Hinduism, unlike the north, appeared less as a monolith than a beleaguered behemoth riven by internal hemorrhage. It is not without significance that the major caste reformers of the nineteenth and twentieth century – Phule, Narayana Guru, EV Ramaswamy Naicker and Ambedkar have been from the south of the Vindhyas. There were other secular reasons for this assertion of equality such as the engagement of lower castes with the cash crop economy (as in the case of the Nadars), the opening up of south east Asia by Natukottai Chettiar capital and the rise of plantations in Ceylon, Malaya and the West Indies raising the possibilities of labour migration (Baker 1984; Hardgrave 1969; Rudner 1994; Menon 1994). The presence of the ocean in general allowed for a larger space of mobility than in the north; particularly the Indo-Gangetic plain where stagnant agrarian hierarchies were the norm till the histories of indentured labour began the engagement with the sea in the nineteenth century.

The discourse of communalism

The previous section has shown how the histories of north and south India diverged around the issue of the addressing of caste inequality. Following on from this, could it be argued that the discourse of communalism in northern India arose from this refusal to engage frontally with hierarchy? How do we engage with the question of the connection between lower caste upward mobility and the phenomenon of 'communalism'? Schematically, one can look at three flashpoints in the period between 1880 and 1947: the Cow Protection Riots of the 1890s in the United Provinces and Bihar; the period of Non-Cooperation in the 1920s in Bengal; and the Partition Riots in Punjab and Bengal in 1946–47. In each of these instances, an economic upturn generated the possibility of upward mobility for lower castes which in turn created intransigence towards the continuing domination by caste superiors. Beleaguered upper caste elites turned to a rhetoric of common symbols and an open Hinduism while at the same time presenting the menace of a resurgent, competitive Islam. In the violence that followed, the problem of internal differentiation and hierarchy in Hinduism was temporarily resolved through the projection of a united Hindu violence against Muslims.

Cow protection in the nineteenth century

The Arya Samaj in the late nineteenth century had carried out militant Hindu proselytizing defining a revived upper caste Hinduism. About 1882, they had started the Cow Protection movement in the Punjab which was as much about inventing a common symbol across castes among the Hindus (though it involved a vilification of Chamars who dealt with the skins of dead cattle) as defining a cow-protecting Hinduism against a cow-killing Islam. This movement spread to the United Province and Bihar which were then the site of massive riots in 1893, particularly in the Bhojpuri speaking regions.[4] This region was characterized by a Rajput, Brahmin and Bhumihar landowning elite, largely communities of smallholders, even though there were a few great landlords with estates like the Rajas of Benares, Hathwa or Bettiah. Their economic dominance was buttressed by their numerical strength, except for western Bhojpur where the untouchable Chamars and the lower caste Ahirs outnumbered them. Over the nineteenth century, the operation of market forces, law courts, and the registration of land rights had led to the assertion of status by lower caste groups as also the Koeris and Chamars. The elite landowning groups meanwhile had been hit by the deindustrialization in the Gangetic plain, the commercialization of agriculture (that benefited middle caste groups) and the closing of service opportunities with the demise of the older political order. A more significant fact was the considerable loss of land through improvidence, debt and the secular operation of market forces.

Lower castes like the Ahirs, Kurmis and Koeris became more assertive through acquiring land; engaging with the Census and its status allocation for castes; and through movements that incorporated ritual procedures like wearing the sacred thread as much as actions with more bite such as the rejection of forced unpaid labour. In this circumstance of a declining elite and a resurgent lower caste group like the Ahirs engaged with the cattle economy, the central issue became the Bakr Id killing of cows by Muslims in 1893.[5] The defence of the cow became the rallying cry to bring together declining elites and militant subalterns among the Hindus against a Muslim community seen narrowly as butchers. The movement for Cow Protection was supported by 'the leading members of the Hindu faith' such as the *rajas* and once prominent landlords and, in Pandey's words, drew upon 'marginally "clean" castes who aspired to full "cleanness" by emphasizing purity of faith'. As Christophe Jaffrelot emphasizes in his study of lower-caste politics in north India, attempts at upward mobility followed the adoption of 'higher' ritual practices, unlike as in south India, where there was a tendency to 'ethnicize' caste and work towards an internal unity and solidarity accompanied by a rejection of upper caste practices (Jaffrelot 2003). Of course, all was not sheer volition and an aspiration for higher status; the cow protection movement was characterized by forms of social coercion like the boycott of those who sold bullocks to Muslims or refused to participate in the protection of mother cow. Needless to add, contingent alliances between caste elites and subordinate castes did not outlast the riots and in some cases, as in Gorakhpur, lower caste groups like the Chamars and Nats were themselves the targets of attack.

Urban strategies of Dalit and shudra groups

In the towns of the United Provinces, lower castes followed two different strategies. In the first instance, untouchable groups turned to *bhakti* devotionalism – the Adi-Hindu movement. As expounded by Swami Achhutanand in the 1920s there were three strategies: the dissociation of untouchables from menial occupations; an assertion that untouchables had been the former rulers of India; and an emphasis on spiritual introspection to understand the irrelevance of social distinctions. The refusal of the Indian National Congress to engage with untouchable leaders, even after the 1920 Nagpur session, meant that they remained within the space of group politics. In Punjab too, Mangoo Ram and the Ad Dharm movement among the untouchables maintained a principled distance from Hinduism as from the Indian National Congress (Juergensmeyer 1982). The second group, the *shudra* poor, on the other hand, positioned as they were squarely within the orthodox Hindu commercial environment, turned towards an affirmation of Hindu militancy expressed in their involvement in the milieu of the wrestling *akharas* (gymnasiums) of UP, as Gooptu's work shows. The Hindu Sabha, presided over by Madan Mohan Malaviya and the Arya Samaj worked to bring these militant Shudras under their wing through collective participation in public festivals like the Ram Lila (see Gooptu 2001). The transformation of earlier shared spaces of religion into zones of recruitment for Hindu militancy and spaces of sectarian demarcation was a process that gathered momentum over the 1920s, following the failed concord of the Gandhian Non-Cooperation/Khilafat movement. Fairs, festivals and spaces of popular religion came to be strictly demarcated as either Hindu or Muslim spaces. Moreover, cities became the site of territorial wars of sound, as the leading of processions and playing of music in front of mosques and temples played out another politics. Here again, an urban *shudra* population of the working poor, tried to work towards larger solidarities in the anomic spaces of the city through an affiliation with militant Hindu organizations (Freitag 1992; Gupta 2001).

Bengal in the early twentieth century

In Bengal, the late nineteenth century had seen the rise of lower caste movements, particularly with the involvement of lower castes like the Kaibartas and Chandalas in the burgeoning jute economy. From the 1870s, apart from moves towards adopting a different nomenclature (Chandalas becoming Namasudras and Kaibarttas assuming the name of Mahishyas), caste associations had begun to boycott upper castes, denying them forced labour and demanding recognition of status. As Sekhar Bandyopadhaya shows in his magnificent monograph on the Namasudras, these groups remained resolutely alienated from the mainstream of nationalist politics, showing disinterest in the largely Hindu upper caste orientation of the Swadeshi movement (1905–11). Here too, the political activity of the Indian National Congress did little to inspire enthusiasm among either lower castes or Muslims. In the late 1920s, over the issue of music before mosques and consequent rioting, it was becoming clear to many upper caste politicians that lower castes like the Mahishyas would prove useful, even if ultimately dispensable, in pitched battles against Muslims. Wooing them towards Hinduism would kill two birds with one stone. Lower caste groups would be less intractable towards social superiors and they could act as a militant force, albeit of contingent loyalty (see Datta 1999).

Given the demographic structure of undivided Bengal, and the fact that Muslims were in a majority in the eastern districts, the *bhadralok* had a lot to fear from the colonial opening up of politics to electoral representation. This fear was to be realized in the first provincial elections in 1937 following the provisions of the Government of India Act of 1935, when the Krishak Praja Party came to power with Fazlul Haque becoming the Chief Minister. As Joya Chatterji has controversially and compellingly argued, the Bengal Congress embodied Hindu nationalism and the *bhadralok laager* mentality in the face of mass politics. Reaching out to the lower rungs of a putative Hindu constituency was left to organizations like the Hindu Sabha which began to be active in the reclaiming of lower castes to Hinduism through *shuddhi* or purification; infinitely condescending, but a gesture nevertheless. The grand old man of Hindu chauvinism, Savarkar, and the Hindu Mahasabha were active with tribal groups like the Santhals, attempting to get them to stop working for the Muslims (see Bandyopadhaya 1997). In the Santhal Rebellion of 1924–32, there was one chilling moment when Jitu Santhal and his followers made their last stand in the Adina Mosque. They performed a 'debased form of worship' in the mosque instituting an image of Kali (see T. Sarkar 1985). From being the outliers of Hinduism (there was considerable debate at the time as to whether the Santhals and other tribals were 'Hindu' in any meaningful sense) the Santhals had reclaimed a mosque for their putative patrons.

In all these instances, then, is there a simple argument to be made about the manipulation of subalterns by upper caste ideologues? Is it just a simple process of the co-opting of lower caste protest and its subsequent deflection on to an imagined enemy? There are three political conjunctures that are crucial in the emergence of a Hindu bloc before the Partition of India in 1947 and the horrific killings that followed. The first is the Census operations from the late nineteenth century that started off at one level a flurry of petitioning the government for social status and the formation of associations towards this end by castes. Classification had a major consequence in curtailing the right to exit from categories as also in ironing out fuzzy identifications: one was either low or high, either Hindu or Muslim and so on (Barrier 1981; Cohn 1996b; Kaviraj 1992). However, the Census operations also fed into the politics of numbers and representation, with the second conjuncture of the opening of colonial government to Indian participation. An emergent rhetoric of the 'dying Hindu' stemmed from the recognition of the importance of numbers in the colonial imagination (Appadurai 1993). In the carving out of constituencies the paranoid Hindu perception was that Muslims would get a greater share of official spoils because of their numbers. Hinduism was represented as a house divided against itself and hemorrhaging through the conversion of its lower sections to other religions. Drawing in outliers like tribal groups and consecrating them as Hindus could help swell numbers at a time when every head counted. The third crucial conjuncture was the Government of India Act of 1935 that opened up the possibility of an electoral politics, albeit with limited suffrage, and provincial ministries. Now was when the principled stand off from nationalist politics on the part of lower caste groups in Bengal, U.P. and Punjab began breaking down as they realized that the time had come to assimilate or be condemned to the wilderness. As Bandyopadhyaya pithily puts it, post 1935, lower caste groups moved from alienation to integration. One consequence of this was as in the 1946 elections in Bengal when the Congress won 27 of the 30 seats in the Scheduled Caste/Scheduled Tribe constituencies. The other and more horrific integration can be seen in the participation of Namasudras in Hindu militant processions from 1945 and their involvement in the massacre of Muslims at Noakhali in 1946. Lower caste entry into Hinduism was through a baptism in blood at the dawn of Independence.

Conclusion

Parallel to the processes of the creation a pan-Hindu identity and the imagination of a unitary Islam in south Asia is the long history of the withdrawal of elites from a space of popular culture and the erosion of spaces of festive, religious and quotidian interaction in themselves. An eighteenth century public sphere of dialogue and negotiation (of which we as yet know very little) had given way to a segregation of the religious from the public sphere by colonial anxieties structured by the trope of 'communalism'. However, we need to look at an attitude towards spaces of popular religion that united a reformist trend from William Jones to the Arya Samaj and Deoband movement through to Gandhi. From the eighteenth century, a process of 'textualization' (to borrow Dirks' pithy phrase) of traditions as well as religion had created a dichotomy in elite perceptions of what constituted an essential Hinduism or Islam (Trautmann 1998). The sphere of abstract, intellectual religious traditions came to be seen as what constituted the fundamentals and the sphere of the everyday, as of pilgrimage and festivals, was perceived as a corrupt set of accretions that marked the devaluation of the abstract ideals in popular practice. This transition was framed by the triangular debate between Christian missionaries and Muslim and Hindu reformers in the public sphere which increasingly moulded an idea of 'religion' around ideas of 'belief', 'text', 'ritual' and singular identity. Almost as much as the Census, the rhetoric of religious reformers narrowed the parameters of faith and 'religion' became increasingly a stand-alone category with its own regulatory mechanisms (Asad 1996; Balagangadhara 1994).

It is the history of the demise of quotidian arenas where differences of class, caste and religion were blurred even if temporarily that we need to chart. And these quoti-dian spaces were shaped by existential concerns inflected as much by difference as sameness, by violence as much as its forgetting and shared spaces of labour as much as exploitation. When we write about communalism we need to bring to bear these his-tories and know too that the existential experience of religion has undergone dramatic transformation over the last two centuries. The neatness of categories like Hindu and Muslim hide the porosity of identities as much as histories of the inner violence of hierarchy. It is through the forgetting, and even the violent suppression of inegalitar-ianism, within putative blocs like Hinduism and Islam that unitary, militant identities are sought to be forged. And in that sense, communalism in India may well be the return of the repressed histories of caste.

Notes

1 This article was originally published in Dilip M. Menon, *The Blindness of Insight: Essays on Caste in Modern India* (Chennai: Navayana Publications, 2006) and has been abridged by the author.
2 I can only raise the question here since as yet we do not have a textured sociological or his-torical account of relations between Dalits and Muslims in both rural and urban environ-ments. Studies tend to collapse these identities under abstract categories of worker or agricultural labourer, which obscure the formation and assertion of notions of self not encompassed by the relations of production. For instance, see the extensive reporting on the Gujarat riots, and how the *Economic and Political Weekly* spoke about Dalit-Muslim antag-onism solely in terms of declining employment opportunities in cities like Ahmedabad and the competition arising from this. A recent work which does look at Chamar perceptions of Muslims in the context of a village is Gottschalk (2001).
3 An important exception is P. Sainath, who has been covering the plight of Dalits all over India in a searing set of articles for the national newspaper *The Hindu* in 2003.
4 The literature on Cow Protection is vast. For a representative range, see McLane (1977) and Freitag (1981). The work of Gyanendra Pandey (1983) is particularly insightful.
5 It is interesting that none of the studies of the Cow Protection Movement actually engage with the 'real' cow as opposed to the cow as 'symbol'. By this I mean that we have no idea of the shifts happening in the cattle economy in northern India in the 19th century which may have had an influence on the rhetoric about preventing cow slaughter. I am grateful for con-versations with Arvind Das and Shahid Amin on this point.

References

Amin, Shahid (2002) 'On retelling the Muslim conquest of northern India', in Partha Chatterjee and Anjan Ghosh (ed.) *History and the Present*, Delhi: Permanent Black.
Appadurai, A. (1993) 'Number in the colonial imagination', in Carol Breckenridge and Peter van der Veer (ed.) *Orientalism and the Post-colonial Predicament*, Delhi: Oxford University Press.
Asad, Talal (1996) *Geneaologies of Religion: Discipline and Reasons of Power in Christianity and Islam*, Baltimore: Johns Hopkins Press.
Baker, C. J. (1984) *An Indian Rural Economy, 1880–1955: The Tamilnad Countryside*, Delhi: Oxford University Press.

Balachandran, Aparna (1999) 'Caste, community and identity formation: the Paraiyars in late 18th and early 19th century Madras', unpublished MPhil dissertation, Jawaharlal Nehru University, New Delhi.

Balagangadhara, S. N. (1994) *'The Heathen in his Blindness ... 'Asia, the West and the Dynamic of Religion*, Leiden: E.J. Brill.

Bandyopadhyaya, Sekhar (1997) *Caste, Protest and Identity in Colonial India: The Namasudras of Bengal, 1872–1947*, London: Curzon Press.

Barrier, Gerald (ed.) (1981) *Census in British India: New Perspectives*, Delhi: Manohar.

Bayly, C. A. (1996) *Empire and Information: Intelligence Gathering and Social Communication in India, 1780–1870*, Cambridge: Cambridge University Press.

—— (1998) 'The pre-history of "communalism" in north India', in *Origins of Nationality in South Asia: Patriotism and Ethical Government in the Making of Modern India*, Delhi: Oxford University Press.

Bayly, Christopher (1994) 'Returning the British to south Asian history: the limits of colonial hegemony', *South Asia*, 17(2).

Bayly, Susan (1989) *Saints, Goddesses and Kings Muslims and Christians in South Indian Society*, Cambridge: Cambridge University Press.

Chakrabarty, Dipesh (1991) 'Open space/public space: garbage, modernity and India', *South Asia*, New Series, 14(1).

Cohn, Bernard (1996a) *An Anthropologist Among the Historians and Other Essays*, Delhi: Oxford University Press.

—— (1996b) 'The census, social structure, and objectification in South Asia', in *An Anthropologist Among the Historians*, Delhi: Oxford University Press.

Dalmia, Vasudha (1997) *The Nationalization of Hindu Traditions: Bharatendu Harishcandra and Nineteenth Century Benares*, Delhi: Oxford University Press.

Das, Veena (1995) *Critical Events: An Anthropological Perspective on Contemporary India*, Delhi: Oxford University Press.

Das, Veena (ed.) (1992) *Mirrors of Violence: Communities, Riots and Survivors in South Asia*, Delhi: Oxford University Press.

Das, Veena and Kleinman, Arthur (eds) (2000) *Violence and Subjectivity*, Berkeley: University of California Press.

Datta, P. K. (1999) *Carving Blocs: Communal Ideology in Twentieth Century Bengal*, Delhi: Oxford University Press.

Dhareshwar, Vivek (1992) 'Caste and the secular self', *Journal of Arts and Ideas,* 25–26.

Dirks, Nicholas B. (2001) *Castes of Mind: Colonialism and the Making of Modern India*, Princeton, NJ: Princeton University Press.

Freitag, Sandria (1981) 'Sacred Symbol as Mobilizing Ideology: The North Indian Search for a "Hindu" community', *Comparative Studies in Society and History*, 22.

—— (1989) *Collective Action and Community: Public Arenas and the Emergence of Communalism in North India*, Berkeley: University of California Press.

—— (1991) 'Introduction', *South Asia*, New Series 14(1), special issue on 'Aspects of the "Public" in Colonial South Asia'.

Geetha, V. and Rajadurai, S. V. (1998) *Towards a Non-Brahmin Millennium: From Iyothee Thass to Periyar*, Calcutta: Samay.

Gooptu, Nandini (2001) *The Politics of the Urban Poor in Early Twentieth Century India*, Cambridge: Cambridge University Press.

Gottschalk, Peter (2001) *Beyond Hindu and Muslim: Multiple Identity in Narratives from Village India*, Delhi: Oxford University Press.

Gupta, Charu (2001) *Sexuality, Obscenity, Community: Women Muslims and the Hindu Public in Colonial India*, Delhi: Permanent Black.

Hansen, Kathryn (1992) *Grounds for Play: The Nautanki Theatre of North India*, Berkeley: University of California Press.

Hansen, Thomas Blom (1999) *Saffron Wave: Democracy and Hindu Nationalism in Modern India*, Princeton, NJ: Princeton University Press.

Hardgrave, Robert (1969) *Nadars of Tamilnad: Political Culture of a Community in Change*, Berkeley: University of California Press.

Jaffrelot, Christophe (2003) *India's Silent Revolution: The Rise of Lower Castes in North India*, New York: Columbia University Press.

Jones, Kenneth (1976) *Arya Dharm: Hindu Consciousness in 19th century Punjab*, Berkeley: University of California Press.

—— (1989) *Socio-Religious Reform Movements in British India*, vol. 3.1, New Cambridge History of India, Cambridge: Cambridge University Press.

Jordens, J. T. F. (1978) *Dayananda Saraswati: His Life and Ideas*, Delhi: Oxford University Press.

Juergensmeyer, Mark (1982) *Religion as Social Vision: The Movement against Untouchability in 20th Century Punjab*, Berkeley: University of California Press.

Kaviraj, Sudipta (1992) 'The imaginary institution of India', in Partha Chatterjee and Gyanendra Pandey (ed.), *Subaltern Studies VII*, Delhi: Oxford University Press.

—— (1996) 'Filth and the public sphere', *Osterreichische Zeitschrift fur Sociologie,* 21(2).

Lelyveld, David (1975) *Aligarh's First Generation: Muslim Solidarity and English Education in Northern India, 1875–1900*, Chicago: Chicago University Press.

Lutgendorf, Philip (1991) *The Life of a Text: Performing the Ramcaritmanas of Tulsidas*, Berkeley: University of California Press.

Menon, Dilip M. (1994) *Caste, Nationalism and Communism in South India: Malabar, 1900–1948*, Cambridge: Cambridge University Press.

—— (2004) 'A place elsewhere: lower caste novels in Malayalam of the 19th century', in Vasudha Dalmia and Stuart Blackburn (eds) *New Literary Histories for South Asia*, Delhi: Permanent Black.

Metcalf, Barbara (1982) *Islamic Revival in British India: Deoband, 1860–1900*, Princeton, NJ: Princeton University Press.

—— (1992) 'Imagining community: polemical debates in colonial India', in Kenneth Jones (ed.) *Religious Controversy in British India: Dialogues in South Asian Languages*, Albany: State University of New York Press.

Orsini, Francesca (2002) *The Hindi Public Sphere, 1920–1940: Language and Literature in the Age of Nationalism*, Delhi: Oxford University Press.

Pandey, Gyanendra (1983) 'Rallying around the cow: sectarian strife in the bhojpuri region c. 1888–1917', in Ranajit Guha (ed.) *Subaltern Studies II*, Delhi: Oxford University Press.

—— (1990) *The Construction of Colonialism in Colonial North India*, Delhi: Oxford University Press.

—— (2001) *Remembering Partition: Violence, Nationalism and History in India*, Cambridge: Cambridge University Press.

Powell, Avril A. (1993) *Muslims and Missionaries in Pre-Mutiny India*, London: Curzon Press.

Raman, Bhavani (1999) 'The emergence of the public in nineteenth century Tamil Nadu', unpublished MPhil dissertation, Jawaharlal Nehru University, New Delhi.

Ramaswamy, Sumathi (1997) *Passions of the Tongue: Language Devotion in Tamil India, 1891–1970*, Berkeley: University of California Press.

Rudner, David (1994) *Caste and Capitalism in Colonial India: The Natukottai Chettiars*, Berkeley: University of California Press.

Sainath, P. (2000) *Everyone Loves a Good Drought*, Delhi: Penguin India.

Sam, N. (1988) *Keralathile Samuhika Navotthanavum Sahityavum* [Social Renaissance in Kerala and Literature], Kottayam.

Sarkar, Sumit (1973) *The Swadeshi Movement in Bengal, 1903–1908*, New Delhi: People's Publishing House.

—— (2002) *Beyond Nationalist Frames: Postmodernism, Hindu Fundamentalism, History*, Bloomington: Indiana University Press.

Sarkar, Tanika (1985) 'Jitu Santhal's movement in Malda, 1924–32: A study in tribal protest', in Ranajit Guha (ed.) *Subaltern Studies IV*, Delhi: Oxford University Press.

Trautmann, Thomas (1998) *The Aryans and British India*, Berkeley: University of California Press.

Varshney, Ashutosh (2002) *Ethnic Conflict and Civic Life: Hindus and Muslims in India*, New Haven: Yale University Press.

Young, Richard F. (1981) *Resistant Hinduism: Sanskrit Sources on Anti-Christian Apologetics in Early Nineteenth Century India*, Vienna: De Nobili Research Library.

9   In search of integration and identity

Indian Muslims since independence[1]

Mushirul Hasan

In the long and impressive history of India's nationalist movement there was a deep ideological schism between ardent communalists and committed champions of a secular and composite Indian state. But the mainstream of Indian nationalism had a decidedly secular orientation. That is why, when the newly created state of Pakistan was fostering its Islamic image in 1947–48, India was engaged in reconstructing a democratic and secular polity amidst the brutal and bloody violence which accompanied independence and partition. Jawaharlal Nehru, the main architect of India's secular state, emphatically declared: 'The Government of a country like India ... can never function satisfactorily in the modern age except on a secular basis'. This was an article of faith with many of his comrades in the Congress and in other political formations.

After 60 years of independence India's secular experiment needs to be reviewed in its implications both for other plural societies endeavouring to tackle their ethnic, regional and religious problems in Asia and Africa, and for the Indian Muslims who form the largest minority segment in the country. We do so without losing sight of the obvious facts that the Indian Muslims do not constitute a single, homogeneous and monolithic entity and that the differentiating features that characterize Indian society as a whole are also to be found within the Muslim community (Khan 1978). At the same time, our concern is to uncover certain broad trends amongst Muslims which would exclude regional, local and class nuances from our analysis.

In the 1940s Mohammad Ali Jinnah led a powerful movement which was meant to advance the interests of his co-religionists after the British withdrawal from the Indian subcontinent. But the final outcome of his campaign proved catastrophic to over 35 million Muslims who chose to remain in post-partition India. Leading industrial families, trading groups and professional men hurried to Pakistan to improve their fortunes, leaving behind a socially fragmented and economically depressed Muslim community. With the introduction of the universal franchise and joint electorates, the Muslims of Uttar Pradesh and Bihar lost their position as a privileged minority – a position they had enjoyed under the British since 1909. There was also a diminution of their influence in government service, for the bulk of the professional groups in these states had migrated to Pakistan. The abolition of the *zamindari* system reduced the rural influence of the former Muslim landlords, even more than that of their Hindu counterparts, because of the smaller number of Muslim peasants in the north and the greater number of urban rentiers among the Muslim landlords (Brass 1974: 235). The dissolution of princely states impoverished a large percentage, if not the majority, of the upper and middle classes.

With the Muslim League dissolved in the north and its leadership drained off to Pakistan, the political trajectory of the Muslim community was defined within the democratic and secular framework; its future lay in coming to terms with the broad contours of Indian secularism, rallying round political parties with avowed secular goals. 'There is absolutely no alternative to secularism, unless communal suicide be considered to be one', wrote an influential Muslim commentator (Ayyub 1965: 15).

But a community nurtured in the tradition of political separatism and religious fundamentalism, exemplified by the Jamaat-i Islami and Muslim League movements, was rather slow in accommodating to the secular Indian framework. One of India's leading lawyer-politicians noted in 1962 that his brethren had 'not yet fully adjusted themselves emotionally to a secular state'.[2] This view was supported by two leading scholars educated in the famous religious seminaries – the Dar al-Ulum at Deoband and the Nadwat al-Ulama in Lucknow (Haq 1972: 11–12; Faruqi 1966: 140). The concept of a secular state was contrary to the fundamentals of Islam, and to be secular was nothing short of being *ghair mazhabi* or *la dini* (irreligious). The modern secular state, stated an official publication of the Jamaat-I Islami, 'rests on the denial of God ... on the denial of the sovereignty of His exclusive title to the obedience of His creatures. ... To owe allegiance to God is to refuse allegiance to every other authority unless the latter acts as His servant and upholds the authority of His law' (Siddiqi 1952: 4–5).

While the rumblings over the acceptance of the secular concept have not quite ceased, relatively few Muslims cling to the idea of an Islamic state. Some hard-headed *ulema* may still cherish the hope of a *dar al-Islam,* but most Muslims have come to regard secularism as a boon on which their welfare depends. The Jamiyat al-ulema propounded the theory of a social contract between Hindus and Muslims to establish a secular state, while the Jamaat-i Islami, after years of diffidence, declared in 1970 that: 'In the present circumstances, the Jamaat-i Islami Hind wants that in contrast to other totalitarian and fascist modes of government, the ... secular democratic mode of government in India should endure' (quoted in Wright 1979: 86).

A keen and sympathetic observer of Indian politics remarked in the mid-1960s that 'informed Muslim opinion is clear that it wants nothing better than the liberty to work out its own destiny within the Indian secular society' (Spear 1967: 47; also see Mir Mushtaq Ahmad, 'Role of Indian Muslims'; Haq 1972: 11–13, 17).

I

In order to assess the Muslims' response to the secular processes, we must turn to an examination of their political preferences as exercised through the general elections.

In the first three general elections, Muslims tied their fortunes to the Congress bandwagon, which had the image of a secular party, and they lent their full support to Jawaharlal Nehru whose secular credentials were never in doubt.[3] In Uttar Pradesh, India's most populous state, Muslim candidates contesting elections on Congress Party tickets constituted the largest proportion among the Muslim political activists, and succeeded in getting elected in larger proportions than the candidates put up by other political parties (Ahmad 1974).

The earlier notion of communal consciousness as a strong element in Muslim voting behaviour (Gupta 1962: 380) stands refuted by recent studies which have shown that Muslims do not operate as a monolithic entity in politics; competitive electoral processes have, moreover, helped to break down their communal solidarity. 'The increasing tendency of Muslim candidates to assume national party identifications shows that the integrative process is at work' (Krishna 1967: 187). Muslim candidates contesting elections on the tickets of the national parties improved their share of the total votes polled by Muslim candidates (ibid.; cf. Ahmad 1967: 523). Equally important was the conscious decision to reject overtly communal organizations and an unmistakable preference for secular parties (Krishna 1986: 187–88, 1972).

The Muslim League disappeared from north India in 1947, and attempts to revive it during 1959 proved futile. Bodies like the Jamiyat al-ulema pursued their traditional nationalist policies and acted in unison with the Congress. Many of its leaders, such as Maulana Hifzur Rahman, were returned to the Lok Sabha as Congress candidates.

In the mid-1960s, however, various Muslim groups in different parts of the country began to question the wisdom of continuing their alliance with and dependence on the Congress. They did so because the Congress had ceased to be a vehicle for their aspirations, and had shown insensitivity towards their specific complaints regarding unequal educational opportunities, discrimination in government employment, and poor representation in central and state governments, in the Indian Administrative Service, the police and the army.[4] Muslims were also victims of organized communal violence, as in Jamshedpur and Rourkela districts (1964), and were aggrieved at the Congress government's failure to curb such persistent assaults. Under the stress of insecurity created by riots there was a growing perception of the community's dwindling fortunes under Congress rule. Summing up Muslim feelings, a leading political scientist noted: 'The Muslims in India are in a quandary. They appear lost and out-of-grips with the evolving reality of contemporary Indian life' (Khan 1968: 25; also see Tyabji 1971: 201, 203).

This disenchantment found expression in the 1967 elections when most Muslims deserted the Congress, especially in Uttar Pradesh, Bihar and Bengal, and vigorously pressed the need for a separate and exclusive platform so that they would send to the legislatures their 'own' representatives who would not be at the mercy of 'non-Muslim parties'. The Muslim Majlis-i Mushawarat, established in August 1964, was meant to articulate Muslim grievances and seek ways of alleviating them through the processes of party and electoral politics.

The Majlis was a loose confederation of diverse political interest groups, including former leaders of the Muslim League, the Jamaat-i Islami, and some Muslim Congressmen backed by the Jamiyat al-ulema. Its demands were embodied in the 1967 *People's Manifesto,* which effectively summarized the main grievances and demands of Muslims, including the revision of textbooks with a Hindu bias, the introduction of proportional representation in elections, protection of the Muslim Personal Law, recognition of Urdu as a second official language in the north Indian states, and preservation of the 'minority character' of the Aligarh Muslim University. It urged Muslim voters to support independent candidates from different parties, 'primarily according to the candidates' attitudes towards the Muslim community'. It stood in favour of those who were free of caste and communal prejudices, subscribed to democratic and secular principles, and were broadly in agreement with the *People's Manifesto* issued by the Majlis.

The Majlis succeeded in stirring up 'political and social consciousness' amongst Muslims (Tyabji 1971: 128), and in 'detouring' them 'from their usual solid support for the Congress' (Quraishi 1968: 981–82). But it was only marginally successful in influencing the outcome of the 1967 elections. The adventurism of the Majlis failed on account of the absence of a unified leadership, the fragmentary nature of the Muslim community with its regional and local specificity, and the small and scattered Muslim votes in most electoral constituencies. Besides, the path of 'contest mobility' (Schermerhorn 1978: 176) was clearly strewn with difficulties because democratic political institutions do not always lend themselves to being used by minority groups in defence of their interests. The Majlis learnt this lesson the hard way when it was stigmatized as a sinister, incipient revival of the old Muslim League, and its demands pushed more votes towards candidates whose appeal was to Hindi and Hindu revivalism. Muslims, it seemed, could not hope to take the political process into their own hands as they thought they could; they had to be content with organizing themselves as pressure groups exerting their influence through other political forces.

At the same time, it was inexpedient to allow Muslim anxieties to grow, for at stake was national unity, the secular image of the Congress, and the country's prestige in other parts of the world, especially in West Asia. Already, the danger signs were too obvious to go unnoticed. The alienation of the minorities and the consequent weakening of the secular elements amongst them, the newly acquired militancy of parochial and sectarian tendencies, the growing intrusion of religion into politics, and the widening gulf that separated Hindus and Muslims lent credence to the view that 'the secularism of India is an aspiration, not yet a reality' (Smith 1965: 10).[5]

II

Just a decade-and-a-half after independence the communal forces, long kept under check by Nehru's leadership, surged forward, causing serious stress to India's secular fabric. Amongst Muslims, the Jamaat-i Islami and the Itehadul Muslimeen derived strength and sustenance from the wave of communal violence which swept through much of north India, leading a perceptive Muslim observer to conclude that 'Muslim communalism ... is now coming to surface again. Its fundamental idea ... is that true Muslim society can exist only in a country where the government is in the hands of Muslims and is carried on according to Islamic law'.

Spearheaded by the cadre-based Rashtriya Swayamsewak Sangh (RSS) and its political wing, the Bharatiya Jana Sangh, Hindu communalism found a substantial ally in the resurgence of nationalist feelings after the Indo-China war of 1962; the alliance was strengthened by the war with Pakistan three years later. Committed to the cause of building a resurgent Hindu nation and a revived Hindi-Hindu culture, the ideology of the RSS and the Jana Sangh was fuelled by the stereotype of an aggressive Islam on the rampage. They repudiated secularism, denounced the Congress for its policy of appeasement under the 'camouflage of secularism',[6] and proposed the 'Indianization' of Muslims to purge them of disloyal tendencies. 'Indianization of the Muslim outlook is the only solution of the socio-religious as well as the political aspect of the communal problem', declared a foremost RSS and Jana Sangh activist (Madhok 1946: 101; 1970: 82).

The communal upsurge in the 1960s was part of the sharpening of existing caste, class and community cleavages, and reflected the limitations of the secularization process which had been boldly initiated through democratic processes, progressive social legislation, rapid industrialization and a massive adult literacy campaign. These cleavages were kept under control during the anti-colonial struggle, with unity and consensus among its central concerns. But not so after independence. The Congress was no longer at the head of a movement: it was overnight turned into a political party whose main aim was to exercise control and dominance over the levers of power and authority. Devising electoral strategies became its prime concern, while populist slogans, radical rhetoric and diffused socio-economic policies were its answers to growing caste/class tensions and increased communal animosities. 'The image of Indian unity', warned the *Economic and Political Weekly,* 'cannot be built merely of eye-catching laces and frills: it must also have the supporting "stays" of harder material'.[7]

The Congress was singularly lacking in ideological coherence, as was signified by the presence of communal and revivalist elements entrenched in the states and districts, and their uneasy relationship with Nehru who was committed to the destruction of communalism and the establishment of a secular state and society. It surged ahead without isolating such elements,[8] without developing any formal or informal structures to effect social transformation, and without evolving instruments to widen the social basis of secularism and thus assuage the fears of the minorities while satisfying the rising aspirations of various social groups. Nehru was no doubt aware of these limitations, but he also dithered on vital issues. He took certain steps or failed to take others which did not fit squarely with his promotion of secularism (Gopal, 'Nehru and secularism': 23). A few years after Nehru's death, the *Economic and Political Weekly* observed:

> The rudest shock comes from the manner in which the Government and the country are allowing themselves to be pushed off the edge of secularism into the abyss of communal reaction, falling back to the frightening atavism of stagnant, dark and medieval ethos of the Hindi-speaking areas.[9]

An easy way out of the communal impasse was to woo sectional and parochial interests and to make occasional friendly gestures towards the minorities, even if it meant heightening their community consciousness. In his keenness to win Muslim confidence, Nehru allowed Muslims a voice in whether or not to provide equality before the law to all Indian women or to promulgate a common civil code, thus precluding either (Gopal, 'Nehru and secularism': 23). He stated in 1954 that he thought a unified civil code was inevitable, but that the time was not ripe to push it through in India! Again, he failed to press his own initiative for the banning of communal parties (Smith 1963: 473–74). The banning of cow-slaughter was also a matter in which Nehru failed to act according to his convictions (Gopal, 'Nehru and secularism': 25). Legislation imposing a total ban on cow slaughter was enacted in Uttar Pradesh, Bihar, Madhya Pradesh and Rajasthan. All of these governments were controlled by the Congress party.

Given the established tradition of using religion as a lever to influence the course of politics, it was not unusual for political parties to collaborate with communal organizations for short-term electoral gains. Opposition parties, too, were often compelled in the sheer interests of survival to fall back on expediency and forge unprincipled alliances. Nehru was sickened and expressed his anguish in no uncertain terms.

III

> Over the years we have been moving towards a society which will soon be ruled by communal bigots.
>
> Udayan Sharma, in *Sunday,* 22–28 June 1986

A wounded India with festering communal sores is limping towards the twenty-first century ... India, today, certainly cannot boast of a heritage and a past which has succeeded in checking the growth of communalism.
Seema Mustafa, in *Sunday,* 28 December 1986–3 January 1987

An all-devouring communal fire is raging across the country, threatening the very existence of a multi-religious, multi-cultural and multi-lingual society.
Kuldeep Kumar, in *Sunday,* 21–27 June 1987

These are not sensational newspaper headlines but serious reflections on India's secular experiment over the last four decades. They portray a picture of Indian society which is both realistic and alarming. Their assessment deserves consideration. There can be no doubt that the last phase of the government of Indira Gandhi witnessed an unprecedented intensification of religious fervor and religiosity, an exacerbation of sectarian feuds, and an increased polarization of Indian society not along class lines, as Nehru had envisaged, but on purely communal grounds.

Equally significant was the rapid growth of Hindu communal organizations with militant overtones. The Vishwa Hindu Parishad and the Virat Hindu Sammelan, were the apex of several right-wing organizations. They vied with each other to emerge as the greatest champion of Hindu communal causes and led aggressive campaigns. These developments suggest that the secular consensus, an imprimatur of the Nehru era, was all but set aside by the new dominant Congress leadership, eager to accommodate Hindu revivalist and obscurantist tendencies in order to isolate and deflect the emergence of alternative political forces surfacing in different parts of the country.

The widely shared Muslim perception has been of a virtual breakdown of the secular consensus embodied in the model of integration worked out by Nehru. Cracks began to appear soon after India's victory over Pakistan in the Bangladesh war, where Indira Gandhi was convinced that she would have to cultivate a Hindu image to strike deep roots in the Indian polity. She went on conspicuous visits to various temples, swiftly banned the use of beef tallow as soon as a ghee-adulteration scandal broke out, adopted Hindu rituals and symbols in state affairs, was lenient towards Hindu revivalism which expressed itself most spectacularly in cross-country marches to 'Save Hinduism', and almost uncharacteristically asserted the 'rights of the majority'. All this was a reversal of the secular traditions that Nehru had tried to establish. 'Far from challenging such revivalism', wrote one of her admirers, Indira Gandhi 'decided to ride it as far as it would take her. And so, there was not even the minor consolation of words of sympathy from Indira Gandhi after Moradabad saw in 1981 one of the worst instances of violence against Muslims in independent India'.[10]

What most angered Muslims is not so much the fact that state patronage of religious fervour had encouraged the fringe of Hindu extremism, but that a long, systematic neglect of their interests had contributed to their economic decline (Faridi 1965). The view that the economic weakness of the Muslims must be seen in the context of the society as a whole, where development is slow, wages are low and unemployment is on the rise, carries no conviction with most Muslim activist groups who argue that opportunities for economic advancement are specifically blocked for their community which has borne the consequences of official neglect and discrimination. In the case of scheduled castes and tribes there are compensatory programmes; there are none for the Muslims. Yet, other categories in north India, such as the Kurmis, Yadavs and Gujars, have been economically weak and have not had access to compensatory programmes. They have, however, in some measure sought to neutralize their weakness through mobilization in the political domain, using their numbers and voting strength to secure attention. To be sure, such mobilization, when it seeks politically allocated resources by way of job quotas and so on, has generated violent controversy in Bihar and elsewhere; but the magnitude of this controversy is small compared to the consequences that await Muslims when they seek to assert themselves, politically or otherwise.

It is possible to debate the causes of the economic decline of the Muslims, but there is no denying that they have been on the lowest rung of the ladder in terms of the basic categories of socio-economic indicators of development (Khan 1978: 1514–15). In modern industry and trade, except for isolated instances, they have not owned large-scale industry or business. As late as the 1980s, there was not a single Muslim house among the fifty industrial groups, while at the lower end of the scale most Muslims are poor and backward (Sanghvi 1984: 28).[11]

When it comes to employment, Muslims present a grim picture of their under-representation, and complain that they have been reduced to being 'the hewers of wood and the drawers of water' (Ansar Harvani quoted in Ahmad n.d.: 25), but the causes of their under-recruitment are still a subject of much dispute. Muslims settle for discrimination as a convenient explanation, though much of the problem in Uttar Pradesh and Bihar is the consequence of the depletion of the Muslim middle classes in the aftermath of partition and the abolition of Urdu as a language of administration and education, which affected the very section of the middle classes that sought employment at the clerical level, in lower government service or in educational institutions. Widespread abandonment of Urdu has also made it difficult for a great many Muslim candidates who have Urdu as their mother tongue to take competitive examinations for government posts. This accounts for the fact that very few Muslims take the examinations at all; another reason, of course, is a constant fear of discrimination if they do take them. The promotion of Urdu, which has been a victim of communal bigotry and linguistic jealousy, is thus not only central to the cultural identity of the Urdu-speaking Muslims but is equally crucial for their material advancement.

The plight of the Muslims is compounded by the fact that nearly all the major communal riots during the last few decades have occurred in towns where they have attained a measure of economic success through their traditional artisanal and entre-preneurial skills: Aligarh, Moradabad, Bhiwandi, Meerut, and of course, Ahmedabad. 'Hindus tend to raise their eyebrows at the assertion of an equal status by a community which they have been used to look down upon as their inferiors in the post-independence era', concludes a report on the Delhi riots of May 1987.[12] 'Economic resurgence' is often ascribed to Islamic fundamentalism and to a new sense of confidence among Muslims, now that their co-religionists in the Gulf have acquired wealth and consider-able global influence. The connection is at best tenuous, though the Hindu petty bour-geoisie has not hesitated to use this argument in order to whip up communal sentiments against the Muslims. The motive is to displace the emerging Muslim entre-preneurial class in certain crucial areas of trade and business and to reduce the possi-bility of keen competition.

Communal riots were not uncommon during the Nehru era, but they were sporadic, localized and easily controllable. This has not been the case in last few decades. The apathy, negligence and complicity of local officials has also grown over the years; wherever public authority is compliant to anti-Muslim forces, the administration has offered weak or inadequate protection to the Muslims.

IV

The articulation of minority interests is often constrained, even in a democracy, as is illustrated by the case of India's Muslims whose identification with the Muslim League movement in the pre-independence period has inhibited them from voicing their grievances in a sustained and organized manner. The formation of the All India Muslim Convention and the Majli-i Mushawarat were bold initiatives, but the strategy of working through the electoral process backfired. The bitter controversy over Urdu, faced by the non-Congress governmental coalitions in Uttar Pradesh and Bihar after 1967, reinforced the proposition that parties identified with minority causes risked alienating many of their constituents. Indira Gandhi was quick to learn this lesson when she talked of a 'Hindu backlash' against any further 'pampering' of the minorities.

Though Parliament and the state legislatures have remained important forums, the part played by Muslim legislators has not been seen in a favourable light by most Muslims. Muslim legislators, though often elected from Muslim-populated constituencies and sponsored as minority representatives, have eschewed the more public forms of protest and rebuffed petitions for help on minority causes. This is because the electoral processes sometimes work in favour of Muslims who are inclined to be docile and reluctant to raise embarrassing issues lest they are denied nomination at the next election (Wright 1966: Chapter 5). The result is that sponsored mobility has improved the political fortunes of a few chosen legislators without advancing the interests of their constituents. 'Hence, when scholars or publicists prepare impressive lists of the Muslim candidates elected over a number of years, they may contribute to group pride, but they signify no more than a Pyrrhic victory' (Schermerhorn 1978: 177–78).

Some formal and informal channels of articulation existed during the first two decades after independence because of Nehru's close links with certain sections of the Muslim leadership and his personal commitment to providing equal opportunities to the minorities and ending discrimination against them. 'All of us', he wrote sadly, 'seem to be getting infested with the refugee mentality or, worse still, the RSS mentality. That is a curious finale to our careers'.[13] Though Nehru's exhortations went unheeded and the grievances of the minorities remained unredressed, Muslims continued to repose their confidence in his leadership and recognized the Congress as the main vehicle of their aspirations.

After Nehru, Congress-Muslim relations were greatly strained, and the links that India's first Prime Minister had established with the minorities were either weakened or altogether severed. Having supported Indira Gandhi in her early years of political dominance, Muslims slowly but steadily drifted away from her. Emergency and the accompanying excesses proved the last straw. Theodore Wright has argued that the 'incongruous coalition of traditionalists, secularists and repentant former Muslim League modernists' who had supported Congress in previous elections was broken up by four features of the emergency: forced sterilization, slum removal, police firing on Muslims, and the suspension of civil liberties, which included the banning of Muslim organizations such as the Jamaat-i Islami (Wright 1977: 1207–20).

V

The gradual weakening of the Congress base amongst Muslims made it possible for the communally-oriented Muslim groups to occupy the political vacuum, while frequent riots and unending discriminatory practices against Muslims lent legitimacy to their activities. This is a familiar pattern. In the 1940s the phenomenal success of the Muslim League and its allies was, in some measure, linked to the fact of Muslim alienation from the Congress after the 1942 Quit India movement. Capitalizing on the 'wrongs' done by the Congress Ministries of 1937–39, the League propaganda machine was able to persuade splinter Muslim groups to join its bandwagon. Nearly three decades later, Muslim organizations of different shades of opinion were able to broaden their base of support by dwelling on the Congress failure to stem the communal tide and its inability to assuage the fears of the minorities.

It is hard to delineate the main contours of Muslim conservatism, though its basic aim has remained unchanged since the advent of British rule in India: the preservation of cultural and religious identity within the defined Islamic framework. Its more tangible manifestation has been in its resistance to modern education, its opposition to the composite and syncretic trends in Indian Islam, and its tendency to thwart reformist initiatives. Muslim organizations and institutions conducted successful mobilization campaigns around these issues and were thus able to insulate the community from the process of social change and modernization, and to resist the secularizing tendencies generated during and after colonial rule. This was a phenomenon unique to Indian Islam, for reformist ideas and movements were not inconsequential in Muslim countries such as Egypt, Turkey and Iran.

Conservative reaction after independence had been most pronounced in opposing the demand for a uniform civil code – an issue which united the three principal organizations in India which were otherwise opposed to each other on fundamental doctrinal matters: the Tablighi Jamaat, the Jamaat-i Islami, and the Jamiyat al-ulema. The Jamaat-i Islami, which takes the most militant position on the issue of change in the Personal Law, argues that even a ban on polygamy cannot be accepted, because Muslims are sure it will be only 'the first step in the direction of erasing every symbol of a separate Muslim culture in India' (quoted in Brass 1974: 220). The Jamiyat al-ulema agrees, though its criticism is reinforced by the argument that any attempt to alter the Personal Law would be an infringement of the 'covenant' of composite nationalism which binds Muslims to India and its Hindu countrymen (Qasmi n.d.). This was echoed at a convention organized in December 1974, and is repeated at every annual session of the Jamiyat.[14] Ziya-ul-Hasan states the position of the Jamiyat by arguing that the demand for a uniform civil code is tantamount to a fundamental departure from the position that in the present day Indian situation where the Muslim community is deeply entangled in a struggle for the search and safeguard of its *self-identity*, it is only the Personal Law that can be a permanent guarantee for its preservation (Faruqi 1983: 23).

Following the December 1974 Convention, an All India Muslim Personal Law Board was set up as a watchdog body to monitor and actively resist any changes that might be brought about in the *Sharia*. Just over a decade later the same Board spearheaded a campaign which signified a massive fundamentalist upsurge, unprecedented in post-Independence India. The immediate provocation was provided by a Supreme Court judgment on 23 April 1985 which seemed to criticize Islamic law and Koranic concepts, in granting maintenance rights to a seventy-three-year old Muslim woman, Shah Bano, who was divorced by her husband after forty-three years of marriage. Muslims everywhere considered this judgment as an assault on the *Sharia* which, in their opinion, makes no such provision in the event of a divorce, and as 'the thin end of the wedge for securing the extinction of the Muslim personal law and its substitution by a common civil code'.[15]

The Rajiv Gandhi government capitulated to the strident clamourings of some Muslims by introducing the retrograde Muslim Women (Protection of Rights on Divorce) Bill in May 1986.[16] It was done in order to stem the rising tide of anger over the Shah Bano verdict which was losing the party its Muslim votes. The electoral defeats of the Congress after the momentous Supreme Court judgment were sharp reminders of this. 'All one can say at present', declared an angry Danial Latifi, a Supreme Court lawyer and an activist in the *Committee for the Protection of Muslim Women*,

> is that some Machiavelli seems to have masterminded this entire operation. That master-mind is not a friend of Islam, of the Muslims or of the Muslim women. Still less is he a friend of the Republic of India. The act that preceded the Bill, of recognition of the so-called Muslim Personal Law Board as a college of cardinals for the Indian Muslims, is not only against Islam but is also the most flagrant exercise of power-drunk autocracy since Caligula installed "Incitatus", his favourite horse, as Governor of Rome. The Muslim intelligentsia who have opposed this act will continue their struggle against this illegitimate papacy.[17]

It is noteworthy that the 'victory' tasted over the Shah Bano issue encouraged Muslim reaction in several different ways. In early January 1987, the volatile Syed Shahabuddin, editor of *Muslim India* and a member of parliament, gave a call to the Muslims to stay away from the Republic Day celebrations on 26 January. 'Come what may', he announced, 'we shall stick to our resolve to stay away from official celebrations of the Republic Day because it is a legal, ethical means to express our agony over the conversion of a historical monument'.[18] This was followed by a call for an all-India strike (*bandh*) on 1 February 1987, the first anniversary of the day when, by an order of the district magistrate, the gates of the Baburi mosque or the Ram Janam Bhoomi in Ayodhya were thrown open for Hindus to offer worship in the mosque's inner sanctum. The same forces which had exerted pressure on Rajiv Gandhi to undo the 'wrong' done by the Supreme Court judgment were in the forefront of attempts to incite communal frenzy amongst Muslims. This was not all. Violence over the Baburi mosque episode, somewhat reminiscent of the 1913 Kanpur mosque agitation, spread to several towns of Uttar Pradesh and Bihar, culminating in a massive congregation of over 300,000 Muslims in Delhi demanding justice and an end to discrimination against their community.

Such stirrings in the Muslim community, perhaps related to fundamentalist movements in the Islamic world and encouraged through an ideological indoctrination (Agwani 1986), symbolize its alienation from the wider democratic and secular processes in the country. The Indian people must wake up to the danger of allowing this alienation to grow. It may be that Jawaharlal Nehru's secular model and the strategy of multi-national integration may still be the answer to India's present communal impasse.

Notes

1 This is an abridged version of the article that appeared in *Third World Quarterly*, April 1988.
2 6 January 1962, typescript, *M C Chagla Papers*, Nehru Memorial and Museum Library.
3 A cynical view is that 'the vote for the Congress had been the protection money Muslims paid in return for the promise of security' (Akbar 1985: 312).
4 Some of these issues were discussed at the All-India Muslim Convention held in Delhi on 10–11 June 1961 and formed part of the resolutions adopted (*Hindustan Times,* 12 June 1961).
5 '[T]he country is far from secular. In fact to impose secularism on a country so balkanized was as likely to prove successful as making an omelette out of hard-boiled eggs' (Baig 1970: 13).
6 *Akhand Bharat or Akhand Pakistan?* Exchange of Population Conference, New Delhi, 28–29 March 1964.
7 *Economic and Political Weekly*, Annual Number, February 1962; and editorial comment in *Hindustan Times,* 3 June 1961.
8 Notice the warning of a veteran Congressmen that 'the Congress authorities should not tolerate the presence in its ranks of people who neither believe in socialism nor in a secular democracy' (Kripalani n.d.: 42).
9 *Economic and Political Weekly,* 5 November 1966.
10 ibid., p. 198.
11 There are only four units owned by Muslim industrialists, in a group of 2,832 industrial houses owned by large corporate units, each with sales of Rs 50 million and above (*Muslim India*, February 1985, p. 82).
12 *Walled City Riots: A Report on the Police and Communal Violence in Delhi, 19–24 May 1987* (1987), p. 1.
13 To Mohanlal Saxena, 10 September 1949, cited in Gopal 'Nehru and secularism', p. 15. For communalism in the Congress, see Smith (1963: 480–81).
14 See presidential address by Maulana Syed Asad Madani, Jamiyat al-ulema session held at Bombay from 14 to 16 January 1983, p. 16; also Nadwi (1969: 209), for opposition to 'change' and 'reform.
15 *Muslim India*, May 1985, p. 195.
16 Significant provisions of the bill introduced in Parliament included:

   ■ Where a Muslim divorced woman is unable to maintain herself after the period of *iddat*, the magistrate, when approached, may make an order for the payment of maintenance by her relatives who would be entitled to inherit her property on her death according to Muslim law in the proportions in which they would inherit her property.

   ■ If any one of such relatives is unable to pay his or her share on the ground of his or her not having the means to pay, the magistrate would direct the other relatives who have sufficient means to pay the shares of these relatives also.

   ■ But where a divorced woman has no relatives or such relatives or any one of them has not enough means to pay the maintenance or the other relatives who have been asked to pay the shares of the defaulting relatives, the magistrate would order the State Wakf Board to pay the maintenance ordered by him or the shares of the relatives who are unable to pay.

17 *Sunday*, 8–14 June 1986.
18 ibid., 25–31 January 1987.

References

Agwani, M. S. (1986) *Islamic Fundamentalism in India*, Chandigarh: Twenty-First Century India Society.
Ahmad, Imtiaz (1967) 'Indian muslims and electoral politics', *Economic and Political Weekly*, 11 March.
—— (1974) 'The muslim electorate and election alternatives in UP', *Religion and Society*, June, 21(2).
—— (n.d.) 'Secular state, communal society', *Communalism: The Razor's Edge*, Bombay: Factsheet Collective.

Ahmad, Mir Mushtaq 'Role of Indian muslims', *Mir Mushtaq Ahmad Papers*, New Delhi: Nehru Memorial and Museum Library.

Ahmed, Bashiruddin (1965) 'Congress defeat in Amroha: a case study in one party dominance', *Economic and Political Weekly*, 22 May.

—— (1967) 'Uttar Pradesh', *Seminar*, July, 95.

Akbar, M. J. (1985) *India: The Siege Within*, London: Penguin.

Alam, Javed (1983) 'Dialectics of capitalist transformations and national crystallization', *Economic and Political Weekly,* January.

Ayyub, Abu Sayeed (1965) 'A long-term solution', *Seminar*, March, 67.

Baig, M. R. A. (1970) 'Enlightened communalism', *Seminar*, January, 125.

Blair, Harry W. (1973) 'Minority electoral politics in a north Indian state: aggregate data analysis and the muslim community in Bihar, 1952–72', *The American Political Science Review,* December, 68(4).

Brass, Paul R. (1974) *Language, Religion and Politics in North India,* Cambridge: Cambridge University Press.

—— (1985) *Caste, Faction and Party in Indian Politics,* vol. 2, Delhi: Chanakya.

Chowdhury, Neerja (1986) 'Growing assertiveness', *Statesman,* 19 April.

Engineer, A. A. (1983) 'Socio-Economic basis of Communalism', *Mainstream*, July, 21(45): 15–18.

—— (ed.) (1984) *Communal Riots in Post-independence India*, Hyderabad: Sangam.

Faridi, S. N. (1965) *Economic Welfare of Indian Moslems*, Agra: Ram Prasad.

Faruqi, Ziya-ul-Hasan (1966) 'Indian Muslims and the ideology of the secular state', in D. E. Smith (ed.) *South Asian Politics and Religion*, Princeton, NJ: Princeton University Press.

—— (1983) 'Orthodoxy and heterodoxy', *Seminar*, April, 284.

Gopal, Sarvepalli 'Nehru and secularism', *Occasional Papers on History and Society*, 62, New Delhi: Nehru Memorial and Museum Library.

—— (1979) *Jawaharlal Nehru: A Biography*, vol. 2, Delhi: Oxford University Press.

Gupta, Sisir K. (1962) 'Moslems in Indian politics, 1947–60', *India Quarterly*, October–December, 28(4).

Haq, Mushirul (1972) *Islam in Secular India*, Simla: Indian Institute of Advanced Study.

Khan, Muneer Ahmad (1965) 'Majlis-e-Ittehadul Muslimeen: a case study in Muslim politics', unpublished PhD thesis, Osmania University, Hyderabad.

Khan, Rasheeduddin (1968) 'Modernization', *Seminar*, June, 106.

—— (1971) 'Muslim leadership and electoral politics in Hyderabad: a pattern of minority articulation', *Economic and Political Weekly*, 10–17 April, 6(15–16).

—— (1978) 'Minority segments in Indian polity: muslim situation and plight of urdu', *Economic and Political Weekly* (Bombay), 2 September.

Kripalani, J. B. (n.d.) *Minorities in India*, Calcutta: Vigil Office.

Krishna, Gopal (1967) 'Electoral participation and political integration', *Economic and Political Weekly,* annual number, February.

—— (1972) 'Muslim politics', *Seminar*, May, 153.

—— (1986) 'Problems of integration in the Indian political community: muslims and the political process', in Dilip K. Basu and Richard Sisson (eds) *Social and Economic Development in India*, Delhi: Sage.

Madhok, Balraj (1946) *Hindustan on the Crossroads*, Lahore: Mehta Brothers.

—— (1970) *Indianization*, Delhi: S. Chand.

Mayer, Peter B. (1981) 'Tombs and dark houses: ideology, intellectuals, and proletarians in the study of contemporary Islam', *Journal of Asian Studies*, May, 40(3).

Nadwi, Maulana Abul Hasan Ali (1969) *Western Civilization: Islam and Muslims*, Lucknow: Academy of Islamic Research & Publications.

Qasmi, Maulana Asrurul Haque (n.d.) *The Community in Retrospect*, Delhi.

Quraishi, Zaheer Masood (1968) 'Electoral strategy of a minority pressure group: the muslim Majlis-e-Mushawarat', *Asian Survey*, 8(12).

Saberwal, Satish and Hasan, Mushirul (1984) 'Moradabad riots: causes and meanings', in A. A. Engineer (ed.) *Communal Riots in Post-independence India*, Hyderabad: Sangam.

Sanghvi, Vir (1984) 'Coming to terms with the hindu backlash', *Imprint,* July.

Saxena, N. C. (1983) 'Public employment and educational backwardness among muslims in India', *Political Science Review*, April-September, 23(2–3).

Schermerhorn, R. A (1978) *Ethnic Plurality in India,* Tucson: University of Arizona Press.

Shah, Ghanshyam (1975) *Caste Association and Political Process in Gujarat*, Bombay: Popular Prakashan.

—— (1984) 'The 1969 communal riots in Ahmedabad: a case study', in A. A. Engineer (ed.) *Communal Riots in Post-Independence India*, Hyderabad: Sangam.

Siddiqi, Mohammad Mazhar-ud-din (1952) *After Secularism What?* Rampur: maktaba-e-Jamaat-I Islamia Hind.

Smith, D. E. (1963) *India as a Secular State*, Princeton, NJ: Princeton University Press.

Spear, Percival (1967) 'The position of the muslims, before and after partition', in Philip Mason (ed.) *India and Ceylon: Unity and Diversity*, London: Oxford University Press.

Tyabji, Badruddin (1971) *The Self in Secularism*, Delhi: Orient Longman.

Walled City Riots: A Report on the Police and Communal Violence in Delhi, 19–24 May 1987 (1987), Delhi.

Weiner, Myron (1984) *India at the Polls 1980: A Study of the Parliamentary Elections*, Delhi: Munshiram Manoharlal.

Wright, Jr., Theodore P. (1966) 'The effectiveness of muslim representation in India', in D. E. Smith (ed.) *South Asian Politics and Religion*, Princeton, NJ: Princeton University Press.

—— (1977) 'Muslims and the 1977 Indian elections: a watershed?', *Asian Survey*, December, 17 (2): 1207–20.

—— (1979) 'Inadvertent modernization of Indian muslims by revivalists', *Journal Institute of Muslim Minority Affairs*, summer.

10 Sikh fundamentalism

Translating history into theory[1]

Harjot Oberoi

Fundamentalism among the Sikhs today is primarily a movement of resistance. While Sikh fundamentalists certainly envision a separate nation-state in the Indian sub-continent, in the last decade much of their energies have been spent in assailing and battling the Indian state. Denied political authority and engaged in constant struggle for survival and legitimacy, Sikh fundamentalists have not succeeded in articulating their vision of the world in any great detail. This lack of an elaborate model, say on the lines of Iranian clerics, of what the world should look like is closely tied to the social origins of Sikh activists. A great majority of them come from the countryside and would be classified as peasants by social anthropologists: Historically, peasants have not been known to come up with grand paradigms of social transformation. Peasant societies are by definition made up of little communities, and their cosmos is invariably parochial rather than universal. To speak of Sikh fundamentalism and its impact is to enter a universe that until recently was largely characterized by marginality, incoherence, and disorder.

In the present context any efforts to grapple with the raw and embryonic universe of Sikh fundamentalism will be considerably shaped by how we define and deploy the term fundamentalism. I use the term not out of any ethnocentrism or lack of understanding of the historical specificities that made it current in the United States at the turn of the century.[2] The current debate surrounding the term fundamentalism is hardly unique in the conceptual history of social sciences. In the past there have been similar discussions regarding the cross-cultural applicability of terms like feudalism, millenarianism, religion, class, state, madness, and so on. Interestingly, the arguments proffered in defense or rejections have not been dissimilar to the recent intellectual exchanges surrounding the term fundamentalism. Those keen on defending these terms have often argued that there was little scope for cross-cultural comparisons if they did not possess a common pool of conceptual vocabulary. Others opposed to the enterprise retorted that the history of the world should not be inscribed in terms of the Euro-American experience alone, for in doing so one would further enhance the hegemony of Euro-American intellectual discourse.

With this background to the contested nature of our conceptual vocabulary, and keenly aware of how loaded and tainted the term fundamentalism can be, I would like to defend my usage of the term Sikh fundamentalism on three grounds. First, in the Punjabi word *mulvad*, Sikhs possess a term that exactly corresponds to fundamentalism and stands in stark opposition to *adharma*, a Punjabi word for secularism. Although the term *mulvad* is of recent coinage, resulting from the need to have a Punjabi counterpart to fundamentalism, Sikh journalists, essayists, and politicians, in discussing contemporary religious and political movements, now constantly use the term *mulvad*, connoting a polity and society organized on the basis of religious (particularly scriptural) authority (for instance, see Azad 1988). Thus, in the Sikh case the commonly voiced objection, that non-Christian religious groups to which the term fundamentalism is applied have no such equivalent in their own lexicon, does not fully hold.

Second, there are strong cultural reasons for adopting the term 'Sikh fundamentalism.' Much like Protestant church groups in the United States that at the turn of the century insisted on the inerrancy of the Bible and opposed liberal theology, Sikh fundamentalists have no patience for hermeneutic or critical readings of Sikh scriptures. Their scriptural absolutism precludes any secular or rational interpretation of what they consider to be a revealed text. K. S. Mann, a secretary of the Institute of Sikh studies in Chandigarh, notes: 'Nobody who has any regard for feelings of the Sikhs, should take liberties to indulge in exercises with the Guru Granth Sahib [the Sikh scripture], literary or otherwise' (1989: 57). Similarly, a recent book written by a group of Sikh civil servants questions the use of Western historiography and textual analysis for the study of Sikh history and sacred texts (see Gurdev Singh 1986, especially pp. 3– 11).[3] It is their firm belief that only those scholars who can strengthen the faith and espouse its 'fundamentals' should study Sikhism. Daljeet Singh, a Sikh writer who for many years has opposed the study of Sikh religion and history within the academy, protests: 'From the point of views the men of religion, such studies would be limited in their scope, partial in their vision and inadequate as a study of man in the totality of his being and functioning, i.e., his spiritual and empirical life' (1989: 21).

Critical scholarship among the Sikhs is under attack, and those who dare to practice it are under constant pressure to relent or face elimination. On 22 February 1984 Summet Singh, the thirty-one-year-old editor of Punjab's oldest literary journal *Preet-Larhi*, was gunned down outside Amritsar. His main fault was his independent-minded interpretation of Sikh theology and tradition. More recent targets have been university professors, poets, artists, and journalists. Theoretically, the Sikh community should be guided divinely in all matters and this divine direction is seen to come from the Sikh scripture, which is perceived as normative for all time and in all place. A critical textual analysis of the Sikh scriptures that may introduce an element of historicity and plurality of interpretations, thus undermining scripturalism, would certainly be construed as an affront – one that would bring quick retribution. Jarnail Singh Bhindranwale (1947–84), a key figure in the rise of Sikh fundamentalism, repeatedly reminded his audience that they should not tolerate any form of insult toward the Sikh scriptures and that, where required, Sikhs were morally obliged to kill an individual who dared to show disrespect toward the holy book.

Third, the current Sikh movement, as will become apparent in this chapter, amply manifests many tendencies like millenarianism, a prophetic vision, puritanism, and antipluralism, trends that have been commonly associated with fundamentalism.[4] For these three reasons – linguistic, cultural, and associative – I think we are justified in speaking and thinking in terms of Sikh fundamentalism.

Having said this, I must stress that in Foucault's terms there is no archaeology to Sikh fundamentalism. It is an episteme that is still in the making, and its canon, ideology, objectives, and practices are being gradually defined. In this sense, for all those who are interested in fundamentalism, the Sikh case is of particular value, for here we can clearly see how a group of fundamentalists invent and reproduce themselves in the late twentieth century. Given its relatively recent origins, the success of

Sikh fundamentalism has been staggering. In less than a decade Sikh fundamentalism not only established a multitude of relationships with ethnicity, political economy and nationalism but also eventually came to encompass these materially and conceptually varied conditions. To speak of Sikh fundamentalism is therefore to address simultaneously issues of Sikh identity, the crisis of agrarian development, class antagonisms, and the process of state formation in India, including popular resistance to this process. All this can be phrased in another way: When today large segments of the Sikh population consider who they are, how to live and die, and how to construct the universe they live in, the answers flow out of what may be termed the discourse and ideology of fundamentalism. Why is this discourse so attractive and powerful? What does this cultural innovation promise? I grapple with these issues in this chapter.

The background

Despite the powerful normative notion of a Sikh collectivity, popularly known in the Punjabi language by the term *panth*, Sikhs are not a monolithic religious community. Much like other religious communities, the Sikhs are divided by geography, ethnicity, social hierarchy, sects, ritual practices, and individual preferences. Consequently, when it comes to political participation, Sikhs have never been represented by a single political party. They have always opted for a wide variety of political platforms, ranging from archconservative to ultraradical.

The first explicitly Sikh political party – the Central Sikh League – was formally established in Amritsar in December 1919. Before the end of the following year the Sikhs had founded two new organizations: the Shiromani Gurdwara Parbandhak Committee (henceforth SGPC) and the Shiromani Akali Dal (henceforth Akali Dal). While the former was technically only supposed to administer major Sikh shrines, it soon turned into an arena within which to wage political battles and to garner social prestige and patronage. Its offshoot, the Akali Dal, initially formed as a body to coordinate Sikh religious volunteers, gradually matured as a political party. By actively participating in the anticolonial nationalist struggle, the Akali Dal gained pan-India recognition. Mahatma Gandhi, impressed by the nonviolent agitation of the Akalis, congratulated them for winning the first decisive battle in India's struggle for freedom (Ganda Singh 1965: 11). Although the growing political influence of the Akalis was often challenged by the Central Sikh League, several breakaway groups, and newly founded Sikh political parties, by the 1940s the Akalis had succeeded in establishing their hegemony among Sikhs. Master Tara Singh (1885–1967), an Akali Dal leader, emerged as the chief spokesman of the Sikhs and formulated Sikh positions on a variety of issues like India's participation in World War II, the demand of the Muslim League for a separate state of Pakistan, and the constitutional parleys when the British decided to pull out of India. When in 1947 the colonial government decided to partition the subcontinent, the Akalis aligned themselves with the Indian National Congress. Thus emerged East Punjab, an entity that was to crystallize into the postcolonial province of Punjab.

In the euphoria of independence many Akalis decided that their party had outlived its historic usefulness and that it should merge with the Congress, India's national party. However, the merger did not secure every Akali Dal member a place in the sun. The Congress had to take care of its own constituency and could not provide the Akalis with all that they aspired to in terms of policies and political power.

Disappointed, many Akali Dal leaders, never shy of hyperbole, incessantly inquired: 'The Hindus got Hindustan [out of independence], the Muslims got Pakistan [out of partition], what did the Sikhs get [out of independence or the partition]?'[5]

One dominant response was the call to set up a 'Punjabi Suba,' a state within the Indian republic where the Punjabi-speaking Sikh population would be a majority. The story of how the Punjabi Suba was finally attained in 1966 despite massive opposition is too well known to be repeated here.[6]

What must be noted is that the establishment of the Punjabi Suba completely transformed the religious demography of the Punjab. Overnight, due to a redistribution of territories, the Sikhs turned from a minority into a majority in the Punjab. In the older, larger Punjab from 1947 to 1966, compared to a 63.7 percent Hindu majority the Sikhs constituted only 33.3 percent of the population. The new state of Punjab reversed the older equations. Now, the Hindus, with 44 percent of the population, became a minority and the Sikhs a majority with 54 percent of the population of the new state. The Akalis never had it so good. With such a large Sikh electoral base, Akali strategists thought political power was going to be theirs for the asking. After all, they had been the 'natural political party of the Sikhs since the 1920s. In their reading they had always tried to secure the interests of the panth; now it was time for the panth to reward them. Master Tara Singh's oft-repeated claim that 'Sikhs were either rulers or rebels' now seemed to have a ring of truth to it. The Sikhs were going to crown the Akalis as the rulers of the new Punjab.

Unfortunately for the Akali Dal, realpolitik proved to be different from the theory of politics. The Congress party, which had governed the Punjab since independence, was not about to let the Akalis walk away with the province. Punjab was too close to the national capital, New Delhi, and invariably what happened in the province had an impact on the neighboring states of Haryana, Himachal Pradesh, and Rajasthan. From 1967 to 1990, a total of 23 years, an Akali-led government ruled the province roughly for one-third of the time (approximately eight years and two months). For the other 15 years the Punjab was either ruled directly by the Congress or put under president's rule. This in practice amounted to unfettered governance by the Congress, since it was the federal ruling party, and it decided on all the policies and key administrative appointments in the province.

Clearly, for some Sikhs the Akalis had badly failed in translating the Sikh demography of Punjab into a permanent political power for Sikhs. In their eyes the democratic option had only further weakened Sikhs, by making them susceptible to factionalism, political manipulation, and extended rule by the Congress. A further complaint was that even when an Akali government ruled the Punjab, it failed to advance Sikh religious interests, because the Akalis almost always had alliances with other political parties, particularly the Jana Sangh, an overtly Hindu political party. A position of compromise and consensus among the Akalis was for some a sure sign of political failure. Disillusioned and angered, some Sikhs were ready to teach the Akalis a few political lessons. After all, the Sikhs had a kingdom of their own in the early nineteenth century and this historical acumen could be once again put to use. The first sign of this came in April 1978, when a group of young Sikh men assembled in Chandigarh and founded the Dal Khalsa.

The founders of the Dal Khalsa justified the founding of the new body by claiming that the government of India had cleverly duped the Sikhs in the name of secularism, when actually all that had happened since India had attained its independence in 1947 from the British was the further extension of 'Hindu imperialism' and the enslavement of Sikhs.[7] In support of this thesis Dal Khalsa activists pointed to a series of abuses: Sikhs were not allowed to freely practice their religion, the sanctity of their holy places had been often violated, Akali governments in the Punjab were never allowed to last for the period of their constitutional term, and Sikhs were being economically discriminated against by the federal government, particularly in areas of employment and budget allocations.

While the Dal Khalsa came to contest the Akali Dal's power over the Sikhs from a largely political-secular context, another body, the Damdami Taksal, under the leadership of Jarnail Singh Bhindranwale sought to humble the Akalis on religious grounds. There is an almost obvious nexus between the success of Bhindranwale and the rise of Sikh fundamentalism. To account for this success is to explain Sikh fundamentalism. And any explanation of Sikh fundamentalism has to be made up of two ingredients: the crisis in Punjab's political economy and its articulation by the Damdami Taksal.

Political economy and Sikh subjectivity

There is no denying the fact that the nature of the contemporary Sikh polity is closely tied to the social and economic transformations undergone by the province of Punjab over the last three decades. Punjab, one of the smallest states in the Indian union, is primarily an agrarian economy, and almost 80 percent of the Sikh population lives here. In 1988–89 over 48.6 percent of the state domestic product was derived from agriculture and livestock, and the same sector generated employment for 59.1 percent of the total labor force.[8] Following the capitalist path of development, the accelerated growth in the agrarian sector made Punjab the first region in South Asia to experience what is commonly known as the 'Green Revolution'. The social costs of such agrarian innovation have been extremely high, and Punjabi society over the last two decades has become highly polarized.

The benefits of agrarian development have primarily accrued to those sectors of rural society which already possessed substantial resources like land and capital. By successfully harnessing their resources to high-yielding varieties (HYV) of seeds and modern technology, the rich cultivators were able to produce large surpluses and further expand their resources, particularly land, the key economic input in Punjab. In 1970–71, rich cultivators having more than 25 acres of land constituted 5.01 percent of the total peasantry and operated approximately 27 percent of the land. Within a decade their proportion of land use increased to 29.17 percent.[9] In contrast to rich cultivators, small and marginal farmers have fared poorly in the Green Revolution. They are faced with a situation where their small land holdings, ranging from two to five acres, have increasingly become less viable. A recent study of agrarian conditions in Punjab points out that while small farmers were faced with an annual loss of 125 rupees per capita, farmers with land holdings between five and ten acres were earning a profit of 50 rupees per capita, while substantial farmers with 20 acres of land or more were producing a profit of 1,200 rupees per capita.[10] The negative returns have made it hard for the small and marginal farmers to sustain their family farms. Consequently, in recent years a large number of small holdings have disappeared. According to agricultural census data, from 1970–71 to 1980–81 operational holdings in Punjab declined by 25.3 percent (Gill 1988b: 441–42).

Suffering this decline were countless Sikh peasants from the small and marginal sector. As yet it is not clear what exactly has been their fate. In classical models of development those who are dispossessed either join the ranks of the agrarian labor force or turn to jobs in the burgeoning industrial sector. In Punjab there is no such simple transition. The bulk of the small and marginal farmers are from the high-status Jat caste, and even when they find themselves without land to cultivate they are most unwilling to become agricultural laborers. This would imply working in the midst of low-caste Harijans, a clear loss of face for the status-conscious Jats. The other alternative – working in the industrial sector – is equally difficult, for two reasons. First, Punjab does not have the large-scale industries which could absorb the depeasantized Sikh cultivators. Second, even where such jobs exist, particularly in medium- and small-scale industries, the work force is made up of migratory labor from the poorer areas of northern India. Given their already depressed conditions, these nonunionized workers are willing to work for subsistence wages for long hours, a prospect which Sikh peasants stoutly resist.

In entering the final quarter of the twentieth century, the Akali Dal, led almost exclusively by rich kulaks, had no solution for the crisis in Punjab's political economy. Parkash Singh Badal, who for a second time became a chief minister of Punjab in 1978 in an Akali Dal-led government, was one of the wealthiest farmers in the whole of India. Many of his cabinet colleagues came from highly privileged backgrounds. For the most part the Akali Dal leadership had prospered from the Green Revolution, and they were unconcerned about those who had lost out in the process (Narang 1983: 198–99). Ronald Herring is quite correct when, in analyzing the issue of redistributive justice in rural India, he observes: 'How can fundamental structural change be effected through the very institutions that service and reproduce the existing society and reflect the existing distribution of power and privilege' (1983: 2)? However, in all fairness to the Akali Dal, it must be acknowledged that the Akalis are part of the general political malaise in the country. India, a social democracy enamored of socialism, has never jettisoned capitalism. This hybrid model of development has only exacerbated poverty and social unrest. In this context the Akali failure to deal with the social inequities in Punjab was perhaps no greater than, say, that of Congress regimes in other provinces across northern India. But while provincial governments in the rest of the country could more easily gloss over the pervasive socioeconomic problems and their long-term failure to alter the situation, the Akalis had no such luck. They were faced with a rural electorate that had often been mobilized and had a bloody history of radical, religious solutions. The rising tide of inequalities in the Punjab did not easily blend with the dominant ethos of Sikh religious tradition, which demands a just moral economy based on an equitable distribution of wealth and resources. From its inception in the early sixteenth century, Sikh discourse has sought the creation of an egalitarian society where all men, if not all women, would be equal and share the ritual, sacred, profane, and economic resources collectively. The appeal of such teachings was considerable in a society where the organizing ideology gave open recognition to principles of human inequality, expressed in the caste system. Over a period of roughly three centuries the Sikh movement launched an offensive against the theory and practice of the 'Hindu' social structure, particularly its acceptance of the notion that inequality was inherent in the human condition. It set up the institution of the *sangat* (congregation) and *langar* (communal consumption) to combat social distinctions and molded a collectivity called the *panth*. The practitioner of faith had equal access to the holy scripture, and there was no institutional priesthood that could act as the sole custodian of the Sikh holy book. During the eighteenth century, Sikh militants further sought to implement the egalitarian paradigm of Sikhism. The Sikh movement attracted the rural poor, the urban underprivileged, and others who persisted on the margins of Punjabi society. No efforts were spared by the peasant armies of the Sikhs to destroy all modes of authority, all order, and all mechanisms of social control. They succeeded in doing away with a whole range of intermediaries, those who extracted the much-hated land revenues for the state and often acted as instruments of oppression. Large estates were dissolved, and the lands distributed to the peasantry.

Whenever this egalitarian thrust within Sikhism has been ably voiced, it has demonstrated an immense power to mobilize the faithful and led them toward the inversion of the status quo, in order to establish a society free of religious and social inequalities. Such an ideology becomes most attractive in periods of intense social change. During the nineteenth and early twentieth centuries under British colonial rule, there were numerous movements within the Sikh community, like the Kukas, Ghadarites, and Babbar Akalis, which sought to recover the original message of Sikhism and establish a society relatively free of human distinctions. The Sikh past endowed its constituents with a highly developed vocabulary of social justice, and the community had a long experience of social movements that fought for greater social equality.

By the early 1970s there was a serious crisis in Punjab's political economy that polarized class distinctions. The scope of this crisis was further enhanced by the nature of the Indian nation-state in general and the pro-rich policies of the Akali Dal in particular. While the crisis may have been more easily accommodated in the rest of India, the egalitarian impulse within the Sikh tradition was to make the voice of redistributive justice more compelling in Punjab. All those who perceived their lived experience in this sequence began increasingly to search for solutions. Eventually in the late 1970s they were to shape a body – the Damdami Taksal – that was to articulate their aspirations forcefully and, by challenging the status quo, to turn the 1980s into a decade of Sikh fundamentalism.

Much as the history of modern Sikh politics is tied to the Akali Dal, so the tenor of contemporary Sikh fundamentalism is most forcefully represented by the Damdami Taksal. Earlier in their history the Sikhs went the way of orthodoxy, traditionalism, reformation, and nativism, but it is, only with the Damdami Taksal in the late 1970s, almost at the same time as the Islamic revolution in Iran, that a considerable segment of the Sikh population, particularly young males, seized on the powerful discourse of fundamentalism. Given the centrality of Damdami Taksal in forging Sikh fundamentalism, this section examines, first, the history of this organization; second, its worldview, particularly its nexus with a millenarian ideology; and, finally, its social makeup.

For all practical purposes the Taksal comes to the fore early this century under Sant Sunder Singh (1883–1930), a figure of great piety and traditional learning. As if almost to foreclose the rapid socioreligious transformation undergone by the Sikhs during this period of British colonial rule, Sunder Singh like many of his contemporaries set out to purge diversity in Sikh doctrine, ritual, and practice, hoping thereby to engender a uniform religious community. Given his special skills in exegesis, Sunder Singh's strategy to negate differentiation among Sikhs was quite simple: abolish all polysemous interpretations of Sikh scriptures and cultivate a univocal reading of texts, in order to shape a more homogeneous community. Accompanying this strategy was the insistence on a standardized Khalsa code of conduct, or *rahit*. Since many others at this juncture – including the leadership of the influential Singh Sabha and the Akali movement – were engaged in a similar task, the Damdami Taksal under Sunder Singh and his two successors, Sant Kartar Singh (1932–37) and Sant Gurbachan Singh (1902–69), continued to be a minor player in this project to manufacture a monolithic Sikh community.

Eclipsed by history, the Damdami Taksal and its cadres were rescued from potential oblivion by three factors: the political failures of the Akali Dal in post-1966 Punjab, the crisis induced by the Green Revolution in Punjab's political economy, and the millenarian teachings of Sant Jarnail Singh Bhindranwale, the new head of Damdami Taksal. Millenarianism is hardly new to Sikhism. Of all the indigenous religious communities in India, Sikhism possesses the most advanced paradigm of millennial thought and practice. For much of their history, at least since the rise of the Khalsa, Sikhs have opted to deal with major social crises – state oppression, economic upheavals, colonialism, collapse of semiotic categories – by invoking the millenarian paradigm. Central to this entire model has been a prophetic figure of extraordinary charisma with the will to establish an alternative social system in which oppression would cease and people would lead a life of harmony, purity, and good deeds. Bhindranwale was heir to this cultural tradition. Perhaps nothing would have come of it without the Green Revolution and the social processes it unleashed. In hindsight it is possible to see how the Sikh past, an expanding network of communications, mechanized farming, and the Sikh identity became inextricably linked in the Punjab of the 1970s. As the first people to experience the Green Revolution in South Asia, Sikhs were confronted with unprecedented change in economy, lived experience, and social relationships. No one had prepared them to handle so much change in so little time. Failed by established political parties, they turned to a messianic leader and his seminary to make sense of a world they had helped create, but one they no longer fully grasped or controlled.

Bhindranwale turned the complex problems faced by the Sikhs into simple homilies. In his worldview, what I shall call the 'Sikh impasse' resulted from the prevalent religious depravity among the Sikhs and the ever-increasing Hindu domination over the Sikhs. As had happened with earlier social movements within, the community, Bhindranwale sought a resolution to this new Sikh impasse by invoking the millenarian charter. In 1982 he agreed to participate in the *dharma yuddh*, or righteous battle, earlier launched by the Akalis. Unlike the Akalis, who viewed the dharma yuddh as a politically expedient campaign, Bhindranwale characterized it as an epic war where good was pitted against evil and only one side was to be victorious. His participation in the campaign was fired by the cultural logic of Sikh millenarianism.

During the eighteenth century many a Sikh activist had chanted the following quatrain: 'The army of the Guru will sit on the throne of Delhi/Over its head will be carried the umbrella of royalty, and its will shall be done/The Khalsa will rule, their enemies will be vanquished/ Only those that seek refuge will be saved'. In February 1984 Bhindranwale echoed that sentiment when he informed a visiting journalist: 'I do not want to rule. I would like the Sikhs to rule; rule Delhi, rule the world: *Raj karega khalsa, baaqi rahe na koe* [The Khalsa will rule, their enemies will be vanquished]. ... In the next ten years Sikhs will get their liberation. This will definitely happen'.[11] Many similar quotes from the speeches of Bhindranwale underscore his unflinching confidence in divine intervention and strong identification with apocalyptic thinking. How else could he believe that the Sikhs, with less than 2 percent of India's population, would rule Delhi or attain liberation within a decade? His refrain 'This will certainly happen', is a hallmark of messianic leaders. As Yonina Talmon, notes in a review essay on millenarian movements:

> Perhaps the most important thing about millenarism is its *attitude towards time*. It views time as a linear process which leads to a final future. … The transition from the present into the final future is not a gradual process of progressive approximations to the final goal. It is a sudden and revolutionary leap onto a totally different level of existence. … The apocalyptic victory will be won by means of a prodigious and final struggle which will destroy the agents of corruption, purge the sinful world and prepare it for its final redemption. Millenarism is thus basically a merger between an historical and non-historical conception of time. Historical change leads to a cessation of all change (1969: 240).

The Damdami Taksal is rooted in the metahistorical time to which Talmon alludes. According to its own version of history, the organization was founded by a cultural hero during the golden age of the Sikhs, the eighteenth century. Similarly, its new cultural hero, Bhindranwale, anticipated a 'decisive phase', a new redemptive age when the Sikhs were to be dramatically ushered in with the foundation of Khalistan. By casting this new utopia in a religious idiom, Bhindranwale recruited to his ranks a wide variety of people from different economic, cultural, and political backgrounds. But the bulk of his following from 1978 to 1984 was made up of those who were at the bottom of the social ladder. Such a constituency confirms a commonplace in the literature on millenarian movements: in class terms they invariably appeal to the disinherited, the marginalized, and the subordinate. Millennial aspirations are a cultural mode for securing self-respect, social dignity, and economic well-being for all those who lack it, particularly in preindustrial agrarian societies. This too is fully supported by Sikh fundamentalism.

The vision

The utopia that fundamentalists envision is not a secular one. Its identity is to be defined in terms of Sikh religious tradition. The 1986 *Declaration of Khalistan* stipulates: 'The Sikh religion will be the official creed of Khalistan. Further, it will be a paramount duty of the Government to see that Sikhism must flourish unhindered in Khalistan' (Panthic Committee 1987: 390). By proclaiming an official religion for the state of Khalistan, Sikh fundamentalists stand in direct opposition to the present secular constitution of India that guarantees freedom of religious practice. Sikh militants are dismayed by several aspects of that constitution. One is its secular content. Another is its association of Sikhs with Hindus. Article 25, section 2b, states that all public Hindu shrines must be open to all Hindus, irrespective of their caste. The clause includes under the category 'Hindu' all persons professing the Sikh, Jain or Buddhist religions. For Sikh fundamentalists there can be no greater affront than being included among the Hindus. In their view, Sikhism and Hinduism are two diametrically opposed religions; there is no common ground between them. Angered by the insensitivity shown them by the constitution, Sikh leaders in February 1984 took to the streets of major cities in Punjab and publicly defaced copies of the Indian constitution in order protest article 25, section 2b. Behind this act of defiance stretches a long history of the Sikh search for a personal law.

I argue that the vision of Sikh fundamentalists is closely related to the problem of Sikh identity. Secular public culture in their view erodes morality and religion. To counter this threat, Sikh fundamentalists seek to inscribe their religious identity on all possible cultural resources: constitutions, dietary habits, and the environment of the body. The objective of all this is to leave no lacuna in definition. For Sikh fundamentalists it is ambiguity that breeds atheism, immorality, and denial of tradition.

There is a fundamental chasm between the worldview of Sikh fundamentalists and what Habermas has described as the 'project of modernity'. A key element in the 'project of modernity' has been its separation of the domain of politics from the sphere of religion. It was this differentiation across 'cultural value spheres' that Max Weber convincingly used to distinguish modern from premodern polities. This distinction between the political and religious domains is anathema to Sikh fundamentalists. For them religion and politics are inseparable. Indeed, the Sikhs have never known a truly secular movement of dissent. Opposition to political authority and the various institutions of the state has always been articulated in religious terms.[12] Whether dealing with the oppression of the Mughal state in the eighteenth century or the economic exploitation of British colonial rule, the Sikhs have always responded with social movements mediated through religion.

Thus the Sikhs have no language of politics free of religion. The categories of thought, the heroic figures, the symbols, the costumes which have motivated Sikhs to react to the demands of the state or come to grips with ongoing social transformations have been of a purely religious nature. The most important qualification for a political leader among the Sikhs is his understanding of Sikh scriptures and his ability to expound on their meaning. It is no coincidence that Bhindranwale, the most important political leader of the Sikhs in the 1980s, belonged to a seminary which instructed Sikh students in the art of exegesis. Politics among the Sikhs is always explained and internalized by referring to the religious history of the *panth* or by quoting from the writings of the Sikh masters. The vocabulary of political discourse and the goals of society are rooted in perceived Sikh experience. What happens outside that experience is unimportant. It is not from classical models of structural change – the French or the Russian revolution – that inspiration is sought. Nor is there an echo of the Indian struggle for freedom from colonial rule. Rather, political mobilization and the search for justice is solely based on Sikh texts and semantics. In recasting the world, Sikh militants today look to the emergence and consolidation of the Sikh movement for their theory and practice.

But it would be wrong to draw from all this the conclusion that the rise of Sikh fundamentalism was inevitable and a logical result of the Sikh past. Much as it would be oversimplistic to ascribe the rise of Nazism to German tradition, similarly Sikh tradition by itself is no explanation for the formation of Sikh fundamentalism. Fundamentalism is a modern ideology, and while it voraciously appropriates the past, the success of Sikh fundamentalism is to be traced to the massive crisis in contemporary Indian society.

The discourse of Sikh fundamentalism is no longer simply rooted in the material conditions of the Punjab. Although these conditions continue to sustain it, fundamentalism is quickly maturing as an ideology and now offers seemingly attractive solutions for the everyday life of both the weak and the powerful. In relating to contemporary struggles, fundamentalism tackles lasting questions of freedom, responsibility, morality, will, faith, righteousness, and collective discipline. It envisions a state of its own, where it would reign supreme in both the private and the public sphere and remake polity, economy, and society.

Notes

1 This article was originally published in Martin E. Marty and F. Scott Appleby (eds) *Fundamentalisms and the State: Remaking Polities, Economies, and Militance* (Chicago: University of Chicago Press, 1993) and has been abridged by the author.

2 On how the term 'fundamentalism' came to be used in the United States and what it encompasses, see Marsden (1980).

3 In a review, Trilochan Singh (1988) states: 'The Sikhs are very tolerant and liberal in all matters but they are not so insensitive and stupid dunces as to go on remaining silent in the face of such nasty and malevolent attacks on Sikh historical traditions, doctrines and scriptures on the basis of … compulsive skepticism [read critical historical and textual scholarship]'.

4 I first explored the millenarian and prophetic aspects of current Sikh fundamentalism in my article 'Two Poles of Akali Politics' (Oberoi 1983).

5 This puzzle is generally attributed to Master Tara Singh. See *Spokesman*, 1961, 11(27): 10, quoted in B. R.Nayar (1966: 102).

6 For details, see Brass (1974: 277–366); Pettigrew (1980); and Jeffrey (1986: 36–45).

7 I base this statement, and the following observations on Dal Khalsa thinking, on my reading of Satnam Singh's deposition before a Pakistani judge in the case of a hijacking of a plane to Lahore on 29 September 1981. Satnam Singh was a founding member of the Dal Khalsa and also a member of its executive committee. The transcript of his lengthy deposition is reproduced in Dilgeer (1989: 130–96).

8 Figures from *Link*, 10 August 1990; and Gill (1988a: 2167).

9 These figures are based on Gill (1988a: 2168).

10 *Punjab da Kisani Masla* (in Punjabi), 13 March 1984, cited in Gill (1988a: 2167).

11 Interview with M. J. Akbar (1985: 185).

12 For the following observations I am indebted to Lewis (1988).

References

Azad, Kirpal Singh (1988) *Sikh Mulvad Bare* (Regarding Sikh Fundamentalism), Chandigarh.

Brass, Paul (1974) *Language, Religion and Politics in North India*, Cambridge: Cambridge University Press.

Dilgeer, Harjinder Singh (1988) *Khalistan di Tawarikh* (The History of Khalistan), Oslo: Guru Nanak-Institute of Sikh Studies.

—— (1989) *Sikh Hijacker* (in Punjabi), Oslo: Guru Nanak Institute of Sikh Studies.

Gill, Sucha Singh (1988a) 'Contradictions of Punjab model of growth and search for an alternative', *Economic and Political Weekly*, 23.

—— (1988b) 'Development crisis in agriculture and its political implications: an enquiry into the Punjab problem', in Paul Wallace and Surendara Chopra (eds) *Political Dynamics and Crisis in Punjab*. Amritsar: Department of Political Science, Guru Nanak Dev University.

Herring, Ronald J. (1983) *Land to the Tiller: The Political Economy of Agrarian Reform in South Asia*, New Haven: Yale University Press.

Jeffrey, Robin (1986) *What's Happening to India?* London: Macmillan.

Lewis, Bernard (1988) 'Islamic Revolution', *New York Review of Books*, 34: 46–50.

Mann, K. S. (1989) 'Compilation of Punjabi poetry', *Sikh Review*, 37: 57.

Marsden, George M. (1980) *Fundamentalism and American Culture: The Shaping of Twentieth-Century Evangelicalism*, New York: Oxford University Press.

Narang, A. S. (1983) *Storm over for Sutlej: The Akali Politics*, New Delhi: Gitanjali Publishing House.

Nayar, B. R. (1966) *Minority Politics in the Punjab*, Princeton, NJ: Princeton University Press.

Panthic Committee (1987) 'Document of the declaration of Khalistan' (trans. from Punjabi), in Gopal Singh (ed.) *Punjab Today*, New Delhi: Intellectual Publishing House.

Pettigrew, Joyce (1980) 'The growth of Sikh community consciousness, 1947–66', *South Asia*, 3: 42–62.

Singh, Daljeet (1989) 'Issues of Sikh studies', in Jasbir Singh Mann and Harbans Singh Saron (eds), *Advanced Studies in Sikhism*, Irvine, CA: Sikh Community of North America.

Singh, Gurdev (ed.) (1986) *Perspectives on the Sikh Tradition*, Patiala: Siddharth Publications.

Talmon, Yonina (1969) 'Pursuit of the millennium: the relation between religious and social change', in Norman Birnbaum and Gertrud Lenzer (eds) *Sociology and Religion*, Upper Saddle River, NJ: Prentice Hall.

Part V
Modernization

11 Gandhi, Newton, and the Enlightenment

Akeel Bilgrami

I

Salman Rushdie once said, no doubt under duress, that secular humanism was itself a religion, thereby selling short both religion and secular humanism in one breath. I reckon (this is a conjecture) that he made that equation so that he could repudiate the charge of apostasy. One cannot, after all, be committing apostasy if one is only opposing one religion with another. Under the threat of execution, one may be allowed a confused thought, but with a clear mind no one with even a vestigial understanding of the mentalities and the realities of religion *or* the aspirations of secular humanism, would be tempted by Rushdie's equation.

Though his equation itself may be quite wrong, I want to briefly pursue with some variation, a theme it opens up.

What I want to ask is really a familiar question, and trace some of the philosophical attitudes and intellectual history that makes it familiar, the question whether there can be in the secular a form of continuity with something in the religious, in my view a continuity which actually stood for a particular form of humane radical politics that was very early on thwarted by a very specific notion of scientific rationality, which I will call a 'thick' notion of scientific rationality. By constantly appealing to this notion of scientific rationality, a dominant orthodox strand in thinking about the Enlightenment has consistently tarnished a certain kind of radical questioning of this orthodoxy with charges of irrationalism. It is worth exposing a sleight of hand in all this.

II

A good place to begin is with Gandhi, a humanist and secularist yet by open declaration opposed to the Enlightenment and also avowedly a Hindu, even if by the lights of high Hinduism, a highly heterodox one. I will be focusing, and focusing selectively, only on Gandhi's thought and writing and not his political interventions during the long freedom movement. I have said this before (Bilgrami 2003) and will say it again at the outset of this chapter: there is something particularly thankless about writing an interpretative essay on someone as intellectually and politically creative, perverse, and prolific, as Gandhi. I have hardly ever spoken on him in public (or indeed in someone's drawing or dining room) without someone offering a refutation by citing either some action or proposal of his during the freedom movement, or by mentioning some attitude of his towards his wife or children or ashram companions, or, more soberly, reminding me of some passage in his writing that is in tension with what I have just said. That is why I am keen to say at the very outset that I will be doing *merely* what I say: focusing selectively on some of his thought and writing with a view to offering a partial (but I hope interesting) interpretation of it that frees us of some of the standard, cliché ways of thinking of him, as a saint on the one hand or a shrewd politician on the other ... a nostalgist and traditionalist, or more specifically, a reactionary holding back the progressive, modernist tendencies in the nationalist movement ... and so on. The idea is not – not by any means – to write anything even approximating a definitive interpretative essay, as if that could be any sensible person's idea. The fact is that Gandhi, remarkable philosopher though he was, was not a systematic thinker, not a philosopher in the sense that the academic subject of philosophy circumscribes. So it is tiresome to keep demanding of him that he be entirely consistent in all his writing. Not only would he have had to be a much less interesting thinker than he was to have that rightly demanded of him, he would have had to be born all over again.

What Gandhi says about the Enlightenment as well as, what he often omnibusly called, 'the West', relates closely to his view of science. In careless moments, Gandhi often said that it was a *predisposition* of science from its earliest days that it would lead to a way of thinking that was disastrous for politics and culture in ways that he outlined in great detail. This notion of a predisposition is obscure because general claims about the predispositions of something like science (something that is at once a theoretical pursuit as well as a practice, something that is defined in terms that are at once conceptual, methodological, and institutional) are hard to pin down and study, leave alone confirm or refute, if they are intended to be empirical hypotheses. I will instead sympathetically read his hunch about such a predisposition by situating it in a certain intellectual history. At the end of this exercise, it will emerge that a far better way to put his point would be in terms, not of an empirical hypothesis about 'science' as a self-standing human cognitive enterprise, but rather to see it as a critique of a certain very specific notion of scientific 'rationality'.

The notion of rationality as it has governed our thought about history and politics and culture has in the past – famously – taken an idealized form, with a progressivist or developmental, conception of these subjects; and for a few decades now that has been under a thoroughly critical scrutiny, as is the notion of modernity with which this idea of 'progress' is so often coupled. Much more often than not the *telos* that defines the progressivist trajectory is in terms of an envisaged ideal or *end-point* and the dialectic by which the end is (or is to be) realized is the large subject of the relevant historiography. Yet it is sometimes more fruitful to focus on the *beginnings* of such a sequence, since it may give a more truthful sense of the notions of rationality that are at stake than those defined by an idealized statement of the normative end. So I will argue.

There is no avoiding the fact that if we even so much as accept the idea of 'modernity' as a genuinely distinctive descriptive and analytical category (whatever side we take on the normative issues of whether modernity is a good thing or not), then we cannot but focus on the genealogy of its beginnings in *early* Modernity.

So let me explore these beginnings briefly by recording the detailed affinities between Gandhi's ideas about science and the metaphysical and political and cultural anxieties that first surfaced at the very site and time of the new science as it first began to be formulated in the seventeenth century in the West. There are many passages in Gandhi's dispatches to *Young India* and also in some passages in his book *Hind Swaraj* that suggest a line of argument something like this.

Sometime in the seventeenth century we were set on a path in which we were given the intellectual sanction to see nature as – to use a Weberian notion – 'disenchanted'. This coincided with the period of the great revolutionary changes in scientific theory, so Gandhi crudely equated it with science itself and its newly and self-consciously formulated experimental methods. He saw in it a conception of nature whose pursuit left us disengaged from nature as a habitus, and which instead engendered a zeal to control it rather than merely live in it. And my claim is that these criticisms by Gandhi have extraordinarily close and striking antecedents in a tradition of thought that goes all the way back to the second half of the seventeenth century in England and then elsewhere in Europe, *simultaneous* with the great scientific achievements of that time. It goes back, that is, to just the time and the place when the outlook of scientific 'rationality' that many place at the defining centre of what they call the 'West', was being formed, and it is that very outlook with its threatening cultural and political consequences that is the target of that early critique.

It should be said emphatically right at the outset that the achievements of the 'new science' of the seventeenth century were neither denied nor opposed by the critique I have in mind, and so the critique *cannot* be dismissed as Luddite reaction to the new science, as Gandhi's critique is bound to seem, coming centuries later, when the science is no longer 'new' and its effects on our lives, which the earlier critique was warning against, seem like a *fait accompli*. What the critique opposed was a development in *outlook* that emerged in the *philosophical surround* of the scientific achievements. In other words, what it opposed is the notion of what I will call a 'thick' rationality that is often described in glowing terms today as 'scientific rationality'. What do I have in mind by calling it a 'thick' notion (a term I am recognizably borrowing from Clifford Geertz [1973])?

To put a range of complex, interweaving themes in the crudest summary, the dispute was about the very nature of nature and matter and, relatedly therefore, about the role of the deity, and of the broad cultural and political implications of the different views on these metaphysical and religious concerns. The metaphysical picture that was promoted by Newton (the official Newton of the Royal Society, not the neo-Platonist of his private study) and Boyle, among others, viewed matter and nature as *brute and inert*. On this view, since the material universe was brute, God was *externally* conceived with all the familiar metaphors of the 'clock winder' giving the universe a push from the *outside* to get it in motion. In the dissenting tradition – which was a *scientific* tradition, for there was in fact no disagreement between it and Newton/Boyle on any serious detail of the scientific laws, and all the fundamental notions such as gravity, for instance, were perfectly in place, though given a quite different metaphysical interpretation – matter was *not* brute and inert, but rather was shot through with an *inner* source of dynamism responsible for motion, that was itself divine. God and nature were not separable as in the official metaphysical picture that was growing around the new science, and John Toland, for instance, to take just one example among the active dissenting voices, openly wrote in terms he proclaimed to be 'pantheistic' (see Toland 1976a, 1976b, 1978; Jacob 1981).

The link with Gandhi in all this is vivid. One absolutely central claim of the freethinkers of this period was about the political and cultural significance of their disagreements with the fast developing metaphysical orthodoxy of the 'Newtonians'. Just as Gandhi did, they argued that it is only because one takes matter to be 'brute' and 'stupid', to use Newton's own terms, that one would find it appropriate to conquer it with nothing but profit and material wealth as ends, and thereby destroy it both as a natural and a human environment for one's habitation. In today's terms, one might think that this point was a seventeenth century predecessor to our ecological concerns but though there certainly was an early instinct of that kind, it was embedded in a much more general point (as it was with Gandhi too), a point really about how nature in an ancient and spiritually flourishing sense was being threatened, and how therefore this was in turn threatening to our moral psychology of engagement with it, including the relations and engagement among ourselves as its inhabitants.

Today, the most thoroughly and self-consciously secular sensibilities may recoil from the term 'spiritually', as I have just deployed it, though I must confess to finding myself feeling no such self-consciousness despite being a secularist, indeed an atheist. The real point has nothing to do with these rhetorical niceties. If one had no use for the word, if one insisted on having the point made with words that we today can summon with confidence and accept without qualm, it would do no great violence to the core of their thinking to say this: the dissenters thought of the *world* not as brute but as *suffused with value*. That they happened to think the source of such value was divine ought not to be the deepest point of interest for us. The point rather is that if it were laden with *value*, it would make *normative* (ethical and social) demands on one, whether one was religious or not; normative demands therefore that did not come merely from our own instrumentalities and subjective utilities. And it is this sense of forming commitments by taking in, *in our perceptions*, an evaluatively 'enchanted' world which – being enchanted in this way – therefore *moved* us to normatively con-strained *engagement* with it, that the dissenters contrasted with the outlook that was being offered by the ideologues of the new science (Bilgrami 2006; McDowell 1985). A brute and disenchanted world could not move us to any such engagement since any perception of it, given the sort of thing it was, would necessarily be a *detached* form of observation; and if one ever came out of this detachment, if there was ever any engagement with a world so distantly conceived, so external to our own sensibility, it could only take the form of mastery and control of something alien, with a view to satisfying the only source of value allowed by this outlook – our own utilities and gain.

In his probing book, *A Grammar of Motives*, Kenneth Burke says that 'the experi-ence of an impersonal outlook was empirically intensified in proportion as the ratio-nale of the monetary motive gained greater authority … ' (Burke 1969: 113). This gives us a glimpse of the sources. As he says, one had to have an impersonal angle on the world to see it as the source of profit and gain, and vice versa. But I have claimed that the sources go deeper. It is only when we see the world as Boyle and Newton did, as against the freethinkers and dissenters, that we understand further why there was no option but this impersonality in our angle on the world. A desacralized world, to put it in the dissenting terms of that period, left us no other angle from which to view it, but an impersonal one. There could be no normative constraint coming upon us from a world that was brute. It could not move us to engagement with it on *its* terms. All the term-making came from us. We could bring whatever terms we wished to such a world; and since we could only regard it impersonally, it being brute, the terms we brought in our actions upon it were just the terms that Burke describes as accompanying such impersonality, the terms of 'the monetary' motives for our actions. Thus it is, that the metaphysical issues regarding the world and nature, as they were debated around the new science, provide the deepest conceptual sources.

The conceptual sources that we have traced are various but they were *not* miscellaneous. The diverse conceptual elements of religion, capital, nature, metaphysics, rationality, science, were *tied together* in a highly *deliberate* integration, that is to say in deliberately accruing worldly *alliances*. Newton's and Boyle's metaphysical view of the new science won out over the freethinkers' and became official only because it was sold to the Anglican establishment and, in an alliance with that establishment, to the powerful mercantile and incipient industrial interests of the period in thoroughly predatory terms. Terms which stressed that how we conceive nature may now be transformed into something, into the *kind* of thing, that is indefinitely available for our economic gain by processes of extraction, processes such as mining, deforestation, plantation agriculture intended essentially as what we today would call 'agribusiness'. None of these processes could have taken on the *unthinking* and yet *systematic* prevalence that they first began to get in this period unless one had ruthlessly revised existing ideas of a world animated by a divine presence. From an *anima mundi*, one could not simply proceed to take at whim and will. Not that one could not or did not, till then, take at all. But in the past in a wide range of social worlds, such taking as one did had to be accompanied by ritual offerings of reciprocation which were intended to show respect towards as well as to restore the balance in nature, offerings made both before and after cycles of planting, and even hunting. The point is that, in general, the revision of such an age-old conception of nature was achieved in tandem with a range of seemingly miscellaneous elements that were brought together in terms that stressed a future of endlessly profitable consequences that would accrue if one embraced this particular metaphysics of the new science and build, in the name of a notion of rationality around it, the institutions of an increasingly centralized political oligarchy (an incipient state) and an established religious orthodoxy of Anglicanism that had penetrated the universities as well, to promote these very specific interests. These were the very terms that the freethinkers found alarming for politics and culture, alarming for the local and egalitarian ways of life, which some decades earlier the radical elements in the English Revolution such as the Levellers, Diggers, Quakers, Ranters, and other groups had articulated and fought for. Gandhi, much later, spoke in political terms that were poignantly reminiscent of these radical sectaries and, in *Hind Swaraj* and other writings, he wrote about science and its relations to these political terms in ways that echoed the alarm of the somewhat later scientific dissenters.

These scientific dissenters themselves often openly avowed that they had inherited the political attitudes of these radical sectaries in England of about 50 years earlier and appealed to their instinctive, hermetic, neo-Platonist, and sacralized views of nature, defending them against the conceptual assaults of the official Newton/Boyle view of matter. In fact, the natural philosophies of Anthony Collins and John Toland and his Socratic Brotherhood (and their counterparts in the Netherlands drawing inspiration from Spinoza's pantheism, and spreading to France and elsewhere in Europe, and then, when strongly opposed, going into secretive Masonic Lodges and other underground movements) were in many details anticipated by the key figures of the radical groups in that most dynamic period of English history, the 1640s, which had enjoyed hitherto unparalleled freedom of publication for about a decade or more to air their subversive and egalitarian views based on a quite different conception of nature. Gerard Winstanley, the most well known among them, declared that 'God is in all motion' and 'the truth is hid in every *body*' (Hill 1975: 293, my italics). This way of thinking about the corporeal realm had for Winstanley, as he puts it, a great 'leveling purpose'. It allowed one to lay the ground, first of all, for a democratization of religion. If God was every-where, then anyone may perceive the divine or find the divine within him or her, and therefore may be just as able to preach as a university-trained divine. But the opposi-tion to the monopoly of so-called experts was intended to be more general than in just the religious sphere. Through their myriad polemical and instructional pamphlets, fig-ures such as Winstanley, John Lilburne, Richard Overton, and others reached out and created a radical rank and file population which began to demand a variety of other things, including an elimination of tithes, a leveling of the legal sphere by a decen-tralizing of the courts and the elimination of feed lawyers, as well as the democratiza-tion of medicine by drastically reducing, if not eliminating, the costs of medicine, and disallowing canonical and monopoly status to the College of Physicians. The later sci-entific dissenters were very clear too that these were the very monopolies and unde-mocratic practices and institutions which would get entrenched if science, conceived in terms of the Newtonianism of the Royal Society, had its ideological victory.

Equally, that is to say, conversely, the Newtonian ideologues of the Royal Society around the Boyle lectures started by Samuel Clarke saw themselves – without remorse – in just these conservative terms that the dissenters portrayed them in. They explicitly called Toland and a range of other dissenters, 'enthusiasts' (a term of oppro-brium at the time) and feared that their alternative picture of matter was an intellectual ground for the social unrest of the pre-Restoration period when the radical sectaries had such great, if brief and aborted, popular reach. They were effective in creating with the Anglican establishment a general conviction that the entire polity would require orderly rule by a state apparatus around a monarch serving the propertied classes and that this was just a mundane reflection, indeed a mundane *version*, of an *externally* imposed divine authority which kept a universe of brute matter in orderly motion, rather than an *immanently* present God in all matter and in all persons, inspiring them with the enthusiasms to turn the 'world upside down', in Christopher Hill's memorable, eponymous phrase. To see God in every body and piece of matter, they anxiously argued, was to lay oneself open to a polity and a set of civic and religious institutions that were beholden to popular rather than scriptural and learned judgement and opi-nion. They were just as effective in forging with the commercial interests over the next century, the idea that a respect for a sacralized universe would be an obstacle to taking with impunity what one could from nature's bounty. By their lights, the only obstacles that now needed to be acknowledged and addressed had to do with the difficulties of mobilizing towards an economy geared to profit. No other factors of a more meta-physical and ideological kind should be allowed to interfere with these pursuits once *nature* had been transformed in our consciousness to a set of impersonally perceived *'natural resources'*.

It would be quite wrong and anachronistic to dismiss initial and early intellectual and perfectly *scientific* sources of critique, from which later critiques of the Enlight-enment derived, as being irrational, unless one is committed to a very specific orthodox understanding of the Enlightenment, of the sort I am inveighing against. It is essential to the argument of this chapter that far from being anti-Enlightenment, Gandhi's early antecedents in the West, going back to the seventeenth century and in recurring het-erodox traditions in the West since then, constitute what is, and rightly has been, called the '*Radical Enlightenment*' (Jacob 1981). To dismiss its pantheistic tendencies as being unscientific and in violation of norms of rationality, would be to run together in a blatant slippage the general and 'thin' use of terms like 'scientific' and 'rational' with just this 'thick' notion of scientific rationality that we have identified above, which had the kind of politically and culturally disastrous consequences that the early dissenters were so jittery about. The appeal to scientific rationality as a defining feature of our modernity trades constantly on just such a slippage, subliminally appealing to the hurrah element of the general and 'thin' terms 'rational' and 'scientific', which we all applaud, to tarnish critics of the Enlightenment such as Gandhi, while ignoring the fact that in their critique the opposition is to the thicker notion of scientific rationality, that was defined in terms of very specific scientific, religious, and commercial alliances.

Were we to apply the *thin* conception of 'scientific' and 'rationality' (the one that I imagine most of us embrace), the plain fact is that *nobody* in that period was, in any case, getting prizes for leaving God out of the worldview of science. That one should think of God as voluntaristically affecting nature from the outside (as the Newtonians did) rather than sacralizing it from within (as the freethinkers insisted), was not in any way to improve on the *science* involved. Both views were therefore just as 'unscientific', just as much in violation of scientific rationality, in the 'thin' sense of that term that we would now take for granted. What was in dispute had nothing to do with science or rationality in that attenuated sense at all. What the early dissenting tradition as well as Gandhi were opposed to was the *metaphysical* orthodoxy that grew around Newtonian science and its implications for broader issues of *culture and politics.* This orthodoxy with all of its implications is what has now come to be called 'scientific rationality' in the 'thick' sense of that term and in the pervasive cheerleading about 'the West' and about the 'Enlightenment', it has been elevated into a defining ideal, dismissing all opposition as irrationalist, with the hope that accusations of irrationality, because of the *general* stigma that the term imparts in its '*thin*' usage, will disguise the very specific and 'thick' sense of rationality and irrationality that are actually being deployed by the opposition. Such (thick) *ir*rationalism is precisely what the dissenters yearned for; and hindsight shows just how admirable a yearning it was.

So the dismissals of Gandhi's critique of the Enlightenment ideals as a kind of irrationalism and nostalgia have blinded us to making explicit the interpretative possibilities for some of his thinking that are opened up by noting his affinities with a longstanding, dissenting tradition in the most radical period in English history. I am not suggesting for a moment that what was radical then could be retained without remainder as being radical today or even at the time when Gandhi was articulating his critique. But I *am* saying that it opens up liberating interpretative options for how to read Gandhi as being continuous with a tradition that was clear-eyed about what was implied by the 'disenchantment' of the world, to stay with the Weberian term. It is a tradition consisting not just of Gandhi and the early seventeenth century freethinkers, but any number of remarkable literary and philosophical voices in between such as Blake, Shelley, Godwin, not perhaps all of Marx but certainly one very central strand in Marx, William Morris, Whitman and Dewey in America, and countless voices of the non-traditional Left, from the freemasons in the early eighteenth century down to the heterodox Left in our own time, voices such as those of E.P. Thompson and Noam Chomsky, and the vast army of heroic but anonymous organizers of popular grass roots movements – in a word, the West as conceived by the 'radical' Enlightenment which has refused to be complacent about the orthodox Enlightenment's legacy of scientific rationality that the early dissenters in England had warned against well over three centuries ago.

III

To move away now from the specific sacralized formulations of Gandhi and his antecedents in intellectual history, we should be asking in a much more general way, what their view amounts to, once we acknowledge that we have our own intellectual demands for more secular formulations. This is a tractable, historically situated, version of the question I began with: is there something interesting in the secular that is continuous with something in the religious? Even so situated, it is a very large question which requires a far more detailed inquiry than I can give in a brief chapter, but I do want to say something now to give at least a very general and preliminary philosophical sense of what I think is the right direction for its answer.

Spinoza, in a profound insight, pointed out that one cannot both intend to do something and predict that one will do it, *at the same time*. Predicting what one will do is done from a detached point of view, when one as it were steps outside of oneself and looks at oneself as others would, from a *third* person point of view. But intending is done from the *first* person point of view of agency itself. And we cannot occupy both points of view on ourselves at once. *Now*, I want to claim that there ought to be *an exactly similar distinction*, not on the points of view that we have *on ourselves,* which was Spinoza's concern, but the points of view we have *on the world*. The world *too* can be seen, on the one hand, from a detached, third person point of view (science being the most systematic version of such a point of view) and, on the other, it can be seen from an engaged, first person point of view, the point of view of practical agency. And it is the availability of the world to us through its *value* properties (which move us to our *first* personal engagement with it) that provides the minimal continuity with the sacralized picture – the rest of which we cannot find palatable any longer.

Thus putting it in the most abjectly simple terms, one might for instance find, from a certain perspective of the study of populations and disease and so on, that this or that segment of a population has a certain average daily caloric intake and that they, as a result, die of old age on average in their late forties, a metaphor for their malnutrition. But that is only one perspective that I could take on the matter, one of detached, roughly scientific, study. I could then switch perspectives and see those very people as being in *need*. And the crucial point is that need is a *value* notion quite unlike the notions of caloric counts and, therefore, it makes *normative* demands on me. To view the world from this quite other perspective is, as I said earlier, to view it from the point of view of engagement rather than detachment. To be able to perceive the evaluative aspects of the world, one therefore has to possess practical agency, one has to have the capacity to respond to its normative force. In fact, we *experience* ourselves as agents in the practical sense partly *in* the perceptions of such a value-laden world.

Our agency and the evaluative enchantment of the world, then, are inseparably linked. That is why Spinoza's insight about ourselves can be extended outwards onto the world. In a long and unsatisfactory philosophical tradition of moral psychology (deriving from philosophers such as Hume and Adam Smith), values are said to be given to us in our desires and moral sentiments. This is precisely the tradition that values are properties in and of the world, to which our practical agency responds. So here, then, is the absolutely crucial point. If my extension of Spinoza's point is right, the *objects* of our desires must be *given to us* as desi*rable,* that is*, as* desi*rabilities* or value elements in the world itself. If they were not, if the objects of our desires were given to us, not as 'desirable' but as 'desir*ed*' (as Hume and Adam Smith's moral psychology claims) then they could only be given to us when we step outside of ourselves and perceive what our desires are from the third person point of view. But that is precisely to abdicate our agency, our *first* person point of view. Agency is possible only if we take the desirabilities or evaluative properties in the world itself as *given to us in the experience* of our desires. Compare my two statements 'This is desired' and 'This is desirable'. The first is a report by me of something in my psychology. I have to step outside of myself and view myself as an object to make the report. In the second, I am not an object to myself, I am a subject expressing (not reporting) what I desire. And it is only the second which has it that the world contains desirabil*ities* – or values. So for us to be agents and subjects rather than mere objects, we have to not only have desires, but our desires have to be responses to desirabilities or values *in the world*.

I have said that these evaluative properties are contained in the world and can be perceived or apprehended as such. But I have also said that this evaluative aspect of the world is nothing, it is darkness, to subjects that do not possess agency, a capacity for normative engagement. One reductive confusion to watch out for here is to think that because subjects capable of agency and engagement alone are capable of perceiving values in the world external to them, that values must therefore *not* be external after all and ultimately come from us. Another – related – confusion is to think that because some people may see some values in the world and others may not (you may see someone as being in need and be moved normatively by it, I may not), it is wrong to think that values are in the world at all and that we respond to them normatively – rather the world is indeed brute and value-free as Newton and Boyle claimed, and it is *we* who through our moral sentiments *make up* values and project them differentially onto the world. This is as confused as saying that because observation of things, of objects in the world, is theory-laden, i.e., because when we hold different physical theories we will perceive different objects in the world, we must therefore in some sense be making up physical objects. These confusions may be natural but they are elementary and are easy to identify and resist.

A more ideological confusion that all this amounts to something unscientific is no less elementary, but being ideological it may be harder to resist. *I have* said that even irreligious people committed to scientific rationality in the *thin* sense of the term[1] can embrace this way of thinking of the enchantment of the world because I insist that there is nothing unscientific about it. To view nature and the world not as brute but as containing value that makes normative demands on our agency is not by any means to be unscientific. It only means that natural science does not have full coverage of nature. In general, it is not unscientific to say that not all themes about nature are scientific themes. It is only unscientific to give unscientific responses to *science's* themes – as hypotheses about creationism or 'intelligent-design' do (being, as they are, responses to scientific questions about the origins of the universe).

The point here is not the same as the perfectly good point many have made before, which is that science has told us how to study nature but not how to study the human subject. The point is rather that there is no studying what is special about human subjectivity *unless we see nature and the world itself* as often describable in terms that are not susceptible to the kind of inquiry that natural science or even social *science* provides. There is a revealing point here about someone like Weber and his legacy. He, among others, is seen as having directed us to what is now fairly widely accepted as an undeniable truth, viz., that what makes the study of *human beings* stand apart from the natural sciences is that such study is 'value-laden'. But – bizarrely – he never linked this now familiar point explicitly with his own remarks about the disenchantment of nature. The fact is that there is no understanding of what makes the study of human society stand apart by its value-ladenness unless we see that fact as being *of a piece* with an equally fundamental insight about a value-laden natural and human environment, in virtue of which our agential engagements with it are prompted. Without that further link the insight that the study of human society stands apart from scientific study in its value-ladenness is incomplete, and the claim to the naturalistic irreducibility of the human subject is shallow.

Under the influence of a familiar orientation in the social sciences, one might aspire to a certain picture of the world that concedes that one does not have to view it as brute. In other words, one can allow that it may contain more than what *natural* science studies, it contains *opportunities* for us to satisfy our desires. Thus, one might say, if I were to take a purely impersonal and scientific perspective on the world, I would see the water in the glass in front of me as H2O, but with the social scientific broadening of this perspective to include a certain expanded notion of scientific rationality, one could also see that very glass of water as an *opportunity* to satisfy a desire of mine, to quench my thirst. This loosens things up a bit to allow the world to contain such strange things as opportunities, something the physicist or chemist or biologist would never allow nor could study, since opportunities, whatever they are, are not the subject-matter of these sciences. Rather they are the subject matter of Economics and more broadly the social and behavioural sciences which could now be seen to be, among other things, the science of desire-satisfaction in the light of (probabilistic) apprehension of the desire-satisfying properties in the world, i.e., opportunities that the world provides to satisfy our wants and preferences.

But this is not the loosening up of our understanding of 'the world' that is needed for a secular *enchantment* of the world that is continuous with the religious. Though it grants that the world is not entirely brute and it grants that the world contains something (opportunities) that escapes the purview of the natural sciences, it doesn't grant enough. It may be a first step but to stop there is merely to extend the reach of scientific rationality in the thick sense, it is not to show its limitations in its conception of nature and the world. Nothing short of seeing the world as containing *values* (an older Aristotelian idea, if recent writers such as McDowell read him rightly) does that limitation get revealed, for it is values not opportunities that put *moral* demands on us. Thus even if we respond to others with a view to gratifying our moral sentiments of sympathy towards them, we are not quite yet on board with the depth of the demand that a perception of others needs is the perception of something that puts normative *demands* on our individual and collective agency. It is in this deep respect that Marx's talk of needs in his slogan 'From each according to his abilities to each according to his needs' went beyond the moral psychology of Hume and Adam Smith. Perceiving opportunities in the world merely tells us that the world is there for satisfying our desires and preferences, however filled with sympathy for others those desires are, but it does not conceive of the desires themselves as responding to what I have described as 'desirabi*lities*' in the world. (This has impoverishing implications for how one may think of more specific questions relevant to politics and political theory, implications I cannot pursue in this chapter.[2]) Nothing short of perceiving in the world *values* that move our agency to respond in ethical terms, then, will re-enchant it and help to arrest our alienation from it, providing the initial steps to a *secular* version of what Gandhi and the freethinkers of the seventeenth century were struggling to find.

That the deliverances of their struggles yielded sacralized and pantheistic conceptions of the world with which we have little sympathy today, does not at all imply that those struggles were not honourable. But to say that their struggles are honourable is to say that they must be the antecedents to our own philosophical struggles to re-characterize the world and nature, and in doing so to reorient our entire range of social scientific and historiographic interests away from the obsessively causal explanatory methods that dominate them. This disciplinary reorientation based on such a re-view of nature may have some chance of laying the ground of resistance to the ubiquitously narrowing effects of the orthodox Enlightenment's legacies not just in the universities but in our moral and political lives generally.

IV

In a previous essay of mine called 'What is a Muslim?' I had tried explicitly to locate the forms of political pacification that come from a loss of agency owing to a picture of things in which a third person, rather than a first person, point of view dominates our conception of *ourselves* and our cultural and political identity. In the present chapter, I have tried to integrate those ideas with the politics that grew around the new science for the first time some centuries ago as a result of an increasingly third person conception not of ourselves, but of the *world and nature*. Many more deep connections between metaphysics, moral psychology and politics and culture still need to be drawn which I could not possibly have drawn here and likely *do not* have the intellectual powers ever to do, before anything of genuinely theoretical ambition is constructed on the subjects of identity, democratic politics, and disenchantment. But even without them it is possible at least to state the issues and aspirations at stake.

What Gandhi's and the seventeenth century radical sectaries' and the somewhat later scientific dissenters' intellectual efforts made *thinkable*, and what I am trying to consolidate in secular terms in my last many remarks, is something that goes measurably beyond what recent scholars have started saying is our best and only bet: the placing of *constraints* on an *essentially utilitarian* framework so as to provide for a social democratic safety net for the worst off. Salutary though the idea of such a safety net is (how could it fail to be given the wretched conditions of the worst off?), it is a project of limited ambition, in which Adam Smith and Hume remain the heroes and Condorcet (among others) is wheeled in as the radical who proposed the sort of requisite constraints we need. In a recent book, Gareth Stedman Jones (2005), chastened by the failures to put into practice more ambitious intellectual frameworks, comes to just these modest conclusions about our world as we have inherited it from these more ambitious theories and their failures. By contrast, the heroes of this lecture, Gandhi and the key radical as well as later dissenting figures of the seventeenth century, through whose lens I have been reading him, wanted it to be at least thinkable that that world could be 'turned upside down' – not entirely, not all at once, but in places where the reach of 'thick' rationality has not been comprehensive and where there might be scope for some reversal and secular re-enchantment. Gandhi in many of his writings had passionately aspired to the argument that India as it first struggled for its freedom and then later came to be poised to gain independence from colonial rule, was just such a place. It would be a reflection both of our moral complacence and our failure of political will to say that what Gandhi aspired to for his times can no longer be an aspiration for ours. I can think of no more urgent task for a political philosophy in

India (the governing theme of this volume) than to aspire to some form of intelligently and judiciously adjusted theorization of what such a 'radical' Enlightenment (within which I am placing Gandhi) amounts to for our own time and place.

Notes

1 By rationality in the 'thin' sense I mean just the standard codifications of deductive rationality and inductive rationality or confirmation theory, and decision theory.
2 In a forthcoming essay in *Economic and Political Weekly*, tentatively entitled 'Value, Disenchantment, and Democracy', I pursue some of those implications.

References

Bilgrami, Akeel (1992) 'What is a Muslim', *Critical Inquiry*, 18 (4).
—— (2003) 'Gandhi, the philosopher', *Economic and Political Weekly*, 38, 4159–65.
—— (2006) *Self-Knowledge and Resentment*, Cambridge, Mass: Harvard University Press.
Burke, Kenneth (1969) *A Grammar of Motives*, Berkeley: University of California Press.
Gandhi, M. K. (1997) *Hind Swaraj and Other Writings*, Anthony Parel (ed.), Cambridge: Cambridge University Press.
Geertz, Clifford (1973) 'Thick description: toward an interpretive theory of culture', in *The Interpretation of Cultures: Selected Essays*, New York: Basic Books, pp. 3–30.
Hill, Christopher (1975) *The World Turned Upside Down*, New York: Penguin Books.
Jacob, Margaret (1981) *The Radical Enlightenment: Pantheists, Freemasons, and Republicans*, London: Allen and Unwin.
Jones, Gareth Stedman (2005) *An End to Poverty? A Historical Debate*, New York: Columbia University Press.
Kaviraj Sudipta (2010) 'An outline of a revisionist theory of modernity', in Aakash Singh and Silika Mohapatra (eds) *Indian Political Thought: A Reader*, London: Routledge.
McDowell, John (1985) 'Values and Secondary Qualities', in Ted Honderich (ed.) *Morality and Objectivity*, London: Routledge and Kegan Paul.
Sabine, G. H. (ed.) (1941) *The Works of Gerard Winstanley*, New York: Cornell University Press.
Toland, J. (1976a) [1704] 'Letters to Serena', *British Philosophers and Theologians of the 17th & 18th Centuries*, 58, New York: Garland Pub.
—— (1976b) [1724] 'Pantheisticon', *British Philosophers and Theologians of the 17th & 18th Centuries*, New York: Garland Pub.
—— (1978) [1696] 'Christianity not mysterious', *British Philosophers and Theologians of the 17th & 18th Centuries*, New York: Garland Pub.

12 Scientific temper

Arguments for an Indian Enlightenment

Meera Nanda

Let the spirit of inquiry overwhelm the respect for traditions ...

M. N. Roy

Science and secularization

The modernist authors of the Constitution imagined a democratic and secular India as a spacious building with many rooms that stood on two sturdy pillars: religious toler-ance, combined with a spirit of skepticism – or what they liked to call 'scientific temper' – regarding all hand-me-down traditions and dogmas.

The words 'scientific temper', just like its twin 'secularism', are not mentioned anywhere in the original draft of the Constitution. It is only the 42nd Amendment, passed under the Emergency rule imposed by Indira Gandhi, that made it a duty of citizens 'to develop the scientific temper, humanism and the spirit of inquiry and reform' (Article 51A, h).

And yet, this chapter will argue, cultivation of a scientific temper was one of the cardinal principles that animated the secular-humanists[1] among the architects of modern India. This group of thinkers considered modern science invaluable not just for its contribution to industrial development, but also for its potential to bring about a cultural revolution in the country. They understood that the hierarchies of caste and gender that pervaded Indian culture presupposed specific metaphysical beliefs about the natural order which, in fact, had been factually disproved by modern science. The secular-humanists believed – and hoped – that scientific demystification of fundamental beliefs about the natural order would lead to a genuine change in the normative order of Indian society, or in simpler words, change in mind would lead to a change of heart.

The objective of this chapter is to place the secular-humanists in the context of the three political-intellectual traditions that dominated mid-20th century India; namely, Gandhism, socialism and dalit-liberation. The resonances and conflicts between these traditions are examined while we try to answer such questions as: Who were the secular-humanists? What aspects of India's dominant culture were they rebelling against? What did they really mean when they exhorted Indians to cultivate a 'scientific temper'?

Indian Enlightenment: radical and moderate wings

The Indian advocates of a scientific temper were part of the worldwide spread of the spirit of the Enlightenment. Like the European Enlightenment, the Indian Enlight-enment, too, had a radical and a moderate wing.

'The Enlightenment' refers to the intellectual-cum-socio-political movement of pro-test against the exercise of all arbitrary authority that started in 18th century Europe in the wake of the Scientific Revolution. Emboldened by the success of the empirical methodology of modern science which had overturned the medieval worldview backed by centuries of scholastic learning, the 'enlighteners' sought to re-evaluate all inherited justifications for social hierarchies, regardless of whether these justifications came from the edicts of kings backed by priestly rituals and holy books, or whether hierarchies were self-enforced by men and women through the force of custom, socialization and habit (Kors 2003).

There were moderate and radical camps in the European Enlightenment. The mod-erate Enlightenment was the kind favored by the mainstream, the governments and even the Churches themselves in countries like Britain, Germany, the Netherlands, Spain and the United States as they modernized. This moderate Enlightenment, in the words of Jonathan Israel:

> aspired to conquer ignorance and superstition, establish toleration and revolutio-nize ideas, education and attitudes ... but in such a way as to *preserve and safe-guard what were judged essential elements of the older structure,* effecting a viable synthesis of old and new, and of reason and faith (2001: 11).

The radical Enlightenment, on the other hand:

> whether on atheistic or deistic basis, *rejected all compromise with the past and sought to sweep away existing structures entirely,* rejecting the Creation as under-stood in the Judeao-Christian civilization ... and refusing to accept that there is any God-ordained social hierarchy, concentration of privilege or land-ownership in noble hands, or religious sanction for monarchy (2001: 11–12).

If the preservation of the Judeo-Christian worldview was what divided the radicals from the moderates in Europe, it was the worldview that legitimized caste that dis-tinguished the moderates from the radicals in India. The moderates, by and large, were content to merely 'cleanse Hinduism of impurities, to chop off the diseased branches of the tree of Brahminical tradition', by fighting against untouchability, while the radicals aimed at nothing less than 'felling the tree' of Hinduism itself because they found it 'Brahminical in essence, caste-bound and irrational' (Omvedt, 1994: 10). The most well-known exponent of such 'cleansing', who combined opposition to untouchability with fulsome defense of Sanatan Dharma and *chaturvarna*, was none other than Mahatma Gandhi himself. Since Gandhi was the most progressive thinker of the neo-Hindu revival, the secular-humanists' position with respect to Gandhi and Gandhism is a good indicator of where they stood on issues of religion and culture.

The Fabian-socialist Jawaharlal Nehru represents the best of the moderate wing of the Indian enlightenment which sought to preserve what they thought was the best of the high Hindu culture, even as they sought to free it of outdated superstitions and social prejudices. The dalit democratic-socialist and neo-Buddhist Bhimrao Ramji Ambedkar remains the undisputed leader of the radical wing, who sought nothing less than a complete annihilation of the worldview that underwrites caste. Other secular-humanists occupied a range of positions between the two poles. The Marxist-turned-radical humanist M. N. Roy, who worked with socialists inside the Congress party, was uncompromising in rejecting Hinduism, old and new, especially that represented by Gandhism. On the other hand, an avowed socialist like Ram Manohar Lohia who saw caste as a crucial issue, accepted the necessity of Gandhi's leadership.

For all their internal disagreements, the Indian secular-humanists were united in rejecting the core of Marxist and Gandhian orthodoxies, the two most dominant intellectual-political traditions of their times. They did not treat religion as Marx's famous 'opium of the people' that eased their pain born of economic exploitation even as it created fantasies of after life. But neither did they see religion, as Gandhi did, as the oxygen that supposedly animates all of life.

The secular-humanists had a much more nuanced appreciation of the role of religion and culture in social life. They saw the dominant religious culture of India, namely Hinduism, as the fourth strand of the seamless triple-helix out of which the Constitution was woven; namely, national unity, democracy and social revolution (Austin 1999: 637). They saw Hinduism as providing a worldview which answered fundamental questions about what the world is like, how to tell right from wrong, and truth from what is not true, and how to live a good life. The Hindu worldview was more than just doctrines written in books; it was enacted in religious rituals, symbolized in myths, coded into social relationships and formal laws. In its pervasiveness, it constituted the commonsense of a people.

It was this underlying worldview, the taken-for-granted assumptions about the world that the Indian secular-humanists wanted to re-evaluate in the light of the worldview that had emerged since the beginnings of the Scientific Revolution. Cultivation of a scientific temper was not a matter of simply teaching more science in schools or funding advanced scientific research. It was rather understood broadly as an attempt to integrate the known facts and the way of thinking into a new worldview, or a new commonsense, that would learn to separate the transcendent or the supernatural both from the workings of nature and from the affairs of men and women in this world. Indian secularists were convinced that India could not be made secular and more democratic simply by adopting a new charter of laws, or by creating new political parties and holding periodic elections. They believed that a new secular commonsense will have to be created which could anchor the secular and democratic laws of modern India. As M. N. Roy insisted:

> Secularism is not a political institution: it is cultural atmosphere, which cannot be created by proclamation of individuals. ... A state can not be secular as long as the people running it remain religious-minded (1968: 155).

To function well, a secular and democratic state needs a secular and democratic culture. The state in India, to use a helpful metaphor from Antonio Gramsci's *Prison Notebooks*, was merely 'an outer ditch, behind which stood the powerful system of fortresses of civil society' made up of the family, castes and religious communities. New ideas needed to percolate into these fortresses of civil society and find a resonance in the hearts and minds of citizens for new laws to become effective.

Lest they be perceived as radical iconoclasts insensitive to their context, some qualifications are in order. While the secular-humanists were passionate in their critique of India's religious temper, they were neither atheists nor naïve positivists who lacked all appreciation of the poetic, imaginative and non-rational aspects of life. Rare exceptions aside, avowed agnostics (e.g. Nehru) and atheists (e.g. Gora) were able to accommodate religion for its social utility exemplified by Gandhi's constructive work in villages, and by the power of religion to mobilize the masses to join the freedom movement. Even B. R. Ambedkar, the most uncompromising and brilliant critic of the religious roots of caste, believed earnestly in the human need for a sense of the sacred. Nor can the secular-humanists be accused of vulgar positivism and scientism. Nehru's writings, for example, are replete with the limits of scientific reason which leaves out human concerns with purposes and meanings. They were not seeking to destroy every aspect of religion, but they were committed to challenging those aspects of the religious world-view – the metaphysics and the religious ways of knowing – that overlapped those of modern science: all *empirical facts* about the nature of the material world that religious metaphysics asserted or assumed, had to be made to pass the muster of modern science.

The political context: putting social reforms on the national agenda

Most contemporary discussions of a scientific temper in India tend to start and end with Jawaharlal Nehru. Nehru is no doubt central to the saga of secularism and rationalism in modern India. His enormous popularity and prestige brought the spotlight on science which he championed, both as a tool for economic progress and as a resource for cultural enlightenment. Furthermore, the socialist wing of the Congress party which came together under Nehru's leadership provided a political home for progressive writers, poets and playwrights who injected an element of cultural critique into politics.

But Nehru was only a representative – and a rather conservative one at that – of the generation of intellectuals, freedom-fighters, political activists and scientists who came of age in the period between the two World Wars that was marked by India's struggle for freedom from the British Raj and the spread of socialist ideals around the world. What sets them apart from the mainstream of Congress Gandhians and other traditionalists was their insistence that *social and religious reforms must precede political reforms*. They wanted the Indian nationalist movement, led by the Indian National Congress, to launch a struggle against religious-cultural sources of oppression and ignorance with at least the same sense of urgency they showed in their struggle against imperialism and economic exploitation. They were committed to the industrial model of modernization (as opposed to the Gandhian village-based small-is-beautiful model), but they did not think industrialization alone will be enough to bring about modern and secular consciousness. They believed, to quote Ambedkar from his *Annihilation of Caste*: 'political revolutions have always been preceded by social and religious revolutions. ... Emancipation of the mind and soul is a necessary preliminary for the political expansion of the people' (1948: 68–69). This revolution of the mind and the soul required, in M. N. Roy's words, an 'organized struggle against superstition' that would 'overwhelm the respect for tradition with a spirit of inquiry' and encourage society-wide 'a criticism of religious thought, subjection of traditional beliefs and the time-honored dogmas of religion to a searching analysis' (nd: 2).

This insistence on the priority of social-religious reform was a radical stand in the face of the cooption, benign neglect and active hostility toward social reform that prevailed in much of the Indian National Congress through much of its history. A case in point is the inglorious record of the National Social Conference, the social reform arm of Indian National Congress. The Social Conference was formed in 1887 on the insistence of liberal-minded, upper-caste reformers including M. G. Ranade, and took on issues like Hindu prohibition against sea-voyages, child marriage, dowry, prohibition against widows marrying again, and very marginally, the social disabilities suffered by the 'depressed classes' (untouchables and shudras). The Conference met for a few years before it was literally driven out by traditionalists (led by Bal Gangahdar Tilak) who threatened to burn down the premises if reformers dared to show up. Even at its peak, the Conference remained deeply split between extremist Hindu nationalists and timid reformers. On the one side were vehement Hindu nationalists like Bal Gangadhar Tilak who saw even the most humane reforms (raising the age of consent for girls from 10 years to 12 years, for instance) as an unbearable admission of Hindu inferiority before the British. Other extremists included influential leaders like Lala Lajpat Rai, B. C. Pal and Sri Aurobindo. (Today's Hindu nationalists revere these extremist leaders, especially Aurobindo and Tilak). The other side was represented by reform-minded traditionalists led by M. G. Ranade and Telang who sought reform, in Ranade's words, 'not as an innovation, but as a return and restoration of our past history' (Heimsath 1964: 184). Any critique of the irrationalities and injustices of 'our past history' was simply not permitted: it was nationalism rather than Enlightenment that was the main driving force behind the national social conference.

The reformist wing of Congress continued to function until M. K. Gandhi emerged as the acknowledged leader of the party in 1916. Gandhi subsumed the social reform platform into his own 'Constructive Programme' which, among other things, promised to improve the lot of the 'depressed classes'. The constructive programme was big on promises, short on funds and paternalistic to boot. From the account Ambedkar provides in his understandably bitter book, *What Congress and Gandhi have done to the Untouchables*, Gandhi's idea of reform amounted to a call to caste Hindus to do good works out of the goodness of their heart. Even later, more mature reformist plans, like the Harijan Sevak Sangh launched by Gandhi in 1932, remained an upper caste affair which aimed to 'uplift' the outcastes by teaching them hygiene and temperance and such, while expressly keeping 'social reforms like abolition of caste, inter-dining ... and inter-caste marriages outside the scope' of its agenda (Ambedkar, 1945: 127).

Paternalism and traditionalism remained the hallmark of Congress on matters of social and cultural issues, leading to the bitter disillusionment of dalit and backward caste movements on the one hand, and socialists on the other. The showdown came over the issue of a separate electorate for untouchables (similar to separate electorates that had already been granted to Muslims, Sikhs and the princely states). The details of the Gandhi-Ambedkar confrontation that resulted in Gandhi going on a fast and Ambedkar having to agree to a compromise (the so-called Poona Pact, signed on September 24, 1932) are not directly relevant here. But following this confrontation, the essentially Hindu nature of Gandhi's social agenda became obvious. Gandhi saw social reform as a 'penance' that the twice-born had to do for having 'neglected the untouchables for ages', while keeping the untouchables firmly in the Hindu fold for the sake of numbers in the electoral democracy that was taking shape during that time.

The Poona Pact only deepened the already existing fissures between the radical critics of caste and the leadership of the Congress party. Gradually, starting with the famous Mahad satyagrah in 1927 when dalits broke the caste taboo against drinking water from upper caste tanks, dalits began to organize themselves and sought entry into skilled industrial work, especially in the textile mills in Maharashtra which became the nucleus of dalit mobilization. The dalit movement emerged as a political force at the same time as working classes and peasantry were forming their organizations. But as Omvedt points out (1994: 166), while non-Brahman, working class and peasant movements were absorbed into the Congress party as a part of the 'anti-imperialist united front', the dalit movement managed to maintain its political and intellectual independence. One hallmark of Ambedkar's leadership of the dalit movement was his fierce rationalism and his search for a new religion which could satisfy the spiritual urges of his people without binding them to the inegalitarian and irrational worldview of Hinduism. This search finally led Ambedkar to embrace a new Buddhism.

Secular-humanists: the complete cast

To focus only on Nehru and Ambedkar will be like reenacting the founding of America by starring only Thomas Jefferson and Tom Paine. There is no doubt that Nehru defined the socialist stream of rationalism and reform, and Ambedkar the stream that emerged from 'below the pollution line', to borrow the very apt description from Aloysius (1997). But both streams had other brilliant and brave men and women including poets, song-writers, novelists and scientists, to say nothing of political acti-vists and social reformers. In addition there were other thinkers who formally belonged to neither camp but have left their own mark.

Apart from Nehru himself, there are at least two other socialist thinkers who have left a valuable legacy. They are Bhagat Singh (1907–31), member of an armed 'terrorist' revolutionary socialist group who was hanged by the British for his subversive activities in 1931, and M. N. Roy (1887–1954) who moved from his youthful involvement in revolutionary 'terrorism' to become the founder of the Communist Party in India but eventually renounced Communism and turned to radical humanism.

Bhagat Singh wrote his well-known tract, *Why I am an Atheist*, literally under the shadow of the gallows in British jails. Bhagat Singh belongs to the select company of rationalists who refuse to take refuge in the consolation of God in their time of perso-nal crisis and strove to 'stand like a man with an erect head to the last, even to the gallows'. Bhagat Singh came to a materialist understanding of the world through his commitment to Marxism and urged his fellow revolutionaries to 'criticize, disbelieve and challenge every item of the old faith', because he found blind faith standing in the way of full development of the intellectual and moral development of the masses.

Manendra Nath Roy was another major Marxist thinker who came to champion the cause of rationalism and humanism. A revolutionary terrorist like Bhagat Sigh, Roy discovered Marxism, rose up in the Comintern under Lenin, and helped to establish the Communist Party in India in 1925. Ideological differences over Soviet policy toward anti-colonial movements in China and India led to his eventual expulsion from Comintern and tensions with the Communist party in India. Roy formally announced his break with Marxism in 1936 by rejecting historical determinism and class war and declared that without a cultural and philosophical revolution, no social or political revolution was possible in India (Haithcox 1971). Roy was welcomed into CSP by Nehru and Jayaprakash Narayan. But Roy and many of his followers who joined CSP seemed to suffer from a sense of political messianism and did not find the party radical enough for their purist understanding of Marxist dogma. Roy himself and his followers gradually parted company from CSP for their own independent political activity out-side the fold of both Congress and the Communists.

One of the contributions of the Congress socialists which outlasted the CSP itself was the encouragement and patronage it provided to the Progressive Writers'

Association that formally came together in 1936 at the Lucknow session of Congress which was presided over by Nehru. The initiative for starting an all India forum form left-leaning writers was taken up by a group of Urdu-speaking intellectuals, headed by Sajjad Zaheer, who drew up a manifesto in 1935 while studying in London. By their own account, as recorded by Mulk Raj Anand, a much admired novelist who was one of the founding members of PWA, they wanted to take a positive stand against the forces of darkness including the worldwide economic depression, Fascism in Europe and colonialism in their homeland. It was in the Nanking restaurant on Denmark Street in London in November 1935 they drew up a manifesto that laid the foundations of PWA.[2] Sajjad Zaheer returned to India with the manifesto and recruited well-known poets, story-tellers and novelists including Premchand (who presided over the first conference of PWA) and Faiz Ahamad Faiz to the cause of 'purposive art', art that aspired to 'rescue literature from the conservative classes' and address the problems of 'hunger and poverty, social backwardness and political subjection', as the Manifesto announced. It is worth quoting from this famous manifesto to get a better idea of what the progressive writers saw their mission as:

(1) It is the duty of Indian writers to give expression to the changes in Indian life and to assist the spirit of progress in the country by introducing scientific rationalistm in literature. They should undertake to develop an attitude of literary criticism which will discourage the general reactionary and revivalist tendencies on questions like family, religion, sex, war and society and to combat literary trends reflecting communalism, racial antagonism, sexual libertinism and exploitation of man by man. ...

(4) All that arouses in us the critical spirit, which examines customs and institutions in the light of reason, which helps us to act, to organize ourselves, to transform, we accept as progressive (Malik 1967).

The movement was immediately attacked as being a pawn of the Communists and as being disrespectful of people's religion, to which PWA responded by insisting that most of the writers associated with it had nothing to do with Communism, and that the PWA did not consider religious faith as a 'disembodied concept' but assessed it in terms of the impact it had on social life (Zaheer: 81). The influence of PWA, even at its peak, remained limited to Urdu writers including Faiz Ahmad Faiz, Sahir Ludhianwi, Rajinder Singh Bedi, Amrita Pritam, Krishan Chander and Upedra Nath Ashk. Hindi writers, perhaps representing Hindu nationalist biases stayed away. The Partition broke the bonds, physically separating the writers in different countries. Even though short-lived, PWA provided a model for engaged artists and intellectuals.

The second, and far more substantial, stream of intellectuals and activists came to the secular humanist position through their first-hand experience of living below the pollution line. British colonialism which simultaneously colluded with upper castes and opened up new opportunities for the lower castes, opened the floodgates to waves of protests against the old order. It was as though the subaltern castes 'were waking up to the fact that they were no longer inhabiting a prison', and that they could break out of the demeaning occupations they had been consigned to based upon their birth (Aloysius, 1998: 77).

A fierce rationalism, often verging on complete atheism, was the hallmark of those anti-caste movements which have had the most lasting impact through the 19th and 20th centuries. The revolutionary neo-Buddhism of Bhimrao Ramji Ambedkar

(1891–1956), one of the architects of India's Constitution, was anticipated by the Satya Shodhak Samaj of Jotirao Phule (1827–90) which combined the rationalism and egalitarianism of Buddha and Kabir with a close reading of Thomas Paine's *The Rights of Man* and *The Age of Reason*, to propagate an alternative to the worldview of Brahminism. Other backward caste leaders, notably Iyothee Thass (1845–1914) and Lakshmi Narasu (1861–1934) in Tamil Nadu also turned to the teachings of the historical Buddha to defy the religious legitimation of caste. The turn to Buddhism found its final culmination in the lifework of Ambedkar.

Dalit rationalism was not always contained within the limits of religion, however enlightened the religious tradition might be. The case in point is the complete atheism of E. V. Ramasamy Naicker (1879–1973), popularly known as 'Periyar', or 'the great man', who founded the Self-Respect League in Tamil Nadu in 1926. Periyar began his career as a Congressman sympathetic to Gandhi's constructive work but became a severe critic of Gandhi's Hindu traditionalism. While he admired the modernist rationalist Buddhism of Iyothee Thass, he refused to propagate Buddhism or any other religion. He completely gave up on all conceptions of god and developed atheism as a 'creative mode of engagement with the problems of faith in a society ruled by caste' (Geetha and Rajadurai 1998: 308). A similar movement away from the enlightened, rationalistic Vedantism can be found among some followers of Narayan Guru (1854–1928) one of the most influential anti-caste reformers of the state of Kerala. Narayan Guru, an ascetic belonging to the lowly Ezhavas caste of toddy tappers, tried to 'de-Brahminize' Hindu gods and rituals by setting up alternative temples open to all castes and by turning these temples into centers for secular learning. Some of Guru's followers, including Kerala's well-known rationalist K. Ayyappan (1889–1968), broke away from the God-centeredness of Guru's teachings. Ayyappan famously changed Narayan Guru's motto of 'One Caste, One Religion and One God for Man' to 'No Caste, No religion and No God for Man'.

Rationalists were pretty unanimously opposed to Gandhian faith-based politics, which they saw as deeply conservative. But Gandhi's 'constructive program' among the rural masses proved to be attractive enough for some committed rationalists and radical critics of caste. The well-known atheist Goparaju Ramchandra Rao, aka Gora (1902–75) who popularized the concept of 'positive atheism' and founded the well-known Atheist Center in Vijaywada in Andhra Pradesh, ended up as an admirer of Gandhi and continued with Gandhian social programs for economic equality even after Gandhi's death. As he describes in his book, *An Atheist with Gandhi*, what brought together the two men with such divergent views regarding God and religion was their pragmatism: Gandhi accepted Gora's atheism as he thought that it could break the barriers between different castes and religious groups, while Gora accepted Gandhi's theism because it did not prevent him from manifesting a free will in practical reforms.

Finally, mention must also be made of the nascent community of Indian scientists. Starting in 1817 with the establishment of Hindu College in Calcutta (which became Presidency College in 1855), a number of important colleges and universities were established in Calcutta, Aligarh, Delhi, Madras and Bombay that introduced the sons of Indian elite to developments in modern science. The growing aspirations of Indian scientists for professional recognition and advancement under the colonial regime, which did not have a high opinion of Indian science, led Mahendra Lal Sircar, a graduate of Calcutta Medical College, to agitate for the formation of the Indian Association of the Cultivation of Science in 1876. By the early decades of the 20th century, India had already chalked up considerable successes on the international scene: Jagdish Chandra Bose, Prafulla Chandra Ray, C. V. Raman had established themselves as international authorities in their fields, with Raman winning the Noble Prize in 1930. By the time of the freedom struggle and independence, India already had a second generation of natural scientists, represented most prominently by Meghnad Saha, P. C. Mahalanobis, Homi Bhabha, among others (Lourdusamy 2004; Baber 1996).

While they won international recognition for their work (which was quite a remarkable achievement, given the British condescension and prejudices they had to fight against), this generation of scientists remained highly ambivalent about their own religious-cultural beliefs. They seemed to be split between rationalism and nationalism, between their allegiance to the universal republic of science and the allegiance they felt toward their culture and religion. While they understood how badly the spiritualist metaphysics, mystical epistemology and caste-based division of labor had retarded the progress of science in India, they were simultaneously driven to defend the scientific abilities of the 'Hindu mind', while denigrating the Islamic contributions to Indian science and technology. While they urged their compatriots to adopt new methods of learning, many (especially P. C. Ray and J. C. Bose) presented modern science largely as a revival of scientific methods of ancient Hindu rishis, often casting themselves as new rishis and their laboratories as temples of learning. With the notable exception of Meghnad Saha, who was outspoken in his critique of Vedic orthodoxy and Gandhian anti-modernism, other scientists of this era did not use their scientific knowledge to examine the validity of the metaphysical truths that served to explain nature for the vast majority of their countrymen.

The meaning of a scientific temper

The phrase 'scientific temper' is not particularly Indian, but it has a uniquely Indian flavor and fervor to it. In the Indian context, the call for cultivating a scientific temper was more than a mere slogan promoting critical thinking in general: it was a call for redefining what constituted truth, evidence and reason. Like the *philosophes* of the Enlightenment, Indian secularists were trying to *re-evaluate the entire episteme of their culture in light of the knowledge made available by modern science.* Their task was much more arduous since they were working in the shadow of the colonial masters, whose ideas they simultaneously admired *and* resisted. The British had looked at India either through the romantic lens of theosophy and spiritualism, or through the lens of Christian missionaries who saw nothing but pagan darkness in Indian culture. The challenge before the Indian enlighteners was to avoid both these extremes. Their task was to develop an understanding of the scientific method and scientific spirit that demarcated it from mystical ways of knowing, but which was not completely cut off from the existing cultural traditions and religious inheritance of the people of India.

The writings of M. N. Roy and to a lesser extent, Nehru, stand out for putting flesh on the idea of a scientific temper and connecting it to the universal history of ideas. On the other hand, the writings of Ambedkar are unique in their attempt to connect modern scientific rationality to a living (albeit minority) religious tradition, namely, Buddhism. Moreover, the neo-Buddhist Ambedkar and the rationalist-atheist Periyar and the 'positive-atheist' Gora have left behind a valuable legacy of new traditions and new rituals of birth, marriage and death that do away with gods and the immortal soul and yet enable ordinary people to find a sense of sacredness.

Nehru's writings, especially his *Discovery of India*, provide many glimpses of his genuine wonder and excitement at the breakthroughs that modern science made in exploring and understanding the world we live in. As a student of history, Nehru understood very well that the scientific revolution had brought about a radical transformation of the criteria of reason which had universal implications. He wanted India to awaken to this revolution in the fullest way possible, which meant not just borrowing new technologies, but questioning the truths we hold sacred and infallible on the authority of the ancients. Nehru described a scientific temper as

> the adventurous and yet critical temper of science [which demands] the search for truth and new knowledge, the refusal to accept anything without testing and trial, the capacity to change previous conclusions in the face of new evidence and the reliance on observed fact and not on preconceived theory, the hard discipline of the mind ... (Nehru, 1956: 525).

While he fully recognized that there are human experiences which lie beyond the reach of science, which deals with the material and sensible world, Nehru insisted that the spirit of science – that is, the spirit of questioning, the spirit of fallibility and willingness to change one's beliefs in proportion with the evidence –

> is necessary for life itself and the solution of its many problems. Too many scientists today, who swear by science, forget all about it outside their particular spheres. The scientific approach and temper are, or should be, a way of life, a process of thinking, a method of acting and associating with our fellow-men. Scientific temper is the temper of a free man ... (DI, 525–26).

M. N. Roy's words, below, also convey the flavor of what scientific outlook meant to the modernist-secularists:

> A philosophical revolution is a precondition for the much delayed but inevitable national renaissance of India ... the adoption of a scientific outlook, the application of the scientific method to the problems of life will necessarily mean the rejection of ideas, ideals, institutions and traditions that are cherished as the peculiar features of Indian culture (Roy 1997: 407).

But what was the 'scientific outlook' and how did it differ from the religious outlook?

> [T]he scientific outlook is essentially materialistic – a term so very misunderstood and piously abhorred in India. Scientific outlook does not take anything for granted. It does not admit miracles, occasional or perpetual. It seeks and eventually finds the cause of every phenomenon. ... It is based on positive knowledge, not on belief, speculation or fantasy. As such, it is hostile to the religious, metaphysical and teleological view of the universe, life, history and society. The religious view is opposed to all free inquiry. Its pivot is authority, which defies or eludes empirical test ... (ibid.: 407–8).

These statements give a flavor of the kind of broad and deep critique of religious reason the modernists had in mind when they talked of modern science and a scientific temper. Clearly, they were arguing for more than merely spreading scientific literacy, and popularizing current scientific facts and figures: they were trying to bring the fundamental metaphysical presuppositions and ways of knowing prescribed by Hinduism in tune with scientific knowledge. They sought to replace the traditional Hindu ideal of 'eternal' and infallible 'Truth' with a more humble and a more fallible view of knowledge which could be backed by the kind of evidence that all people, using their ordinary five senses and basic rules of logic, could ascertain for themselves.

The fate of the scientific temper

In this concluding section, we will ask a simple question: What happened to the legacy of secular-humanists?

The short answer is: nothing much. The organized attack on superstition that the secular-humanist championed never materialized. India acquired the trappings of a modern nation-state without undergoing a classic class revolution. Or rather, the mostly upper-caste bourgeoisie took control of the machinery of the state, the industry and the civil society without demanding or encouraging any serious revision of the essentials of elite, Sanksritic Hinduism. Indeed, rather than deploy a scientific temper to purge Indian culture of the Hindu myths and metaphysical claims, as the rationalists tried so valiantly, science has been used mostly to *bolster* these false myths and metaphysical schemes.

The obvious question is *why* secular-humanist ideas failed to engage the imagination and conscience of the urban industrial and commercial bourgeoisie, the rural owner-producers or even the white-collar mental workers/intellectuals in the agencies of the state and civil society. The greatest mystery of all is why even those with advanced degrees in natural sciences have shown no great enthusiasm for cultivating a scientific outlook. Even on such matters that directly overlap with science's territory – the existence of atman, the truth of reincarnation and karma, the possibility of miracles, the efficacy of rituals and prayers, the mystical ways of knowing etc. – the Indian scientific community has been largely conspicuous by its silence.

Part of the explanation surely lies in the dismal state of education, including science education. Learning science is more a matter of the memorization of facts rather than mastering the critical thinking and careful weighing of evidence that science requires. Moreover, in conditions of rather severe deprivation that many millions still suffer, there is not much motivation to deny the gods and their miracles.

But there are at least two other more serious factors, specific to Indian society, that seem to have played a role in dampening the momentum for rationalism. To begin with, there seems to be an elective affinity between those on the lower rungs of caste hierarchy and scientific rationalism. It is true that not all anti-caste movements have been rationalist, but all rationalist movements have been stridently anti-caste and all have attracted intellectuals and activists from anti-caste movements. Most Indian scientists and intellectuals come from privileged upper-caste backgrounds and feel quite at home in the inherited religious traditions and do not feel the existential or emotional need to examine these traditions critically.

Secondly, leading voices of protest and transformation in India have come from the Marxist tradition. While theoretically very sophisticated, Indian Marxists have remained stuck in a rather mechanical understanding of Marxism and not paid sufficient attention to the role of religion, culture and ideas in general in perpetuating *caste* inequities. This neglect of ideas has been compounded by the nationalistic and populist strains in the non-Marxist, Gandhian intellectuals who in recent past have spent more time and energy in condemning the Orientalism of the British imperialists rather than fighting the indigenous force of custom and habit.

In conclusion, the project of the Indian Enlightenment remains incomplete.

Notes

1 By 'secular-humanist' I simply mean someone who believes that 'the affairs of human beings should be governed not by faith in the supernatural but by reliance of reason and evidence adduced from the natural world' (Jacoby 2004: 4).
2 The original signatories in London included: Jyoti Ghosh, Mulk Raj Anand, Promode Sengupta, Mohammad Din Taseer and Sajjad Zaheer. See the memoir-cum-history of PWA by Sajjad Zaheer titled *Roshnai* that he wrote in a Pakistani prison.

References

Aloysius, G. (1997) *Nationalism without a Nation*, New Delhi: Oxford University Press.
Ambedkar, Bhimrao R. (1936) *The Annihilation of Caste*, Jalandhar: Beem Patrika.
—— (1945) *What Congress and Gandhi have done to the Untouchables*, Bombay: Thacker and Co.
Austin, Granville (1999) *Working a Democratic Constitution: A History of Indian Experience*, New Delhi: Oxford University Press.
Baber, Zaheer (1996) *The Science of Empire*, Albany: State University of New York.
Geetha, V. and Rajadurai, S. V. (1998) *Toward a non-Brahmin Millennium*, Calcutta: Samya Press.
Gora (Goparaju Ramchandra Rao) (n.d.) *An Atheist with Gandhi*, http://positiveatheism.org.
Haithcox, John P. (1971) *Communism and Nationalism in India: M.N. Roy and Comintern Policy, 1920–1939*, Princeton: Princeton University Press.
Heimsath, Charles (1964) *Indian Nationalism and Hindu Social Reform*, Princeton, NJ: Princeton University Press.
Israel, Jonathan (2001) *Radical Enlightenment: Philosophy and the Making of Modernity, 1650–1750*, New York: Oxford University Press.
Jacoby, Susan (2004) *Freethinkers: History of American Secularism*, New York: Free Press.
Kors, Alan C. (2003) Preface, *Encyclopedia of the Enlightenment*, vol. 1, New York: Oxford University Press.
Lourdusamy, J. (2004) *Science and the National Consciousness in Bengal, 1870–1930*, New Delhi: Orient Longman.
Malik, Hafeez (1967) 'The Marxist literary movements in India and Pakistan', *Journal of Asian Studies*, 24(4): 649–64.
Nehru, Jawaharlal (1951) *Discovery of India*, London: Meridian.
Omvedt, Gail (1994) *Dalits and the Democratic Revolution: Dr. Ambedkar and the Dalit Movement in Colonial India*, New Delhi: Sage Publications.
Ray, Sibnarayan (ed.) (1997) *Collected Works of M.N. Roy, Vol. IV, 1932–36*, New Delhi: Oxford University Press.
Roy, M. N. (1968) 'Secularism, indeed!' in V. K. Sinha (ed.) *Secularism in India*, Bombay: Lalvani Publishing House.
—— (n.d.) *Science and Superstition*, Dehradun: Indian Renaissance Association Ltd.
Zaheer, Sajaad (2006) *Roshnai: The Light: A History of the Movement for Progressive Literature in the Indo-Pak Subcontinent* (A translation of *Roshnai* by Amina Azfar), Karachi: Oxford University Press.

13 Outline of a revisionist theory of modernity[1]

Sudipta Kaviraj

Outline of the theory that needs revision

What this chapter offers is, in a literal sense, an outline. It needs fuller theoretical elaboration (Kaviraj 2000, 1994). It also needs more detailed discussion of historical evidence. Its focus is a question usually neglected in current social theory. How should a theory of modernity cope with historical difference? My dissatisfaction with received modernization theories has been driven by my parochial interest in Indian history, just as that theory was devised by the need to understand the equally parochial interest of making sense of primarily European history. But if modernity is viewed as a process that expands from the West to other parts of the world, this raises not merely a historical but also a theoretical question. It is certainly necessary to understand the history of modernity in other settings, but also to ask what shape the theory should assume if it is to deal with this expanding historical diversity. The original theory went through two later extensions. The first appears legitimate: the application of the European theory of modernity to cover non-European societies that originated and functioned as extensions of the Western world – like Canada, America and Australia – on the partially correct ground that their social histories were sufficiently similar to Europe's. But some historical sociologists have objected to this simple transfer.[2] There was a second extension of the 'European' theory of modernity which was of a very different character. This was the widespread application of this theory in the 1950s to non-European societies in the form of sociological theories of modernization, political theories of 'political development' and economic theories of growth (Shils 1968). To put it schematically, but not inaccurately, all these were theories of 'transition'. All such theories expected societies which started their transformation towards modernity later to follow the examples and, to be more precise, the institutional forms of European history of the nineteenth century, especially, the manner in which social theory interpreted the history of these forms. To put it in Marx's graphic phrase, modern European history showed to the societies of Asia, Africa and Latin America 'the images of their future' (Marx 1969a: 19).

Disaggregating the general theory of modernity

At the most abstract level, the 'general theory of modernity' can be seen to consist of two large proposals about modern history. The *first thesis* states that the transformation of European societies was not just another instance of usual historical change; it was a new kind of newness. Marx, Weber, and earlier writers like Guizot agreed that the birth of modern Europe saw the emergence of a new civilization which altered the relations of forces between the various cultures or civilizations of the world. This thesis is mainly inward looking, comparing modern Europe with previous European social forms. There is a *second thesis* that was, in a strict sense, absent from the work of earlier thinkers like Kant, Hegel or Guizot and really emerged in the works of Marx and Weber. In these earlier thinkers there was certainly a vivid sense of the growing superiority of the newly emergent European civilization, often so strong that it affected the linguistic usage of the term 'civilization'. Before this conceptual and theoretical change, the European Christian civilization was contrasted to others like the Islamic, Chinese or Hindu; but after this change, European self-definition altered this usage crucially, and contrasted the *civilized* society of Europe with other societies which were rude (including those which would have been regarded as different civilizations before) or where civilization was merely rudimentary or clearly inferior.

This move achieved two changes simultaneously – both in the direction of losing differentiation and towards homogeneity. First, this encouraged a falsely homogeneous picture of modern European civilization. Second, correspondingly, using this contrast as a major characteristic, it produced a falsely homogeneous picture of other civilizations by emphasizing their 'rudeness' – i.e., pre-modernity. By this conceptual re-description, this new theory recast the relation between Europe and other parts of the world. Europe now contained a new kind of civilization that was universalistic in several ways. It was based on universal principles in two senses. First, they were based on and justifiable by appeals to rules of a universal reason; and secondly, as a corollary, its achievements could be in principle achieved by all other human societies. This was accompanied by a strong belief that as reason and enlightenment spread across the world, these achievements – both practical and moral – would be owned by other peoples and realized in their societies. Modernity would thus be a universal civilization, and the rest of the world was now seen as future recipients of this civilization of modernity. In the works of Marx and Weber this rather general historical expectation was given more explicit and theoretical form.

This theory common to Marx and Weber reflected with greater accuracy the new relation of power that had emerged between modern Europe and its colonial possessions. By the end of the nineteenth century the theory had two parts: the first provided a 'theory' of the causes, present character and probable future trends of modernity in Europe; the second offered a *hypothesis* that this form had the power to destroy earlier social forms in the rest of the world and install a universal social form. I wish to suggest that we should accept the first part of this theory because, between its many versions – from Hegel down to Foucault, Western social theory is still answering those questions – it provides powerful, rich and still evolving conceptions of modern European history. However, in the light of our constant difficulties, we should reject the second part suggesting an easy diffusionist teleology, and install in its place a theory which holds that there is a logic of self-differentiation in modernity. The more modernity expands and spreads to different parts of the world the more it becomes differentiated and plural. To invoke Dipesh Chakravarty's phrase, Europe can be 'provincialized' (Chakrabarty 2002) only if we recognize that although its origins were certainly European, modernity's subsequent global expansion forces it increasingly to leave behind and forget its origins.

In fact, the two sub-theories that the common theory housed within itself were of quite different character. The first theory was working on actual historical evidence, and applied casts of interpretative/explanatory understanding on an historical process *after the fact*. The second theory contained a body of hypothetical ideas about the expected transformation of non-European societies, where the processes of modernity had not yet begun: the theorization was therefore *prognostic* and primarily speculative. It extrapolated trends from the European case to other cultures, without close inspection of what actually happened when modernity began to appear in these social contexts. The two theories, though plausibly connected by an abstract frame of expectation, were really of rather different kinds, based on different kinds of evidence and followed different methods of reasoning.

Structure and history in Marx's thought: the idea of 'trajectories'

In one sense, the kind of thinking I am proposing is not altogether new. Antecedents of this form of analysis can be found in the classical theories, though, for understandable reasons, these remained mere sketches, and were not elaborated at full length. In all three significant thinkers of historical modernity, traces of such analyses about varying forms and trajectories can be found. I shall illustrate this by analyzing some parts in Marx's writings on capitalism, and then make a case that we should take up that strand, and develop it in the case of non-European cultures (Roy 2000).

Two types of theoretical arguments can be found in Marx's sprawling works on the rise of capitalism. It is well known that the precise methods of analysis differ between Marx's economic and political writings. When commenting on the constant ebb and flow of politics – in France or Germany – he maintains an *historicist* method[3] of describing events which are unique in their agents, in the forces which act in them, and in their historical outcomes. Although there are attempts, particularly when dealing with Germany, to discern a long-term pattern (Marx 1969b) there is a sense that the fluctuations of political life are too sudden and chaotic to plot onto serene designs of progress. When writing about economic life, by contrast, Marx's mode of presentation is predominantly *structural*, delineating in persistent detail the fundamental arrangement of relationships in the capitalist economy, describing its elements and the determinate relations between them to produce an invariant architecture. Sketches of historical analyses of capitalist development are interspersed throughout the argument but generally subordinated to this structural view. But if we look closely, it is possible to suggest a significant difference between the two ways of thinking about capitalism in Marx's works. Although the structural form of writing encourages a view that capitalism is a 'universal form', i.e., wherever it arises, it eventually produces an economy of the same structural design, the historical analyses seem to suggest a very different implication.

If we look at Marx's understanding of the *history* of capitalism, as opposed to its *structure*, two rather different ways of thinking can be distinguished in his reflections about the evolution of capitalist social forms. In Marx's early writings, down to the middle period, there is a clear expectation that, although the capitalist mode of production emerged in different times and conditions in specific European societies, and social and political institutions associated with the rise of the capitalist economy take even more complex patterns of evolution, eventually all societies tend historically towards a single structural form in which social relations are commoditized or become, in some sense, abstract and commodity-like (Lukacs 1971; Habermas 1986: Chapter IV). It is possible then to extend this in Lukacs's style to conceive of a necessary pattern of interconnected structures of capitalist economy, bureaucratized states, market-dominated cultures, nuclear families – all as part of a global design of modernity. The rise of capitalism therefore meant the establishment of a similar kind of society in all European countries. In later writings, Marx takes an increasingly more complex view about this historical question; and it appears that, instead of a belief in an equi-final trajectory of capitalist evolutions, it moves towards a more plural vision of historical paths. Finally, this perception led to the well-known distinction in the final chapters of *Capital I* and parts of *Capital III* between the 'first way' of capitalist development, which Marx designates as 'really revolutionary', and a separate path designated as 'late capitalism' in which both the purely economic logic of capitalist evolution of the economy and associated sociological and political transformations settle into a distinctive 'second way' (Marx 1971: 334). In the 'first way', capitalism drives forward the political forces of democracy; in the second, it retards and obstructs them (Marx and Engels 1972, 1942). If we read this division in European modernity not as a partial and temporary obstruction but as a dynamic pattern, we arrive at an interesting theoretical conclusion. At least by implication, this is then the beginning of a theory of 'multiple modernities' within the Western world itself, and inside the canonical traditions of Western social theory. This would suggest that although the impulses towards a capitalist economy, urbanization, and political democracy are all general tendencies in the history of modern Europe, there are different configurations of their complex figuration, and even differential *trajectories* within the history of European modernity.

It is this second theory in Marx which seems to have more explanatory power in understanding the modern history of Europe. Paths of German, Italian and Russian modernity, taken in this wider and more complex sense, diverged significantly from the earlier English and French trajectories, and led to an immense historical conflict in Europe about which of these could establish itself as dominant and 'universal', until this contest was decided by the violence of the Second World War. This will also lay to rest the unconvincing idea of a spontaneous combustion of democracy in all European cultures that pervades the less historically sensitive version of social science common sense. Drawing on this alternate theory, we can ask: if the history of the West itself shows a tendency for forms of modernity to diffract, how can we reasonably expect them to be homogeneous when modernity goes out of the frame of European history into other continents and cultures (Taylor 2004). Let me make this point independently of Marx's theory.

Two views of Western modernity

Symmetry and sequence

Theorists who analyze modern European history acknowledge that the phenomenon called modernity is not a single, homogeneous process, but a combination of several which can be isolated and distinguished. When we are talking about modernity, we are talking about a number of processes of social change which can be studied or analyzed independently of each other – such as, capitalist industrialization, the increasing centrality of the state in the social order (Foucault's 'governmentality'), urbanization, sociological individuation, secularization in politics and ethics, the creation of a new order of knowledge, vast changes in the organization of family and intimacy, and changes in the fields of artistic and literary culture. If modernity is shown to be analytically decomposable into these constituent processes, that raises a further and crucial question: how should we view the relationship among them?

Broadly, there are two ways of answering this question, which I shall designate as 'theories' of *symmetry* and *sequence*. The conventional theory that dominates the common sense of social science accepts the *symmetrical* view. It suggests, first, that these separate processes are linked by a *functional* relation of interdependence, and second, in consequence, these processes develop *symmetrically*.

Functionalist conceptions of modernity

To put it schematically, if modernity consists of five distinct isolable processes, say A, B, C, D and E, this theory holds that they are *functionally dependent* on each other, i.e., either all of them would emerge, evolve and survive interdependently, or none at all. Besides, the emergence of *any one* or more of these constituents creates conditions for the emergence of the others, leading eventually to the establishment of the whole constellation. Finally, since they tend to emerge simultaneously, their historical development is likely to be parallel and symmetrical. In some theoretical models, as in Weber, these are all seen as instantiations of some larger, more abstract, general principle like 'rationality'. The rise of a capitalist economy based on economic rationality is not accidentally related to the growth of bureaucratization in state practices; they are deeply linked because bureaucratic rationality is simply the application of the same general rational principles to the sphere of the state's activity. The rise of secular ethics, or the decline of religious culture in spheres of social and family life, can then be seen as being related to this process, as a further instance of a general, comprehensive 'rationalization' of life. Despite the well-known differences between Marx and Weber's theoretical pictures of a capitalist society, there can be a powerful overlap. Clearly, this is precisely how the capitalist society is viewed by an influential strand in Western Marxism. Lukacs conceives of the capitalist society as an 'expressive totality' in Althusser's phrase, 'a circle of circles', with the principle of rationality in the axial circle at the centre of this design (Lukacs 1971; cf. Althusser 1969). These processes can be given separate histories, but they are not really causally separate; because of their strong functional connection, their histories are bound to be symmetrical. Early capitalist economies are found to be linked to the rise of liberal ideologies, and early impulses towards constitutionalism (anachronistically over-interpreted as democracy), the first signs of *gesellschaft*-based associationism, and experiments with state secularism. The period from the fifteenth to the seventeenth centuries is thus a period of the rise of *modernity* in the literal comprehensive sense, i.e. the simultaneous rise of all these processes, each supporting the others. It is not surprising that slowly all these interdependent processes literally mature and eventually assume the enchanting form that we recognize as advanced capitalist democracies of today, which have ended history by becoming the collective object of desire of all human beings.

The sequential view

The symmetrical view still remains the dominant view in social theory, almost a default setting to which social science literature reverts absentmindedly (Shils 1968; Toulmin 1992). However, historical research about European modernity over the last few decades has moved in a different direction and calls, by implication, for a radically different theoretical model. Change in historical interpretation has been fuelled, among other things, by critical discussions on the relation between capitalism and democracy. Although conventional Marxist understanding regarded democratic institutions initially as functionally connected to the capitalist economy – as the ideal political superstructure of the capitalist mode of production – a heterodox line of thought claimed that democratic forms were not simply functional reflexes of the bourgeois economy, but political practices imposed upon a reluctant and hostile bourgeoisie by popular struggles of the working class (Thompson 1974). This view of a more contradictory rather than functional relation between capitalism and democracy has been subsequently widely accepted amongst historians, disrupting the benign hypothesis of capitalism inevitably creating the conditions for the growth of democratic politics. If the second view is accepted, the real history of European modernity comes out in a far more complicated way. It would then appear that the rise of capitalism was decisive and transformative for the economy precisely because of the *absence* of democracy in political life. In the absence of even rudimentary rights of resistance and legitimate protest against the intensifying demands of capitalist industrial work discipline, an unwilling and resisting peasantry, driven out of the countryside by economic distress, could be forcibly shaped into the familiar sociological form of the modern industrial proletariat. To put it schematically, the initial success of the capitalist productive organization was due precisely to the general absence of democratic institutions. Once capitalist industry was entrenched, and had reshaped the structure of the whole European economy into a general bourgeois form, working class political movements gradually drew democratic rights as concessions from the entrepreneurial classes and political elites. To characterize democracy as a necessary functional concomitant of capitalist economy is an astonishingly rationalizing and indolent way of viewing historic upheavals like the Chartist movement. It produces an ideologically rationalizing picture of capitalism as producing inevitable democratic political effects, showing it in a better light than it deserves historically. And it is indolent because it simply projects anachronistically into the past a state of affairs that has existed for a limited period since the 1920s. By the late nineteenth century, proletarian and lower class movements in major parts of Western Europe had secured substantial rights of political participation; and when the universal suffrage was conceded in early twentieth century, the poor in industrial capitalist societies could use their votes strategically to demand and eventually achieve the structure of a welfare state. This revisionist view of the historical relation between the economic logic of capitalism and the political logic of democracy leads to two further implications.

The narrower conclusion is that instead of emerging and evolving *symmetrically*, and being related *functionally*, capitalism and democracy had a contradictory at least oppositional relation for a long period in the early history of modernity. They could only develop *sequentially*. But after the rise of democracy modified some of the worst features of early capitalist iniquity, some (but not all) Western European societies developed the familiar outline of the 'advanced capitalist society', which combines the advantages of capitalist wealth and democratic freedom. According to a sequential reading of the history of Western modernity, this achievement was possible precisely because, in the West, all the different features of modern society did not emerge at the same time. These elements could not have been functionally related.

Let me show what the wider theoretical implications of this revisionist reading of history will be by taking up briefly the single example of thinking about democracy in

India. In political science literature, authors often point to the existence of various *preconditions* for the success of democracy. If we turn the conditions that are known to have existed at the time of the rise of European democracy, and treat them as preconditions for all other subsequent cases, the explanation of the sheer existence of Indian democracy becomes inordinately difficult. The conditions under which democracy arises in the West and in India are different in several significant respects:

1 In the West real democracy came to a capitalist society which was already economically converted into a capitalist form of production and already fairly wealthy in international terms of comparison (whether this was because of colonialism or not is a contested question that we can leave aside because that is irrelevant to my argument).
2 By the time universal suffrage democracy emerged, the sectoral structure of the economy was already transformed by the industrial revolution, and a relatively small agricultural sector existed against a much larger industrial working force (see Varshney 1995).
3 The secular *state* as a political device was long established, and secular legal arrangements established on the basis of a social consensus (cf. Nandy 1998; Madan 1998; Bhargava 2001b; Kaviraj 1998: 293–98).
4 Literacy levels were high, if not universal, while in India, at the time of the adoption of the constitution, literacy levels were below 3 percent, and that meant an ability just to sign one's name.
5 Processes of social individuation were far advanced, and medieval communal bonds were already in serious decline.
6 To use Foucault's terminology, European societies had already established 'states of governmentality'.
7 What Weber termed a bureaucratic state or a *rechtstaat* already existed in many Western European countries.

Were these differences in the historical conditions when democratic institutions were introduced likely to cause serious differences in the pattern in which democracy functioned and evolved?

Sequence and structure

Answering that question depends on how we conceive the relation between sequence and structure. Theorists who believe in the symmetrical model recognize that there is often a difference in sequence in which key modern processes are introduced in a particular society. However, to their way of thinking, this does not make a material difference in the longer term. Because of the functional connection, through which different elements of the modernist paradigm support and reinforce each other, after a time, when most of the essential elements are put in place, modern societies tend to look very similar. But it would follow from the sequential reading of European modernity that the sequence did matter substantially. Instead of the difference being gradually whittled down, the difference of origins and the set of initial conditions settled into radically different paths, so significant that while 'first way' capitalism led to the growth of political democracy in England and France, 'second way' capitalism in Germany, Italy and Russia preempted the growth of democratic institutions altogether, a dark prediction made with some force in Engels's last writings in the 1890s (Engels 1969).

Alterations to the theory

Four reasons for historical differentiation

In the next part of this chapter I shall offer four reasons for differentiation of trajectories, and provide some illustrations of such complexity from the history of modern India. These are not exhaustive; there can conceivably be other reasons for the differentiation of paths and institutional forms. But these show us why a revisionist theory is required.

Two meanings of 'initial conditions'

The first reason is connected to the diversity of 'initial conditions'. Modernity is a transition into a transformed set of institutions from a prior set that were different. In some theories of modernity, universality is seen as a feature of modern institutions, but certainly not of pre-modern ones. Clearly, pre-modern is a *secondary* description of such societies, and a naïve reading of this term might suggest that it is an invariant condition; but clearly it is not. Modernity might be uniform, but what exists before it must be structurally diverse. This is a suggestion that should be acceptable to both sides, those who believe in theories of symmetry and sequence. These structures constitute the 'initial' or prior conditions from which modern institutions begin to arise.

   The phrase 'initial conditions', used widely in historical explanations, appears unproblematic at first, but it is possible to detect two meanings in the use of this phrase. First, initial conditions might refer to those conditions that simply happen to exist as surrounding circumstances when a historical process of modern transformation starts. In this case, it is normal to expect that as the new process establishes itself its effects will slowly obliterate those initial circumstances. These would be initial in the sense that these conditions would exist at the start, when the process is weak, or immature, but would not leave any serious consequence when it matures. The initial character implies that these conditions are to be transcended. But in historical thinking initial conditions can also be used with a much stronger meaning. In this case, initial historical conditions in which processes of modernity begin to work impart to those processes and institutions specific qualities and forms which condition their further evolution. Initial conditions, to use Gadamer's terminology, remain 'effective-historical' (1981: 305ff).

The 'translation' of practices

Initial conditions in which modern institutions and processes arrive in particular societies determine the subsequent shape of their modernity to a substantial extent. In fact, there is no new unused 'place' to write modern practices on. Practices are 'written' upon pre-existing practices. Postcolonial theorists sometimes refer to this general pattern of events as 'hybridity'. But hybridity is an excessively general term, and does not distinguish between the many distinct ways in which the traditional and the European-derived modern might relate and configure. At times, the older and newer practices might tend in the same direction, and become miscible, as, for instance, in the case of the idioms of traditional religious toleration and modern secular institutions in India. In other cases, they might be more oppositional or contradictory. Consequently, while accepting that the idea of hybridity captures a historically significant fact, it is essential to emphasize the need for further conceptual refinement. A second conceptual strategy to capture this process is to regard them as a form of 'translation', which is a suggestive way of thinking about them, but with some attendant difficulties. In a literary translation too, two languages interact, and what is produced as the end effect is generally acknowledged to be more a fusion of meanings, rather than a simply one-way writing of the meanings of a text into an entirely different passive language. Language is never passive to that extent. Even in literary translations, it is impossible to turn off the connotative effectivity of the receiving language to ensure the transfer of meanings from the language of the text. The historical argument is largely similar: the social effectiveness of the prior practices are never entirely neutralized by the reception of new ways of doing things.

Specificities of sequence

The second reason for differentiation is simply drawn from the earlier discussion about sequencing. If sequencing plays a causative role in the specific formation of modernity in each particular society, it follows that the exact pattern of the interweaving or braiding of the processes would be of crucial importance. For example, several current discussions about Indian democracy can instantiate a larger debate about the precise sequencing effects of the component processes. To take but one example, observers have pointed out that one of the major problems for government policy is that Indian democracy operates in an economic environment in which the major part of the population still pursues agricultural occupations. Because of their electoral weight, the agrarian sector extracts huge subsidies from elected governments; yet such subsidies, apart from their efficiency, run up against a more fundamental limit, because a smaller sector of the economy – around 25 percent – cannot indefinitely subsidise a sector that is much larger in size (Varshney 1995). This is a sequence problem because Indian democracy arose at a time when the economy was largely agricultural.

Improvization

Third, modernity in traditional societies introduces processes of institutional change that are driven either by some kind of structural logic – like the operation of a market in which capitalist firms produce the primary products for the society's consumption – or an institutional norm – like democratic government, or secular states where institutions are deliberately organized around certain general principles. In the second type of cases, the historical evolution of modernity takes the form of 'generative' processes: they are centred around acceptance of distinctive fundamental *principles* which groups of actors – politicians, classes, communities – constantly seek to fit to their determinate historical circumstances. In the construction and running of institutions, the principles are more fundamental than external forms. Following these norms does not make any sense, unless these are translated into institutional forms, and institutional forms operate under initial conditions of intelligibility specific to these societies. Improvization, in this sense, i.e., not simply copying them from other successful democracies, but fitting them to a society's peculiar circumstances, is of the essence of the unfolding of the modern. As a result of such historical improvisation, it is likely that institutions of democracy or capitalism or secularism would tend to develop unprecedented features and institutional idiosyncrasies in different historical settings. Unlike conventional political science, the proper way of judging them is not to take a map of European institutions and decide whether the new forms are 'correct' or not – by judging if they fitted the European 'norm' – but to test them more abstractly and philosophically against the relevant principles.

To take a well-known Indian example, K. C. Wheare, the English political scientist, measured Indian federalism against the 'dominant' American-derived model, and decided to characterize it as 'quasi-federal' (1963), causing much avoidable anguish to a generation of Indian constitutionalists who made heroic attempts to defend the conceptual respectability of the Indian federation. Obviously, the correct response to Wheare was not to try to prove that the Indian system was really like the American one and that Wheare had empirically misjudged it. The correct response would have been to recognize that Wheare had used an inappropriate measure, and to theoretically endorse the Indian politicians' improvisation on the received architecture of federalism to suit the Indian political context. After all, the real test for a political institution of one country is not whether it resembled another, but if it could respond effectively to the political demands it was likely to encounter. Quite often, the only way of entrenching an institutional system in a different culture is precisely to break away from a slavish adherence to European precedents. What would have appeared unacceptably heterodox to the Euro-normal thinking of conventional political science in Wheare's time should be seen as a case of major success in imaginative political architecture.

Reflexivity

Finally, it is commonly acknowledged that one of the major features of the culture of modernity is the principle of reflexivity. This is a difficult and many-sided notion, and quite different aspects of modern culture and its typical institutions are regarded as reflexive in different senses. I shall deal with a few features, but there could conceivably be some others, which are left out of my discussion. Theories of modernity, which offer different judgments about it in descriptive or evaluative terms, concur that a central principle driving different spheres of modern culture was rational questioning or criticism. Appeals to authority were culturally undermined in vastly divergent fields – from art to scientific enquiry – and an appeal to rational argument and critical judgment finally decided acceptance of a proposition or a point of view. Weberian sociology suggests that this principle of rational-critical judgment animates the politics of liberal democracy, modern scientific culture, the constant search for economic efficiency, and modernity's re-foundation of ethics on human reason. Precisely because it is a common principle that organizes institutions in such divergent fields, this also provides a kind of overarching normative link between various aspects of the modern civilization.

This capacity for rational consideration and arriving at judgments that are argumentative, dialogical, provisional and revisable has another obvious field of application. In modern cultures people turn their capacity for rational reasoning and criticism upon themselves – at least in two ways. Reflexivity leads to assessments of their own conduct from an *exterior* point of view, which was unavailable to non-European societies before the arrival of Western ideas. New influences broke the obviousness and the immovability of cultural habitus, the impossibility of conceiving the world in any except an 'internal' way. Reflexivity however cannot stop there, simply using Western modernity as an exterior point of view that comprehensively undermines traditional cultures. The capacity for critical reflection extends to assessments of institutions and practices of Western modernity as well, leading to two further results. Reflection on the precise conditions in which a group of people or even individuals wish to realize some modern principle does give rise to improvisation and proliferation of new forms. If the Japanese develop techniques of running modern capitalist firms in innovative ways, saying that they do not conform to earlier known management patterns is hardly an effective argument.

Indeed, proliferation of new forms of this kind feed back into the older versions of institutions as well – extending the repertoire of capitalist management. More significantly, latecomers into modernity have the vast expanse of the historical experience of modern European civilization open for critical examination before them. If they take the impulse of critical reasoning and rejection of authority seriously, they will recognize that the unquestioned prestige of Western modernity, at least of its dominant ideological narrative, is a most formidable authority in contemporary culture which works exactly like other sources of authority, and needs critical evaluation. In fact, the powerful idea that animates the modern ideal – that individuals and societies should live an elective life, as they choose or think fit – requires this critical response. Turning the faculty of critical reasoning upon oneself, one's own situation, conduct, ideals, on one's own society and its practices, thus results in a critical reading of all history, including that of the modern West. Modern culture leads to an application of the same critical criteria to the experiences of Western modernity itself, though advocates of Western modernity are unnecessarily startled by this assertion. The peculiar popularity of Marxism among the intelligentsia of the colonial world is perhaps linked to the fact that it offered them a way of being both modern and anti-Western. It is entirely conceivable that a late entrant into modernity might not applaud every aspect of modern European civilization. They might reject some major proposals of modern politics or ethics, after subjecting them to rational criticism. The intellectual results of this kind of critical reasoning are not expressions of opposition to modernity, but an essential continuation of its spirit. The final reason for the deviation of new modernities from the old European ones is disillusionment with the overall pattern of life that European modernity itself has gradually elaborated over the last centuries. Disillusionment with aspects of Western modernity is likely to encourage the logic of institutional improvization even further. The historically declining imaginative power of the West, despite its military dominance, makes it unlikely that diverging trajectories of the modern in other parts of the world can be folded back into recognizable Western patterns – that people can be persuaded to force their futures into versions of the Western past.

Conclusion

A second threshold of social theory

If true, this argument has large implications. It appears that social theory in the widest sense – not merely in the explicit form of 'theory', but also as the inexplicit assumptions and methods that animate social science research in general – has entered an interesting critical period, because of a fundamental imbalance. One of the major new developments in social knowledge has been the addition of a vast body of careful historical knowledge about non-European societies to the immense documentation of Western life that already existed. But this extension has also led to an underlying theoretical crisis, because the more interesting and perceptive work on other societies is evincing increasing discomfort with the structure of received theory, simply because its major presuppositions, arguments, examples and generalizations were all drawn, quite naturally, from the stock of European historical experience. It is proving impossible to force this new body of intractable evidence into the received theoretical architecture. This might suggest that social sciences have imperceptibly reached a significant threshold. The methodological dispute in German sociology in the early twentieth century indicated that the common methods of natural science do not easily cross over into the very different field and materials of social science; scientific enquiry needed a methodological retuning when it crossed this boundary. In contemporary social science, we have reached a similar boundary between the West and other societies – a threshold that requires the social sciences to have significantly different concepts and theoretical generalizations. Producing what I have called 'secondary' descriptions is not a particularly promising response to this problem. It is necessary to preserve and continue the great tradition of Western theory without being imprisoned within its borders.[4]

In the last analysis, what this chapter suggests may be a matter of historical common sense. But the imaginative power of social theory is so overwhelming that much of contemporary mainstream social science – particularly the hinge that crucially links modern social theory, which developed in Europe to the emerging social science research of other societies – simply disregards this central question. It is time that this view, now a heterodoxy, becomes a new commonsense.

Notes

1 This is an abridged version of the article that appeared in *European Journal of Sociology*, 46(3), 2005.
2 S. N. Eisenstadt (2000) has suggested that if we think closely about American history, we are forced to recognize the first case of emendation in the direction of a theory of 'multiple modernities' (cf. Gaonkar 2001; Bhargava 2001a): i.e., there were peculiarities in American history and colonialism, the presence of three different races, the resultant use of endemic violence against racially subordinated communities or peoples – which made American modernity sufficiently different from the standard European cases to call for a serious attempt at theoretical differentiation.
3 Historicist in the strict sense used by German thinkers like Dilthey, not in the very different sense used by Popper (1945) in his Cold War study. In the first sense, historicism means staying away from law-like generalizations specific to natural sciences, and treating each historical situation as unique. Popper's idiosyncratic use means almost the opposite – a belief in inexorable historical teleology. Unfortunately, in much contemporary writing, the second sense has overshadowed the first.
4 In recent debates in Indian political thought, several authors have suggested a comparable programme. See for instance, Partha Chatterjee's attempt to theorize a distinction between civil and political society, in a way that is entirely different from European precedents: Chatterjee 2004; Chakrabarty 2002: Chapter I, where he explains what he means by 'provincializing'; Rajeev Bhargava's work on secularism points to significant changes in the theory of secularism in Indian nationalist discourse (Bhargava 2001). I make a similar point in 'In search of civil society' (Kaviraj and Khilnani 2001: Chapter 15).

References

Althusser, Louis (1969) 'The materialist dialectic', *For Marx*, London: Allen Lane, Penguin.
—— (1974) 'The outline of a theory of historical time', in Louis Althusser and Etienne Balibar (eds) *Reading Capital*, London: NLB.

Bhargava, Rajeev (2001a) 'Are there alternative modernities?' in N. N. Vohra (ed.) *Culture, Democracy and Development in South Asia*, Delhi: India International Centre/Shipra, pp. 9–26.

—— (ed.) (2001b rpt) *Secularism and its Critic*, Delhi: Oxford University Press.

—— (ed.) (1998) *Secularism and Its Critics,* Delhi: Oxford University Press.

Chakrabarty, Dipesh (2002) *Provincializing Europe,* Princeton, NJ: Princeton University Press.

Chatterjee, Partha (2004) *The Politics of the Governed,* New York: Columbia University Press.

Eisenstadt, S. N. (2000) 'Multiple Modernities', *Daedalus* (Winter).

Engels, Friedrich (1942) *Revolution and Counter-Revolution in Germany,* in Karl Marx and Friedrich Engels, *Selected Works,* Vol. I, London: Lawrence and Wishart.

—— (1969) 'Introduction to K. Marx, *Class Struggles in France* [1895]', in K. Marx and F. Engels, *Selected Works, Volume I*, Moscow: Progress Publishers, pp. 186–204.

Gadamer, Hans Georg (1981) *Truth and Method*, London: Sheed and Ward.

Gaonkar, Dileep (ed.) (2001) *Alternative Modernities*, Durham: Duke University Press.

Habermas, Jurgen (1986) *A Theory of Communicative Action,* Vol. I, Cambridge: Polity Press.

Kaviraj, Sudipta (1983) 'On the status of Marx's writings on India', *Social Scientist,* 124.

—— (1994) 'Dilemmas of democratic development', in Adrian Lefwich (ed.) *Democracy and Development*, Cambridge: Polity Press.

—— (2000) 'Modernity and politics in India', *Daedalus* (Winter).

—— (2001) 'In search civil society', in Sudipta Kaviraj and Sunil Khilnani (eds) *Civil Society: History and Possibilities*, Cambridge: Cambridge University Press.

—— (ed.) (1998) *Politics in India*, Delhi: Oxford University Press.

Lukacs, Georg (1971) 'Reification and the consciousness of the proletariat' in *History and Class Consciousness*, London: Merlin.

Madan, T. N. (1998) 'Secularism in its place', in Sudipta Kaviraj (ed.), *Politics in India*, Delhi: Oxford University Press.

Marx, Karl and Engels, Friedrich (1971) *Articles on Britain*, Moscow: Progress Publishers.

—— (1972) *Articles from the Neue Rhenische Zeitung, 1848–49*, Moscow: Progress Publishers.

Marx, Karl (1969a) *Capital,* Vol. I, Moscow: Progress Publishers.

—— (1969b) 'Revolution and counter-revolution in Germany (1851–52)', in Karl Marx and Friedrich Engels, *Selected Works,* Vol. I, Moscow: Progress Publishers.

—— (1971) *Capital,* Vol. III, Moscow: Progress Publishers.

—— (1973) *Grundrisse,* trans. Martin Nicolaus, Harmondsworth: Penguin.

Nandy, Ashis (1998) 'Politics of secularism and the recovery of religious tolerance', in Sudipta Kaviraj (ed.) *Politics in India*, Delhi: Oxford University Press.

Popper, Karl (1945) *The Open Society and Its Enemies*, London: Routledge and Kegan Paul.

Roy, M. N. (2000) *Selected Works of M. N. Roy, Volume I, 1917–1922*, Delhi: Oxford University Press.

Shils, Edward (1968) *Political Development in the New States*, Mouton: Paris.

Taylor, Charles (2004) *Modern Social Imaginaries*, Durham: Duke University Press.

Thompson, E. P. (1974) *The Making of the English Working Class*, Harmondsworth: Penguin.

Toulmin, Stephen (1992) *Cosmopolis*, Chicago: University of Chicago Press.

Varshney, Ashutosh (1995) *Democracy, Development and the Countryside*, Cambridge: Cambridge University Press.

Weber, Max (1994) *Political Writings*, Cambridge: Cambridge University Press.

Wheare, K. C. (1963) *Federal Governments*, London: Oxford University Press.

Part VI
Reconstruction

14 Reconstructing childhood

A critique of the ideology of adulthood[1]

Ashis Nandy

I

There is nothing natural or inevitable about childhood. Childhood is culturally defined and created; it, too, is a matter of human choice. There are as many childhoods as there are families and cultures, and the consciousness of childhood is as much a cultural datum as patterns of child-rearing and the social role of the child. However, there are political and psychological forces which allow the concept of childhood and the perception of the child to be shared and transmitted. And it is with the political psychology of this shared concept and this transmission that I am concerned in the following analysis.

In the modern world, the politics of childhood begins with the fact that maturity, adulthood, growth and development are important values in the dominant culture of the world. They do not change colour when describing the transition from childhood to adulthood. Once we have used these concepts and linked the processes of physical and mental change to a valued state of being or becoming, we have already negatively estimated the child as an inferior version of the adult – as a lovable, spontaneous, delicate being who is also simultaneously dependent, unreliable and willful and, thus, as a being who needs to be guided, protected and educated as a ward. Indirectly, we have also already split the child into two: his childlikeness as an aspect of childhood which is approved by the society and his childishness as an aspect of childhood which is disapproved by the society. The former is circumscribed by those aspects of childhood which 'click' with adult concepts of the child; the latter by those which are independent of the adult constructions of the child. Childlikeness is valued, sometimes even in adults. Childishness is frowned upon, sometimes even in children.

In much of the modern world the child is not seen as a homunculus, as a physically smaller version of the adult with a somewhat different set of qualities and skills. To the extent adulthood itself is valued as a symbol of completeness and as an end-product of growth or development, childhood is seen as an imperfect transitional state on the way to adulthood, normality, full socialization and humanness. This is the theory of progress as applied to the individual life-cycle. The result is the frequent use of childhood as a design of cultural and political immaturity or, it comes to the same thing, inferiority (Nandy 1983: Chapter 1). Much of the pull of the ideology of colonialism and much of the power of the idea of modernity can be traced to the evolutionary implications of the concept of the child in the Western worldview. Much of the modern awe of history and of the historical can also be traced to the same concept. Let me give two examples from the two centuries of British colonialism in India.

No better representative can be found than James Mill (1773–1836) for the sincerity of purpose which some social reformers brought into the culture of British rule in India. The nineteenth century liberal and Utilitarian thinker's view of his private responsibility as a father meshed with his view of Britain's responsibility to the societies under its patriarchal suzerainty. Mill chose to provide, almost single-handed, an intellectual framework for civilizing India under British rule. Yet he was no xenophobe. In fact, he saw the Indian empire as a training ground and an opportunity for both colonizers and colonized. Only there was a clear difference between his perceptions of the two sets of trainees. He saw Britain as the elder society guiding the young, the immature and, hence, primitive Indian society towards adulthood or maturity, and he felt that Indian culture required more fundamental restructuring than that required by relatively advanced Western cultures. It is thus that he provided his powerful, if indirect, ideological defence of British imperialism.

Mill's gentle civilizational mission was not the only metaphor of childhood that legitimized colonialism. Cecil Rhodes put it more clearly and, one might add, darkly: 'The native is to be treated as a child and denied franchise. We must adopt the system of despotism … in our relations with the barbarous of South Africa' (Chinweizu 1978: 403). I am unable to believe that the equation Rhodes made between childhood and barbarism was only a matter of racism. It also conveyed, I suspect, a certain terror of childhood. Rhodes was one of those persons who sensed – and had to sense – that children could be dangerous. Not merely do children define childhood, they also symbolize, once we have seen through our constructions of childhood, a persistent, living, irrepressible criticism of our 'rational', 'normal', 'adult' visions of desirable societies. Whoever does not know that 'childhood is the promise of a new world – and that new world can only be destroyed before it is born' (Evgeny 1976: 282)? Colonial ideology required savages to be children, but it also feared that savages could be like children.

Rudyard Kipling (1865–1936) sought to establish a relationship between the metaphor of childhood and British Imperialism on an altogether different plane. He was another one of those pathetic adults who wanted to reclaim, through his utopian vision of British rule, a lost childhood that had once been his own. Kipling, who was brought up primarily as an Indian child and whose experience in England as a child had been devastatingly cruel, spoke of the Indian as 'half savage and half child' – the former requiring civilization, the latter socialization. As I have argued elsewhere, to the extent the Indian was half child, he represented Kipling's own Indian childhood and his Indian experiences which he wanted to recover as an adult in his heroes; to the extent the Indian was half savage, he represented Kipling's fear of his authentic Indianized self, a self he wanted to disown for the sake of his inauthentic English – and Imperialist – self, with the help of his overemphasis on laws and rules, unconditional obedience to authority, and his idea of legitimate violence inflicted or suffered for a cause (see Nandy 1983).

Mill and Kipling only used the growing ideological links between evolutionism and biological stratification in their culture (Nandy 1983). The doctrine of progress, in the guise of models of biological and psychological development, had already promoted in post-medieval Europe, particularly in the nineteenth century, the use of the metaphor of childhood as a major justification of all exploitation. As Calvinism and the spirit of Protestantism consolidated their hold over important aspects of the European consciousness, the growth of the idea of the adult male as the ultimate in God's creation and as the this-worldly end-state for everyone was endorsed by the new salience of the productivity principle and Promethean activism, both in turn sanctified by far-reaching changes in Christianity. By about the sixteenth century the imagery of the child Christ, like that of the androgynous Christ, started becoming recessive in European Christianity. Instead, a patriarchal God, with a patriarchal relationship with his suffering and atoning son, became the dominant mode in the culture. In such a culture, the child's physical weakness was already being seen as coeval with his moral and emotional weakness, which needed.to be corrected with the help of mature persons. Without this correction, the child was seen to stand midway between the lower animals and humanity. In a culture in which nature, including non-human living beings, was seen as a lower stratum of God's creation, meant for man, the chosen species of God, the child as a being closer to nature was naturally considered usable – economically, socially and psychologically.

In his well-known work, Lloyd deMause faults Philippe Aries for suggesting that childhood, as we know it, is a modern creation (deMause 1975: 5–6; Aries 1962). deMause argues that children have been ill-treated throughout history, and the modern world, if anything, is somewhat kinder to the child. He is here stating an old argument which offsets modern violence against various traditional forms of institutionalized violence.

deMause is partly correct. Viewed from this side of history, the tradition of childhood is indeed the tradition of neglect, torture and infanticide. So-called parental care and education have often been a cover for the widespread social and psychological exploitation of children. Many past societies saw children as the property of their parents, sometimes without any legal protection against parental oppression. This in turn legitimized every variety of institutional violence. Mutilation of children in some societies – in the form of castration, circumcision or beautification through folk surgery – was the norm, rather than the exception. Terrorization of children for fun or for ensuring conformity was widespread. So were sodomy and other sexual abuses of children. Often these took place with the full consent not only of the victim's parents but also of society. And, above all, infanticide was not only common; it was often a way of life. It took place in the 'civilized' West and in 'pacifist' India till the middle of the nineteenth century. (Indirect female infanticide exists in many pockets of India and other traditional third-world societies even now.)

All this does suggest that mankind has progressed towards better treatment of children and that modern societies have been kinder to children than traditional societies. Such an argument, however, ignores the qualitative changes in human oppression brought about by new, impersonal, centralizing and uniformizing forces released by the modern state system, technology and, more recently, by a social consciousness dominated by mass communications. It ignores that anomic, mechanical, dispassionate, 'banal' oppression, to adapt Hannah Arendt's overworked term, is mainly a contribution of our times to the global culture. Unlike the traditional or savage oppressor, the modern oppressor is empty within. He lives with a schizoid sense of unreality of his self and that of others. He himself is an instrument; he uses others as instruments; his reason is instrumental and he legitimizes his actions in terms of instrumentality. In sum, he lives in a world of instruments, instrumentalities and instrumentation. Such a world induces a sharp discontinuity between the oppressor and the oppressed, who no longer share the same framework of values as in the medieval witch-hunt or in pre-modern feudal land relations. They speak to each other from two sides of a soundproof glass wall. The estimated 1000 children who die every year at the hands of their parents in Britain – or the estimated casualty rate in the United States, ranging between 200,000 and 500,000 for physical abuse and between another 465,000 and 1,175,000 for severe neglect and sexual abuse – are not victims of mystification, black magic or false religious values (as in ritual child sacrifice or indirect female infanticide in India) or of poverty leading to neglect or murder (Light 1973 quoted in Steiner and Milius 1976: 85–86). They are victims of meaninglessness, the collapse of inter-generational mutuality, unlimited individualism and a system which views children as intrusions into what is increasingly considered the only legitimate dyad in the family – namely the conjugal unit. They are victims of a worldview which sees the child as an inferior, weak but usable version of the fully productive, fully performing, human being who owns the modern world.

Aries is, after all, not so specious when he speaks of childhood as a product of the post-medieval consciousness. Modern childhood did come into its own with the growth of industrialism, the spread of Protestant values, the emergence of modern technology and consolidation of colonialism. Children formed one of the first social groups on which the model of the brave new world promised by these forces was tried out. For the first time in important parts of the world, normal modern adulthood could no longer be conceptualized without conceptualizing its opposite, modern childhood.

The resulting construction of childhood was not a matter of genuine false-consciousness. It did not arise from real limits to human awareness at a particular time or space. On the contrary, it involved a refusal to admit easily available data and experiences incongruent with the new ideology. If it was a false consciousness, it had built-in resistance to the recognition of its falsity.

For instance, when the Industrial Revolution gave rise to widespread use of child-labour in England, it also produced apologists of child-labour who wrote ornate, flowing prose on the good that industrial employment did to the child. Children slaving in the mills for more than twelve hours a day supposedly learned the virtues of productive work, thrift, honesty, and discipline.[2] But many of these apologists also sensed that it was not incidental that the 'moral growth' of the allegedly reprobate, unsaved and savage children also helped a labour-scarce economy and produced wealth for their employers. Parents who habitually sent their children to other families to work as domestic servants and in exchange took in others' children for the same purpose, as in eighteenth-century England, mostly knew what they were doing. It was not genuine unconsciousness; it was primarily rational cost-calculations with a very thin, easily penetrable, veneer of rationalization.

I do not wish to underplay the suffering of the child in non-modern societies. Nor do I want to split hairs on the actual quanta of oppression involved in different societies and times. But I do doubt the glib assumptions of a theory of progress which is surreptitiously applied to life-cycles of both persons and societies. I am conscious that if the early industrial societies introduced economies of scale in the exploitation of children, most other societies, too, have tried their hand at social and emotional exploitation of their children. There is a continuity between pre-modern and modern societies, maintained through the social inculcation in the child of culturally preferred adaptive devices, such as what psychoanalysis calls the mechanisms of ego defence. Though euphemistically called training in cultural values and cognitive styles, and seen as products of family socialization and organized education, there can be little doubt that many elements of such training would have been described as institutionalized brain-washing if the trainees were adults.

In spite of this continuity between the traditional and the modern ill-treatment of the child, the modern worldview is distinctive in stressing four special uses of children. Each of these uses can also be found in traditional cultures, but modern technology and communications and the spread of the values of modern life – particularly the growing instrumental view of interpersonal relationships – have given them a new reach and legitimacy.

First, there is greater sanction now for the use of the child as a projective device. The child today is a screen as well as a mirror. The older generations are allowed to project into the child their inner needs and to use him or her to work out their fantasies of self-correction and national or cultural improvement. For instance, parents may try to realize through the child their own status ambitions or to negate through him or her their own sense of economic and psychological insecurity, or they may 'bring up' the child as a double who has marital, professional and other life choices no longer open to them. Such a system can be both effective and lasting, because parents constitute the immediate environs of the child. The society, too, perceives them as providing a bene-volent capsulating context for childhood. So when a parent acts out his or her inner conflicts on the child or tries to face the oppressions of society by using the child as a shield, he or she has the support of the entire society. Bruno Bettelheim once said that neither Hamlet's father nor King Lear had any business to impose on their progenies, on Hamlet and Cordelia respectively, the responsibility of avenging the wrongs done to the earlier generation. The parents in both cases tried to put reins on the next genera-tion and 'saddle it with a burden of gratitude'. Hamlet's father, like Lear, 'put a private burden on his child's too weak shoulders'. And it is poetic justice, Bettelheim says, that Cordelia, willing to serve age by forgoing her right to a life of her own, suffers destruction along with her father (Bettelheim 1963: 69–70).

Unlike young adults such as Hamlet and Cordelia, younger children do not often have the option of breaking out of the social or educational 'traps' set for them. Their physical, emotional and socioeconomic vulnerability does not give them much chance of escape and they have to play out the institutional games devised for them. In many societies, by the time they gain social and economic autonomy, it is already too late for psychological autonomy; they continue to carry within them the passions, hates and loves of their earliest authorities. Even when oppression becomes obvious and, thus, some subjective basis for a search for autonomy is created, as in Shakespeare's *Romeo and Juliet*, the society may turn on the young with some savagery to ensure that the search is not actualized in practice. At one time, this probably was the ultimate meaning of all blood feuds and all attempts to settle historical scores. Today, it is the source of all attempts to use children to satisfy the grandest of personal and national aspirations.

Second, as already noted, childhood has become a major dystopia for the modern world. The fear of being childish dogs the steps of every psychologically insecure adult and of every culture which uses the metaphor of childhood to define mental illness, primitivism, abnormality, underdevelopment, non-creativity and traditionalism. Perfect adulthood, like hyper-masculinity and ultra-normality, has become the goal of most over-socialized human beings, and modern societies have begun to produce a large number of individuals whose ego-ideal includes the concept of adult maturity as defined by the dominant norms of the society. (Evgeny Bogat makes the important point that while every child is unique and while one expects that 'differences among persons and differences in character, should become more apparent as people grow older ... this is not the case. The differences sadly fade away, leaving only the memory of the wonderfully unique world of childhood' [Bogat 1976a: 285]). Thus, the idea of childhood as a dystopia subtly permeates most popular myths about the lost utopia of childhood and most compensatory ideas about the beauties of childlike innocence and spontaneity. As deMause points out in a different context, the idea of childhood as a lost utopia – found not in autobiographies but mainly in literature, myths and fantasies – is often built out of small episodes in remembered childhoods to serve as a wish-fulfilling fantasy and as a defence against traumatic childhood memories (deMause 1975). More dominant is the idea of a fearsome childhood to which one might any time regress.

Thirdly, with greater and more intense cross-cultural contacts, childhood now more frequently becomes a battleground of cultures. This is especially true of many third-world societies where middle-class urban children are often handed over to the modern world to work out a compromise with cultures successfully encroaching upon the traditional life-style. For instance, even traditional rural parents may begin to send their children to modern urban schools for Western education – partly to fulfill their status ambitions and partly to create a manageable bicultural space or an interface with the modern world within the family. Nobody who has read the lives of the reformers, political leaders and writers of nineteenth century India can fail to notice that the Indian middle-class child became, under the growing cultural impact of British rule, the arena in which the battle for the minds of men was fought between the East and the West, the old and the new, and the intrinsic and the imposed. The autobiographies of Rabindranath Tagore (1944) and M. K. Gandhi (1927) provide excellent accounts of childhood as an area of adult experimentation in social change in mid-nineteenth century India. Both exemplify how the authors as children bore the brunt of conflicts precipitated by colonial politics, Westernized education and exogenous social institutions.

Nineteenth century Indian childhood was not an exception. Throughout the southern world children are being made a means of reconciling the past and the present of their societies. With the accelerating pace of social change, even in many modern societies children are expected to help their elders cope, with the contradictory social norms introduced into the society by large-scale techno-cultural changes, and to vicariously satisfy their elders' needs for achievement, power and self-esteem. (These are the needs a modern society implants in all its members but can allow only a handful to satisfy. The mythology of modernity rests on the belief that these needs can be satisfied if only an individual works hard, is adaptable and psychologically healthy. That is, there is no insurmountable institutional constraint on anyone having a sense of achievement, potency and personal worth; all failures in this respect, the modern belief goes, are actually failures of culpable individuals, not of structures.) As the modern society typically promises to meet these needs in exchange for productive, impersonal, monetized, industrial work in a competitive setting, the culture of productive work gradually takes over all other areas of life. It is in modern society that we see the remarkable spectacle of even the child's early attainments in the area of sphincter control, speech, literacy and school work becoming instruments of parental drive for performance, competition, productivity and status. This is the tacit politics in the psychopathology of everyday life in many societies today.

Fourthly, societies dominated by the principle of instrumental reason and consumerism mystify the idea of childhood more than the idea of the child. This differential mystification ensures that the idea of the child is more positively cathected than the real-life child. The image of the child is in fact split and those aspects of childhood which are incongruent with the culture of adult life are defined as part of a natural savage childhood and excluded from the mythological idea of the child as a fully innocent, beautifully obedient, self-denying and non-autonomous being. In its most extreme form, the child is appreciated when he or she is least genuinely childish or authentic – in fact, only when he or she meets the adult's concept of a good child.

The concept of a good child, derived from the objective and subjective demands of adults, finds expression in various ways. For instance, in many traditional societies such as the Indian and the Chinese, the child may be seen as a reincarnation of some familial spirit, most frequently of one's parents' parents.[3] But even when the child is seen as a good omen or as the incarnation of a good spirit, there may be a touch of instrumentality to it. Thus, a male child in a patriarchal system may be seen as a means of ensuring the continuity of lineage. He may be expected to prepare himself to look after the welfare of his ancestors, and ensure their safe passage to the life after death or look after their after-life comforts from this world through proper rituals and other religious ceremonies.

Modern parents also see children as sources of economic security, old-age insurance and as allies in the cruel world of competition, work and day-to-day politics. Many cultures and individuals have elaborate defences against recognizing this aspect of their relationship with children. Of course, all interdependence is not tainted. Economic and social mutuality is no less legitimate than psychological mutuality. But when cultures help individuals to repress the contractual aspects of the adult-child relationship and help institutionalize a totally benevolent, self-sacrificing concept of parenthood, social consciousness gets used to perceiving only a one-way flow of material benefits from parents to the child. The child, too, is socialized to such perceptions of benevolence and sacrifice and is constantly expected by the outside world as well as by his inner self to make reparative gestures towards his parents.

Thus, we seem to have come full circle to the first use of childhood we have described. If Hamlet seems too mythical a figure telling too apocryphal a story, every age has produced its version of the myth of the obligated progeny sacrificing his life to right real or imaginary wrongs done to his parents or to his parents' generation.

II

Until recently, in most societies, high birth and high mortality rates ensured a plurality or near-plurality of children in the population. When the ideology of adulthood is superimposed on such social profiles, it beautifully sanctifies a subtle abridgement of democratic rights. Even in societies not dominated by this ideology – in societies where the child has often enjoyed a certain dignity, autonomy and, as in India, a clear touch of divinity[4] – the encroachment of the modern world on the traditions of nurture and child-rearing is helping to turn the childhood of the third world into an ethnic variant of the first world.

Thus, children are getting homogenized as a target as well as a metaphor of oppression and violence. Their story is becoming, to borrow Elise Boulding's expression for the history of women, another underside of history. Though some awareness of the role of the child in human civilization is reflected in religions and myths, it is mostly the lesser minds of the modern times that have empathized with the child: an occasional

Engels, not Marx, examining the political economy of the family and, indirectly, of childhood; an-occasional Dickens, not Dostoevsky or Thomas Mann, anticipating twentieth century authoritarianism in the treatment meted out to the nineteenth century child.

It is an indicator of the power of modern consciousness that even Gandhi's Gandhism failed when it came to his own children. Though his model of social change was a majestic indictment of the metaphor of childhood legitimizing colonialism and modernity, his attempt to introduce the concept of social intervention or service in the Indian worldview did presume a non-traditional, almost Calvinist concept of the sinful, selfish child who had to be moulded into a socially useful being. Corollary-wise, in his personal life, too, Gandhi forced his sons to live in a way that would concretize his own concept of the ideal child and atone for their birth in the sin of sexuality (see Erikson 1969; Payne 1968). In consequence, Gandhi's eldest son Haridas was fully destroyed. He tried his hardest not to play out Gandhi's scenario for an eldest son's life, preferring to pursue to its nadir a lifestyle defined by blind negation of his enveloping father (Payne 1968). Alcohol, prostitutes, rejection of Hinduism, and a self-centred hedonism were not only the passions of Haridas but also his flawed instruments of a self-destructive search for autonomy. In the process, he provided a classic instance of oedipal conflict in a culture which had traditionally shown a low salience of such conflicts.

If Gandhi, too, partly gave in to the modern concept of childhood, one can imagine the universalizing and homogenizing power of the concept. Here was a man who had not only rejected the ideology of modernity but had also defied the implied homology between the adult-child relationship and the West–East encounter under colonialism. Yet he was unable to extend his dissent against the ideology of adulthood from aggregates to persons, as he did so successfully in the case of the man-woman relationship and the ideology of hyper-masculinity (Nandy 1980).

For intimations of that other dissent against the ideology of adulthood one is forced to turn, paradoxically, to the best-known ideologue of normality and adulthood of our century, Sigmund Freud. Unlike Gandhi, Freud was totally oblivious of the larger political use being made of the ideology of adulthood. But then he was perfectly aware of the micropolitics of the family and that of the process of socialization.

It was Freud who first spelt out for the moderns the way exploitation of children ensures the persistence of a tortured childhood within each adult as a flawed consciousness. He called such consciousness abnormal personality, one which could not own up the remnants of an oppressed childhood within it, because it also included norms internalized from the ideology of adulthood. Psychopathology, in such a model, is a *double entendre*. It is an apparently apolitical, rational attempt to cope with inescapable memories of oppression, the so-called reality principle being not, as social consensus and psychiatric expertise would have it, a value-neutral objectivity, but a compromised apperception of reality erected by the inescapable structures of oppression. Secondly, psychopathology is a non-critical adaptation to the pathology of a fractured interpersonal world where the unreality of conventional reality and the abnormality of conventional normality organize a child's early environment.

The double meaning of psychopathology is one of Freud's major legacies. Patriarchal and conservative in personal life and overtly committed to normality and adulthood, Freud left behind in this dialectics of meaning an instrument of dissent from the ideology of normality and adulthood. It was this legacy which made the social critic Freud, in spite of all attempts to institutionalize him as a positivist applied psychologist, a reluctant political rebel and visionary of a just world. In that rebellious, 'savage' Freud, a part of the culture of modern science suspended its social-evolution-ism – to affirm that childhood and adulthood were not two fixed phases of the human life-cycle (where the latter had to inescapably supplant the former) but a continuum which, while diachronically laid out on the plane of life history, was always synchro-nically present in each personality. And that the repression of children in the name of socialization and education was the basic model of all 'legitimate' modern repression, exactly as the ideology of adulthood (including the glorification of work, performance and productivity as normal and mature) was the prototypical theory of progress, designed to co-opt on behalf of the oppressors the visions of the future of their victims. Admittedly, the metaphor of oppression was not used by Freud, impressed as he was by the rather simple, mechanistic versions of historicism and scientism (which blunted the critical edge of his concepts such as infantile sexuality, civilization as repression, and the reality principle). But, then, all social criticism does not have the obligation to be either self-aware or self-consistent.

In sum, Freud implied (1) that the use of children for acting out the emotional con-flicts of adulthood, in turn built on the ruins of an oppressed childhood, distorted the world of the child; (2) that 'mental illness' was only a means of protecting oneself from the inescapable arbitrary victimhood experienced in childhood; and (3) that the oppression of socialization was the root of the civilizational discontents of our times and the ultimate psychopathology of everyday life. The repression within, to use a now worn-out expression, invariably found its social counterpart in repression without.

I suspect that the early hostility to Freud was only partly due to his concept of infantile sexuality, which in any case was implied in the Western concept of the savage, sinful child. Freud's stress on such sexuality only provided a humane interpretation of the fearful awareness that was already there in the recesses of the Western mind. The hostility to Freud was also due to his theories which hinted at the oppressiveness of the idea of adulthood and the hollowness of the theory of progress when applied to a per-son's life-cycle. Human childhood, Freud's meta-psychology seemed to suggest, was the basic design of a society where physical and material dominance set the pace for emo-tional and cultural life, by forcing human subjectivity to adapt to the physical and material dependency of the child. It is the modern childhood-which-survives-childhood from which Freud sought to liberate his civilization.

On this plane, Freud tried to do for the person what Gandhi tried to do for the aggregate: to free humanity from the institutionalized violence which used the meta-phor of childhood and the doctrine of progress as spelt out in the dominant post-medieval concept of history. Both tacitly agreed that childhood was a culture, a quality of living and a distinctive collection of cognitive skills, emotional and motivational patterns which modernity sought to disown or repress. Liberating the child or the savage was, thus, a means of liberating the adult and the civilized from the straitjacket of 'normal' adulthood and civility (Nandy 1983: Chapter 1).

I doubt if any other ideological formulation could have been more subversive of the language of modernity at that point of time. The formulation sought not only to pro-tect the child and the savage but also to alter the language of social change and to unmask the universalism of modernity as only another legitimacy for ethnocides. If we see children as carriers of a culture which is politically and socially vulnerable but is nonetheless intrinsically valuable, we also change the nature of our search for secular salvation. Analogously, cultures have a right to live not because they can be saved or promoted to a higher state of civilization but because of the alternatives they give us in their distinctive philosophies of life. Because ultimately they *are* willing to live out these alternatives on our behalf.

Freud was not a cultural relativist. In his model, childhood can be assessed in terms of the unique orientation to the natural and interpersonal worlds it represents. Cultural criticism of childhood, too, is legitimate; only it has to be ventured in the context of the biological, environmental and interpersonal demands of childhood – that is, in the context of both the psycho-ecology of childhood and the politics of cultures in our times. The model fears the arrogance of parents or societies which presume to 'bring up' their children; it sees family as a psycho-social space within which the culture of the adult world intersects and, sometimes, confronts the world of the child. Ideally, this sharing of space should take place on the basis of mutual respect. That it does not is a measure of our fear of losing our own selfhood through our close contacts with cultures which dare to represent our other selves, as well as a measure of our fear of the liminality between the adult and the child which many of us carry within ourselves. This is the liminality Freud worked through in his interpretation of psychopathology. This is also the liminality Gandhi had to face openly while battling the ideology of colonialism.

Liberation from the fear of childhood is also liberation from the more subtly institutionalized ethnocentrism towards past times. Elsewhere, I have discussed the absolute and total subjection of the subjects of history, who can neither rebel against the present times nor contest the present interpretations of the past. I have argued that the corollary of the modern attitude to the child is the tendency of the modern child within each modern adult to apply to past times the same doctrine of progress which is applied to the child by the adult (Nandy 1987; also 1983: Chapter 1). The other name of modern childhood is personal history. Not knowing this is to be caught in the causality of history; knowing this is to reduce history to non-causal remembered past (cf. Keen 1978). The struggle to disown one's 'childish' past in personal life is also an attempt to disown one's collective past as a pre-history or as a set of primitivisms and traditions. The struggle to own up the child within oneself is an. attempt to restore wholeness in ruptured human relationships and experiences.

Is all attempt to improve or educate children, then, also an attempt to self-improve? Is every violation of children an attempt to self-destruct? Perhaps. One accepts in children what one accepts in oneself; one hates in children what one hates in oneself. Turn this into a conscious process and what looks like educating and rearing children turns out to be a pathetic attempt to compensate for unfulfilled and unrealized self-images and private ideals. Children, too, bring up their elders.

I must not end this argument leaving the impression that there is something intrinsically glamorous about childhood, or even about the innocence and victimhood of the child. That glamorization, too, is a defence against feared memories of childhood. The use of the child as a symbol of counter-cultures or utopias has often been a correlate of the use of the child as a symbol of dystopias. Children represent the contradictions and pathologies of cultures as part of an inescapable struggle for self-preservation. Adults, too, may sometimes need to be protected from them. Though the need for such protection has not arisen in the past, it may do so in the future. The vulnerability of the child in the past was primarily physical. As the importance of physical power diminishes in modern social relations, the power relations between age groups may change in the same way that it is changing between the sexes. So, while the inequality between the adult and the child may not automatically decline, it may come to depend less on brute force and more on institutions, technologies and the politics of age in the future. (Witness for instance the case of the youth. The youth 'revolutions' of the late 1960s in the West were also an effort to institutionalize the growing power of the youth in the Western political economy as consumers and as voters who were becoming more numerous and mobilizable both in absolute terms and in comparison, with other sections of the population.)

Until now the main force behind the ill treatment of children has been the social structures and processes which have forced large sections of men and women to lose their self-esteem, and then forced them to seek that lost self-esteem through their children. From the violence-prone Spartan society (which saw its children only as future warriors for Sparta and, to test their 'toughness', exposed a large proportion of them to death at birth) to the English miners at the time of the Industrial Revolution (working fifteen to eighteen hours a day and coming back to beat up or rape their own children), violated, brutalized adulthood has been the other side of violated, brutalized children.

We thus come full circle. If violated men and women produce violated children, violated children in turn produce violated adults. Fortunately, this apparently vicious circle can be read the other way too. The ideology of adulthood has hidden the fact that children see through our hypocrisy perfectly and respond to our tolerance and respect fully. Our most liberating bonds can be with our undersocialized children. And the final test of our skill to live a bicultural or multicultural existence may still be our ability to live with our children in mutuality.

A plea for the protection of children is, thus, a plea for an alternative vision of the good society on the one hand, a vision in which the plurality of cultures and paradoxically that of visions themselves are granted, and a plea for recognizing the wholeness of human personality on the other.

Notes

1 This is an abridged version of the article that appeared in Ashis Nandy, *Traditions, Tyranny, and Utopias: Essays in the Politics of Awareness* (Delhi; New York: Oxford University Press, 1987).
2 Exactly as employers of child labourers in South Indian match and fire-works factories have recently produced elegant justifications for their employment practices in response to an indictment published by a civil rights worker. See the controversy following the publication of Kothari (1983a, 1983b).
3 deMause (1975) even has a name for this; he calls it the 'reversal reaction'.
4 For example, on the Indian tradition of child rearing see Kakar (1979).

References

Aries, Philippe (1962) *Centuries of Childhood: A Social History of Family Life*, New York: Knopf.
Bettelheim, B. (1963) 'The problem of generations', in E. H. Erikson (ed.) *Youth: Change and Challenge*, New York: Basic Books, pp. 64–92.
Bogat, Evgeny (1976a) 'Boys and girls', in *Eternal Man: Reflections, Dialogues, Portraits*, Moscow: Progress Publishers, pp. 279–87.
—— (1976b) 'The great lesson or childhood', in *Eternal Man: Reflections, Dialogues, Portraits*, Moscow: Progress Publishers, pp. 288–93.
Chinweizu (1978) *The West and the Rest of Us*, London: NOK.

deMause, Lloyd (1975) 'The evolution of childhood', in Lloyd deMause (ed.) *The History of Childhood*, New York: Harper, pp. 1–76.

Erikson, Erik H. (1969) *Gandhi's Truth*, New York: Norton.

Gandhi, M. K. (1927) *An Autobiography or The Story of My Experiments with Truth*, Ahmedabad: Navjeevan.

Kakar, Sudhir (1979) *Indian Childhood: Cultural Ideals and Social Reality*, New Delhi: Oxford University Press.

Keen, Earnest (1978) 'The past in the future: consciousness and tradition', *Journal of Humanistic Psychology*, 18: 5–18.

Kothari, Smithu (1983a) 'Facts about Shivakasi Child Labour', *Indian Express*, 14 February.

—— (1983b) 'There's blood on those matchsticks: child labour in Shivakasi', *Economic and Political Weekly*, 2 July, 18: 1191–1202.

Light, Richard J. (1973) 'Abused and neglected children in America: a study of alternative policies', *Harvard Educational Review*, 43: 566–67.

Mazlish, Bruce (1975) *James and John Mill: Father and Son in the Nineteenth Century*, New York: Basic Books.

Nandy, Ashis (1980) 'The final encounter: the politics of the assassination of Gandhi', in *At the Edge of Psychology*, New Delhi: Oxford University Press, pp. 70–98.

—— (1983) *The Intimate Enemy: Loss and Recovery of Self under Colonialism*, New Delhi: Oxford University Press.

—— (1987) 'Towards a third world utopia', in *Traditions, Tyranny, and Utopias: Essays in the Politics of Awareness*, New Delhi: Oxford University Press.

Payne, Robert (1968) *The Life and Death of Mahatma Gandhi*, New York: Dutton.

Steiner, Gilbert Y. and Milius, Pauline H. (1976) *The Children's Cause*, Washington, D.C.: Brookings Institute.

Tagore, Rabindranath (1944) *Chhelebela*, Calcutta: Visvabharati University.

15 Subaltern Studies as postcolonial criticism[1]

Gyan Prakash

To note the ferment created by Subaltern Studies in disciplines as diverse as history, anthropology, and literature is to recognize the force of recent postcolonial criticism. This criticism has compelled a radical rethinking of knowledge and social identities authored and authorized by colonialism and Western domination. Of course, colonialism and its legacies have faced challenges before. One has only to think of nationalist rebellions against imperialist domination and Marxism's unrelenting critiques of capitalism and colonialism. But neither nationalism nor Marxism broke free from Eurocentric discourses.[2] As nationalism reversed Orientalist thought, and attributed agency and history to the subjected nation, it staked a claim to the order of Reason and Progress instituted by colonialism. When Marxists turned the spotlight on colonial exploitation, their criticism was framed by a historicist scheme that universalized Europe's historical experience. The emergent postcolonial critique, by contrast, seeks to undo the Eurocentrism produced by the institution of the West's trajectory, its appropriation of the other as History. It does so, however, with the acute realization that its own critical apparatus does not enjoy a panoptic distance from colonial history but exists as an aftermath, as an after – after being worked over by colonialism. Criticism formed as an aftermath acknowledges that it inhabits the structures of Western domination that it seeks to undo. In this sense, postcolonial criticism is deliberately interdisciplinary, arising in the interstices of disciplines of power/knowledge that it critiques. This is what Homi Bhabha calls an in-between, hybrid position of practice and negotiation (1994a: 22–26), or what Gayatri Chakravorty Spivak terms catachresis: 'reversing, displacing, and seizing the apparatus of value-coding' (1990b: 228).

The dissemination of Subaltern Studies, beginning in 1982 as an intervention in South Asian historiography and developing into a vigorous postcolonial critique, must be placed in such a complex, catachrestic reworking of knowledge. The challenge it poses to the existing historical scholarship has been felt not only in South Asian studies but also in the historiography of other regions and in disciplines other than history. The term 'subaltern' now appears with growing frequency in studies on Africa, Latin America, and Europe, and subalternist analysis has become a recognizable mode of critical scholarship in history, literature, and anthropology.

The formation of subaltern studies as an intervention in South Asian historiography occurred in the wake of the growing crisis of the Indian state in the 1970s. The dominance of the nation-state, cobbled together through compromises and coercion during the nationalist struggle against British rule, became precarious as its program of capitalist modernity sharpened social and political inequalities and conflicts. Faced with the outbreak of powerful movements of different ideological hues that challenged its claim to represent the people, the state resorted increasingly to repression to preserve its dominance. But repression was not the only means adopted. The state combined coercive measures with the powers of patronage and money, on the one hand, and the appeal of populist slogans and programs, on the other, to make a fresh bid for its legitimacy. These measures, pioneered by the Indira Gandhi government, secured the dominance of the state but corroded the authority of its institutions. The key components of the modern nation-state – political parties, the electoral process, parliamentary bodies, the bureaucracy, law, and the ideology of development – survived, but their claim to represent the culture and politics of the masses suffered crippling blows.

In the field of historical scholarship, the perilous position of the nation-state in the 1970s became evident in the increasingly embattled nationalist historiography. Attacked relentlessly by the 'Cambridge School', which represented India's colonial history as nothing but a chronicle of competition among its elites, nationalism's fabric of legitimacy was torn apart.[3] This school exposed the nationalist hagiography, but its elite-based analysis turned the common people into dupes of their superiors. Marxists contested both nationalist historiography and the 'Cambridge School' interpretation, but their mode-of-production narratives merged imperceptibly with the nation-state's ideology of modernity and progress. This congruence meant that while championing the history of the oppressed classes and their emancipation through modern progress, the Marxists found it difficult to deal with the hold of 'backward' ideologies of caste and religion. Unable to take into account the oppressed's 'lived experience' of religion and social customs, Marxist accounts of peasant rebellions either overlooked the religious idiom of the rebels or viewed it as a mere form and a stage in the development of revolutionary consciousness. Thus, although Marxist historians produced impressive and pioneering studies, their claim to represent the history of the masses remained debatable.

Subaltern Studies plunged into this historiographical contest over the representation of the culture and politics of the people. Accusing colonialist, nationalist, and Marxist interpretations of robbing the common people of their agency, it announced a new approach to restore history to the subordinated. Started by an editorial collective consisting of six scholars of South Asia spread across Britain, India, and Australia, Subaltern Studies was inspired by Ranajit Guha. A distinguished historian whose most notable previous work was *A Rule of Property for Bengal* (1963), Guha edited the first six *Subaltern Studies* volumes. After he relinquished the editorship, Subaltern Studies was published by a rotating two-member editorial team drawn from the collective. Guha continues, however, to publish in Subaltern Studies, now under an expanded and reconstituted editorial collective.

The establishment of subaltern studies was aimed to promote, as the preface by Guha to the first volume declared, the study and discussion of subalternist themes in South Asian studies (1982b: vii). The term 'subaltern', drawn from Antonio Gramsci's writings, refers to subordination in terms of class, caste, gender, race, language, and culture and was used to signify the centrality of dominant/dominated relationships in history. Guha suggested that while Subaltern Studies would not ignore the dominant, because the subalterns are always subject to their activity, its aim was to 'rectify the elitist bias characteristic of much research and academic work' in South Asian studies (ibid.). The act of rectification sprang from the conviction that the elites had exercised dominance, not hegemony, in Gramsci's sense, over the subalterns. A reflection of this belief was Guha's argument that the subalterns had acted in history *'on their own, that is, independently of the elite*'; their politics constituted 'an *autonomous* domain, for it neither originated from elite politics nor did its existence depend on the latter' (Guha 1982a: 3–4).

While the focus on subordination has remained central to Subaltern Studies, the conception of subalternity has witnessed shifts and varied uses. Individual contributors to the volumes have also differed, not surprisingly, in their orientation. A shift in interests, focus, and theoretical grounds is also evident through the many volumes of essays produced so far and several monographs by individual subalternists (Guha 1982–89; Pandey and Chatterjee 1992; Arnold and Hardiman 1993; Guha 1983a; Chatterjee 1986, 1993; Chakrabarty 1989; Hardiman 1987; and Pandey 1990). Yet what has remained consistent is the effort to rethink history from the perspective of the subaltern.

How the adoption of the subaltern's perspective aimed to undo the 'spurious primacy assigned to [the elites]' was not entirely clear in the first volume. The essays, ranging from agrarian history to the analysis of the relationship between peasants and nationalists, represented excellent though not novel scholarship. Although all the contributions attempted to highlight the lives and the historical presence of subaltern classes, neither the thorough and insightful research in social and economic history nor the critique of the Indian nationalist appropriation of peasant movements was new; Marxist historians, in particular, had done both (Siddiqi 1978; Banaji 1977). It was with the second volume that the novelty and insurgency of Subaltern Studies became clear.

The second volume made forthright claims about the subaltern subject and set about demonstrating how the agency of the subaltern in history had been denied by elite perspectives anchored in colonialist, nationalist, and or Marxist narratives. Arguing that these narratives had sought to represent the subaltern's consciousness and activity according to schemes that encoded elite dominance, Guha asserted that historiography had dealt with 'the peasant rebel merely as an empirical person or member of a class, but not as an entity whose will and reason constituted the praxis called rebellion' (1983b: 2). Historians were apt to depict peasant rebellions as spontaneous eruptions that 'break out like thunder storms, heave like earthquakes, spread like wildfires'; alternatively, they attributed rebellions as a reflex action to economic and political oppression. 'Either way insurgency is regarded as *external* to the peasant's consciousness and Cause is made to stand in as a phantom surrogate for Reason, the logic of consciousness' (ibid.: 2–3).

How did historiography develop this blind spot? Guha asked. In answering this question, his 'Prose of Counter-Insurgency' offers a methodological *tour de force* and a perceptive reading of the historical writings on peasant insurgency in colonial India. Describing these writings as counter-insurgent texts, Guha begins by distinguishing three types of discourses – primary, secondary, and tertiary. These differ from one another in terms of the order of their appearance in time and the degree of their acknowledged or unacknowledged identification with the official point of view. Analyzing each in turn, Guha shows the presence, transformation, and redistribution of a 'counter-insurgent code'. This code, present in the immediate accounts of insurgency produced by officials (primary discourse), is processed into another time and narrative by official reports and memoirs (secondary discourse) and is then incorporated and redistributed by historians who have no official affiliation and are farthest removed from the time of the event (tertiary discourse). The 'code of pacification', written into the 'raw' data of primary texts and the narratives of secondary discourses, survives, and it shapes the tertiary discourse of historians when they fail to read in it the presence of the excluded other, the insurgent. Consequently, while historians produce accounts that differ from secondary discourses, their tertiary discourse also ends up appropriating the insurgent. Consider, for example, the treatment of peasant rebellions. When colonial officials, using on-the-spot accounts containing 'the code of pacification', blamed wicked landlords and wily moneylenders for the occurrence of these events, they used causality as a counter-insurgent instrument: to identify the cause of the revolt was a step in the direction of control over it and constituted a denial of the insurgent's agency. In nationalist historiography, this denial took a different form, as British rule, rather than local oppression, became the cause of revolts and turned peasant rebellions into nationalist struggles. Radical historians, too, ended up incorporating the counter-insurgent code of the secondary discourse as they explained peasant revolts in relation to a revolutionary continuum leading to socialism. Each tertiary account failed to step outside the counter-insurgent paradigm, Guha argues, by refusing to acknowledge the subjectivity and agency of the insurgent (1983b: 26–33).

Clearly, the project to restore the insurgent's agency involved, as Rosalind O'Hanlon pointed out in a thoughtful review essay, the notion of the 'recovery of the subject' (1988). Thus, while reading records against their grain, these scholars have sought to uncover the subaltern's myths, cults, ideologies, and revolts that colonial and national- ist elites sought to appropriate and that conventional historiography has laid waste by the deadly weapon of cause and effect. Ranajit Guha's *Elementary Aspects of Peasant Insurgency in Colonial India* (1983) is a powerful example of scholarship that seeks to recover the peasant from elite projects and positivist historiography. In this wide-ran- ging study full of brilliant insights and methodological innovation, Guha returns to nineteenth century peasant insurrections in colonial India. Reading colonial records and historiographical representations with an uncanny eye, he offers a fascinating account of the peasant's insurgent consciousness, rumors, mythic visions, religiosity, and bonds of community. From Guha's account, the subaltern emerges with forms of sociality and political community at odds with nation and class, defying the models of rationality and social action that conventional historiography uses. Guha argues per- suasively that such models are elitist insofar as they deny the subaltern's autonomous consciousness and that they are drawn from colonial and liberal-nationalist projects of appropriating the subaltern.

It is true that the effort to retrieve the autonomy of the subaltern subject resembled the 'history from below' approach developed by social history in the West. But the subalternist search for a humanist subject-agent frequently ended up with the discovery of the failure of subaltern agency: the moment of rebellion always contained within it the moment of failure. The desire to recover the subaltern's autonomy was repeatedly frustrated because subalternity, by definition, signified the impossibility of autonomy: subaltern rebellions only offered fleeting moments of defiance, 'a night-time of love', not 'a life-time of love' (Das 1989: 315). While these scholars failed to recognize fully that the subalterns' resistance did not simply oppose power but was also constituted by it, their own work showed this to be the case. Further complicating the urge to recover the subject was the fact that, unlike British and U.S. social history, Subaltern Studies drew on anti-humanist structuralist and poststructuralist writings. Ranajit Guha's deft readings of colonial records, in particular, drew explicitly from Ferdinand de Sassure, Claude Levi-Strauss, Roman Jakobson, Roland Barthes, and Michel Foucault. Partly, the reliance on such theorists and the emphasis on 'textual' readings arose from, as Dipesh Chakrabarty points out, the absence of workers' diaries and other such sources available to British historians (1992b: 102). Indian peasants had left no sources, no documents from which their own 'voice' could be retrieved. But the emphasis on 'readings' of texts and the recourse to theorists such as Foucault, whose writings cast a shroud of doubt over the idea of the autonomous subject, contained an awareness that the colonial subaltern was not just a form of 'general' subalternity. While the operation of power relations in colonial and metropolitan theaters had parallels, the conditions of subalternity were also irreducibly different. Subaltern Studies, therefore, could not just be the Indian version of the 'history from below' approach; it had to conceive the subaltern differently and write different histories.

This difference has grown in subsequent Subaltern Studies volumes as the desire to recover the subaltern subject became increasingly entangled in the analysis of how subalternity was constituted by dominant discourses. Of course, the tension between the recovery of the subaltern as a subject outside the elite discourse and the analysis of subalternity as an effect of discursive systems was present from the very beginning (Spivak 1985b: 337–38). It also continues to characterize Subaltern Studies scholarship today, as Florencia Mallon notes in her essay in this issue of the *AHR*. Recent volumes, however, pay greater attention to developing the emergence of subalternity as a discursive effect without abandoning the notion of the subaltern as a subject and agent. This perspective, amplified since *Subaltern Studies III*, identifies subalternity as a position of critique, as a recalcitrant difference that arises not outside but inside elite discourses to exert pressure on forces and forms that subordinate it.

The attention paid to discourse in locating the process and effects of subordination can be seen in Partha Chatterjee's influential *Nationalist Thought and the Colonial World* (1986). A study of how Indian nationalism achieved dominance, this book traces critical shifts in nationalist thought, leading to a 'passive revolution' – a concept that he draws from Gramsci to interpret the achievement of Indian independence in 1947 as a mass revolution that appropriated the agency of the common people. In interpreting the shifts in nationalist thought, Chatterjee stresses the pressure exerted on the dominant discourse by the problem of representing the masses. The nationalists dealt with this problem by marginalizing certain forms of mass action and expression that run counter to the modernity-driven goals that they derived from the colonial discourse. Such a strategy secures elite dominance but not hegemony over subaltern culture and politics. His recent *The Nation and Its Fragments* (1993) returns once again to this theme of appropriation of subalternity, sketching how the nation was first imagined in the cultural domain and then readied for political contest by an elite that 'normalized' various subaltern aspirations for community and agency in the drive to create a modern nation-state.

Investigating the process of 'normalization' means a complex and deep engagement with elite and canonical texts. This, of course, is not new to Subaltern Studies. Earlier essays, most notably Guha's 'Prose of Counter-Insurgency', engaged and interrogated elite writings with enviable skill and imagination. But these analyses of elite texts sought to establish the presence of the subalterns as subjects of their own history. The engagement with elite themes and writings, by contrast, emphasizes the analysis of the operation of dominance as it confronted, constituted, and subordinated certain forms of culture and politics. This approach is visible in the treatment of the writings of authoritative political figures such as Mahatma Gandhi and Jawaharlal Nehru and in the analyses of the activities of the Indian National Congress – the dominant nationalist party. These strive to outline how elite nationalism rewrote history and how its rewriting was directed at both contesting colonial rule and protecting its flanks from the subalterns (see Amin 1984, 1987). Another theme explored with a similar aim is the intertwined functioning of colonialism, nationalism, and 'communalism' in the partition of British India into India and Pakistan – a theme that has taken on added importance with the recent resurgence of Hindu supremacists and outbreaks of Hindu-Muslim riots (see Pandey 1990, 1992).

Subalternity thus emerges in the paradoxes of the functioning of power, in the functioning of the dominant discourse as it represents and domesticates peasant agency as a spontaneous and 'pre-political' response to colonial violence. No longer does it appear outside the elite discourse as a separate domain, embodied in a figure endowed with a will that the dominant suppress and overpower but do not constitute. Instead, it refers to that impossible thought, figure, or action without which the dominant discourse cannot exist and which is acknowledged in its subterfuges and stereotypes.

This portrait of subalternity is certainly different from the image of the autonomous subject, and it has emerged in the confrontation with the systematic fragmentation of the record of subalternity. Such records register both the necessary failure of subalterns to come into their own and the pressure they exerted on discursive systems that, in turn, provoked their suppression and fragmentation. The representation of this discontinuous mode of subalternity demands a strategy that recognizes both the emergence and displacement of subaltern agency in dominant discourses. It is by adopting such a strategy that the Subaltern Studies scholars have redeployed and redefined the concept of the subaltern, enhancing, not diminishing, its recalcitrance.

The Subaltern Studies' relocation of subalternity in the operation of dominant discourses leads it necessarily to the critique of the modern West. For if the marginalization of 'other' sources of knowledge and agency occurred in the functioning of colonialism and its derivative, nationalism, then the weapon of critique must turn against Europe and the modes of knowledge it instituted. It is in this context that there emerges a certain convergence between Subaltern Studies and postcolonial critiques originating in literary and cultural studies. To cite only one example, not only did Edward Said's *Orientalism* provide the grounds for Partha Chatterjee's critique of Indian nationalism (1986: 36–39), Said (1988) also wrote an appreciative foreword to a collection of Subaltern Studies essays. It is important to recognize that the critique of the West is not confined to the colonial record of exploitation and profiteering but extends to the disciplinary knowledge and procedures it authorized – above all, the discipline of history.

It is important to note that 'Europe' or 'the West' in Subaltern Studies refers to an imaginary though powerful entity created by a historical process that authorized it as the home of Reason, Progress, and Modernity. To undo the authority of such an entity, distributed and universalized by imperialism and nationalism, requires, in Chakrabarty's words, the 'provincialization of Europe'. But neither nativism nor cultural relativism animates this project of provincializing Europe; there are no calls for reversing the Europe/India hierarchy and no attempts to represent India through an 'Indian', not Western, perspective. Instead, the recognition that the 'third-world historian is condemned to knowing 'Europe' as the original home of the 'modern', whereas the 'European' historian does not share a comparable predicament with regard to the pasts of the majority of humankind', serves as the condition for a deconstructive rethinking of history (Chakrabarty 1992a: 19). Such a strategy seeks to find in the functioning of history as a discipline (in Foucault's sense) the source for another history.

This move is a familiar one for postcolonial criticism and should not be confused with approaches that insist simply on the social construction of knowledge and identities. It delves into the history of colonialism not only to document its record of domination but also to identify its failures, silences, and impasses; not only to chronicle the career of dominant discourses but to track those (subaltern) positions that could not be properly recognized and named, only 'normalized'. The aim of such a strategy is not to unmask dominant discourses but to explore their fault lines in order to provide different accounts, to describe histories revealed in the cracks of the colonial archaeology of knowledge (see Bhabha 1994b).

This perspective draws on critiques of binary oppositions that, as Frederick Cooper notes, historians of former empires look upon with suspicion. It is true, as Cooper points out, that binary oppositions conceal intertwined histories and engagements across dichotomies, but the critique must go further. Oppositions such as East/West and colonizer/colonized are suspect not only because these distort the history of engagements but also because they edit, suppress, and marginalize everything that upsets founding values. It is in this respect that Jacques Derrida's strategy to undo the implacable oppositions of Western dominance is of some relevance.

> Metaphysics – the white mythology which reassembles and reflects the culture of the West: the white man takes his own mythology, Indo-European mythology, his own *logos*, that is, the *mythos* of his idiom, for the universal form that he must still wish to call Reason. ... White mythology – metaphysics has erased within itself the fabulous scene that has produced it, the scene that nevertheless remains active and stirring, inscribed in white ink, an invisible design covered over in the palimpsest (Derrida 1982: 213).

If the production of white mythology has nevertheless left 'an invisible design covered over in the palimpsest', Derrida suggests that the structure of signification, of 'differance', can be rearticulated differently than that which produced the West as Reason. Further, the source of the rearticulation of structures that produce foundational myths (History as the march of Man, of Reason, Progress) lies inside, not outside, their ambivalent functioning. From this point of view, critical work seeks its basis not without but within the fissures of dominant structures. Or, as Gayatri Chakravorty Spivak puts it, the deconstructive philosophical position (or postcolonial criticism) consists in saying an 'impossible "no" to a structure, which one critiques, yet inhabits intimately' (1990a: 28).

The potential of this deconstructive position has been explored effectively in the recent readings of the archival documents on the abolition of *sati*, the Hindu widow sacrifice in the early nineteenth century. The historian encounters these records, as I have suggested elsewhere, as evidence of the contests between the British 'civilizing mission' and Hindu heathenism, between modernity and tradition, and as a story of the beginning of the emancipation of Hindu women and about the birth of modern India.[4] This is so because, Lata Mani (1987) shows, the very existence of these documents has a history that entails the use of women as the site for both the colonial and the indigenous male elite's constructions of authoritative Hindu traditions. The questions asked of accumulated sources on *sati* – whether or not the burning of widows was sanctioned by Hindu codes, did women go willingly to the funeral pyre, on what grounds could the immolation of women be abolished – come to us marked by their early nineteenth century history. The historian's confrontation today with sources on *sati*, therefore, cannot escape the echo of that previous rendezvous. In repeating that encounter, how does the historian today not replicate the early nineteenth century staging of the issue as a contest between tradition and modernity, between the slavery of women and efforts toward their emancipation, between barbaric Hindu practices and the British 'civilizing mission'? Mani tackles this dilemma by examining how such questions were asked and with what consequences. She shows that the opposing arguments assumed the authority of the law-giving scriptural tradition as the origin of Hindu customs: both those who supported and those who opposed *sati* sought the authority of textual origins for their beliefs. In other words, the nineteenth century debate fabricated the authority of texts as Hinduism without acknowledging its work of authorization; indigenous patriarchy and colonial power colluded in constructing the origins for and against *sati* while concealing their collusion. Consequently, as Spivak states starkly, the debate left no room for the widow's enunciatory position. Caught in the contest over whether traditions did or did not sanction *sati* and over whether or not the widow self-immolated willingly, the colonized subaltern woman disappeared: she was literally extinguished for her dead husband in the indigenous patriarchal discourse, or offered the choice to speak in the voice of a sovereign individual authenticated by colonialism (see, especially, Spivak 1988: 299–307). The problem here is not one of sources (the absence of the woman's testimony) but of the staging of the debate: it left no position from which the widow could speak.

The silencing of subaltern women, Spivak argues, marks the limit of historical knowledge (see Spivak 1985a). It is impossible to retrieve the woman's voice when she was not given a subject-position from which to speak. This argument appears to run counter to the historiographical convention of retrieval to recover the histories of the traditionally ignored – women, workers, peasants, and minorities. Spivak's point, however, is not that such retrievals should not be undertaken but that the very project of recovery depends on the historical erasure of the subaltern 'voice'. The possibility of retrieval, therefore, is also a sign of its impossibility. Recognition of the aporetic condition of the subaltern's silence is necessary in order to subject the intervention of the historian-critic to persistent interrogation, to prevent the refraction of 'what might have been the absolutely Other into a domesticated Other' (Spivak 1985c: 253).

These directions of postcolonial criticism make it an ambivalent practice, perched between traditional historiography and its failures, within the folds of dominant discourses and seeking to rearticulate their pregnant silence – sketching 'an invisible design covered over in the palimpsest'. This should not be mistaken for the postmodern pastiche, although the present currency of concepts such as decentered subjects and parodic texts may provide a receptive and appropriative frame for postcolonial criticism. Postcolonial criticism seizes on discourse's silences and aporetic moments neither to celebrate the polyphony of native voices nor to privilege multiplicity. Rather, its point is that the *functioning* of colonial power was heterogeneous with its founding oppositions. The 'native' was at once an other and entirely knowable; the Hindu widow was a silenced subaltern who was nonetheless sought as a sovereign subject asked to declare whether or not her immolation was voluntary. Clearly, colonial discourses operated as the structure of writing, with the structure of their enunciation remaining heterogeneous with the binary oppositions they instituted.

This perspective on history and the position within it that the postcolonial critic occupies keeps an eye on both the conditions of historical knowledge and the possibility of its reinscription. It is precisely this double vision that allows Shahid Amin to use the limits of historical knowledge for its reinscription. His monograph on the 1922 peasant violence in Chauri Chaura is at once scrupulously 'local' and 'general'. It offers a 'thick description' of a local event set on a larger stage by nationalism and historiographical practice. Amin seizes on this general (national) staging of the local not only to show that the Indian nation emerged in its narration but also to mark the tension between the two as the point at which the subaltern memory of 1922 can enter history. This memory, recalled for the author during his field work, is not invoked either to present a more 'complete' account of the event or to recover the subaltern. In fact, treating gaps, contradictions, and ambivalences as constitutive, necessary components of the nationalist narrative, Amin inserts memory as a device that both dislocates and reinscribes the historical record. The result is not an archaeology of nationalism that yields lifeless layers of suppressed evidence and episodes. Instead, we get a stage on which several different but interrelated dramas are performed, jostling for attention and prominence; curtains are abruptly drawn on some, and often the voices of the peasant actors can only be heard in the din of the other, more powerful, voices.

To read Amin's work in this way shows, I hope, that his deconstructive strategy does not 'flatten' the tension that has existed, as Florencia Mallon notes correctly, in this scholarship from the very beginning. To be sure, Amin's account is not animated by the urge to recover the subaltern as an autonomous subject. But he places his inquiry in the tension between nationalism's claim to know the peasant and its representation of the subalterns as the 'criminals' of Chauri Chaura. The subaltern remains a recalcitrant presence in discourse, at once part of the nation and outside it. Amin trafficks between these two positions, demonstrating that subaltern insurgency left its mark, however disfigured, on the discourse – 'an invisible design covered over in the palimpsest'.

Neither Amin's retelling of the 1922 event nor Chakrabarty's project of 'provincializing Europe' can be separated from postcolonial critiques of disciplines, including the discipline of history. Thus, even as Subaltern Studies has shifted from its original goal of recovering the subaltern autonomy, the subaltern has emerged as a position from which the discipline of history can be rethought. This rethinking does not entail the rejection of the discipline and its procedures of research. Far from it. As Chakrabarty writes, 'it is not possible to simply walk out of the deep collusion between "history" and the modernizing narrative(s)' (1992a: 19). Nor is it possible to abandon historical research so long as it is pursued as an academic discipline in universities and functions to universalize capitalism and the nation-state. There is no alternative but to inhabit the discipline, delve into archives, and push at the limits of historical knowledge to turn its contradictions, ambivalences, and gaps into grounds for its rewriting.

If Subaltern Studies' powerful intervention in South Asian historiography has turned into a sharp critique of the discipline of history, this is because South Asia is not an isolated arena but is woven into the web of historical discourse centered, as Chakrabarty argues, in the modern West. Through the long histories of colonialism and nationalism, the discourse of modernity, capitalism, and citizenship has acquired a strong though peculiar presence in the history of the region. The institutions of higher education in South Asia, relatively large and thriving, have functioned since the mid-nineteenth century in relation to the metropolitan academy, including centers for South

Asian studies in the West. For all these reasons, India's historical scholarship has been uniquely placed to both experience and formulate searching critiques of metropolitan discourses even as its object remains the field of South Asia. To its credit, Subaltern Studies turned South Asia's entanglement with the modern West as the basis for rendering its intervention in South Asian history into a critique of discourses authorized by Western domination.

Subaltern Studies has arrived at its critique by engaging both Marxism and post-structuralism. But the nature of these engagements is complex. If the influence of Gramsci's Marxism is palpable in the concept of the subaltern and in treatments of such themes as hegemony and dominance, Marxism is also subjected to the post-structuralist critique of European humanism. It should be noted, however, as Spivak points out, that while 'there is an affinity between the imperialist subject and the subject of humanism', the European critique of humanism does not provide the primary motive force for the Subaltern Studies project (1985b: 337). Thus, even as this project utilizes Foucault's genealogical analysis to unravel the discourse of modernity, it relies on the subaltern as the vantage point of critique. The recalcitrant presence of the subaltern, marking the limits of the dominant discourse and the disciplines of representation, enables Subaltern Studies to identify the European provenance of Marx's account of capital, to disclose Enlightenment thought as the unthought of his analysis. It is outside Europe, in subaltern locations, that Marx's emancipatory narrative is disclosed as a *telos* deeply implicated in a discourse that was once part of colonialism and now serves to legitimate the nation-state (Chakrabarty 1989: 224–29). Such a critical and complex engagement with Marxism and poststructuralism, deriving its force from the concept of the subaltern, defines the Subaltern Studies project.

Clearly, Subaltern Studies obtains its force as postcolonial criticism from a catachrestic combination of Marxism, poststructuralism, Gramsci and Foucault, the modern West and India, archival research and textual criticism. As this project is translated into other regions and disciplines, the discrepant histories of colonialism, capitalism, and subalternity in different areas would have to be recognized. It is up to the scholars of these fields, including Europeanists, to determine how to use Subaltern Studies' insights on subalternity and its critique of the colonial genealogy of the discourse of modernity. But it is worth bearing in mind that Subaltern Studies itself is an act of translation. Representing a negotiation between South Asian historiography and the discipline of history centered in the West, its insights can be neither limited to South Asia nor globalized. Trafficking between the two, and originating as an ambivalent colonial aftermath, Subaltern Studies demands that its own translation also occur between the lines.

Notes

1 This is an abridged version of the article that appeared in *The American Historical Review*, 99 (5), 1994.
2 In calling these accounts Eurocentric, I do not mean that they followed the lead of Western authors and thinkers. Eurocentricity here refers to the historicism that projected the West as History.
3 The classic statement of the 'Cambridge School' is to be found in Anil Seal's study *The Emergence of Indian Nationalism: Competition and Collaboration in the Later Nineteenth Century* (1968), which contended that Indian nationalism was produced by the educated elites in their competition for 'loaves and fishes' of office. This was modified in Gallagher, Jognson

and Seal (1973), which advanced the view that nationalism emerged from the involvement of local and regional elites in colonial institutions. As the official institutions reached down to the locality and the province, the elites reached up to the central level to secure their local and regional dominance, finding nationalism a useful instrument for the articulation of their interests.

4 This discussion of *sati* draws heavily on my 'Postcolonial Criticism and Indian Historiography' (Prakash 1992: 11).

References

Amin, Shahid (1984) 'Gandhi as mahatma: Gorakhpur district, eastern UP, 1921–22', in Ranajit Guha (ed.) *Subaltern Studies III*, Delhi: Oxford University Press, pp. 1–61.

—— (1987) 'Approver's testimony, judicial discourse: the case of Chauri Chaura', in Ranajit Guha (ed.) *Subaltern Studies V*, Delhi: Oxford University Press, pp. 166–202.

—— (1995) *Event, Metaphor, Memory: Chauri Chaura 1922–1992*, Berkeley: University of California Press.

Arnold, David and Hardiman, David (eds) (1993) *Subaltern Studies VIII*, Delhi: Oxford University Press.

Banaji, Jairus (1977) 'Capitalist domination and small peasantry: Deccan districts in the late nineteenth century', *Economic and Political Weekly*, 12(33).

Bhabha, Homi K. (1994a) *The Location of Culture*, London: Routledge.

—— (1994b) 'Of mimicry and man: the ambivalence of colonial discourse', in *Location of Culture*, pp. 85–92.

Chakrabarty, Dipesh (1989) *Rethinking Working-Class History: Bengal 1890–1940*, Princeton, NJ: Princeton University Press.

—— (1992a) 'Postcoloniality and the artifice of history: who speaks for "Indian" pasts?' *Representations*, Winter, 37.

—— (1992b) 'Trafficking in history and theory: subaltern studies', K. K. Ruthven (ed.) *Beyond the Disciplines: The New Humanities*, Canberra: Australian Academy of the Humanities.

Chatterjee, Partha (1986) *Nationalist Thought and the Colonial World: A Derivative Discourse?* London: Zed.

—— (1993) *The Nation and Its Fragments: Colonial and Postcolonial Histories*, Princeton, NJ: Princeton University Press.

Cooper, Frederick; Isaacman, Allen F.; Mallon, Florencia E.; Roseberry, William and Stern, Steve J. (eds) (1993) *Confronting Historical Paradigms: Peasants, Labor, and the Capitalist World System in Africa and Latin America*, Madison: University of Wisconsin Press.

Das, Veena (1989) 'Subaltern as perspective', in Ranajit Guha (ed.) *Subaltern Studies VI*, Delhi: Oxford University Press.

Derrida, Jacques (1982) *Margins of Philosophy*, trans. Alan Bass, Chicago: University of Chicago Press.

Gallagher, J.; Jognson, G. and Seal, Anil (eds) (1973) *Locality, Province and Nation: Essays on Indian Politics, 1870–1940*, Cambridge: Cambridge University Press.

Guha, Ranajit (1963) *A Rule of Property for Bengal*, Paris: Mouton.

—— (1974) 'Neel darpan: the image of a peasant revolt in a liberal mirror', *Journal of Peasant Studies*, 2: 1–46.

—— (1982a) 'On some aspects of the historiography of colonial India', in Ranajit Guha (ed.) *Subaltern Studies I*, Delhi: Oxford University Press.

—— (ed.) (1982b) *Subaltern Studies I*, Delhi: Oxford University Press.

—— (1983a) *Elementary Aspects of Peasant Insurgency in Colonial India*, Delhi: Oxford University Press.

—— (1983b) 'The prose of counter-insurgency', in Ranajit Guha (ed.) *Subaltern Studies II*, Delhi: Oxford University Press.

—— (ed.) (1982–89) *Subaltern Studies I-VI*, Delhi: Oxford University Press.

Hardiman, David (1987) *The Coming of the Devi: Adivasi Assertion in Western India*, Delhi: Oxford University Press.

Mani, Lata (1987) 'Contentious traditions: the debate on sati in colonial India', *Cultural Critique*, Fall, 7: 119–56.

Nehru, Jawaharlal (1946) *Discovery of India*, New York: The John Day Company.

O'Hanlon, Rosalind (1988) 'Recovering the subject: subaltern studies and histories of resistance in colonial south Asia', *Modern Asian Studies*, 22: 189–224.

Pandey, Gyanendra (1990) *The Construction of Communalism in Colonial North India*, Delhi: Oxford University Press.

—— (1992) 'In defense of the fragment: writing about Hindu-Muslim riots in India today', *Representations*, Winter, 37: 27–55.

Pandey, Gyanendra and Chatterjee, Partha (eds) (1992) *Subaltern Studies VII*, Delhi: Oxford University Press.

Prakash, Gyan (1990) *Bonded Histories: Genealogies of Labor Servitude in Colonial India*, Cambridge: Cambridge University Press.

—— (1992) 'Postcolonial criticism and Indian historiography', *Social Text*, 31–32.

—— (1995) 'Introduction: after colonialism', in Gyan Prakash (ed.) *After Colonialism: Imperial Histories and Postcolonial Displacements*, Princeton, NJ: Princeton University Press.

Said, Edward (1988) 'Foreword', in Ranajit Guha and Gayatri Chakravorty Spivak (eds) *Selected Subaltern Studies*, New York, pp. v–x.

Seal, Anil (1968) *The Emergence of Indian Nationalism: Competition and Collaboration in the Later Nineteenth Century*, Cambridge: Cambridge University Press.

Siddiqi, Majid (1978) *Agrarian Unrest in North India: The United Provinces, 1918–22*, Delhi: Vikas.

Spivak, Gayatri Chakrabarty (1985a) 'The rani of Sirmur: an essay in reading the archives', *History and Theory*, 24: 247–72.

—— (1985b) 'Subaltern studies: deconstructing historiography', in Ranajit Guha (ed.) *Subaltern Studies IV*, Delhi: Oxford University Press.

—— (1985c) 'Three women's texts and a critique of imperialism', *Critical Inquiry*, 12.

—— (1988) 'Can the subaltern speak?' in Cary Nelson and Lawrence Grossberg (eds) *Marxism and Interpretation of Culture*, Urbana: University of Illinois Press, pp. 271–313.

—— (1990a) 'The making of Americans, the teaching of english, the future of colonial studies', *New Literary History*, 21.

—— (1990b) 'Poststructuralism, marginality, postcoloniality and value', in Peter Collier and Helga Geyer-Ryan (eds) *Literary Theory Today*, London: Polity.

16 The commitment to theory[1]

Homi Bhabha

I

There is a damaging and self-defeating assumption that theory is necessarily the elite language of the socially and culturally privileged. It is said that the place of the academic critic is inevitably within the Eurocentric archives of an imperialist or neo-colonial West. The Olympian realms of what is mistakenly labelled 'pure theory' are assumed to be eternally insulated from the historical exigencies and tragedies of the wretched of the earth. Must we always polarize in order to polemicize? Are we trapped in a politics of struggle where the representation of social antagonisms and historical contradictions can take no other form than a binarism of theory vs politics? Can the aim of freedom of knowledge be the simple inversion of the relation of oppressor and oppressed, centre and periphery, negative image and positive image? Is our only way out of such dualism the espousal of an implacable oppositionality or the invention of an originary counter-myth of radical purity? Must the project of our liberationist aesthetics be forever part of a totalizing Utopian vision of Being and History that seeks to transcend the contradictions and ambivalences that constitute the very structure of human subjectivity and its systems of cultural representation?

Between what is represented as the 'larceny' and distortion of European 'metatheorizing' and the radical, engaged, activist experience of Third World creativity (Taylor 1987), one can see the mirror image (albeit reversed in content and intention) of that ahistorical nineteenth century polarity of Orient and Occident which, in the name of progress, unleashed the exclusionary imperialist ideologies of self and other. This time round, the term 'critical theory', often untheorized and unargued, is definitely the Other, an otherness that is insistently identified with the vagaries of the depoliticized Eurocentric critic. Is the cause of radical art or critique best served for instance, by a fulminating professor of film who announces, at a flashpoint in the argument, 'We are not artists, we are political activists'? By obscuring the power of his own practice in the rhetoric of militancy, he fails to draw attention to the specific value of a politics of cultural production; because it makes the surfaces of cinematic signification the grounds of political intervention, it gives depth to the language of social criticism and extends the domain of 'politics' in a direction that will not be entirely dominated by the forces of economic or social control. Forms of popular rebellion and mobilization are often most subversive and transgressive when they are created through oppositional *cultural* practices.

Before I am accused of bourgeois voluntarism, liberal pragmatism, academicist pluralism and all the other '-isms' that are freely bandied about by those who take the most severe exception to 'Eurocentric' theoreticism (Derrideanism, Lacanianism, poststructuralism …), I would like to clarify the goals of my opening questions. I am convinced that, in the language of political economy, it is legitimate to represent the relations of exploitation and domination in the discursive division between the First and Third World, the North and the South. Despite the claims to a spurious rhetoric of 'internationalism' on the part of the established multinationals and the networks of the new communications technology industries, such circulations of signs and commodities as there are, are caught in the vicious circuits of surplus value that link First World capital to Third World labour markets through the chains of the international division of labour, and national comprador classes. Gayatri Spivak is right to conclude that it is 'in the interest of capital to preserve the comprador theatre in a state of relatively primitive labour legislation and environmental regulation' (Spivak 1987: 166–67).

I am equally convinced that, in the language of international diplomacy, there is a sharp growth in a new Anglo-American nationalism which increasingly articulates its economic and military power in political acts that express a neo-imperialist disregard for the independence and autonomy of peoples and places in the Third World. I am further convinced that such economic and political domination has a profound hegemonic influence on the information orders of the Western world, its popular media and its specialized institutions and academics. So much is not in doubt.

What does demand further discussion is whether the 'new' languages of theoretical critique (semiotic, poststructuralist, deconstructionist and the rest) simply reflect those geopolitical divisions and their spheres of influence. Are the interests of 'Western' theory necessarily collusive with the hegemonic role of the West as a power bloc? Is the language of theory merely another power ploy of the culturally privileged Western elite to produce a discourse of the Other that reinforces its own power-knowledge equation?

I want to take my stand on the shifting margins of cultural displacement – that confounds any profound or 'authentic' sense of a 'national' culture or an 'organic' intellectual – and ask what the function of a committed theoretical perspective might be, once the cultural and historical hybridity of the postcolonial world is taken as the paradigmatic place of departure.

Committed to what? At this stage in the argument, I do not want to identify any specific 'object' of political allegiance – the, Third World, the working class, the feminist struggle. Although such an objectification of political activity is crucial and must significantly inform political debate, it is not the only option for those critics or intellectuals who are committed to progressive political change in the direction of a socialist society. It is a sign of political maturity to accept that there are many forms of political writing whose different effects are obscured when they are divided between the 'theoretical' and the 'activist'. It is not as if the leaflet involved in the organization of a strike is short on theory, while a speculative article on the theory of ideology ought to have more practical examples or applications. They are both forms of discourse and to that extent they produce rather than reflect their objects of reference. The difference between them lies in their operational qualities. The leaflet has a specific expository and organizational purpose, temporally bound to the event; the theory of ideology makes its contribution to those embedded political ideas and principles that inform the right to strike. The latter does not justify the former; nor does it necessarily precede it. It exists side by side with it – the one as an enabling part of the other – like the recto and verso of a sheet of paper, to use a common semiotic analogy in the uncommon context of politics.

My concern here is with the process of 'intervening ideologically', as Stuart Hall describes the role of 'imagining' or representation in the practice of politics in his response to the British election of 1987 (1987: 30–35). For Hall, the notion of hegemony implies a politics of *identification* of the imaginary. This occupies a discursive space which is not exclusively delimited by the history of either the right or the left. It exists somehow in-between these political polarities, and also between the familiar divisions of theory and political practice. This approach, as I read it, introduces us to an exciting, neglected moment, or movement, in the 'recognition' of the relation of politics to theory; and confounds the traditional division between them. Such a movement is initiated if we see that relation as determined by the rule of repeatable materiality, which Foucault describes as the process by which statements from one institution can be transcribed in the discourse of another (1972: 102–5). Despite the schemata of use and application that constitute a field of stabilization for the statement, any change in the statement's conditions of use and reinvestment, any alteration in its field of experience or verification, or indeed any difference in the problems to be solved, can lead to the emergence of a new statement: the difference of the same.

In what hybrid forms, then, may a politics of the theoretical statement emerge? What tensions and ambivalences mark this enigmatic place from which theory speaks? Speaking in the name of some counter-authority or horizon of 'the true' (in Foucault's sense of the strategic effects of any apparatus or *dispositif*), the theoretical enterprise has to represent the adversarial authority (of power and/or knowledge) which, in a doubly inscribed move, it simultaneously seeks to subvert and replace. In this complicated formulation I have tried to indicate something of the boundary and location of the event of theoretical critique which does not *contain* the truth (in polar opposition to totalitarianism, 'bourgeois liberalism' or whatever is supposed to repress it). The 'true' is always marked and informed by the ambivalence of the process of emergence itself, the productivity of meanings that construct counter-knowledges *in medias res*, in the very act of agonism, within the terms of a negotiation (rather than a negation) of oppositional and antagonistic elements. Political positions are not simply identifiable as progressive or reactionary, bourgeois or radical, prior to the act of *critique engagée*, or outside the terms and conditions of their discursive address. It is in this sense that the historical moment of political action must be thought of as part of the history of the form of its writing. This is not to state the obvious, that there is no knowledge – political or otherwise – outside representation. It is to suggest that the dynamics of writing and textuality require us to rethink the logics of causality and determinacy through which we recognize the 'political' as a form of calculation and strategic action dedicated to social transformation.

'What is to be done?' must acknowledge the force of writing, its metaphoricity and its rhetorical discourse, as a productive matrix which defines the 'social' and makes it available as an objective of and for, action. Textuality is not simply a second-order ideological expression or a verbal symptom of a pre-given political subject. That the political subject – as indeed the subject of politics – is a discursive event is nowhere more clearly seen than in a text which has been a formative influence on Western democratic and socialist discourse – Mill's essay 'On Liberty'. His crucial chapter, 'On The Liberty of Thought and Discussion', is an attempt to define political judgement as the problem of finding a form of *public rhetoric* able to represent different and opposing political 'contents' not as a priori preconstituted principles but as a dialogical discursive exchange; a negotiation of terms in the on-going present of the enunciation of the political statement:

> [If] opponents of all important truths do not exist, it is indispensable to imagine them. ... [He] must feel the whole force of the difficulty which the true view of the subject has to encounter and dispose of; *else he will never really possess himself of the portion of truth which meets and removes that difficulty*. ... Their conclusion may be true, but it might be false for anything they know: they have never thrown themselves into the *mental position* of those who think differently from them ... and consequently they do not, in any proper sense of the word, *know the doctrine which they themselves profess* (Mill 1972: 93–94; my emphases).

What is unexpected is the suggestion that a crisis of identification is initiated in the textual performance that displays a certain 'difference' within the signification of any single political system, prior to establishing the substantial differences *between* political beliefs. A knowledge can only become political through an agnostic process: dissensus, alterity and otherness are the discursive conditions for the circulation and recognition of a politicized subject and a public 'truth'.

It is true that Mill's 'rationality' permits, or requires, such forms of contention and contradiction in order to enhance his vision of the inherently progressive and evolutionary bent of human judgement. (This makes it possible for contradictions to be resolved and also generates a sense of the 'whole truth' which reflects the natural, organic bent of the human mind.) It is also true that Mill always reserves, in society as in his argument, the unreal neutral space of the Third Person as the representative of the 'people', who witnesses the debate from an 'epistemological distance' and draws a reasonable conclusion. Even so, in his attempt to describe the political as a form of debate and dialogue – as the process of public rhetoric – that is crucially mediated through this ambivalent and antagonistic faculty of a political 'imagination', Mill exceeds the usual mimetic sense of the battle of ideas. He suggests something much more dialogical: the realization of the political idea at the ambivalent point of textual address, its emergence through a form of political projection.

Rereading Mill through the strategies of 'writing' that I have suggested, reveals that one cannot passively follow the line of argument running through the logic of the opposing ideology. The textual process of political antagonism initiates a contradictory process of reading between the lines; the agent of the discourse becomes, in the same time of utterance, the inverted, projected object of the argument, turned against itself. It is, Mill insists, only by effectively assuming the mental position of the antagonist and working through the displacing and decentring force of that discursive difficulty that the politicized 'portion of truth' is produced. This is a different dynamic from the ethic of tolerance in liberal ideology which has to imagine opposition in order to contain it and demonstrate its enlightened relativism or humanism. Reading Mill, against the grain, suggests that politics can only become representative, a truly public discourse, through a splitting in the signification of the subject of representation; through an ambivalence at the point of the enunciation of a politics.

I have chosen to demonstrate the importance of the space of writing, and the problematic of address, at the very heart of the liberal tradition because it is here that the myth of the 'transparency' of the human agent and the reasonableness of political action is most forcefully asserted. Despite the more radical political alternatives of the right and the left, the popular, commonsense view of the place of the individual in relation to the social is still substantially thought and lived in ethical terms moulded by liberal beliefs. What the attention to rhetoric and writing reveals is the discursive ambivalence that makes 'the political' possible. From such a perspective, the problematic of political judgement cannot be represented as an epistemological problem of appearance and reality or theory and practice or word and thing. Nor can it be represented as a dialectical problem or a symptomatic contradiction constitutive of the materiality of the 'real'. On the contrary, we are made excruciatingly aware of the ambivalent juxtaposition, the dangerous interstitial relation of the factual and the projective, and, beyond that, of the crucial function of the textual and the rhetorical. It is those vicissitudes of the movement of the signifier, in the fixing of the factual and the closure of the real, that ensure the efficacy of stategic thinking in the discourses of *Realpolitik*. It is this to-and-fro, this *fort/da* of the symbolic process of political negotiation, that constitutes a politics of address. Its importance goes beyond the unsettling of the essentialism or logocentrism of a received political tradition, in the name of an abstract free play of the signifier.

A critical discourse does not yield a *new* political object, or aim, or knowledge, which is simply a mimetic reflection of an a priori political principle or theoretical commitment. We should not demand of it a pure teleology of analysis whereby the prior principle is simply augmented, its rationality smoothly developed, its identity as socialist or materialist (as opposed to neo-imperialist or humanist) consistently confirmed in each oppositional stage of the argument. The language of critique is effective not because it keeps forever separate the terms of the master and the slave, the mercantilist and the Marxist, but to the extent to which it overcomes the given grounds of opposition and opens up a space of translation: a place of hybridity, figuratively speaking, where the construction of a political object that is new, *neither the one nor the other*, properly alienates our political expectations, and changes, as it must, the very forms of our recognition of the moment of politics. The challenge lies in conceiving of the time of political action and understanding as opening up a space that can accept and regulate the differential structure of the moment of intervention without rushing to produce a unity of the social antagonism or contradiction. This is a sign that history is *happening* – within the pages of theory, within the systems and structures we construct to figure the passage of the historical.

When I talk of *negotiation* rather than *negation*, it is to convey a temporality that makes it possible to conceive of the articulation of antagonistic or contradictory elements: a dialectic without the emergence of a teleological or transcendent History, and beyond the prescriptive form of symptomatic reading where the nervous tics on the surface of ideology reveal the 'real materialist contradiction' that History embodies. In such a discursive temporality, the event of theory becomes the *negotiation* of contradictory and antagonistic instances that open up hybrid sites and objectives of struggle, and destroy those negative polarities between knowledge and its objects, and between theory and practical-political reason (Laclau and Mouffe 1985: Chapter 3). If I have argued against a primordial and previsionary division of right or left, progressive or reactionary, it has been only to stress the fully historical and discursive différance between them. I would not like my notion of negotiation to be confused with some syndicalist sense of reformism because that is not the political level that is being explored here. By negotiation I attempt to draw attention to the structure of *iteration* which informs political movements that attempt to articulate antagonistic and oppositional elements without the redemptive rationality of sublation or transcendence (Gasché 1986).

The temporality of negotiation or translation, as I have sketched it, has two main advantages. First, it acknowledges the historical connectedness between the subject and object of critique so that there can be no simplistic, essentialist opposition between ideological miscognition and revolutionary truth. The progressive reading is crucially determined by the adversarial or agonistic situation itself; it is effective because it uses the subversive, messy mask of camouflage and does not come like a pure avenging angel speaking the truth of a radical historicity and pure oppositionality. If one is aware of this heterogeneous emergence (not origin) of radical critique, then – and this is my second point – the function of theory within the political process becomes double-edged. It makes us aware that our political referents and priorities – the people, the community, class struggle, anti-racism, gender difference, the assertion of an anti-imperialist, black or third perspective – are not there in some primordial, naturalistic sense. Nor do they reflect a unitary or homogeneous political object. They make sense as they come to be constructed in the discourses of feminism or Marxism or the Third Cinema or whatever, whose objects of priority – class or sexuality or 'the new ethnicity' – are always in historical and philosophical tension, or cross-reference with other objectives.

Indeed, the whole history of socialist thought which seeks to 'make it new and better' seems to be a different process of articulating priorities whose political objects can be recalcitrant and contradictory. Within contemporary Marxism, for example, witness the continual tension between the English, humanist, labourist faction and the 'theoreticist', structuralist, new left tendencies. Within feminism, there is again a marked difference of emphasis between the psychoanalytic/semiotic tradition and the Marxist articulation of gender and class through a theory of cultural and ideological interpellation. I have presented these differences in broad brush-strokes, often using the language of polemic, to suggest that each position is always a process of translation and transference of meaning. Each objective is constructed on the trace of that perspective that it puts under erasure; each political object is determined in relation to the other, and displaced in that critical act. Too often these theoretical issues are peremptorily transposed into organizational terms and represented as sectarianism. I am suggesting that such contradictions and conflicts, which often thwart political intentions and make the question of commitment complex and difficult, are rooted in the process of translation and displacement in which the object of politics is inscribed. The effect is not stasis or a sapping of the will. It is, on the contrary, the spur of the negotiation of socialist democratic politics and policies which demand that questions of organization are theorized and socialist theory is 'organized', *because there is no given community or body of the people whose inherent, radical historicity emits the right signs.*

This emphasis on the representation of the political, on the construction of discourse, is the radical contribution of the translation of theory. Its conceptual vigilance never allows a simple identity between the political objective and its means of representation. This emphasis on the necessity of heterogeneity and the double inscription of the political objective is not merely the repetition of a general truth about discourse introduced into the political field. Denying an essentialist logic and a mimetic referent to political representation is a strong, principled argument against political separatism of any colour, and cuts through the moralism that usually accompanies such claims. There is literally, and figuratively, no space for the unitary or organic political objective which would offend against the sense of a socialist *community* of interest and articulation.

In Britain, in the 1980s, no political struggle was fought more powerfully, and sustained more poignantly, on the values and traditions of a socialist community than the miners' strike of 1984–85. The battalions of monetarist figures and forecasts on the profitability of the pits were starkly ranged against the most illustrious standards of the British labour movement, the most cohesive cultural communities of the working class. The choice was clearly between the dawning world of the new Thatcherite city gent and a long history of the working man, or so it seemed to the traditional left and the new right. In these class terms the mining women involved in the strike were applauded for the heroic supporting role they played, for their endurance and initiative. But the revolutionary impulse, it seemed, belonged securely to the working-class male. Then, to commemorate the first anniversary of the strike, Beatrix Campbell, in the *Guardian*, interviewed a group of women who had been involved in the strike. It was clear that their experience of the historical struggle, their understanding of the historic choice to be made, was startlingly different and more complex. Their testimonies would not be contained simply or singly within the priorities of the politics of class or the histories of industrial struggle. Many of the women began to question their roles within the family and the community – the two central institutions which articulated the meanings and mores of the tradition of the labouring classes around which ideological battle was enjoined. Some challenged the symbols and authorities of the culture they fought to defend. Others disrupted the homes they had struggled to sustain. For most of them there was no return, no going back to the 'good old days'. It would be simplistic to suggest either that this considerable social change was a spin-off from the class struggle or that it was a repudiation of the politics of class from a socialist-feminist perspective. There is no simple political or social truth to be learned, for there is no unitary representation of a political agency, no fixed hierarchy of political values and effects.

My illustration attempts to display the importance of the hybrid moment of political change. Here the transformational value of change lies in the rearticulation, or translation, of elements that are *neither the One* (unitary working class) *nor the Other* (the politics of gender) but something else besides, which contests the terms and territories of both. There is a negotiation between gender and class, where each formation encounters the displaced, differentiated boundaries of its group representation and enunciative sites in which the limits and limitations of social power are encountered in an agonistic relation. When it is suggested that the British Labour Party should seek to produce a socialist alliance among progressive forces that are widely dispersed and distributed across a range of class, culture and occupational forces – without a unifying sense of the class for itself – the kind of hybridity that I have attempted to identify is being acknowledged as a historical necessity. We need a little less pietistic articulation of political principle (around class and nation); a little more of the principle of political *negotiation*.

Such negotiations between politics and theory make it impossible to think of the place of the theoretical as a metanarrative claiming a more total form of generality. Nor is it possible to claim a certain familiar epistemological distance between the *time and place* of the intellectual and the activitist, as Fanon suggests when he observes that 'while politicians situate their action in actual present-day events, men of culture take their stand in the field of history' (1967: 168). It is precisely that popular binarism

between theory and politics, whose foundational basis is a view of knowledge as totalizing generality and everyday life as experience, subjectivity or false consciousness, that
I have tried to erase. It is a distinction that even Sartre subscribes to when he describes
the committed intellectual as the theoretician of practical knowledge whose defining
criterion is rationality and whose first project is to combat the irrationality of ideology
(1973: 16–17). From the perspective of negotiation and translation, *contra* Fanon and
Sartre, there can be no final discursive *closure* of theory. It does not foreclose on the
political, even though battles for power-knowledge may be won or lost to great effect.
The corollary is that there is no first or final act of revolutionary social (or socialist)
transformation.

I hope it is clear that this erasure of the traditional boundary between theory/poli-
tics, and my resistance to the en-*closure* of the theoretical, whether it is read negatively
as elitism or positively as radical supra-rationality, do not turn on the good or bad
faith of the activist agent or the intellectual *agent provocateur.* I am primarily concerned with the conceptual structuring of the terms – the theoretical/the political – that
inform a range of debates around the place and time of the committed intellectual. I
have therefore argued for a certain relation to knowledge which I think is crucial in
structuring our sense of what the *object* of theory may be in the act of determining our
specific political *objectives.*

II

What is at stake in the naming of critical theory as 'Western'? It is, obviously, a des-
ignation of institutional power and ideological Eurocentricity. Critical theory often
engages with texts within the familiar traditions and conditions of colonial anthropology either to universalize their meaning within its own cultural and academic discourse, or to sharpen its internal critique of the Western logocentric sign, the idealist
subject, or indeed the illusions and delusions of civil society. This is a familiar manoeuvre of theoretical knowledge, where, having opened up the chasm of cultural difference, a mediator or metaphor of otherness must be found to contain the effects of
difference. In order to be institutionally effective as a discipline, the knowledge of
cultural difference must be made to foreclose on the Other; difference and otherness
thus become the fantasy of a certain cultural space or, indeed, the certainty of a form
of theoretical knowledge that deconstructs the epistemological 'edge' of the West.

More significantly, the site of cultural difference can become the mere phantom of a
dire disciplinary struggle in which it has no space or power. Montesquieu's Turkish
Despot, Barthes's Japan, Kristeva's China, Derrida's Nambikwara Indians, Lyotard's
Cashinahua pagans are part of this strategy of containment where the Other text is
forever the exegetical horizon of difference, never the active agent of articulation. The
Other is cited, quoted, framed, illuminated, encased in the shot/reverse-shot strategy of
a serial enlightenment. Narrative and the *cultural* politics of difference become the
closed circle of interpretation. The Other loses its power to signify, to negate, to initiate
its historic desire, to establish its own institutional and oppositional discourse. However
impeccably the content of an 'other' culture may be known, however anti-ethnocen-
trically it is represented, it is its *location* as the closure of grand theories, the demand
that, in analytic terms, it be always the good object of knowledge, the docile body of
difference, that reproduces a relation of domination and is the most serious indictment
of the institutional powers of critical theory.

There is, however, a distinction to be made between the institutional history of critical theory and its conceptual potential for change and innovation. Althusser's critique of the temporal structure of the Hegelian-Marxist expressive totality, despite its functionalist limitations, opens up the possibilities of thinking the relations of production in a time of differential histories. Lacan's location of the signifier of desire, on the cusp of language and the law, allows the elaboration of a form of social representation that is alive to the ambivalent structure of subjectivity and sociality. Foucault's archaeology of the emergence of modern, Western man as a problem of finitude, inextricable from its afterbirth, its Other, enables the linear, progressivist claims of the social sciences – the major imperializing discourses – to be confronted by their own historicist limitations. These arguments and modes of analysis can be dismissed as internal squabbles around Hegelian causality, psychic representation or sociological theory. Alternatively, they can be subjected to a translation, a transformation of value as part of the questioning of the project of modernity in the great, revolutionary tradition of C.L.R. James – *contra* Trotsky or Fanon, *contra* phenomenology and existentialist psychoanalysis. In 1952, it was Fanon who suggested that an oppositional, differential reading of Lacan's Other might be more relevant for the colonial condition than the Marxist reading of the master-slave dialectic.

It may be possible to produce such a translation or transformation if we understand the tension within critical theory between its institutional containment and its revisionary force. The continual reference to the horizon of other cultures which I have mentioned earlier is ambivalent. It is a site of citation, but it is also a sign that such critical theory cannot forever sustain its position in the academy as the adversarial cutting edge of Western idealism. What is required is to demonstrate another territory of translation, another testimony of analytical argument, a different engagement in the politics of and around cultural domination. What this other site for theory might be will become clearer if we first see that many poststructuralist ideas are themselves opposed to Enlightenment humanism and aesthetics. They constitute no less than a deconstruction of the moment of the modern, its legal values, its literary tastes, its philosophical and political categorical imperatives. Secondly, and more importantly, we must rehistoricize the moment of 'the emergence of the sign', or 'the question of the subject', or the 'discursive construction of social reality' to quote a few popular topics of contemporary theory. This can only happen if we relocate the referential and institutional demands of such theoretical work in the field of cultural difference – not cultural diversity.

Such a reorientation may be found in the historical texts of the colonial moment in the late eighteenth and early nineteenth centuries. For at the same time as the question of cultural difference emerged in the colonial text, discourses of civility were defining the doubling moment of the emergence of Western modernity. Thus the political and theoretical genealogy of modernity lies not only in the origins of the *idea* of civility, but in this history of the colonial moment. It is to be found in the resistance of the colonized populations to the Word of God and Man – Christianity and the English language. The transmutations and translations of indigenous traditions in their opposition to colonial authority demonstrate how the desire of the signifier, the indeterminacy of intertextuality, can be deeply engaged in the postcolonial struggle against dominant relations of power and knowledge. In the following words of the missionary master we hear, quite distinctly, the oppositional voices of a culture of resistance; but we also hear the uncertain and threatening process of cultural transformation. I quote from A. Duff's influential *India and India Missions* (1839):

Come to some doctrine which you believe to be peculiar to Revelation; tell the people that they must be regenerated or born again, else they can never 'see God'. Before you are aware, they may go away saying, 'Oh, there is nothing new or strange here; our own Shastras tell us the same thing; we know and believe that we must be born again; it is our fate to be so.' But what do they understand by the expression? It is that they are to be born again and again, in some other form, agreeably to their own system of transmigration or reiterated births. To avoid the appearance of countenancing so absurd and pernicious a doctrine, you vary your language, and tell them that there must be a second birth – that they must be twice-born. Now it so happens that this, and all similar phraseology, is preoccupied. The sons of a Brahman have to undergo various purificatory and initiatory ceremonial rites, before they attain to full Brahmanhood. The last of these is the investiture with the sacred thread; which is followed by the communication of the Gayatri, or most sacred verse in the Vedas. This ceremonial constitutes, 'religiously and metaphorically, their second birth'; henceforward their distinctive and peculiar appellation is that of the twice-born, or regenerated men. *Hence it is your improved language might only convey the impression that all must become perfect Brahmans, ere they can 'see God'* (Duff 1839: 560; my emphasis).

The grounds of evangelical certitude are opposed not by the simple assertion of an antagonistic cultural tradition. The process of translation is the opening up of another contentious political and cultural site at the heart of colonial representation. Here the word of divine authority is deeply flawed by the assertion of the indigenous sign, and in the very practice of domination the language of the master becomes hybrid – neither the one thing nor the other. The incalculable colonized subject – half acquiescent, half oppositional, always, untrustworthy – produces an unresolvable problem of cultural difference for the very address of colonial cultural authority. The 'subtle system of Hinduism', as the missionaries in the early nineteenth century called it, generated tremendous policy implications for the institutions of Christian conversion. The written authority of the Bible was challenged and together with it a post-enlightenment notion of the 'evidence of Christianity' and its historical priority, which was central to evangelical colonialism. The Word could no longer be trusted to carry the truth when written or spoken in the colonial world by the European missionary. Native catechists therefore had to be found, who brought with them their own cultural and political ambivalences and contradictions, often under great pressure from their families and communities.

This revision of the history of critical theory rests, I have said, on the notion of cultural difference, not cultural diversity. Cultural diversity is the recognition of pre-given cultural contents and customs; held in a time-frame of relativism, it gives rise to liberal notions of multiculturalism, cultural exchange or the culture of humanity. Cultural diversity is also the representation of a radical rhetoric of the separation of totalized cultures that live unsullied by the intertextuality of their historical locations, safe in the Utopianism of a mythic memory of a unique collective identity.

The concept of cultural difference focuses on the problem of the ambivalence of cultural authority: the attempt to dominate in the *name* of a cultural supremacy which is itself produced only in the moment of differentiation. And it is the very authority of culture as a knowledge of referential truth which is at issue in the concept and moment of *enunciation*. The enunciative process introduces a split in the performative present of cultural identification; a split between the traditional culturalist demand for a model, a tradition, a community, a stable system of reference, and the necessary negation of the certitude in the articulation of new cultural demands, meanings, strategies in the political present, as a practice of domination, or resistance. The struggle is often between the historicist teleological or mythical time and narrative of traditionalism – of the right or the left – and the shifting, strategically displaced time of the articulation of a historical politics of negotiation which I suggested above.

The enunciation of cultural difference problematizes the binary division of past and present, tradition and modernity, at the level of cultural representation and its authoritative address. It is the problem of how, in signifying the present, something comes to be repeated, relocated and translated in the name of tradition, in the guise of a pastness that is not necessarily a faithful sign of historical memory but a strategy of representing authority in terms of the artifice of the archaic. That iteration negates our sense of the origins of the struggle. It undermines our sense of the homogenizing effects of cultural symbols and icons, by questioning our sense of the authority of cultural synthesis in general.

The reason a cultural text or system of meaning cannot be sufficient unto itself is that the act of cultural enunciation – *the place of utterance* – is crossed by the *différance* of writing. This has less to do with what anthropologists might describe as varying attitudes to symbolic systems within different cultures than with the structure of symbolic representation itself – not the content of the symbol or its social function, but the structure of symbolization. It is this difference in the process of language that is crucial to the production of meaning and ensures, at the same time, that meaning is never simply mimetic and transparent.

The linguistic difference that informs any cultural performance is dramatized in the common semiotic account of the disjuncture between the subject of a proposition (*énoncé*) and the subject of enunciation, which is not represented in the statement but which is the acknowledgement of its discursive embeddedness and address, its cultural positionality, its reference to a present time and a specific space. The pact of interpretation is never simply an act of communication between the I and the You designated in the statement. The production of meaning requires that these two places be mobilized in the passage through a Third Space, which represents both the general conditions of language and the specific implication of the utterance in a performative and institutional strategy of which it cannot 'in itself' be conscious. What this unconscious relation introduces is an ambivalence in the act of interpretation. The pronominal I of the proposition cannot be made to address – in its own words – the subject of enunciation, for this is not personable, but remains a spatial relation within the schemata and strategies of discourse. The meaning of the utterance is quite literally neither the one nor the other. This ambivalence is emphasized when we realize that there is no way that the content of the proposition will reveal the structure of its positionality; no way that context can be mimetically read off from the content.

The implication of this enunciative split for cultural analysis that I especially want to emphasize is its temporal dimension. The splitting of the subject of enunciation destroys the logics of synchronicity and evolution which traditionally authorize the subject of cultural knowledge. It is often taken for granted in materialist and idealist problematics that the value of culture as an object of study, and the value of any analytic activity that is considered cultural, lie in a capacity to produce a cross-referential, generalizable unity that signifies a progression or evolution of ideas-in-time, as well as a critical self-reflection on their premises or determinants.

The intervention of the Third Space of enunciation, which makes the structure of meaning and reference an ambivalent process, destroys this mirror of representation in which cultural knowledge is customarily revealed as an integrated, open, expanding code. Such an intervention quite properly challenges our sense of the historical identity of culture as a homogenizing, unifying force, authenticated by the originary Past, kept alive in the national tradition of the People.

It is only when we understand that all cultural statements and systems are constructed in this contradictory and ambivalent space of enunciation, that we begin to understand why hierarchical claims to the inherent originality or 'purity' of cultures are untenable, even before we resort to empirical historical instances that demonstrate their hybridity. It is that Third Space, though unrepresentable in itself, which constitutes the discursive conditions of enunciation that ensure that the meaning and symbols of culture have no primordial unity or fixity; that even the same signs can be appropriated, translated, rehistoricized and read anew.

It is significant that the productive capacities of this Third Space have a colonial or postcolonial provenance. For a willingness to descend into that alien territory – where I have led you – may reveal that the theoretical recognition of the split-space of enunciation may open the way to conceptualizing an international culture, based not on the exoticism of multiculturalism or the *diversity* of cultures, but on the inscription and articulation of culture's hybridity. To that end we should remember that it is the 'inter' – the cutting edge of translation and negotiation, the *inbetween* space – that carries the burden of the meaning of culture. It makes it possible to begin envisaging national, anti-nationalist histories of the 'people'. And by exploring this Third Space, we may elude the politics of polarity as we encounter something much more challenging – the difference "within", the otherness that constitutes our experience of ourselves. Exceeding a polarising politics that singularises 'difference' ("gender", "generation", "race", "class", "regionality" etc.) enables individuals and groups to commit themselves to associations (and negotiations) that aspire to the subaltern politics of solidarity and *survivance* rather than displaying an adamantine attachment to identitarian claims to sovereignty and autonomy. For those who have been denied their sovereignty as subjects and citizens, the price of freedom demands nothing less than the revision of what it means, in the first place, to be an in-dependent person.

Note

1 This is an abridged version of the article that appeared in Homi Bhabha, *The Location of Culture* (London: Routledge, 1994).

References

Duff, Rev. A. (1839) *India and India Missions: Including Sketches of the Gigantic System of Hinduism etc.*, Edinburgh: John Johnstone.
Fanon, F. (1967) [1961] *The Wretched of the Earth*, Harmondsworth: Penguin.
Foucault, M. (1972) *The Archaeology of Knowledge*, London: Tavistock.
Gasché, R. (1986) *The Tain of the Mirror*, Cambridge, MA.: Harvard University Press.
Hall, S. (1987) 'Blue election, election blues', *Marxism Today*, July.

Laclau, E. and Mouffe, C. (1985) *Hegemony and Socialist Strategy*, London: Verso.

Mill, J. S. (1972) 'On Liberty', in *Utilitarianism, Liberty, Representative Government*, London: Dent & Sons.

Sartre, J. P. (1973) [1948] *Politics and Literature*, London: Calder & Boyars.

Spivak, G. C. (1987) *In Other Worlds*, London: Methuen.

Taylor, C. (1987) 'Eurocentrics vs new thought at Edinburgh', *Framework*, 34.

Part VII
Emancipation

17 The justice of human rights in Indian constitutionalism[1]

Upendra Baxi

Prefatory observations

Talking about the 'justice' of rights runs many a narrative risk. For one thing, the formations of erudite 'Indian political thought' remain relatively unmarked with any sustained theoretical/philosophic attention to approaches to justice and human rights.[2] Nor is it easy to fall back upon the resources of practical reason provided by such organic intellectuals as Phule, Gandhi, Ambedkar, Nehru, Acharya Narendra Dev, Ram Manohar Lohia, M. N. Roy, Vinoba Bhave and Jayaprakash Narayan; they engaged preciously with 'injustice' of the liberal and libertarian theories of rights, but it remains an open question whether they, save Ambedkar (see Baxi 1995; 2002a), proposed any general theory of justice and rights, at least in the way contemporaneously understood (Parekh and Pantham 1987). In any event, future tasks of the retrieval of their praxes should remain relevant to 'context sensitive' contrasted with 'context freedom' oriented organic knowledges concerning ideas of freedom, justice and rights.

Further, contemporary liberal theoretical approaches to justice/rights remain richly diverse and not fully exhausted by distinctions/divisions into 'libertarian' and 'liberal', cosmopolitan as well as communitarian – too formidable a territory to be visited here, even if one had the necessary cognitive/epistemic visa at hand! At least then from the edges, borders, outsides of this vast philosophic continent, an intrepid observer may venture to say that the discourse concerning the justice of rights has moved away from the paradigm of justice as a virtue of individual human conduct to the notion of justice as a virtue of the 'basic' structure of a just society, assuring fair and equal arrangement for production/reproduction of ongoing social cooperation and collaboration. Overall, these approaches seek to reconcile, in diverse ways, the conflicted domains of 'liberty' and 'equality', and insist that a just social and political order remains inconceivable outside recognition and respect for equal worth and dignity of all human beings, regardless of the happenstance of birth, blood and belonging. Justice cannot be thought of any longer outside some affirmation of respect for human rights, regardless of the multifarious disagreements concerning the nature, number, limits, and negotiability of human rights.[3] Put another way, the issue now concerns the ethical viability of the 'thin' as contrasted with the 'thick' descriptions of rights, in all their accompanying varied justifications.

Constitutionalism: the history of nothing?

In trying to situate my understanding of the justice of rights in contexts of constitutionalism, I risk non-conversation with the other practitioners of 'Indian political thought' represented in the present volume. Contemporary Indian political and social theory resolutely bypasses the many discursive worlds of the Indian constitutional development and the place of justice and rights within these. To be sure, the worlds of constitutionalism remain exigent and normatively untidy; yet the same worlds have cross-fertilized disciplines other than 'Indian political thought'. The reasons for this inadvertence – or in Parekh's terms, the 'poverty of theory' – summon future sociology of knowledge type labours. However, some fresh starts in the understanding of state, law and rights were provided by social anthropologists writing in the traditions of thought constituted from M. N. Srinivas to Veena Das. It is another matter that unfortunately Srinivas is all but forgotten; and Das seems to have moved away from her early agendum of serious grappling of these concerns to a mode of understanding that finally relegates 'the discourse of justice and rights' primarily to 'a series of part-nerships through which state and community mutually engage in self-creation and maintenance' (Das 2004: 251).

I remain aware that at the very outset the term 'constitutionalism' raises some stunning perplexities. By this notion I wish to simply refer to three intersecting orders of norm and fact: constitutional texts (C1), constitutional interpretation (C2), and theory or ideology underlying these (C3), which I name elsewhere (Baxi 2000a) in terms of the dialectical relation between the three Cs, briefly put as the state of play and war between the normative, institutional, and social movement/struggle types of relation-ship among the text, interpretation, and theory/ideology. These states of 'play' and 'war' further require us to develop some workable distinctions between – borrowing from Derrida (1992) – the *foundational* and *reiterative* aspects of constitutionalism, or the making of a constitution and its subsequent working. Both offer vast spheres of proliferating narratives. By 'foundational', I signify the myriad exertions of constituent power, the labours of the originary moment, when the contexts and the texts of con-stitution are composed. Reiterative labours invite attention to the semiotic and the social (that is, material) fact that the composition of the text of the constitution marks the beginnings of all subsequent labours of interpretation and renovation (Baxi 2003: 557, 575–84). Constitutionalism then, in my view, furnishes various sites of *labours of production* of political and social meanings/significations clustered around four vast thematics: governance, rights, development and justice that address the futures of the 'politics of production' and 'production of politics' (to borrow from Michael Burawoy 1985). Perhaps the notion of labouring practice as defining the realms and tasks of constitutionalism may offer the beginnings of a *materialist theory of constitutionalism* (Baxi 1993).

Doing a materialist interpretation of the act of constitution-making is always a dif-ficult task, as the trend towards archival retrieval of the massive Indian Constituent Assembly Debates [CADS] – from B. Shiva Rao (1967) and Granville Austin (1966) – already suggests. We also know from recent political science/cultural theory resurgence of interest in the CADS that these are read in terms of who said what and when, not *why* they said what they said and left unsaid what may have been after all more fully said. Thus at best, the CADS narratives exemplify so many forms of objectified and politically commoditized 'dead labour'. The forensic and adjudicatory CADS usages do surely constitute hermeneutic practices of 'living labour'. But in the main, all this presents a master progress narrative, in which the making of India's Constitution fur-nishes a saga of normative and institutional insurrection against India's co-equally violent colonial and precolonial past. The power of critical acts of reading of the

CADS in the genre of Marxian narratology (e.g. Chaube 1973; Gupta 1979) continues to be negated by the habits of the romantic reading. The current engagement with the CADS now leads to a free-for-all post-ideological type revisitation of the foundational constitutional moment. The CADS are now being read in some post-historic ways; the contexts of high feminist, post-modern, and even ecological critique, uncongenial to the makers of the Constitution, furnish ironic modes of who-said-what-and-why type narrative, interspersed further with ad hoc and exigent commentation from the present whatever standpoint. The new project of reading seeks different understandings of both the constitutional promise and the betrayal, yet at the same moment failing to revisit the constitutional past in terms of grasping the material contradictions. I speak to this with some care in what follows.

The question then arises: What sort of reflexivity may inform diverse acts/practices/performatives of reading the CADS? May some rather forbidding Hegelian practices of reading universal history wholly inform these? How may we receive in this mode the question of the 'nature' of 'postcolonial reason' as Gayatri Spivak now summons us to fully understand? Do the CADS already mark then the originary moment of 'failed decolonization' and thus provide, as it were, the genetic blueprint for all subsequent progressive postcolonial liberal constitutionalisms? Is the originary moment then fraught with a world-historic significance? Further, how may one relate this sort of reading of the foundational moment to the inaugural postcolonial reading in Gandhi's *Hind Swaraj,* which radically framed 'Western' parliamentary governance as an aspect of Westoxification and denied the logics of competitive liberal party politics in his later insistence that the Indian National Congress dissolve as a party and convert itself into a people's movement? How may the rhetoric of 'failed decolonization' help us grasp the varieties of Indian socialist, Marxian, and radical humanist thought, which hailed the foundational moment as a truly revolutionary one, in which self-determination signified (in the terms of Antonio Negri 2003) the production of the insurgent 'proletarian' time in confrontation with the 'productive' time of global capitalism? How may we read the Nehruvian imagery of the same originary moment as an aspect of nation-building, that gave us both a just and a strong state (Baxi 1992a)?

Or, may we revisit/resist the CADS in some privileged Walter Benjamin mode approaching history always as radically fragmented, standing always in some redemptive relation with the 'present' and the 'future'? Benjamin presents the originary moment of liberation also as moments of 'horror' (1969: 256–57). No serious reading of the making of the Indian Constitution may escape this 'horror' of the Partition of India. Veena Das captures this moment of horror rather acutely when she asserts that: 'If men emerged from colonial subjugation as autonomous citizens of an independent nation, they emerged simultaneously as monsters' (1997: 86). Yet, most current practices of reading the *Debates* constructing the collective authorial intent (if such things can ever be), in the main, sanitize the 'horror' simply, and cruelly, as a bygone affair of the 'past', as if of little relevance today. Were we further to note with Benjamin's reading of the 'angel of history' whose face is turned to the past so that he may 'awaken the dead' (1969: 257–58), the question surely arises: What *dead* do we *awaken* by our acts of reading the CADS, and with what future specific Indian pertinences? Put another way, how may our acts of reading the CADS revive the 'future memory' (as Benjamin named it) of the foundational moment of several types of suppression: for example, of the militarization of governance and of the early forms of the Hindutva dissidence?

Or, do acts of reading the CADS invite, with Reinhardt Kosselleck, some difficult practices of devising resources for 'timing history' and 'spacing concepts' that trace conceptual and social histories of pre-or proto-constitutional past? Is it the case that the famous Preamble of the Constitution – proclaiming the values of justice, equality, freedom and fraternity – remains merely mimetic of the Euro-American historic pasts, and the languages, of their originary moments? If not, in which future history modes may we read the CADS as offering any disruptive articulations of these very conceptions? Indeed, how may we begin to pursue Kosselleck-type conceptual, semantic and semiotic labours that may ground a distinctive understanding of the perambulatory values?[4]

Another important question thus emerges: In what ways do the CADS enact exclusions silencing the myriad subaltern voices and instituting a new hegemonic discourse concerning justice/rights? What voices of suffering were silenced, how many registers of insurgencies erased, and what cacophonies of a 'strong' state were thus orchestrated in the making of the Constitution and to what/which future effect? How do we institute careful, responsible, minuscule and fiduciary ways of reading the constitutional past in terms of a present which is not and a future yet to be?

In sum, how may we practice ethically inoffensive readings of the labours of the founding moment and reiterative practices of constitutional development? As I have demonstrated inter alia in my meditations on Jawaharlal Nehru, Mahatma Gandhi and Babasaheb Ambedkar (Baxi 1995, 1992a: 1–10, 226–41), the choice here is indeed difficult. I find myself drawn to the possibility of some sustained Marxian readings that impute the *Debates* with a collective authorial/deliberative intent, which programme and install some mystifying rhetoric universalizing constellations of specific (arid strategically positioned) particular class interests as 'the' public interest or the common good and even managing the self-presentation of the state as 'neutral' and as pro-proletariat (see Gupta 1979; Chaube 1973; Baxi 1993). From this perspective, I miss in these contemporary readings of CADS and the Indian constitutional development a sense of dialectical understanding of the constitutional unfoldment.

Prescinding this, we still need to invent some distinctly postcolonial ways of reading the CADS (cf. Rajan 2003). Is it the case that any such moral reading of constituent labours may suggest a decisive break marking a triumphant normative reversal of mercantilist colonial state formation? If the constitutional Indian state was intended to furnish an assemblage of governance structures and practices outlawing predatory ruling classes who seek to violently appropriate and distribute the resources of the nation among themselves and networks of their artificial affines and kins, it failed (and still continues to fail) even to *name* governance corruption as a distinct violation of its conceptions of human rights and accompanying freedoms. Constitutional conceptions of rights and justice as originally envisioned and still now practiced the enthronement of a predatory and corrupt sovereign. This almost altogether renders conceptions of governance state/regime-oriented, rather than human rights and justice-friendly. The constitution-makers regarded plebiscitary forms of democracy as the primary mechanism, even perhaps the sole one, to ensure both integrity in governance and in the protection and promotion of human rights. No other more specific mechanisms were thought necessary, such as those that would ensure systemic constitutional surveillance over political corruption in high places (Baxi 1990). The constitution-makers did not deploy the foundational moment, outside the badge of probity somehow offered by periodic elections, any salience to the values of transparency in governance. In this, they continued the colonial inheritance and further innovated new cultures of impunity. In a memorable interview with Andre Malraux, Nehru defined in one sentence the foundational constitutional moment when he said that the postcolonial task was to build a *strong state,* which pursued the ends of justice. Note that he did not say *a strong state that pursued this task with just means.*

How, then, may the originary self-presentations of the constitutional Indian state and governance relate to its several reiterative moments? These specific configurations raise all over again the Nehruvian dialectic of the power of justice and justice of power, if one may so put this, posing in turn many an intractable question. All I can say here by way of a prolegomena is that the reiterative discourse manifests the colliding worlds of the material labours of C2, here further revised as connoting the *insurgent* citizen interpretation of Cl. One hopes for, but rarely finds, any fully-fledged articulation of relationship between rights and justice even in C3. In these multiple universes of these reiterative three Cs the problem emerges more in terms of *conflict of rights* than directly as the problem of *the justice of rights.* On the whole, an ongoing constitutional discourse does not engage in providing justifications for enshrining human rights; rather it remains primarily concerned with the nature and number of rights thus enshrined and the permissible modes of the negotiation of their limits. In contrast, the problem of the justice of rights arises for deep and wide deliberation in moments of originary constitution choice-making, that is, making of a new constitution or amending an existing one.

I read the CADS, as early as 1967, as illustrating the vicissitudes of the construction of a 'constitutionally desired just social order'. This was, of course, a wholly pre-Lacanian reading, on my part, of the politics of constitutive desire because it was simply then not available to me! I did not then grasp Lacan's ways of telling stories of desire, constituting always a mobile horizon that marked the impossibility of its attainment, although I was able even then to lisp the disorder of the constituent desire. Perhaps, 'Indian political thought' may then benefit in re-locating the appetites of political desire thriving on the politics of microfascism of governance, contrasted with the 'emancipative' disorder of popular human rights desire within Lacanian grammars. Perhaps, also this may be informed by some revisitation of the classical Buddhist thought concerning the karmic overload of political desires (the *maya, sunnyata,* and the *dukkha* of desire as such) (cf. Hallward 2001). I instantly apologize for this heavily rolled-up formulation, but I do think that we ought to grasp constitutionalism as in some sense being *passional* rather than entirely *rational.* Constitutionalisms, forever, construct and reconstruct the violent 'orders' of the desiring subjects.

Innovations: a summary overview

Forms of Indian constitutionalism, especially at some cutting edges of Indian judicial activism ...

i.   Creatively *modify* the classic liberal human rights model into politically inclusive adjudicative, negotiated constitutional secularism.
ii. *Structure* extensions of human rights beyond naming organized political community (the state) as the seat and source of human – and human rights – violations to the storehouse, the *fons et origio*: civil society. (How else may we grasp Article 17 outlawing practices of untouchability, and Article 23 banning practices of agrestic serfdom and related practices of debasing human beings?).

iii.   *Assert* a progressive role for the law and state in the reform of majority (Hindu) religious practices.
iv.   *Enunciate* 'near-absolute' rights of minorities to establish and administer educational institutions (Article 30).
v.   *Authorize* the scope both for runaway practices of political management in devising programmes of affirmative action, while at the same time permitting strict judicial scrutiny.
vi.   *Enshrine*, irreversibly, some rights of political participation, though the device of legislative reservations for the Scheduled Castes and Tribes, the right to return their own elected representatives to state legislatures and Indian Parliament.
vii.   *Renovate* judicial review with the daring of enunciative regimes that not merely limit the plenary power of the Indian Parliament to amend the Constitution but also to exercise constituent power, a form where apex justices may even declare a particular amendment constitutionally invalid (Baxi 2003).
viii.   *Create* a model of fundamental rights forever vulnerable to the creeping imposition of 'reasonable regulation', on constitutionally stated grounds, of these very rights, subject, from time to time, to both the regimes of 'strict' and 'relaxed' judicial review scrutiny.
ix.   *Devise* constestatory forms of 'cooperative' administrative, fiscal and legislative federalism, always subject to apex judicial interpretation.
x.   *Fashion* modes of judicial review that legitimate judicial governance via adjudication that contests all forms of executive, legislative and constitutive (in the sense of the Supreme Court's invigilation over the over-reach of the amending power).

Manifestly, some of these features (especially the first eight) constitute a distinctive break with received high colonial legal-liberal inheritance, even when raising in turn a cornucopia of troublesome theory questions. In these, I believe, indwells the originality of the Indian constitutional imagination that also, moreover, contributes in a significant measure a framework for many an Asian and Anglophonic African constitutional design and development.

I recognize at the outset two general questions. First, are there available theories of justice of human rights according to which we may adjudge the justice of constitutional arrangements? Second, were this the case, how may these be made to inform by way of practical or pragmatic reason that finally collapses the 'foundational'/'reiterative' dichotomy (Baxi 2000c)?

Diversity

Would it be true to say that the making of the Indian Constitution normatively annihilates some orders of civilizational diversity? If so, were the choices thus after all made, *just* and if so, on whose *say-so,* and *why?* How far ought the making of the Indian Constitution have attended to the classical Hindu, Buddhist, Jain, Islamic, Judaic, Parsee, Christian and indigenous civilization traditions in its value aspirations?

How may we speak to the problematic of the Uniform Civil Code (UCC)? The Constitution makes two basic moves: first it manages to preserve the 'personal law system' of Muslim minorities, while, second, it acts (in Marc Galanter's words) as a 'charter of reform' for Hinduism. Clearly, while the first is understandable at the moment of Partition, which jeopardized 'minority' rights, the lack of any movement towards the progressive realization of the promise of UCC, over more than 50 years, raises the question of the constitutional insincerity of the elected public officials and Justices. Prescinding different readings of acts of political expediency, the UCC discourse raises a bouquet of poignant questions concerning the nature and scope of 'minority rights' and their justice qualities: Should the communitarian logics of rights of conscience, religion, and identity justify departures, and even denials, of women's rights as human rights, imperiling in the very process the constitutive ideals of constitutional secularism (see Baxi 2002a: 80–87; 2005b; Menski 2003)?

Citizenship

In what ways may we read Indian constitutional development as providing any *just* conceptions of citizenship? Any such conception ought to embrace not just the concept of human beings endowed with human rights but also citizens as bearing human rights responsibilities towards co-citizens (co-nationals) and in certain situations towards non-citizens (non-nationals). Granted that the very notion of 'citizenship' remains no more than just over half a century old in India, how may any understanding of Indian constitutionalism at work in several ways reconcile the libertarian notion of citizenship (a category of rights without responsibilities) with its communitarian reconfiguration in which we may install co-citizen human rights responsibilities? How may we in this context read the 42nd Amendment insinuating Part IV-A (Fundamental Duties of Citizens) as an act redressing the initial failure or as a radical constitutional innovation? In either event, how may courts, citizens and ways of governance capaciously feminize the conceptions of citizenship in ways which abate, frustrate and foil, the social reproduction of what Veena Das names as 'citizen monsters'? Further, and now in a globalizing India, how ought our notions of citizenship inform the new-fangled notions of 'corporate citizenship'?

The right to political participation

The constitutional paradigm of the justice of rights, no doubt, richly innovating the classical liberal inheritance, fatefully invents at least three orders of distinction: (1) here-and-now fundamental rights (Part III rights); (2) promises of uncertain futures for social, economic, and cultural rights (Part IV rights and the Directive Principles of State Policy); and, (3) constitutional rights (the rights to citizenship, the right to adult suffrage, the right to trade and commerce throughout the territory of India). How far, and with what democratic justifications may performances of judicial activism mutate these hierarchies of rights? Do these performances contribute at all to any enhanced fulfillment of the Part IV-A charter of the Fundamental Duties of Indian Citizens?[5]

Take, for example, the right to adult suffrage, the cornerstone of democratic India, conventionally understood both as a right to vote as well as to contest elections. Under the constitutional schema, this right is a *constitutional,* not a *fundamental* right. This means that the Indian Parliament may, by a simple majority, change its content and scope – and, indeed, the transformations of the Indian Representation of the Peoples Act all too often accomplished this, especially concerning the forms of administrative disenfranchisement through the venality of the preparation of the electoral rolls, or the difficult judicial monitoring of the muscle and money power in election campaigns, or further through somewhat capricious judicial oversight over the nomination of candidates with a history of criminal indictment. All these arrangements of power raise some basic issues concerning the justice of voting rights, which constitute, when at all, the hinterland of 'Indian political thought'!

What, may we say, are the grounds of the justice of rights to political participation in the Indian Constitution? On the one hand, it proclaims horizontal human rights of citizens in terms of the right to adult suffrage. On the other hand, it also authorizes a system of electoral reservations under which the right to contest elections stands limited by the justice considerations of political participation that entail that certain constituencies may be reserved for the candidates belonging to the Scheduled Castes and Tribes, a time-bound provision initially restricted to the first constitutional decade, and now infinite in duration. How may, incidentally, any approach to the justice of rights justify this infinite reservation? A veteran trade union leader, who then ascended to the status of Indian Presidency, once contended the justice of this provision on the bar of equality rights; the Supreme Court of India negated this claim.[6] On what normative grounds may we then adjudge the resultant situation of the justice of rights? May we attend to this in terms of a justifiable arrangement of group rights trumping individual citizen rights as a mode of historic form of reparative justice? The available Euro-American repertoire of Rawls, and post Rawls, response (see Williams 1995; Thompson 2004) remains unhelpful simply because the forms of legislative reservations, Indian-style, remain rather exotic in their distinctive justice/rights discursivity.

Equally, the ongoing discourse on the multiply aborted constitutional amendments seeking to provide legislative reservations for women in the Indian Parliament and state legislatures raises some serious normative questions (as well as some empirical ones). Ought we, for example, to regard, or relegate, women as identifiable justice constituencies of millennially hurt and harmed constituencies? If so, in what sense may women constitute a class/culture/religion-based 'minority' group/collectivity justified to an order of 'reservation' rights? Does this forever then essentialize this category? Put another way, are *all* women, regardless of their class and history location, to be considered worthy of empowerment through electoral reservations or may we (and if so how) draw some justifiable distinctions across the categories of historically and contemporaneously disempowered women.

Hierarchies

The complex and contradictory notion of universality, inalienability, indivisibility and interdependence of human rights in sum, the 'community of rights' as Gewirth (1996) enunciates this haunts any agendum contemplating the justice of human rights in Indian constitutional development. The very process of the making of the Indian Constitution frames, as already noted, this agenda via fragmentation of the 'universality etc.' of human rights via the partition enacted by Part III and Part IV. Different approaches to notions of justice have created contested terrains for the scope of constitutionally enunciated human rights and also the scope of justice considerations that may determine state and law based enforcement of constitutionally enshrined human rights.

Untouchability

The problem of the justice of rights haunts Indian constitutionalism on several registers. The abolition of 'untouchability' (Article 17 itself puts this term in quotation marks!) is indeed a direct onslaught on the dominant Hindu religious beliefs concerning purity and pollution. Insofar as histories (rather, narratives) can, the history of the nationalist movement had indeed settled the question of the justification of constitutional outlawing of 'untouchability'. What was not settled was the question of how any constitutional imagination may after all address the varieties of 'untouchability'. Because blood secretion was somehow defined as polluting, menstruating women remained 'untouchable'. Contact with a human corpse was similarly viewed as defiling; so was contact with *mlecha,* a foreigner, and by extension visits to a foreign land. The priestly powers, of course, ordained purificatory rites in temporally bound practices of 'untouchability'. The Constitution-makers, wisely but not altogether well, attended only to 'untouchability' arising by birth in certain lower castes. Further, what they perhaps wisely choose to forbid was not religious *belief* but its outward *practice;* the Constitution targets discrimination arising on the ground of 'untouchability'. Spectacularly, also, it provides for equal access of all to Hindu temples (Article 26); this continues even today to raise issues concerning the relationship between state and religion because many Hindu beliefs and traditions (and not just these) practice restrictions on access to the *sanctum sanctorum* in the name of the collective 'right' of the ritually 'pure' religious belief and practice. The Supreme Court of India has indeed inveighed heavily on the exclusion of access by the ritually 'impure' castes to the Hindu temples; it has even ruled that duly qualified non-Brahmins may administer rituals of worship.[7]

Conscience and conversion

The arena of religious conversion further complicates the multiplex issue concerning the justice of rights. How may the state/law combinatory regime regulate the exercise of the right to conscience when this extends to the practices of both individual and mass (collective) religious conversion? In the abstract, the right to the 'freedom of conscience' may seem to be near-absolute, if only because 'conscience' may not be regulated by expedient acts of sovereign power. But the Indian state/law combine has asserted, and won, the claim to regulate, and even criminalize, conversions by 'force and fraud'.[8]

Article 25 of the Indian Constitution authorizes the state to regulate religious freedom and even the right to conscience on the grounds of public order, health and *morality.* This raises an overarching question: What *'morality'* may justify state power, and legal authority, over the freedom of *conscience,* in its radically ethical sense? What non-agentative ethic may we construct for state/law regulation of conscientious conduct? How may/ought we derive a superior collective ethic that may justifiably regulate, discipline, and punish agnosticism, apostasy, conscientious objection to war-like operations, and religious conversions? Precisely because of this, the question then arises in terms of even practical reason: when may state regulation of religious *belief/practice* be said to violate *the right to conscience?* This is a different question because it is hard to tell when state regulation of *practice* of a religion may in turn profoundly affect or indeed stand apperceived as a sustained assault on religious *belief.* The rarefied world of 'Indian political thought' has done little to foreground this as an affair of political philosophy.

Minority rights

The practices of identity politics continue to raise vexed questions concerning the 'legitimacy' of the rights assured to 'minority' communities. Many questions of the justice of rights here crowd the discourse. How may the recognition of collective rights extend to justification and endorsement of denial of rights to individual members of a given community? Should individual agency authorize authentic acts of acceptance of denial of rights by individuals thus interpellated within a community? Should we legitimate state coercion that disallows such individual acts constituting a 'waiver' or 'renunciation' of human rights? Does state intervention here reek of flawed state/law moral paternalism, such that may be said to endanger the ethical existence of a moral/religious community?

Here also we encounter the problematic of a *just conceptualization of collectivities,* fashioned by social and political histories, as bearers of human rights. What shall we say about the justice-qualities of Indian constitutionalism's penchant for describing these in terms of 'socially and educationally backward classes' and 'other backward classes'? What conceptions of secularity stand here entailed? What may we say of the standards of ethical appraisal involved in judgements concerning the 'justice' of affirmative action programmes, Indian style? The discourse raises the question whether we may think of justice as prior to politics or of justice in and through the practices of politics (Williams 1995; Thompson 2004)? How justifiable remain the constitutional choreographies of the politics of identity and difference? In what ways may we understand the forms of the production of textual/sexual constitutional politics?

Conclusionary remarks

There are no easy ways at hand, then, to address (let alone resolve) in the Indian context the justice of rights, especially via a transportation of the messages of the liberal and cosmopolitan approaches to justice (see Chandhoke 1999; Mahajan 1998; Bhargava 1985; Rajan 2003). How may we seek to avoid the imposition of sameness that denies deference to the logics of difference through the strident identification of the 'Indian' with the politically constructed 'Hindu' identity formation? How may we marshal hermeneutic understandings of the Indian traditions (Christian, Buddhist, Judaic, Parsee, Islamic and a thousand-fold variety of Indian indigenous traditions)? Where may we situate the organic knowledges concerning the justice of rights arising from the Old (mostly labour movement histories) and the New Social Movements (in the main, civil and democratic human rights, ecological, gender, identity politics, ecofeminism movements) on the tableau of the erudite 'Indian political thought'?

Finally, how may we locate, within variegated landscapes of globalization (germinally traced by Arjun Appadurai) any assertion of ontological robustness of 'Indian' thought and praxes, outside its totalizing (and therefore tyrannical and violent) enunciative performances?

Notes

1 This is an abridged version of the article that appeared in Vrajendra Raj Mehta and Thomas Pantham (eds) *Political Ideas in Modern India: Thematic Explorations* (New Delhi: Sage Publications, 2006).

2 I cannot recall a single treatise specifically focused on the theory of justice or rights by an Indian social or political theorist, though some Indian philosophers have written insightfully: Daya Krishna (1991), Satish Saberwal (1998), Vinit Haksar (2001), and Chattrapati Singh (1986), notable among them. However, some approaches towards a theory of justice and rights remain implicit in the works exploring: (*a*) 'Classical' Hindu theory: Debi Prasad Chattopadhyaya (1977, 1989), D. D. Kosambi (1962, 1965), Maharishi Kane (1941), Romila Thapar (1978, 1985, 2003); (*b*) Gandhian thought: B. N. Ganguli (1977), V. R. Mehta (1999), Thomas Pantham (1995), Bhikhu Parekh (1999), Anthony Parel (1997), Partha Chatterjee (1986); (*c*) Nehruvian tradition: S. Gopal (1989), Partha Chatterjee (1986), Ravinder Kumar (1986) and Akeel Bilgrami (1995); (*d*) Comparative political theory project: Ranajit Guha, Veena Das (2004), Satish Saberwal (1998), Ashis Nandy (1990), Sudipta Kaviraj (2000), Yogendra Singh (1985), T. K. Oommen (1984, 2004), Pratap Bhanu Mehta (2007), Rajeswari Sunder Rajan (2003), Rajeev Bhargava (1985), Gurpreet Mahajan (1998), Neera Chandhoke (1999). Outside the corpus of A. A. A. Fyzee (2005), there is not much writing concerning rights and justice in Islamic law in India. I do not wish to burden this footnote by references, howsoever sparse, concerning justice and rights conceptions of indigenous peoples.

3 By 'nature' I mean here primarily distinctions made between 'enforceable' and not directly 'justiciable' rights. By 'number', I refer to the distinction between 'enumerated' and 'unenumerated' rights, the latter often articulated by practices of judicial activism. By 'limits' I indicate here the scope of rights thus enshrined, given that no constitutional guarantee of human rights may confer 'absolute' protection. The 'negotiation' process is indeed complex; it refers to at least three distinct though related aspects: (*a*) judicially upheld definitions of grounds of restriction or regulation of the scope of rights, (*b*) legislatively and executively unmolested judicial interpretation of the meaning, content, and scope of rights and (*c*) the ways in which the defined bearers of human rights chose or chose not to exercise their rights, this in turn presupposing that they have the information concerning the rights they have and the capability to deploy them in various acts of living.

4 I suspect that some order of juxtaposition of the thought-ways of diverse thinkers such as Debi Prasad Chattopadhyaya, D. D. Kosambi, Ananda Coomaraswamy, Ranajit Guha, Partha Chatterjee, and Sudipta Kaviraj, for example, may here provide some clues.

5 See, *Bijoe Emmanuel vs. State of Kerala* (1086) 3 SCC 615; and *Rangnath Mishra vs. Union of India and Others* (2003) 7 SCC 1333.

6 See, *V. V. Gin* vs. *D. Suri Dora,* AIR 1959 SC 1313.

7 Not without jurisprudential twists and turns. See *M. Adithyan vs. Travancore Devaswom Board* (2002) 8 SCC 106.

8 See *Yulitha Hyde* vs. *State of Orrisa,* AIR 1973 SC 116; in part overruled in *Rev. Stainislaus* vs. *State of M.P.* [1977] 1 SCC 677.

References

Appadurai, Arjun (1997) *Modernity at Large: Cultural Dimensions of Globalization,* New Delhi: Oxford University Press.

Austin, Granville (1966) *The Indian Constitution: Cornerstone of a Nation,* New Delhi: Oxford University Press.

—— (2001) 'Religion, personal law, and identity in India', in Gerald James Larson (ed.) *Religion and Personal Law in India: A Call to Judgement,* Bloomington and Indianapolis: Indiana University Press.

Baxi, Upendra (1967) 'The little done, the vast undone: reflection on reading Granville Austin's *The Indian Constitution*', *Journal of the Indian Law Institute.* 9: 323–430.

—— (1990) *Liberty and Corruption: The Antulay Case and Beyond,* Lucknow: Eastern Book Co.

—— (1992a) 'Dare not be little: Jawaharlal Nehru's constitutional vision and its relevance in the eighties and beyond', in Rajeev Dhavan and Thomas Paul (eds) *Nehru and the Indian Constitution,* New Delhi: The Indian Law Institute.

—— (1992b) 'The recovery of fire: Nehru and legitimation of power in India', in Rajeev Dhavan and Thomas Paul (eds) *Nehru and the Indian Constitution,* New Delhi: The Indian Law Institute.

—— (1993) *Marx, Law and Justice*. Bombay: N. M. Tripathi.

—— (1995) 'Emancipation as justice: Babasaheb Ambedkar's legacy and vision', in Upendra Baxi and Bhikhu Parekh (eds) *Crisis and Change in Contemporary India*, New Delhi: Sage Publications, pp. 122–50.

—— (2000a) 'Constitutionalism as a site of state formative practices', *Cardozo Law Review,* 21 (1183).

—— (2000b) 'Postcolonial constitutionalism', in H. Schwartz and S. Ray (eds) *Blackwell Companion to Postcolonial Studies*, Oxford: Blackwell.

—— (2000c) 'The avatars of judicial activism: explorations in the geography of (in) justice', in S. K. Verma and Kusum (eds) *Fifty Years of the Supreme Court of India: Its Grasp and Reach*, New Delhi: Oxford University Press and Indian Law Institute, pp. 156–209.

—— (2002a) *The Future of Human Rights*, New Delhi: Oxford University Press.

—— (2002b) 'The (im)possibility of constitutional justice: seismographic notes on Indian constitutionalism', in Z. Hasan, E. Sridharan and R. Sudarshan (eds) *India's Living Constitution*, New Delhi: Permanent Black, pp. 31–63.

—— (2003) '"A known but an indifferent judge": situating Ronald Dworkin in contemporary Indian jurisprudence', *International Journal of Constitutional Law,* 1: 557–58.

—— (2004) 'Protection of human rights and production of human rightlessness in India', in Randall Peerenboom; Carole J. Petersen; Albert H. Y. Chen (eds) *Human Rights in Asia, France, and the US*, London: Routledge.

—— (2005a) 'The Gujarat catastrophe: notes on reading politics as democidal rape culture', in Kalpana Kannabiran (ed.) *The Violence of the Normal Times: Essays on Women's Lifeworlds*, New Delhi: Women Unlimited, pp. 382–85.

—— (2005b) 'Siting secularism in the uniform civil code', in Rajeswari Sunder Rajan and Anuradha Needham (eds), *Secularism in India*, Durham, NC: Duke University Press.

Benjamin, Walter (1969) [1968] *Illuminations: Essays and Reflection*, New York: Schocken Books.

Bhargava, Rajeev (1985) 'Religious and secular identities', in Upendra Baxi and Bhikhu Parekh (eds) *Crisis and Change in Contemporary India*, New Delhi: Sage, pp. 317–49.

Bilgrami, A. and Nandy, A. (1995) *Secularism, nationalism, and modernity*, RGICS paper, no. 29, New Delhi: Rajiv Gandhi Institute for Contemporary Studies.

Burawoy, Michel (1985) *The Politics of Production: Factory Regimes under Capitalism and Socialism*, London: Verso.

Chandhoke, Neera (1999) *Beyond Secularism: The Rights of Religious Minorities*, New Delhi: Oxford University Press.

Chatterjee, Partha (1986) *Nationalist Thought in the Colonial World: A Derivative Discourse?* New Delhi: Oxford University Press.

Chattopadhyaya, Debi Prasad (1977) *Science and Society in Ancient India*, Calcutta: Research India Publications.

—— (1989) *In Defence of Materialism in Ancient India*, New Delhi: People's Publishing House.

Chaube, S. K. (1973) *Constituent Assembly of India: Springboard of Revolution*, New Delhi: People's Publishing House.

Das, Veena (1997) 'Language and body transactions in the construction of pain', in Arthur Kleinman, Veena Das and Margaret Lock (eds) *Social Suffering,* vol. 67, Berkeley: University of California Press.

—— (2004) 'The signature of the state: the paradox of legibility', in Veena Das and Deborah Poole (eds), *Anthropology in the Margins of State*, New Delhi: Oxford University Press, pp. 225–52.

Derrida, Jacques (1992) 'The force of law: the mystical foundations of authority', in Drucilla Cornell, Michel Rosenfeld and David Gray Carlson (eds) *Deconstruction and the Possibility of Justice*, New York: Routledge.

Fyzee, A. A. A. and Mahmood, T. (2005). *Cases in the Muhammadan law of India, Pakistan, and Bangladesh*, New Delhi: Oxford University Press.

Ganguli, B. N. (1977) *Indian Economic Thought*, New Delhi: Tata McGraw-Hill.

Gewirth, Allan (1996) *The Community of Rights*, Chicago: University of Chicago Press.

Gopal, S. (1989) *The Nehru Era: A Symposium on an Assessment of Nehru*, Seminar, 363, New Delhi: Singh.

Gupta, Sobhanlal Datta (1979) *Justice and Political Order in India*, Calcutta: Firma Mukhopadhyaya.

Haksar, Vinit (2001) *Rights, Communities and Disobedience: Liberalism and Gandhi*, New Delhi: Oxford University Press.

Hallward, Peter (2001) *Absolutely postcolonial: Writing between the Singular and the Specific*, Manchester: Manchester University Press.

Kane, P. V. (1941) *History of Dharmaśāstra: Ancient and Mediaeval Religions and Civil Law in India*, Poona: Bhandarkar Oriental Research Institute.

Kaviraj, S. (2000) 'Modernity and politics in India', *Daedalus: Proceedings of the American Academy of Arts and Sciences.* 129, 137.

Kosambi, D. D. (1962) *Myth and Reality: Studies in the Formation of Indian Culture*, Bombay: Popular Prakashan.

—— (1965) *The Culture and Civilisation of Ancient India in Historical Outline*, London: Routledge & Kegan Paul.

Kosselleck, Reinhardt (2000) *The Practice of Conceptual History: Timing History, Spacing Concepts*, Stanford: Stanford University Press.

Krishna, Daya (1991) *Indian Philosophy: A Counter Perspective*, New Delhi: Oxford University Press.

Kumar, R. (1986) *Jawaharlal Nehru, the Indian National Congress, and the Anti-fascist Struggle, 1939–1945*, Occasional papers on history and society, no. 25, New Delhi: Nehru Memorial Museum and Library.

Mehta, P. B. (2007) 'The rise of judicial sovereignty', *Journal of Democracy*, 18, 70–83.

Madan, T. N. (1987) 'Secularism in its place', *Journal of Asian Studies*, 46: 747.

Mahajan, Gurpreet (1998) *Identities and Rights: Aspects of Liberal Democracy in India*, New Delhi: Oxford University Press.

Mehta, V. R. (1999) *Foundations of Indian Political Thought*, New Delhi: Manohar.

Menski, Werner (2003) *Hindu Law: Beyond Tradition and Modernity*, New Delhi: Oxford University Press.

Nandy, Ashis (1990) 'The politics of secularism and the recovery of religious tolerance', in Veena Das (ed.) *Mirrors of Violence*, New Delhi: Oxford University Press.

Negri, Antonio (2003) *A Time for Revolution?* London: Continuum Books.

Oommen T. K. (1984) *Social Structure & Politics: Studies in Independent India*, Delhi: Hindustan Pub. Corp.

—— (2004) 'Futures India: society, nation-state, civilisation', *Futures.* 36, 745.

Pantham, Thomas (1995) *Political Theories and Social Reconstruction: A Critical Survey of the Literature on India*, New Delhi: Sage.

Parekh, Bhikhu (1999) *Colonialism, Tradition and Reform*, New Delhi: Sage.

Parekh, Bhikhu and Pantham, Thomas (eds) (1987) *Political Discourse: Explorations in India and Western Political Thought*, New Delhi: Sage.

Parel, A. J. (1997) *Gandhi: Hind Swaraj and Other Writings*, Cambridge: Cambridge University Press.

Rajan, Rajeswari Sunder (2003) *Scandal of the State: Women, Law, and Citizenship in Postcolonial India*, Durham, NC: Duke University Press.

Rao, B. Shiva (1967) *The Framing of India's Constitution, Select Documents*, New Delhi: Indian Institute of Public Administration.

Rawls, John (1993) *Political Liberalism*, New York: Columbia University Press.

—— (1999) *The Law of Peoples*, Cambridge, MA: Harvard University Press.

Saberwal, Satish and Sievers, H. (eds) (1998) *Rules, Laws, Constitutions*, New Delhi: Sage.

Singh, Chattrapati (1986) *Law from Anarchy to Utopia*, New Delhi: Oxford University Press.

Singh, Yogendra (1985) *Image of Man: Ideology & Theory in Indian Sociology*, Delhi: Chanakya Publications.

Spivak, Gayatri Chakravorty (1999) *A Critique of Postcolonial Reason: Towards a History of Vanishing Present*, New York: Columbia University Press.

Thapar, Romila (1978) *Ancient Indian Social History: Some Interpretations*, New Delhi: Orient Longman.

—— (1985) *From Lineage to State: Social Formations of the Mid-First Millennium B.C. in the Ganges Valley*, New Delhi: Oxford University Press.

—— (2003) *Cultural Pasts: Essays in Early Indian History*, New Delhi: Oxford University Press.

Thompson, Janna (2004) *Taking Responsibility for the Past: Reparation and Historic Justice*, Cambridge: Polity.

Williams, Melissa (1995) 'Justice towards groups: political, not juridical', *Political Theory*, 23: 67–71.

18 Emancipatory feminist theory in postcolonial India

Unmasking the ruse of liberal internationalism[1]

Ratna Kapur

The attack by liberal intellectuals on critical theory, which aims at introducing a more philosophical analysis into the reading and understanding of culture and other disciplines, has become a significant feature of liberal feminism in both the 'West' and non-West. The work of liberal feminist scholars such as Martha Nussbaum, characterize the way in which this attack has been choreographed in feminist scholarship.

I specifically engage with Nussbaum's views for two reasons. The first is to take on board the critique of some feminist scholars who have argued that the feminist challenge to liberal legalism has been at times guilty of 'straw-manning' its liberal target (Munro 2007: 51–54; Lacey 1998: 69). Secondly, Nussbaum has been academically engaged with India for many years, and written about the feminist liberal project in that context with considerable zeal and intensity. Given her defense of the liberal position as integral to the pursuit of social justice within the context of postcolonial India, her work becomes all the more significant with which to engage.

Nussbaum's most aggressive attack on critical theory is found in her polemical critique of Judith Butler's book *Excitable Speech,* in the February 22, 1999 issue of *The New Republic,* entitled 'The Professor of Parody'. Nussbaum attacked Butler for being highly theoretical, invoking jargon without adding clarity, and introducing no new ideas to feminist theory. She assailed Butler for being anti-political, embracing a 'hip defeatism', and a 'collaborator with evil' (1999: 45). Butler was pilloried for her impenetrable writing style, her daring to venture into an arena outside of her discipline – that is, law – her failure to produce a normative theory of social justice, and the lack of connection between her 'fancy words on paper' and feminist political struggle on the ground. According to Nussbaum, Butler's work was illustrative of how theory had become divorced from practice and hence of little value, amounting to nothing more than the couched ravings of intellectuals from their lofty ivory towers.

In this chapter, I do not provide a comprehensive response to Nussbaum's critique of Butler. My central concern is to challenge the way in which Nussbaum invokes the struggle of Indian feminists to justify her principal argument against critical theory as well as some of the claims made in this process about Indian feminism and liberalism's universal appeal.

In defense of liberal internationalism

In 'The Professor of Parody' Nussbaum positioned herself as a spokesperson for the Indian feminist movement and the kind of theory with which Indian women lived and worked. She implied it was a theory that replicated the good theory of Catherine

MacKinnon and refused to 'collaborate with evil', supposedly unlike Butlerian feminism. She argued Indian feminists were attracted to the MacKinnon position based on the idea of 'patriarchy' and men's sexual subordination of women. She argued that Indian feminists had to be more sensitive to women's material conditions and understood the need for practical solutions, the practical solutions that have driven MacKinnon's theory.

Nussbaum's position has been and continues to be based on a robust defense of what she has characterized as 'liberal internationalism' that no longer faces any ideological resistance in the post-Cold War era. In her text *Sex and Social Justice,* she developed an argument in favour of a capabilities approach to human development. Her theory of justice and human rights emerged from her reading of Amartya Sen's concept of substantial freedoms or capabilities, which he developed to address questions of justice and human development (Sen 1999).

The capabilities approach identifies 'a kind of basic human flourishing' based on a list of central capabilities drawn up by Nussbaum from which she generates some specific political principles. It includes the following ten criteria: to be able to live for a normal human life span; have good reproductive health, nourishment, and adequate shelter; move freely from place to place and be free from sexual violence; think, reason and do these things in a 'truly human way'; love, grieve, experience longing, gratitude and justified anger; form a conception of the good and critically reflect on how to plan one's life; live for and in relation to others and have a social basis of self-respect and non-humiliation; live with a concern for and in relation to animals, plants and nature; play, which includes laughing and enjoying recreational activities; and have control over one's political and material environment (Nussbaum 1999a: 40–41). These capabilities are construed as substantive freedoms and cannot be accounted for merely within the gross national product or determined in terms of income-deprivation. This approach emphasizes that the central goal of public policy must be to promote the capabilities of each citizen to be able to perform all of these important human functions. Each capability must be equally promoted by society in order to ensure an individual's claim to a good life in which 'the dignity of the human being is not violated by hunger or fear or the absence of opportunity' (Nussbaum 1999a: 40).

The capabilities approach considers people one by one, and does not lump them together in families or communities. The capabilities approach is also based on choice, where the government does not direct the citizen into acting in a specific way, but simply makes sure that the citizen has all the resources and conditions that are required for acting in those ways. Society is obliged to provide individuals with the basic infrastructure in order to enable them to make choices (Nussbaum, 1999a:45). Nussbaum advocates this capabilities approach for all members of humanity, a liberal internationalism that is not just confined to one's own context. As she states, 'I believe that individuals have moral obligations to promote justice for people outside their national boundaries and that their governments do also' (Nussbaum 1999a: 6).

Nussbaum's position is based on two primary assumptions about humans that lie at the heart of the liberal tradition as articulated by Immanuel Kant and John Rawls – all individuals have worth because of their power of moral choice; and secondly, society and politics must respect and promote this choice and equal worth of the choosers (Nussbaum 1999a: 57). Nussbaum acknowledges that there are some important critiques of liberalism put forward by feminists that must be confronted if her argument is to be persuasive. The first is the idea that liberalism is based on individualism, and treats the subject as existing *a priori* to social relations, outside of any social ties (Nussbaum 1999: 59). Nussbaum's response to this critique is that feminists should be concerned about the fact that liberalism has not been nearly individualist enough when it comes to women and family. Nussbaum relies on J. S. Mill's argument in the *Subjection of Women* to illustrate how this liberal thinker was in fact concerned with the well being of the individual as well as the individual family members and argued that law should be used to advance the fair treatment of every individual including women in the family.

The second critique put forward by feminists is that the liberal vision is abstract and formalistic, and does not take account of important differences such as class, caste, religion, gender or race. Such an approach could for example justify segregation. Nussbaum argues that it is a mistake to think that liberalism has been committed to ahistorical abstraction, even though some liberal thinkers have been guilty of such an error. She argues that liberal philosophers have rejected such a notion of pure formal equality and that liberalism affords individuals the right to demand equality from their government in ways that take into consideration material prerequisites – that it aims at 'equality of capabilities'. A true liberal position on equality, promotes equal worth, which requires that society work towards promoting the capacities of people to choose a life that accords with their own thinking.

A third feminist critique focuses on liberalism's emphasis on human beings as reasoning subjects. Although reasoning has helped women to secure their equality, it does tend to place too much emphasis on something that is considered a male trait, and denigrates traits such as emotion and imagination that are traditionally associated with females (Nussbaum 1999a: 72). Nussbaum does not reject the liberal emphasis on reason, though she does reject excessive male rationalization. She seeks to create a liberal construction of emotions that represents a balance between reason and feelings as opposed to emotions, which are imposed on women through tradition, convention, and patriarchal social conditioning (Nussbaum 2004).

Nussbaum argues that the thing women must most mistrust is habit, disguised in the form of tradition, as it has invariably been used to their disadvantage. Women need to recognize that tradition has often been articulated by men and used to subordinate women to do men's bidding. And the most regressive traditions are located in the 'Third World'. She proclaims that:

> We [American women] would never tolerate a claim that women in our own society must embrace traditions that arose thousands of years ago – indeed, we are proud that we have no such traditions. Isn't it condescending, then, to treat Indian and Chinese women as bound by the past in ways that we are not (Nussbaum 1999a: 37)?

Nussbaum is willing to suffer the label of a Western imperialist, rather than to 'stand around in the vestibule waiting for a time when everyone will like what we are going to say' (Nussbaum 1999a: 30). She states categorically that any tradition that objects to the universal obligation to protect human functioning and its dignity and the dignity of women as being equal to that of men, is unjust. Liberalism must be used to challenge tradition and the social formation of sexual desire to ensure that women think first before they give themselves away to another. Reason thus becomes the antidote for unreflective and habitual action.

A recurring refrain in Nussbaum's argument is that the liberal position is not *per se* flawed, but that there has been a profound inconsistency in what liberalism stands for and how it has operated in relation to women. However, her responses fail to engage with two very significant concerns. The first is the role of power and how it operates at multiple levels and not in a linear manner. Nussbaum fails to pay attention to the subtle operations of power and how liberal feminism cannot begin to bring about political repair through the application of one simple antidote – inclusion. We need to understand the role of power in law and its ability to shape and inform different liberal values and rights. The second shortcoming is her failure to engage with the work of postcolonial feminists, postcolonial theory and subaltern scholarship, which have exposed the limitations of liberalism, in particular, its inability to transcend assumptions about the 'Other' on which legal reasoning and the liberal project are based.

Feminist theory in postcolonial India

Nussbaum's assumption that postmodernism is not relevant among feminists in India, or that feminists have already dismissed it, betrays a naive assumption that feminist theorizing in India operates on the basis of consensus and with one common end in view. In fact the strength of the movement has been the ability of Indian feminists to debate, disagree and keep pushing the boundaries, always recognizing that the 'evil' resides in the dominant structures of power that we seek to challenge, transform or alter. It cannot be assumed that Butler's theories have no relevance in India or the 'Third World', just as it cannot be assumed that feminists in India completely align with the liberal feminism of Nussbaum. Indeed, the postcolonial feminist critiques have exposed liberalism's historical entanglements with the project of Empire and thus challenge its claim to be an exclusively liberating or emancipating project. The history of the colonial encounter illustrates how the rule of law and the liberal premise on which it is based has been used to subjugate and not just to liberate. This double-consciousness enables Indian feminists to develop a devastating critique of liberal internationalism while at the same time, not fear that such a critique will produce pessimism or push us into a theoretical abyss. Dialectics, skepticism and debate have been a part of philosophical thought in the subcontinent, and not something that is feared or directed towards one end or used to sustain one, exclusive normative vision.

In her critique of Butler's work, Nussbaum makes several assumptions about feminist theory in India. She states:

> In India, for example, academic feminists have thrown themselves into practical struggles, and feminist theorizing is closely tethered to practical commitments such as female literacy, the reform of unequal land laws, changes in rape law (which, in India today, has most of the flaws that the first generation of American feminists targeted), the effort to get social recognition for problems of sexual harassment and domestic violence. These feminists know that they live in the middle of a fiercely unjust reality; they cannot live with themselves without addressing it more or less daily, in theoretical writing and in their activities outside the seminar room (Nussbaum 1999: 37–38).

Any feminist in India reading the above statement would be puzzled and surprised at its casual assumptions. It reflects a lack of insight into the kind of feminist theorizing being conducted in India. Many academic feminists in India theorize the material condition. But they do not draw exclusively on one theory, nor for that matter do they unanimously reject and condemn Butlerian feminism.

Feminist academics in India engage in a whole host of other theories precisely because the myopia and liberal feminist pieties advocated by Nussbaum have been largely unsuccessful in the Indian legal domain. Feminist legal scholarship as it is emerging in India has engaged with liberal theories but it has also drawn on new and alternative theories and scholarship, including subaltern studies, postcolonial feminist theory, postmodernism of the Butler variety as well as various philosophical traditions present in the subcontinent. It is drawing on a broad range of disciplines outside of law to produce dynamic ideas about justice and social reform, partly because of the failure of the legal academy to put forth an adequate theory for the empowerment of women in India (Sarkar 1996; Mani 1998). This point belies Nussbaum's critique of Butler for daring to venture beyond the boundaries of her own discipline – that is, philosophy. Indeed, some of the most important theoretical work being done by feminists in India that is informing the development of feminist legal theory emerges from the disciplines of Indian philosophy, sociology and history.

Nussbaum's reference to our 'practical struggles' and achievements in the form of rape laws or sexual harassment laws and literacy, are left uninterrogated and dehistoricized. Feminists in India have become acutely aware of how practical-oriented solutions, aimed at the empowerment of all women, can have a reactionary potential that has revealed itself under the emergence and rule of the Hindu Right, a nationalist political movement aimed at establishing a Hindu State in India (Hansen and Jaffrelot 2004; Cossman and Kapur 2001; Basu et al. 1993; Bhargava 1998). When the BJP led the coalition government from 1999–2004, their proposals included advocating the death penalty for rape, and communalizing the crime by largely targeting Muslim men for the rape of Hindu women. Their support for broad-based guidelines against sexual harassment in the workplace produced a conservative backlash against women's sexual behavior with complainants succeeding only if they demonstrated that the harassment violated principles of decency, morality and modesty. A complainant was more likely to succeed in her grievance if she demonstrated an appropriate lack of familiarity with sex.[2] And their move towards banning images regarded as vulgar and obscene in the name of women's rights to equality served to compromise women's rights to bodily integrity, freedom of speech and expression. The rights to equality, secularism and free speech, rights which all 'real' liberals would support, were successfully deployed by the Hindu Right as part of its strategy for combating violence against women. Such agendas have not proved liberating for women, and are increasingly leading many feminists to turn to theories that assist in developing a more specific and contextual analysis.

By simply listing decontextualized and circumscribed reforms in the name of women's rights as proof of the achievements of Indian feminists, Nussbaum provides a skewed picture. The movements to reform the laws relating to women's rights in India cannot be held out as either a simple success or failure. Nussbaum's analysis does not reveal the complex and contradictory nature of these struggles and their outcomes. For this reason, some feminist theorists in India have turned to discourse theory and postmodernism, enabling a more complex understanding of law and social reform and highlighting the contradictory results they may produce for women.

Nussbaum also makes some unfortunate assumptions about women in India, often stripping them of claims to agency and subjectivity until they have fully embraced the liberal project. It is assumed that only liberal individualism can enable the subject. Indeed there is an unfortunate moment in Nussbaum's article (1999: 42) where, carried away by her animus against Butler, we read:

> Well parodic performance is not so bad when you are a powerful tenured academic in a liberal university. But here is where Butler's focus on the symbolic, her proud neglect of the material side of life, becomes a fatal blindness. For women who are hungry, illiterate, disenfranchised, beaten, raped, it is not sexy or liberating to reenact, however parodically, the condition of hunger, illiteracy, disenfranchisement, beating and rape. Such women prefer food, schools, votes, and integrity of their bodies. I see no reason to believe that they long sadomasochistically for a return to the bad state. If some individuals cannot live without the sexiness of domination, that seems sad, but it is not really our business. But when a major theorist tells women in desperate conditions that life offers them only bondage, she purveys a cruel lie, and a lie that flatters evil by giving it much more power than it actually has.

This sentence betrays an utter lack of imagination regarding women who exist in disadvantaged situations. It assumes that they are defined only in terms of their disadvantage and parody has no role to play in their lives as a liberating tool. I cannot help but think of how Hindi commercial films provide the ultimate parodic space for millions of people in India (and elsewhere), rich and poor, where the subversive song and dance sequences are replayed over and over again in the gullies and mohallahs (alleys and neighborhoods) and mansions, long after the film is over (Bose 2007; Ghosh 2007, 1999).

Nussbaum's assumption about women in disadvantaged situations as victims devoid of choice or agency fails to engage with a vast sea of critical scholarship that has been produced on this issue in the postcolonial context. An important feature of postcolonial theory is its challenge to the unitary liberal subject. The liberal project has been successfully built on the idea that the subject is atomized, decontextualized, ahistorical and reasoning. 'He' is also a universally valid subject.

The postcolonial project affords the possibility of conceptualizing the subject in ways that directly challenges the autonomous, reasoning subject of liberal rights discourse (Nessiah 2003). It focuses on the resistive subject – that is – one who produces resistance in coercive circumstances, a deeply layered and multifaceted subject. It is at this juncture that postcolonial theory joins with subaltern studies (Said 1983: v–x). The subaltern studies project further complicates our understanding of the subject who is excluded by the liberal project and the imperial narratives of history (Guha and Spivak 1988; Sarkar 1985). The subaltern project exposes how certain voices have been excluded from the dominant narratives and telling of history. The project regards hegemonic history as part of modernity's power/knowledge complex, which in the context of colonialism, has been deeply implicated in imperialism's violent encounters with other regimes of power (McClintock 1995:6). In the context of law, the subaltern project also brings a normative challenge to the assumptions about universality, neutrality and objectivity on which legal concepts are based, exposing the cultural specificity of such assumptions.

One stream of the subaltern studies project influenced by the work of Michel Foucault came to focus on contesting the Eurocentric, metropolitan and bureaucratic systems of knowledge (Chakrabarty and Bhabha 2005; Chakrabarty 2000; Chakrabarty 1995). The new tradition was concerned with challenging all traditions and disciplines defined within the logic and rationale of the Enlightenment project. One aspect of this new tradition was to unmask the universal subject of liberal rights discourse. It destabilized the humanist subject and brought into critical consideration a host of other categories, including gender, class, ethnicity, and race. Subaltern studies did not remain pre-occupied with the idea of a peasant rebel as an autonomous political subject who writes her own history as suggested by some scholars (Sen 2005). It shifted away from economic analysis as the primary zone of power that characterized an earlier stream of subaltern studies, and began to unpack the multiple sites and locations of power through a discursive and textual analysis. The scholarship continued to expand and began to address and challenge the neo-imperialism of the late twentieth century and problems of agency, subject position, and hegemony in an era of globalization (Ludden 2002; Chakrabarty and Bhabha 2002; Lal 2002; Mignolo 2000).

The subaltern subject provides a normative challenge to the subject of liberal rights discourse. It is a subject who occupies an ambivalent position, whose resistance or presence can be read in different ways. The subaltern project analyzes the terms by which the formerly colonized subject comes to engage with her past, as well as how she challenges the simple dichotomies of us and them, of the invader and the native. She denaturalizes the liberal subject, revealing its instability and culturally specific location. At a more radical level, this subject brings about a conscious normative challenge, intent on resisting the assimilative gestures of the imperial and liberal project, produc-ing a subject that is quite distinct and unlike the sovereign autonomous subject of liberal rights discourse. Indeed it is this ambivalence which provides a central lens through which subject constitution in law in the postcolonial world can be understood.

Nussbaum is well known as a sensitive and acute observer and someone who tries to live up to the philosopher's ideal of self-awareness. Yet she has apparently not fully escaped from a patronizing First World response to women in the Third World, who are presented by her only as victims, only as women in situations of starvation, poverty and abuse. This reveals a lack of sensitivity to the way in which women live in India and elsewhere, despite their situations of impoverishment and need. In Nussbaum's well meaning stereotype, there can be no 'Bandit Queen', nor understanding of those dress rehearsals in which the wretched of the earth prepare to tackle their oppressors. When sex workers perform the roles of Hindi film heroines among themselves and their friends, this may be a very modest gesture of self-recovery, but nonetheless an impor-tant one. The *hijra* (transsexual) dances and sings publicly in the streets despite the grueling poverty and disadvantage in which most of them live. How would Nussbaum respond to Nepali women keen to participate in the Miss Nepal Beauty pageant 2008 and prevented from doing so by Maoist women intent on 'cleaning up culture' and 'obscenity' in Nepali public space? Or the raid on women activists in Kathmandu who sought to protest the violent and brutal slaying of a woman human rights defender in July 2008, by threatening to strip in public as a way of drawing attention to the case and issues of violence against women? How would she respond to them as ('Third World') performers in a pageant space, or public protestors shattering her neatly sculpted image of the victim-subject? Would they also stand accused of not being sen-sitive to their sisters' material condition? Why is 'material condition' assumed to refer only to women's experience of oppression and impoverishment? Perhaps Nussbaum would characterize the pageant women performers as 'sad' for finding what she describes as 'sexiness in domination' or the women activists as misguided in their strategies and in need of support from their liberal feminist sisters?

Pleasure and performance are not 'evil' *per se* as Nussbaum would have us believe, whether in her reading of Butler or in the lived material reality of women's lives in India or elsewhere on the subcontinent. They are extremely important dimensions to women's lives in postcolonial India. Indeed the very recognition of this aspect of women's reality subverts Nussbaum's projection of such women as existing always and exclusively as poor, unhappy and unfortunate. It is this image that has burdened feminist politics in India and elsewhere as it exposes little understanding of the material and social conditions of women's lives, the very condition that Nussbaum prides herself on comprehending and from which her theory emerges. If her theory is built on the image of the suffering and emaciated 'Third World' woman, no wonder there is a longing for a new politics and theory that would disrupt if not demolish this uninformed (and I might add, unsexy) representation. Such an image exists in the work of those who require a victim on which to build their theories, rather than to provide a theory with which to empower 'the victim'.

Nussbaum is concerned that subversion is insufficient if not accompanied by a normative theory of social justice and human dignity. Without such a theory, all acts of subversion would be regarded as the same – they would all be good. Thus subversiveness through parodic performance to 'proclaim the repressiveness of heterosexual gender norms' would rank equally with subversive performance to evade compliance with tax norms, or treating fellow human beings indecently. However, if power operates from multiple and dispersed locations, then the articulation of a single logic or normative theory would serve only to obscure or mask this reality. Subversion and subversive practices operate to expose the obfuscatory function of metanarratives, and universalizing theories and explanations. Subversion contains within it the seeds of altering the meaning of the world and providing a story that will challenge if not displace dominant narratives. The most obvious evidence of such efforts is in the writing of subaltern history and the continuing work of the Subaltern Studies group in India.

Efforts at articulating an alternative theory of social justice and human dignity are laudable. But the meaning of these theories will ultimately be determined by one's historical and political context. In India, feminists assumed that we had a clear-cut theory of equality for women and disadvantaged groups. However, the meaning of equality has been altered by the Hindu Right, not through force or coercion, but through the use of liberal rights discourse as well as democratic means and processes, in ways that operate against persecuted or discriminated groups. More specifically, they have advocated a model of equality based on formal equal treatment and sameness that has encouraged attacks on special measures that exist in favor of religious minorities, in particular for Muslims. This result does not mean we must evict equality and find an alternative model of social justice. But, it does reveal the ways in which equality is a site of discursive struggle, a place where different visions of the world are fought out, and a site in which we have engaged and must continue to engage.

Neither Butler's idea of subversion nor the postcolonial idea of the resistive subject amount to a surrender or acceptance that it is impossible to alter structures of power and subordination; that the best we can hope for is a space of resistance, which will not lead to institutional change. Subversive politics pushes change by inches rather than by leaps and bounds. When we read against the grain viewing a formula Hindi commercial film, we can derive pleasure conscious of the fact that there are certain normative arrangements in place that will resist such a reading. Yet the act of reading against the grain has the potential for altering the meaning and location of pleasure and destabilizing the surety of normative structures that determine what does or does not constitute pleasure. In concrete terms, when a sex worker identifies with the main protagonist in Muzafar Ali's classic film *Umrao Jaan,* which recounts the life story of an exquisite courtesan of nineteenth century Lucknow, she participates in providing a subaltern reading of the script and hence alters its dominant meaning.[3] She is reading the film in a way that validates and brings to the centre her own marginalized existence.

Alternative intellectual traditions

Given the limits of the liberal internationalism, it is necessary not to reinforce a 'Yes, I know. But … ' politics for fear that we may end up in a nihilistic space or remain stuck in a politics of despair (Brown 2001: 16). At this juncture, there is a critical role to be played by the postcolonial feminist theorist as well as space available to engage with different philosophical articulations about emancipation drawn from the various intellectual traditions of the subcontinent. This role is defined by at least three exercises. Firstly, it is necessary for advocates of the liberal intellectual tradition to turn the gaze back on the tradition, and ask how it has been implicated in creating the mess we are in. What is the role of this project in producing the hatred and animosities today? An honest and urgent critique of this tradition is warranted rather than a self-laceration driven by guilt or a flight from the homeland to more pristine niches on the globe to 'do good' or help the 'wronged ones', including the poor, victimized 'Third World' woman.

A second exercise is to be willing to engage with theories and critiques of the liberal project. Such engagements should not merely be restricted to incorporating suggestions with the goal of simply 'fixing' the project, but to be willing to engage with the dark and dirty side of liberal internationalism, acknowledge its more and many histories, and seriously engage with alternative or excluded ideas about emancipation that cannot be captured by the liberal imaginary (Mahmood 2007).

A third related exercise is both a task and a tool – to seriously look for and learn from alternative traditions. The subcontinent is also home to some extraordinary philosophical and intellectual traditions. Unfortunately, philosophical traditions other than from the West have invariably been regarded as exotic, esoteric or rooted in religion. This view fails to recognize the religious tone of intellectuals in Western traditions, or appreciate the significant distinction made in non-Western traditions between philosophy and religion (Matilal 1986). Some of these traditions are immersed in systems of logic, inference and dialectics that can be traced from well before the Buddha, who was an agnostic,[4] to Amartya Sen, a noble laureate in economics. Sen traces this tradition of dialectics, debate and even skepticism in the *Argumentative Indian* which, he concludes, illustrates that everything is open to question (Sen 2005).

While these traditions are in no way homogenous, I end by briefly postulating at least three distinct aspects they posses. Firstly, the critique of epistemology and metaphysics – the very basis from which knowledge proceeds – is an integral and not renegade feature of some of these traditions.[5] Challenges to epistemological issues in the West have often been castigated as ravings of the post-modern, post-Enlightenment intellectual as demonstrated in Nussbaum's critique of Butlers work. Yet this level of inquiry existed well before the post-modernists became the nuisance.

A second distinction is the notion of the Self as indivisible – one, organic, non-fragmented whole, who ultimately is not exclusively just an intellectual, nor just an activist, nor this or that, but all of these. She pursues an emancipatory vision of all through the knowledge of the self and her relationship with the 'Other', which is integral and potentially liberating, rather than frightening, fearful and exclusive. This idea of non-dualism was expounded by the brilliant philosopher Sankara in the ninth century.[6]

And finally, neither history nor time are unilinear in such traditions. The consolidation of unilinear, progressive teleological and Eurocentric history as the dominant mode of experiencing time and being is the hallmark of liberal internationalism. In this project, others' present are seen as Europe's past while Europe's present is posited as others' future. It is a construction where nations and individuals only attain maturity when they are fully conscious of themselves as subjects of unilinear and progressive history, and it is only such individuals who can realize freedom. Those placed outside of this history have no claims or rights and may rightfully be subjugated even if to bring them into the stream of the Eurocentric history of Europe.

Some philosophical traditions posit time very differently. Firstly, they centre the individual within the framework of reflection, rather than reason or rationality, in order to bring about discernment. Nussbaum argues that rationality or reason provide women the tools with which to cast off tradition, but she does not simultaneously inquire into whether the liberal project has indeed been a liberating project, nor does her work provide any space for pursuing such an inquiry. It is simply regarded as *per se* progressive, as a step forward in the pursuit of female emancipation. Alternative traditions shift away from any notion of progress, of linear movement and a sense of moving forward from a dark, more primitive era that has been the hallmark of liberal thought. Instead, they recognize that there is consistent change, where the relationship with time and space is critical because there is no linearity. Progress does not mean a march forward, but as an exercise of going deeper, here and now.

Each of these aspects can provide another metaphysical basis from which to articulate a project of emancipation and freedom. They offer ways in which to emancipate feminist politics from the constraints of liberal internationalism and its deeply problematic claims. It is a move to pursue goals of social justice, freedom and equality from a different historical and metaphysical trajectory and to help stage the sorely needed intellectual insurrection that the contemporary moment and progressive politics demands.

Notes

1 This is an author revised version of the article that appeared as 'Imperial Parody' in *Feminist Theory*, 2(1), 2001.

2 See the decision of the Supreme Court of India, *Apparel Export Promotion Council* v. *A. K. Chopra* (1999) 1 SCC 759, where the woman succeeded in her sexual harassment claim partly on the grounds that she was single and would not have knowledge about matters of sex and therefore could not have welcomed the conduct.

3 *Umrao Jaan,* played by Rekha, the darling of Indian movie-going audiences, is the story of a woman who performs as a dancer and singer at the 'Kota' of Khanum Jan, the madam, and develops a number of liaisons with the nobles of Lucknow, a major city in northern India. Her exquisite singing and dancing skills as well as her talent in composing Urdu poetry attracts the attention of the Royal Court of Avadh. She develops a relationship with one nobleman, and the story of their affair is set against the backdrop of the 1857 'Indian Mutiny'.

4 Venkata Ramana discusses the ideas of the third century philosopher, Nagarjuna, who contested the notion of an absolute position or truth, and argued in favour of the awareness of the possibility of different formulations of one and the same truth from different standpoints as a way in which to rise above an exclusive clinging to any one formulation as absolute (Venkata Ramana 1966).

5 Dinnaga, c. 400–480. Author of *Pramanasamuccaya, Hetucakradamaru, Nyayamukha*, a major contributor to the development of 'Buddhist Logic', where he put his theory of logic within the broader context of his view on epistemology – the source or means of knowing (*pramana*).

6 See the 'Crest-Jewel of Discrimination' or *Viveka Chudamani*, one of his most famous works, which summarizes his ideas of non-dualism (Pande 1994).

References

Basu, T., Datta, P., Sarkar, S., Sarkar, T, and Sen, S. (1993) *Khaki Shorts, Saffron Flags: A Critique of the Hindu Right*, New Delhi: Orient Longman.

Bhargava, R. (ed.) (1998) *Secularism and its Critics*, New York, London and New Delhi: Oxford University Press.

Bose, Brinda (2007) 'The desiring subject: female pleasures and feminist resistance in Deepa Mehta's Fire', in Brinda Bose (ed.) *The Phobic and the Erotic: The Politics of Sexualities in Contemporary India*, London, New York, Calcutta: Seagull, pp. 437–50.

Brown, W. (2001) *Politics Out of History*, Princeton, NJ: Princeton University Press.

Butler, J. (1997) *Excitable Speech: A Politics of the Performative*, London, New York: Routledge.

Chakrabarty, D. (2000) *Provincializing Europe*, Princeton, NJ: Princeton University Press.

—— (1995) 'Radical histories and question of enlightenment rationalism', *Economic and Political Weekly,* 30(14): 751.

Chakrabarty, D., and Bhabha, H. (2002) *Habitations in Modernity: Essays in the Wake of Subaltern Studies,* Chicago, Illinois: University of Chicago Press.

Chandra Pande, G. (1994) *Life and Thought of Sankaracarya*, Delhi: Motilal Banarsidass.

Cossman, B. and Kapur, R. (2001 rpt). *Secularism's Last Sigh? Hindutva and the [Mis]rule of Law*, New York, London and New Delhi: Oxford University Press.

Ghosh, S. (2007) 'False appearances and mistaken identities: the phobic and the erotic in Bombay cinema's queer vision,' in Brinda Bose (ed.) *The Phobic and the Erotic: The Politics of Sexuality in Contemporary India*, London, New York, Calcutta: Seagull, pp. 417–36.

—— (1999) 'The troubled existence of sex and sexuality: feminists engage with censorship', in Christiane Brosius and Melissa Butcher (eds) *Image Journeys: Audio-Visual Media and Cultural Change in India*, pp. 233–60, Thousand Oaks, CA, London and New Delhi: Sage.

Guha, R. and Spivak, G. S. (1988) *Selected Subaltern Studies*, New York and Oxford: Oxford University Press.

Hansen, T. B. and Jaffrelot, C. (eds) (2004) *Omnibus: Hindu Nationalism and Indian Politics*, New Delhi: Oxford University Press.

Hartsock, N. (1983) *Money, Sex and Power: Towards a Feminist Historical Materialism*, Boston, MA: Northeastern University Press.

Kapur, Ratna and Cossman, Brenda (1996) *Subversive Sites: Feminist Engagements with Law in India*, Thousand Oaks, CA, London and New Delhi: Sage.

Lacey, Nicola (1998) 'Closure and critique in feminist jurisprudence: transcending the dichotomy or a foot in both camps?' in *Unspeakable Subjects: Feminist Essays in Legal and Social Theory,* Oxford: Hart.

Lal, V. (2002) *Empire and Knowledge: Culture and Plurality in the Global Economy*, Sterling, Virginia: Pluto Press.

Ludden, D. (ed.) (2002) *Reading Subaltern Studies: Critical History, Contested Meaning and the Globalization of South Asia*, London: Anthem Press.

Mani, L. (1998) *Contentious Traditions: The Debate on Sati in Colonial India*, New York, London and New Delhi: Oxford University Press.

Matilal, B. K. (1986) *Perception: An Essay on Classical Indian Theories of Knowledge*, Oxford: Clarendon Press.

McClintock, A. (1995) *Imperial Leather: Race, Gender and Sexuality in the Colonial Contest*, New York: Routledge.

Mignolo, W. (2000) *Local Histories/Global Designs*, Princeton, NJ: Princeton University Press.

Mahmood, S. (2007) *The Politics of Piety: The Islamic Revival and the Feminist Subject,* Princeton, NJ: Princeton University Press.

Munro, Vanessa (2007) *Law and Politics at the Perimeter: Re-Evaluating Key Debates in Feminist Theory*, Oxford and Portland, Oregon: Hart.

Nessiah, V. (2003) 'The ground beneath her feet: TWAIL feminisms', in A. Anghie, B. Chimni, and O. Mickelson (eds) *The Third World International Order: Law, Politics and Globalizations*, pp. 133–43, London: Kluwer Law International.

Nussbaum, M. (2004) *Hiding from Humanity: Disgust, Shame, and the Law*, Princeton, NJ: Princeton University Press.

—— (1999a) *Sex and Social Justice*, New York, Oxford: Oxford University Press.

—— (1999b) 'The professor of parody', *The New Republic*, February 22.

Parashar, A. (1992) *Women and Family Law in India: Uniform Civil Code and Gender Equality*, Thousand Oaks, CA, London and New Delhi: Sage.

Sarkar, T. (1996) 'Colonial lawmaking and lives/deaths of Indian women: different readings of law and community', in Ratna Kapur (ed.) *Feminist Terrains in Legal Domains: Interdisciplinary Essays on Women and Law*, Thousand Oaks, CA, London and New Delhi: Sage.

Said, E. (1993) *Culture and Imperialism*, London: Chatto and Windus.

Sen, A. (2005) *The Argumentative Indian: Writings on Indian History, Culture and Identity*, New York: Farrar, Strauss and Giroux.

—— (1999) *Development as Freedom*, New York: Random House.

Venkata Ramana, K. (1966) *Nagarjuna's Philosophy*, Rutland, Vermont: Charles E. Tuttle Company.

19 Righting wrongs[1]

Gayatri Chakravorty Spivak

The primary nominative sense of *rights* cited by the *Oxford English Dictionary* is 'justifiable claim, on legal or moral grounds, to have or obtain something, or to act in a certain way'. There is no parallel usage of *wrongs*, connected to an agent in the possessive case – 'my wrongs' – or given to it as an object of the verb to have – 'she has wrongs'.

Rights entail an individual or collective. *Wrongs*, however, cannot be used as a noun, except insofar as an other, as agent of injustice, is involved. The verb *to wrong* is more common than the noun, and indeed the noun probably gets its enclitic meaning by back-formation from the verb.

The word *rights* in 'Human Rights, Human Wrongs', the title of the 2001 Oxford Amnesty Lectures series in which this chapter was first presented, acquires verbal meaning by its contiguity with the word *wrongs*.[2] The verb *to right* cannot be used intransitively on this level of abstraction. It can only be used with the unusual noun *wrong*: 'to right a wrong', or 'to right wrongs'. Thus 'Human Rights' is not only about having or claiming a right or a set of rights; it is also about righting wrongs, about being the dispenser of these rights. The idea of human rights, in other words, may carry within itself the agenda of a kind of social Darwinism – the fittest must shoulder the burden of righting the wrongs of the unfit – and the possibility of an alibi. Only a 'kind of' Social Darwinism, of course. Just as 'the white man's burden', undertaking to civilize and develop, was only 'a kind of' oppression. It would be silly to footnote the scholarship that has been written to show that the latter may have been an alibi for economic, military, and political intervention. It is on that model that I am using the concept-metaphor of the alibi in these introductory paragraphs.

Having arrived here, the usual thing is to complain about the Eurocentrism of human rights. I have no such intention. I am of course troubled by the use of human rights as an alibi for interventions of various sorts. But its so-called European provenance is for me in the same category as the 'enabling violation' of the production of the colonial subject (Spivak 1999a: 217 n33).[3] One cannot write off the righting of wrongs. The enablement must be used even as the violation is renegotiated.

Colonialism was committed to the education of a certain class. It was interested in the seemingly permanent operation of an altered normality. Paradoxically, human rights and 'development' work today cannot claim this self-empowerment that high colonialism could. Yet, some of the best products of high colonialism, descendants of the colonial middle class, become human rights advocates in the countries of the South. [...]

The end of the Second World War inaugurated the postcolonial dispensation. [...] For the eighteenth century Declaration of the Rights of Man and of the Citizen by the National Assembly of France the 'nation is essentially the source of sovereignty; nor can any individual, or any body of men, be entitled to any authority which is not expressly derived from it' (cited in Paine 1992: 79). A hundred and fifty years later, for better or for worse, the human rights aspect of post-coloniality has turned out to be the breaking of the new nations, in the name of their breaking-in into the international community of nations.[4] This is the narrative of international maneuvering. Thomas Risse, Stephen Ropp, and Kathryn Sikkink's book, *The Power of Human Rights* (1999), takes the narrative further. In addition to the dominant states, they argue, since 1993 it is the transnational agencies, plus nongovernmental organizations (NGOs), that subdue the state.

Nevertheless, it is still disingenuous to call human rights Eurocentric, not only because, in the global South, the domestic human rights workers are, by and large, the descendants of the colonial subject, often culturally positioned against Eurocentrism, but also because, internationally, the role of the new diasporic is strong, and the diasporic in the metropolis stands for 'diversity', 'against Eurocentrism'. Thus the work of righting wrongs is shared above a class line that to some extent and unevenly cuts across race and the North-South divide. I say 'to some extent and unevenly' because, to be located in the Euro-U.S. still makes a difference. In the UN itself, 'the main human rights monitoring function [has been] allocated to the OSCE'. The presuppositions of Risse, Ropp, and Sikkink's book also make this clear. The subtitle – 'International Norms and Domestic Change' – is telling. The authors' idea of the motor of human rights is 'pressure' on the state 'from above' – international – and 'from below' – domestic. (It is useful for this locationist privilege that most NGOs of the global South survive on Northern aid.) [...]

This is pressure 'from below', of course. Behind these 'societal actors' and the state is 'international normative pressure.' I will go on to suggest that, unless 'education' is thought differently from 'consciousness-raising' about 'the human rights norm' and 'rising literacy expand[ing] the individual's media exposure', 'sufficient habitualization or institutionalization' will never arrive, and this will continue to provide justification for international control (Risse, Ropp and Sikkink 1999: 167).

Thinking about education and the diaspora, Edward Said has recently written that 'the American University generally [is] for its academic staff and many of its students the last remaining utopia' (2000: xi). The philosopher Richard Rorty as well as Lee Kuan Yew, the former prime minister of Singapore – who supported 'detention without trial ... [as] Confucianist' – share Professor Said's view of the utopianism of the Euro-U.S. university. I quote Rorty, but I invite you to read Premier Lee's *From Third World to First: The Singapore Story: 1965–2000* to savor their accord: 'Producing generations of nice, tolerant, well-off, secure, other-respecting students of [the American] sort in all parts of the world is just what is needed – indeed all that is needed –to achieve an Enlightenment utopia. The more youngsters like that we can raise, the stronger and more global our human rights culture will become' (Rorty 1993: 127).[5]

If one wishes to make this restricted utopianism, which extends to great universities everywhere, available for global social justice, one must unmoor it from its elite safe harbors, supported by the power of the dominant nation's civil polity, and be interested in a kind of education for the largest sector of the future electorate in the global South – the children of the rural poor – that would go beyond literacy and numeracy and find a home in an expanded definition of a 'Humanities to come'.

Education in the Humanities attempts to be an *uncoercive* rearrangement of desires. If you are not persuaded by this simple description, nothing I say about the

Humanities will move you. This is the burden of the second section of this chapter. This simple but difficult practice is outlined there. It is only when we interest ourselves in this new kind of education for the children of the rural poor in the global South that the inevitability of unremitting pressure as the *primum mobile* of human rights will be questioned.

If one engages in such empowerment at the lowest level, it is in the hope that the need for international/domestic-elite pressure on the state will not remain primary forever. We cannot necessarily expect the old colonial subject transformed into the new domestic middle-class urban radical, defined as 'below' by Risse, Ropp, and Sikkink and by metropolitan human rights in general, to engage in the attempt I will go on to describe. Although physically based in the South, and therefore presumably far from the utopian university, this class is generally also out of touch with the mindset – a combination of episteme and ethical discourse – of the rural poor below the NGO level. To be able to present a project that will draw aid from the North, for example, to understand and state a problem intelligibly and persuasively for the taste of the North, is itself proof of a sort of epistemic discontinuity with the ill-educated rural poor. (And the sort of education we are thinking of is not to make the rural poor capable of drafting NGO grant proposals!) This discontinuity, not skin color or national identity crudely understood, undergirds the question of who always rights and who is perennially wronged.

I have been suggesting, then, that 'human rights culture' runs on unremitting Northern-ideological pressure, even when it is from the South; that there is a real epistemic discontinuity between the Southern human rights advocates and those whom they protect.[6] In order to shift this layered discontinuity, however slightly, we must focus on the quality and end of education, at both ends; the Southern elite is often educated in Western or Western-style institutions. We must work at both ends – both in Said/Rorty's utopia and in the schools of the rural poor in the global South.

I will argue this by way of a historical and theoretical digression.

As long as the claim to natural or inalienable human rights was reactive to the historical alienation in 'Europe' as such – the French ancien régime or the German Third Reich – the problem of relating 'natural' to 'civil' rights was on the agenda. Since its use by the Commission on Decolonization in the 1960s, its thorough politicization in the 1990s, when the nation-states of the South, and perhaps the nation-state form itself, needed to be broken in the face of the restructuring demands of globalization, and its final inclusion of the postcolonial subject in the form of the metropolitan diasporic, that particular problem – of relating 'natural' to 'civil' rights – was quietly forgotten. In other words, that the question of nature must be begged (assumed when it needs to be demonstrated), in order to use it historically, has been forgotten. [...]

I have not the expertise to summarize the long history of the European debate surrounding natural/civil rights. With some hesitation I would point at the separation/ imbrication of nature and liberty in Machiavelli, at the necessary slippage in Hobbes between social contract as natural fiction and social contract as civil reality, at Hobbes's debate on liberty and necessity with Bishop Bramhill. Hobbes himself places his discussions within debates in Roman law and I think we should respect this chain of displacements – rather than a linear intellectual history – that leads to the rupture of the first European Declaration of Human Rights.[7] I am arguing that such speculative lines are not allowed to flourish within today's global human rights activities where a crude notion of cultural difference is about as far as grounds talk will go.

Academic research may contest this trend by tracking rational critique and/or individualism within non-European high cultures. This is valuable work. But the usually silent victims of pervasive rather than singular and spectacular human rights violations are generally the rural poor. These academic efforts do not touch their general cultures, unless it is through broad generalizations, positive and negative. Accessing those long-delegitimized epistemes requires a different engagement. The pedagogic effort that may bring about lasting epistemic change in the oppressed is never accurate, and must be forever renewed. Otherwise there does not seem much point in considering the Humanities worth teaching. And, as I have already signaled, the red thread of a defense of the Humanities as an attempt at uncoercive rearrangement of desires runs through this chapter.

Attempts at such pedagogic change need not necessarily involve confronting the task of undoing the legacy of a specifically *colonial* education. Other political upheavals have also divided the postcolonial or global polity into an effective class apartheid. The redressing work of Human Rights must be supplemented by an education that can continue to make unstable the presupposition that the reasonable righting of wrongs is inevitably the manifest destiny of groups – unevenly class-divided, embracing North and South – that remain poised to right them; and that, among the receiving groups, wrongs will inevitably proliferate with unsurprising regularity. Consequently, the groups that are the dispensers of human rights must realize that, just as the natural Rights of Man were contingent upon the historical French Revolution, and the Universal Declaration upon the historical events that led to the Second World War, so also is the current emergence, of the human rights model as the global dominant, contingent upon the turbulence in the wake of the dissolution of imperial formations and global economic restructuring. The task of making visible the begged question grounding the political manipulation of a civil society forged on globally defined natural rights is just as urgent; and not simply by way of *cultural* relativism.

[...] What we are describing is a simplified version of the aporia between ethics and politics. An aporia is disclosed only in its one-way crossing. This essay attempts to make the reader recognize that human rights is such an interested crossing, a containment of the aporia in binary oppositions.[8]

A few words, then, about supplementing metropolitan education before I elaborate on the pedagogy of the subaltern. By *subaltern* I mean those removed from lines of social mobility.[9]

I will continue to insist that the problem with U.S. education is that it teaches (corporatist) benevolence while trivializing the teaching of the Humanities. The result is, at best, cultural relativism as cultural absolutism ('American-style education will do the trick'). Its undoing is best produced by way of the training of reflexes that kick in at the time of urgency, of decision and policy. However unrealistic it may seem to you, I would not remain a teacher of the Humanities if I did not believe that at the New York end – standing metonymically for the dispensing end as such – the teacher can try to rearrange desires noncoercively – as I mentioned earlier – through an attempt to develop in the student a habit of literary reading, even just 'reading,' suspending oneself into the text of the other – for which the first condition and effect is a suspension of the conviction that I am necessarily better, I am necessarily indispensable, I am necessarily the one to right wrongs, I am necessarily the end product for which history happened, and that New York is necessarily the capital of the world. A training in literary reading is a training to learn from the singular and the unverifiable. Although literature cannot speak, this species of patient reading, miming an effort to make the text respond, as it were, is a training not only in poiesis, accessing the other so well that probable action can be prefigured, but teleo-poiesis, striving for a response from the distant other, without guarantees.

I have no moral position against grading, or writing recommendation letters. But if you are attempting to train in specifically literary reading, the results are not directly ascertainable by the teaching subject, and perhaps not the taught subject either. In my experience, the 'proof 'comes in unexpected ways, from the other side. But the absence of such proof does not necessarily 'mean' nothing has been learned. This is why I say 'no guarantees'. And that is also why the work of an epistemic undoing of cultural relativism as cultural absolutism can only work as a supplement to the more institutional practice, filling a responsibility shaped gap but also adding something discontinuous. As far as human rights goes, this is the only prior and patient training that can leaven the quick-fix training institutes that prepare international civil society workers, including human rights advocates, with uncomplicated standards for success. This is not a suggestion that all human rights workers should have institutional Humanities training. As it stands, Humanities teaching in the United States is what I am describing only in the very rare instance. And the mode is 'to come'.

It is in the interest of supplementing metropolitan Humanities pedagogy, rather than from the perspective of some fantasmatic cultural difference, that we can say that the 'developed postcapitalist structure' of today's world must 'be filled with the more robust imperative to responsibility that capitalist social productivity was obliged to destroy. We must learn to redefine that lost imperative as defective for the emergence of capitalism, rather than necessarily precapitalist on an interested sequential evolutionary model' (Spivak 1999b: 68). In the simplest terms, being defined by the call of the other – which may be a defining feature of such societies – is not conducive to the extraction and appropriation of surplus. Making room for *otium* and living in the rhythm of the eco-biome does not lead to exploration and conquest of nature. And so on. The method of a specifically literary training, a slow mind-changing process, can be used to open the imagination to such mindsets.[10]

One of the reasons international communism failed was because Marx, an organic intellectual of the industrial revolution, could only think the claiming of rights to freedom from exploitation by way of the public use of reason recommended by the European Enlightenment. The ethical part, to want to exercise the freedom to redistribute, after the revolution, comes by way of the sort of education I am speaking of. [...] A desire to redistribute is not the unproblematic consequence of a well-fed society. In order to get that desire moving by the cultural imperative of education, you have to fix the possibility of putting not just *wrong* over against *right*, with all the genealogical lines compressed within it, but also to suggest that another antonym of *right* is *responsibility*, and further, that the possibility of such responsibility is underived from rights. [...]

The responsibility I speak of is not necessarily the one that comes from the consciousness of superiority lodged in the self, [...] but one that is, to begin with, sensed before sense as a call of the other.

Instead, varieties of the Churchillian sense of 'responsibility' – 'The price of greatness is responsibility' – nearly synonymous with duty, have always also been used from within the Rights camp. Machiavelli and Hobbes both wrote on duty. The 1793 version of the Declaration of the Rights of Man already contained a section on the duties of man and of the citizen. The UN issued a Declaration of Responsibilities – little more than a reinscription of the rights as duties for their establishment – in 1997. There is a scientists' Declaration of Duties. And so on. This is the trajectory of the idea of 'responsibility' as assumed, by choice, by the group that can right wrongs. However, even a liberal vision (like that of Amnesty International) is obliged to admit that there is no continuous line from rights to responsibilities. This notion of responsibility as the 'duty of the fitter self' toward less fortunate others (rather than the predication of being-human as being called by the other, before will) is not my meaning, of course. I remain concerned, however, by one of its corollaries in global social movements. The leaders from the domestic 'below' – for the subaltern an 'above' – not realizing the historically established discontinuity between themselves and the subaltern, counsel self-help with great supervisory benevolence. This is important to remember because the subalterns' obvious inability to do so without sustained supervision is seen as proof of the need for continued intervention. It is necessary to be involved in the everyday working (the 'textuality') of global social movements to recognize that the seeming production of 'declarations' from these supervised groups is written to dictation and no strike against class apartheid. 'To claim rights is your duty' is the banal lesson that the above – whether Northern or Southern – then imparts to the below. The organization of international conferences with exceptionalist tokenization to represent collective subaltern will is a last-ditch solution, for both sides, if at all. And, sometimes, […] the unwitting native informant is rather far from the subaltern. […]

It can seem at first glance that if the Euro-U.S. mindset modifies itself by way of what used to be called, just yesterday, Third Way politics, providing a cover for social democracy's rightward swing, perhaps the dispensers of human rights would at least modify their arrogance. As George W. Bush claims Tony Blair as his chum on Bush's visit to Britain in July 2001, I believe it is still worth examining this impulse, however briefly, so that it is not offered as a panacea. Let us look at a few crucial suggestions from *Beyond Left and Right* by Anthony Giddens, the academic spokesperson of the Third Way (1994: 165, 247, 184, 185, 190, 194).[11]

Giddens mentions the virtues of Third World poverty and therefore may seem at first glance to be recommending learning from the subaltern. Criticizing the welfare state, he quotes Charles Murray with approval: 'Murray, whose work has been influenced by experiences in rural Thailand, asks the question, what's wrong with being poor (once people are above the level of subsistence poverty)? Why should there be such a general concern to combat poverty?' I hope it is clear that I have no interest in keeping the subaltern poor. To repeat, it is in view of Marx's hope to transform the subaltern – whom he understood only as the worker in his conjuncture – into an agent of the undoing of class apartheid rather than its victim that this effort at educating the educator is undertaken.

[…] How is Professor Giddens going to persuade global finance and world trade to jettison the culture of economic growth? This question is particularly pertinent in 2009. He is, of course, speaking of state policy in Europe, but his book tries to go beyond into other spaces: 'The question remains whether a lifestyle pact as suggested here for the wealthy countries could also work when applied to the divisions between North and South. Empirically, one certainly could not answer this question positively with any degree of assurance. Analytically speaking, however, one could ask, what other possibility is there?'[12]

However utopian it might seem, it now appears to me that the only way to make these sweeping changes – there is nothing inherently wrong with them, and, of course,

I give Professor Giddens the benefit of the doubt – is for those who teach in the Humanities to take seriously the necessary but impossible task to construct a collectivity among the dispensers of bounty as well as the victims of oppression. Learning from the subaltern is, paradoxically, through teaching. In practical terms, working across the class-culture difference, trying to learn from children, and from the behavior of class 'inferiors', the teacher learns to recognize, not just a benevolently coerced assent, but also an unexpected response. For such an education speed, quantity of information, and number of students reached are not exclusive virtues. Those 'virtues' are inefficient for education in the responsibilities in the Humanities, not so much a sense of being responsible *for*, but of being responsible *to*, before will. Institutionally, the Humanities, like all disciplines, must be subject to a calculus. It is how we earn our living. But where 'living' has a larger meaning, the Humanities are without guarantees.

Speaking with reference to the Rights of Man and the Universal Declaration, I am insisting that in the European context, it used to be recognized that the question of nature as the ground of rights must be begged in order to use it historically. The assumption that it is natural to be angled toward the other, before will, the question of responsibility in subordinate cultures, is also a begged question. Neither can survive without the other, if it is a just world that we seem to be obliged to want. Indeed, any interest in human rights for others, in human rights and human wrongs, would do better if grounded in this second begged question, to redress historical balance, as it were, than in the apparent forgetting of the other one. In the beginning are two begged questions. [...]

In the 'real world', there is, in general, a tremendously uneven contradiction between those who beg the question of nature as rights for the self and those who beg the question of responsibility as being called by the other, before will.

If we mean to place the latter – perennial victims – on the way to the social productivity of capital, we need to acknowledge the need for supplementation there as well, rather than transform them willy-nilly, consolidating already existing hierarchies, exporting gender struggle, by way of the greed for economic growth. (I have argued earlier in this chapter that these cultures started stagnating because their cultural axiomatics were defective for capitalism. I have also argued that the socialist project can receive its ethical push not from within itself but by supplementation from such axiomatics. I have argued that in their current decrepitude the subaltern cultures need to be known in such a way that we can suture their reactivated cultural axiomatics into the principles of the Enlightenment. I have argued that socialism belongs to those axiomatics. That socialism turns capital formation into redistribution is a truism.[13] It is by this logic that supplementation into the Enlightenment is as much the possibility of being the agent of the social productivity of capital as it is of the subjectship of human rights).

The general culture of Euro-U.S. capitalism in globalization and economic restructuring has conspicuously destroyed the possibility of capital being redistributive and socially productive in a broad-based way. As I have mentioned here, 'the burden of the fittest' – a reterritorializing of 'the white man's burden' – does also touch the economic sphere. [...]

Meanwhile, the seriousness of training into the general culture is reflected by the fact that Morgan Stanley Dean Witter, Merrill Lynch, and other big investment companies are accessing preschoolers; children are training parents to manage portfolios. There is a growing library of books making it 'fun' for kids to invest and giving them detailed instructions how to do so. The unquestioned assumption that to be rich is to be happy and good is developed by way of many 'educational' excuses. [...]

Such a training of children builds itself on the loss of the cultural habit of assuming the agency of responsibility in radical alterity. It is followed through by the relentless education into business culture in academic and on-the-job training, in management, consumer behavior, marketing, prepared for by the thousands and thousands of business schools all over the global South as well as the North, training undergraduates into business culture, making the supplementation of the responsibility-based subaltern layer by the ethics of class-culture difference altogether impossible, consolidating class apartheid. The Declaration of the Right to Development is part of such acculturation into the movements of finance capital. Third Way talk floats on this base. Culturalist support is provided on the Internet – in book digests on 'market Taoism' and 'Aristotle for capitalism'.[14] It is provided in the sales presentations of countless telecommunication marketing conferences. It connects to the laughing and frequent exhortations to 'follow the money' at women's rights meetings at the UN. We should keep all this in mind when we give Professor Giddens the benefit of the doubt. [...]

Such a training of children is also a legitimation by reversal of our own insistence on elementary pedagogy of the rural poor. Supplementation by the sort of education I am trying to describe becomes necessary here, so that the relationship between child investors and child laborers is not simply one of righting wrongs from above. How does such supplementation work? If in New York, the subterranean task is to supplement the radical responsibility-shaped hole in the education of the dispenser of rights through literary reading, and making use of the Humanities, what about the education of those whose wrongs are righted?

Some assumptions must first be laid aside. The permeability of global culture must be seen as restricted. There is a lack of communication between and among the immense heterogeneity of the subaltern cultures of the world. Cultural borders are easily crossed from the superficial cultural relativism of metropolitan countries, whereas, going the other way, the so-called peripheral countries encounter bureaucratic and policed frontiers. The frontiers of subaltern cultures, which developed no generative public role, have no channels of interpenetration. Here, too, the problem is not solved in a lasting way by the inclusion of exceptional subalterns in South-based global movements with leadership drawn from the descendants of colonial subjects, even as these networks network. These figures are no longer representative of the subaltern stratum in general. [...]

We must question the assumption that, if the sense of doing for the other is not produced on call from a sense of the self as sovereign, packaged with the sense of being fittest, the alternative assumption, romantic or expedient, of an essence of subalternity as the source of such a sense, denies the depradations of history. [...] We must be on guard against subalternist essentialism, both positive and negative. If the self-permission for continuing to right wrongs is premised implicitly on the former – they will never be able to help themselves – the latter nourishes false hopes that will as surely be dashed and lead to the same result: an unwilling conclusion that they must always be propped up. Indeed, in the present state of the world, or perhaps always and everywhere, simply harnessing responsibility for accountability in the South, checking up on other directedness, as it were, without the persistent training, of 'no guarantees', we reproduce and consolidate what can only be called 'feudalism', where a benevolent despot like Lee Kuan Yew can claim collectivity rather than individualism when expedient. [...]

Declarations like the Bangkok NGO Declaration, entitled 'Our Voice', and cataloging what 'their right to self-determination' would be for 'Indigenous People in general',[15] may, like many UN Declarations, be an excellent tool for political maneuvering, but it will not touch the entire spectrum of Asian aboriginals, each group as culturally absolutist as the rural audience at the biodiversity festival. In order to make the political maneuverings open to the ethical, we must think the supplementation toward which we are now moving. [...]

Subordinate cultures of responsibility – a heuristic generalization as precarious as generalizations about the dominant culture – base the agency of responsibility in that outside of the self that is also in the self, half-archived and therefore not directly accessible. I use the word *subordinate* here because, as I have been arguing throughout this chapter, they are the recipients of human rights bounty, which I see as 'the burden of the fittest', and which, as I insist from the first page on down, has the *ambivalent* structure of enabling violation that anyone of goodwill associates with the white man's burden. I will rely on this argument for this second part of my chapter, which concerns itself with the different way in to the damaged episteme.

[...] I am asking readers to shift their perception from the anthropological to the historico-political and see the same knit textile as a torn cultural fabric in terms of its removal from the dominant loom in a historical moment. That is what it means to be a subaltern. My point so far has been that, for a long time now, these cultural scripts have not been allowed to work except as a delegitimized form forcibly out of touch with the dominant through a history that has taken capital and empire as telos. My generalization is therefore precarious, though demonstrable if the effort I go on to describe is shared. These concept-metaphors, of suturing a torn fabric, of recoding a delegitimized cultural formation, are crucial to the entire second half of my argument.

Subordinate cultures of responsibility, then, base the agency of responsibility in that outside of the self that is also in the self, half-archived and therefore not directly accessible. Such a sentence may seem opaque to (Christianized) secularists who imagine ethics as internalized imperatives; they may seem silly to the ordinary language tradition that must resolutely ignore the parts of the mind not accessible to reason in order to theorize. It may be useful to think of the archived exteriority, in terms of your unmediated knowledge, of the inside of your body. The general premise of the Oxford Amnesty series the *Genetic Revolution and Human Rights*, for example, was that genes are digitalized words that are driving our bodies, our selves (Burley 1999). Yet they are inaccessible to us as objects and instruments of knowledge, insofar as we are sentient beings. Think also of our creative invention in the languages that we know well. The languages have histories before us, and futures after us. They are outside us, in grammar books and dictionaries. Yet the languages that we know and make in are also us, and in us. These are analogies for agency that is out of us but in us – and, like all analogies, imperfect, but I hope they will suffice for now. In responsibility-based subordinate cultures the volatile space of responsibility can be grasped through these analogies, perhaps.

These [...] analogies [...] work in the following way: if we can grasp that all human beings are genetically written before will; and if we can grasp that all human children access a language that is 'outside', as mother-tongue; then, on these structural models, we might grasp the assumption that the human being is human in answer to an 'outside call'. We can grasp the structure of the role of alterity at work in subordinate cultures, by way of these analogies. The word *before* in 'before the will' is here used to mean logical and chronological priority as well as 'in front of'. The difference is historical, not essential. It is because I believe that right/responsibility can be shared by everyone in the persistent mode of 'to come' that I keep insisting on supplemental pedagogy, on both sides.

In its structure, the definitive predication of being-human by alterity is not with reference to an empirical outside world. Just as I cannot play with my own genes or access the entire linguisticity of my mother tongue, so 'is' the presumed alterity radical in the general sense. Of course it bleeds into the narrow sense of 'accountability to the outside world', but its anchor is in that imagined alterity that is inaccessible, often transcendentalized and formalized (as indeed is natural freedom in the rights camp).

I need not be more specific here. The subordinate subaltern is as diversified as the recipients of Human Rights activity. I need not make too many distinctions. For they are tied by a Universal Declaration. [...]

I am suggesting that human rights activism should be supplemented by an education that should suture the habits of democracy onto the earlier cultural formation. [...] I think that the real effort should be to access and activate the tribals' indigenous 'democratic' structures to *parliamentary* democracy by patient and sustained efforts to learn to learn from below. *Activate* is the key word here. There is no tight cultural fabric (as opposed to group solidarity) among these disenfranchised groups after centuries of oppression and neglect. Anthropological excavation for description is not the goal here. (I remain suspicious of academic golden-agism from the colonial subject.) I am not able to give scholarly information. Working hands-on with teachers and students over long periods of time on their own terms without thinking of producing information for my academic peers is like learning a language 'to be able to produce in it freely ... [and therefore] to move in it without remembering back to the language rooted and planted in [me, indeed] forgetting it' (Marx 1973: 147; translation modified). [...]

Even if the immense labor of follow-up investigation on a case-by-case basis is streamlined in our era of telecommunication, it will not change the epistemic structure of the dysfunctional responsibility-based community, upon whom rights have been thrust from above. It will neither alleviate the reign of terror nor undo the pattern of dependency. The recipient of human rights bounty [...], an agent of counterterrorism and litigious blackmail at the grassroots, will continue not to resemble the ego ideal implied by the Enlightenment and the UDHR. As long as real equalization through recovering and training the long-ignored ethical imagination of the rural poor and indeed, all species of subproletarians on their own terms – is not part of the agenda to come, she or he has no chance of becoming the subject of human rights as part of a collectivity, but must remain, forever, its object of benevolence. We will forever hear in the news, local to global, how these people cannot manage when they are left to manage on their own, and the new imperialism, with an at best embarrassed social Darwinist base, will get its permanent sanction.

The seventh article of the Declaration of the Rights of Man and of the Citizen, following eighteenth century European radical thought, says that 'the law is an expression of the will of the community' (Paine 1992: 79). Among the rural poor of the global South, one may attempt, through that species of education without guarantees, to bring about a situation where the law can be imagined as the expression of a community, always to come. Otherwise the spirit of human rights law is completely out of their unmediated reach. The training in 'literary reading' in the metropolis is here practiced, if you like, in order to produce a situation, in the mode of 'to come', where it can be acknowledged that 'reciprocally recognized rating [to acknowledge a corresponding integrity in the other] is a condition without which no civil undertaking is possible' (Sacksteder 1988: 103).

The supplementary method that I will go on to outline does not suggest that human rights interventions should stop. It does not even offer the impractical suggestion that the human rights activists themselves should take time to learn this method. Given the number of wrongs all the world over, those who right them must be impatient. I am making the practical suggestion for certain kinds of humanities teachers, here and there, diasporics wishing to undo the delinking with the global South represented by impatient benevolence, second-generation colonial subjects dissatisfied by the divided postcolonial polity. Only, whoever it is must have the patience and perseverance to learn well one of the languages of the rural poor of the South. This, I hope, will set them apart from the implicit connection between world governance and the self-styled international civil society.

One of the languages. For the purposes of the essential and possible work of righting wrongs – the political calculus – the great European languages are sufficient. But for access to the subaltern episteme to devise a suturing pedagogy, you must take into account the multiplicity of subaltern languages.

This is because the task of the educator is to learn to learn from below, the lines of conflict resolution undoubtedly available, however dormant, within the disenfranchised cultural system; giving up convictions of triumphalist superiority. It is because of the linguistic restriction that one is obliged to speak of just the groups one works for; but, in the hope that these words will be read by some who are interested in comparable work elsewhere, I am always pushing for generalization. The trainer of teachers will find the system dysfunctional and corrupted, mired in ritual, like a clear pond choked with scum. For their cultural axiomatics as well as their already subordinated position did not translate into the emergence of nascent capitalism. We are now teaching our children in the North, and no doubt in the North of the South, that to learn the movement of finance capital is to learn social responsibility. It is in the remote origins of this conviction – that capitalism is responsibility – that we might locate the beginning of the failure of the aboriginal groups of the kind I am describing: their entry into (a distancing from) modernity as a gradual slipping into atrophy.[16]

This history breeds the need for activating an ethical imperative atrophied by gradual distancing from the narrative of progress – colonialism/capitalism. This is the argument about cultural suturing, learning from below to supplement with the possibility of the subjectship of rights.[17]

Now I go back to my broader argument – a new pedagogy. The national education systems are pretty hopeless at this level because they are the detritus of the postcolonial state, the colonial system turned to rote, unproductive of felicitous colonial subjects like ourselves, at home or abroad. This is part of what started the rotting of the cultural fabric of which I speak. Therefore, I am not just asking that they should have 'the kind of education we have had'. The need for supplementing metropolitan education – 'the kind of education we have had' – is something I am involved in every day in my salaried work. And when I say 'rote', I am not speaking of the fact that a student might swot as a quick way to do well in an exam. I am speaking of the scandal that, in the global South, in the schools for middle-class children and above, the felicitous primary use of a page of language is to understand it; but in the schools for the poor, it is to spell and memorize. [...]

The teachers on this ground level at which we work tend to be the least successful products of a bad system. Our educator must learn to train teachers by attending to the children. It is through learning how to take children's response to teaching as our teaching text that we can hope to put ourselves in the way of 'activating' democratic structures. [...]

The effort at education that I am describing [...] hopes against hope that a permanent sanction of the social Darwinism – 'the burden of the fittest' – implicit in the Human Rights agenda will, perhaps, be halted if the threads of the torn cultural fabric are teased out by the uncanny patience of which the Humanities are capable at their best, for the 'activation' of dormant structures.

Indeed, this is the 'Humanities component,' attending upon the object of investigation as other, in all labor. Here is the definitive moment of a Humanities 'to come', in the service of a Human Rights, that persistently undoes the asymmetry in our title 'Human Rights, Human Wrongs' by the uncoercive rearrangement of desires in terms of the teaching text described earlier in this chapter. [...]

To suture thus the torn and weak responsibility-based system into a conception of human dignity as the enjoyment of rights one enters ritual practice transgressively, alas, as a hacker enters software. The description of ritual-hacking may seem silly, perhaps. But put yourself on the long road where you *can* try it, and you will respect us – you will not dismiss as 'nothing but' this or that approach on paper. Insofar as this hacking is like a weaving, this, too, is an exercise in *texere*, textil-ity, text-ing, textuality. I must continue to repeat that my emphasis is on the difficulties of this texting, the practical pedagogy of it, not in devising the most foolproof theory of it for you, my peers. Without the iterative text of doing and devising in silence, the description seems either murky or banal.

Subordinate cultural systems are creative in the invention of ritual in order to keep a certain hierarchical order functioning. With the help of the children and the community, the trainer must imagine the task of recoding the ritual-to-order habits of the earlier system with the ritual-to-order habits of parliamentary democracy, with a teaching corps whose idea of education is unfortunately produced by a terrible system. One learns active ritual as one learns manners. The best example for the readership of this anthology might be the 'wild anthropology' of the adult metropolitan migrant, learning a dominant culture on the run, giving as little away as possible. The difference here is that we learn from the vulnerable archaic (Raymond Williams's word captures the predicament better than the anthropological *primitive*), but also without giving much away. The point is to realize that democracy also has its rituals, exaggerated or made visible, for example, when in our metropolitan life we seek to make politically correct manners 'natural', a matter of reflex.

[...] I will not be able to produce anthropologically satisfying general descriptions here because no trainer can provide satisfactory descriptions of the grammar of a language that s/he is learning painfully. This *is* the distinction I want to convey. [...] What follows must remain hortatory – an appeal to your imagination until we meet in the field of specific practice, here or there. Of course we all know, with appropriate cynicism, that this probably will not be. But a ceremonial lecture allows you to tilt at windmills, to insist that such practice is the only way that one can hope to supplement the work of human rights litigation in order to produce cultural entry into modernity.

Fine, you will say, maybe Human Rights interventions do not have the time to engage in this kind of patient education, but there are state-sponsored systems, NGOs, and activists engaging in educational initiatives, surely? The NGO drives count school buildings and teacher bodies. The national attempts also do so, but only at best.

Activists, who care about education in the abstract and are critical of the system, talk rights, talk resistance, even talk nationalism. But instilling habits in very young minds is like writing on soft cement. Repeating slogans, even good slogans, is not the way to go, alas. It breeds fascists just as easily. UNESCO's teaching guides for Human Rights are not helpful as guides.

Some activists attempt to instill pride, in these long-disenfranchised groups, in a pseudohistorical narrative. This type of 'civilizationism' is good for gesture politics and breeding leaders, but does little for the development of democratic reflexes.[18] These pseudohistories are assimilated into the aetiological mythologies of the Aboriginals without epistemic change. Given subaltern ethnic divisions, our teaching also proceeds in the conviction that, if identitarianism is generally bad news here, it is also generally bad news there. [...]

My project seems to have defined itself as the most ground-level task for the breaking of the production and continuation of class apartheid. I now understand why, in Marx's world, Marx had come down to something as simple as the shortening of the working day as 'the grounding condition [*die Grundbedingung*]' when he was speaking of such grand topics as the Realm of Freedom and the Realm of Necessity (Marx, *Capital* 3: 959; translation modified). [...]

I am often reprimanded for writing incomprehensibly. There is no one to complain about the jargon-ridden incomprehensibility of children's textbooks in this subaltern world. If I want you to understand the complete opacity of that absurd history lesson about 'National Liberation Struggles in Many Countries,' devised by some state functionary at the Ministry of Education, for example, I would have to take most of you through an intensive Bengali lesson so that you are able to assess different levels of the language. Without venturing up to that perilous necessity, I will simply recapitulate: first, the culture of responsibility is corrupted. The effort is to learn it with patience from below and to keep trying to suture it to the imagined felicitous subject of universal human rights. Second, the education system is a corrupt ruin of the colonial model. The effort is persistently to undo it, to teach the habit of democratic civility. Third, to teach these habits, with responsibility to the corrupted culture, is different from children's indoctrination into nationalism, resistance-talk, identitarianism.

I leave this chapter with the sense that the material about the rural teaching is not in the acceptable mode of information retrieval. The difficulty is in the discontinuous divide between those who right wrongs and those who are wronged. [...]

I am so irreligious that atheism seems a religion to me. But I now understand why fundamentalists of all kinds have succeeded best in the teaching of the poor – for the greater glory of God. One needs some sort of 'licensed lunacy' (Orlando Patterson's phrase) from some transcendental Other to develop the sort of ruthless commitment that can undermine the sense that one is better than those who are being helped, that the ability to manage a complicated life support system is the same as being civilized. But I am influenced by deconstruction and for me, radical alterity cannot be named 'God', in any language. Indeed, the name of 'man' in 'human' rights (or the name of 'woman' in 'women's rights are human rights') will continue to trouble me.

'Licensed lunacy in the name of the unnamable other', then. It took me this long to explain this incomprehensible phrase. Yet the efforts I have described may be the only recourse for a future to come when the reasonable righting of wrongs will not inevitably be the manifest destiny of groups that remain poised to right them; when wrongs will not proliferate with unsurprising regularity.

Notes

1 This article is a severely reduced version of the original, as included in 'Righting wrongs', *South Atlantic Quarterly* 103(2/3), (2004). The editors have placed a [...] at every point where text has been cut. This chapter was originally presented in the Oxford Amnesty Lectures series 'Human Rights, Human Wrongs', Spring 2001.

2 George Shelton incidentally provides a gloss on the native English-speaker's take on the word *wrong* (1992: 128–29). See also Raphael (1988: 164–65). Alex Callinicos (1999) gives other examples of social Darwinism.

3 This is a much-revised version of earlier work. The initial thinking and writing of the piece took place in 1982–83. In other words, I have been thinking of the access to the European Enlightenment through colonization as an enablement for 20 odd years. I am so often stereotyped as a rejecter of the Enlightenment that I feel obliged to make this clear at the outset. [...]

4 The identity of the nation and the state is generally associated with the Peace of Westphalia (1648), often thought of as one of the inaugurations of the Enlightenment. See, for example, Churchill (1988: 17).

5 See also, Lee (2000); the sentiment about detention is to be found on p. 488. Meanwhile, general pieces like Eide (1998), share neither Rorty's wit nor the realism of the rest.

6 Anthony de Reuck comments on the discontinuity between subaltern and elite (using a 'periphery/center' vocabulary) as 'styles of perceptual incoherence ... on the threshold of a cultural anthropology of philosophical controversy' and veers away from it: 'That, as they say, is another story!' (1988: 59–63). My essay lays out the practical politics of that other story, if you like. [...]

7 In his reading of Rousseau in *Of Grammatology* Derrida has indicated Rousseau's place on this chain (1976: 95–316). Locke's view of natural rights is another well-known concatenation on this chain (see Locke 1990 for how Locke taught the issue; for a scholarly account, see Simmons 1992). [...]

8 I use *aporia* to name a situation where there are two right ways that cancel each other and that we, by being agents, have already marked in one way, with a decision that makes us rather than we it. There are other, more philosophically complex ways of formalizing aporia.

9 For a more extensive definition, see Spivak (1999: 269–74).

10 As I will mention later in connection with Anthony Giddens's *Beyond Left and Right* (1994), I am not extolling the virtues of poverty, not even the Christian virtues of poverty, as does Sahlins by association (Sahlins 1972: 32–33). I am only interested in bringing those virtues above, and concurrently instilling the principles of a public sphere below; teaching at both ends of the spectrum. For, from the point of view of the asymmetry of what I am calling class apartheid in the global South, a responsibility-based disenfranchised stagnating culture left to itself can only be described, in its current status within the modern nation-state, as 'a reversal of "possessive individualism",' 'the tragedy "of negative individuality" or individualism' (Balibar n.d.).

11 'Third Way' was, I believe, coined in a Fabian Society pamphlet (Blair 1998) confined to policies of a European Britain. I am grateful to Susan M. Brook for getting me this pamphlet. It was used by Bill Clinton in a round-table discussion sponsored by the Democratic Leadership Council in Washington, D.C., on 25 April 1999.

12 I have discussed the role of teaching in the formation of collectivities (Spivak 2000). Necessary but impossible tasks – like taking care of health although it is impossible to be immortal; or continuing to listen, read, write, talk, and teach although it is impossible that everything be communicated – lead to renewed and persistent effort. I use this formula because this is the only justification for Humanities pedagogy. This is distinct from the 'utopian mode', which allows us to figure the impossible.

13 Marx, *Capital* (3: 1015–16) puts it in a paragraph, in the mode of 'to come'.

14 Clark (n.d.) and Morris (1997). Examples can be multiplied.

15 'Our Voice', Bangkok NGO Declaration, available online at www.nativenet.uthsca.edu/archive/nl/9307.

16 For an uncritical summary of this cultural formation as universal history, see Reagan (1979).

17 We should not forget that Kant fixed the subject of the Enlightenment as one who could write for posterity and the whole world *as a scholar* (1996: 60–61). As the reader will see, our effort is to suture a cultural inscription rather unlike Kant's into the thinking and practice of

the public sphere and an education that will not preserve class apartheid. An unintended posterity, a world not imagined by him as participant in the cosmopolitical.
18 I am grateful to Henry Staten for the felicitous word *Civilizationism*.

References

Blair, Tony (1998) *New Politics for the New Century*, London: College Hill Press.

Burley, Justine (ed.) (1999) *The Genetic Revolution and Human Rights*, Oxford: Oxford University Press.

Callinicos, Alex (1999) *Social Theory: A Historical Introduction*, Oxford: Blackwell.

Churchill, R. Paul (1988) 'Hobbes and the assumption of power', in Peter Caws (ed.) *The Causes of Quarrel: Essays on Peace, War, and Thomas Hobbes*, Boston: Beacon Press.

Clark, John P. (n.d.) *Going with the Cash Flow: Taoism and the New Managerial Wisdom*; available online at www.britannica.com (accessed May 2000).

de Reuck, Anthony (1988) 'Culture in conflict', in Peter Caws (ed.) *The Causes of Quarrel: Essays on Peace, War, and Thomas Hobbes*, Boston: Beacon Press.

Derrida, Jacques (1976) *Of Grammatology*, trans. Gayatri Chakravorty Spivak, Baltimore: The Johns Hopkins University Press.

Eide, Asbjørn (1998) 'Historical significance of the universal declaration', *International Social Science Journal*, December, 50(4): 475–96.

Giddens, Anthony (1994) *Beyond Left and Right: The Future of Radical Politics*, Stanford: Stanford University Press.

Kant, Immanuel (1996) 'An answer to the question: what is enlightenment?' in James Schmidt (ed.) *What Is Enlightenment? Eighteenth-Century Answers and Twentieth-Century Questions*, Berkeley: University of California Press, pp. 60–61.

Lee, Kuan Yew (2000) *From Third World to First: The Singapore Story, 1965–2000*, New York: Harper.

Marx, Karl (1973) 'The eighteenth brumaire of Louis Bonaparte', in *Surveys From Exile*, trans. David Fernbach, New York: Vintage.

Morris, Thomas V. (1997) *If Aristotle Ran General Motors: The New Soul of Business*, New York: Henry Holt.

Paine, Thomas (1992) *Rights of Man*, Indianapolis: Hackett.

Raphael, D. D. (1988) 'Hobbes on justice', in G. A. J. Rodgers and Alan Ryan (eds) *Perspectives on Thomas Hobbes*, Oxford: Clarendon.

Reagan, Ronald (1979) 'Free enterprise', *Radio Essay*, www.newyorktimes.com.

Risse, Thomas; Ropp, Stephen C. and Sikkink, Kathryn (eds) (1999) *The Power of Human Rights: International Norms and Domestic Change*, New York: Cambridge University Press.

Rorty, Richard (1993) 'Human rights, rationality, and sentimentality', in Stephen Shute and Susan Hurley (eds) *On Human Rights*, New York: Basic Books.

Sacksteder, William (1988) 'Mutually acceptable glory', in Peter Caws (ed.) *The Causes of Quarrel: Essays on Peace, War, and Thomas Hobbes*, Boston: Beacon Press.

Sahlins, Marshall (1972) *Stone Age Economics*, New York: de Gruyter.

Said, Edward W. (2000) *Reflections on Exile and Other Essays*, Cambridge: Harvard University Press.

Shelton, George (1992) *Morality and Sovereignty in the Philosophy of Hobbes*, New York: St. Martin's.

Simmons, A. John (1992) *The Lockean Theory of Rights*, Princeton: Princeton University Press.

Spivak, Gayatri Chakravorty (1999a) *A Critique of Postcolonial Reason: Toward a History of the Vanishing Present*, Cambridge: Harvard University Press.

—— (1999b) *Imperatives to Reimagine the Planet*, Vienna: Passagen.

—— (2000) 'Schmitt and post stucturalism: a response', *Cardozo Law Review*, May, 21(5–6): 1723–37.

Part VIII
Conclusion

20 The poverty of Western political theory

Concluding remarks on concepts like 'community' East and West[1]

Partha Chatterjee

Community in the West

I must confess that when the debate raged in Anglo-American academic circles some 15 years ago between liberal individualists and communitarians, I found little in it to sustain my interest. It seemed to me an utterly provincial debate, repetitious and largely predictable in its arguments, playing out all over again a set of confrontations that students of Western political philosophy in the rest of the world had become familiar with for at least a hundred years. Today, I think I was perhaps a little too impatient. Had I not been so dismissive of the significance of the debate for the future advance of political theory, I might have noticed then, as I do now, that in rehearsing once more the fundamental antinomies of political theory in the West, the debate was in fact pointing to some of the ways in which practices of modern politics in non-Western countries might be theorized and perhaps even institutionalized.

I will not spend any time here going over the various arguments and counter-arguments of this debate on which much has been written (Sandel 1984; Avineri and de-Shalit 1992). Let me come straight to the point that is most relevant for my discussion. The communitarian attack on liberal individualism had two prongs – one, methodological, and the other, normative. From the methodological angle, the communitarians argued that the image of the individual self as constructed by liberal theorists was false. Individuals were not, as liberals would have it, sovereign subjects, unencumbered by involuntary obligations, freely choosing between available options on the basis of their individual preferences. On the contrary, those preferences were shaped by a network of social attachments into which people were born; not all attachments were freely chosen. The very constitution of the individual self became a false abstraction if it was removed from the actual social circumstances that provided the cultural and moral resources with which individual wills were formed. Arguing from the normative angle, communitarians charged that by constructing the individual self as one unencumbered by any prior social attachments, the liberal theorist had emptied the idea of political obligation of all genuine moral content. If one's ties with the community in which one was born had no intrinsic moral value, how would the liberal individualist explain why people were so often prepared to make sacrifices for their family or kin or ethnic group or country? More generally, communitarians argued, individuals needed the community to give moral meaning to their lives; even personal autonomy was more satisfactorily achieved within the community than outside it. Above all, communitarians were unprepared to accept the liberal premise that the protection of individual freedom required that considerations of right must have priority over questions of the common good. The latter, they insisted, were at the very heart of modern participatory politics and liberal attempts to constrain and devalue them as something potentially divisive and dangerous had only laid the ground for widespread apathy among citizens and manipulative politics by powerful organized interests in most liberal democracies in the West.

The reply of the liberal individualists to the methodological criticism of the communitarians was that the latter's image of the self as one shaped by the experience of life in a community could well be true, but this was only a particular theoretical position designed to make a particular case about the common good. There were several other contending positions on the common good and so deep were the divisions between them that there could not be any general consensus in society on these questions. The liberal argument was that the only situation in which all these contending views could get an equal and fair chance to represent themselves was one in which the procedures were neutral between individuals. This was the basis for the methodological claims of liberal individualism.

On the moral plane too, the liberal individualists did not altogether reject the importance of community for individual lives. Some agreed that community was a need; others argued that the goals of community could be realized even in a liberal society. Their main concern was that by undermining the liberal system of rights and the liberal policy of neutrality on questions of the common good, communitarians were opening the door to majoritarian intolerance, the perpetuation of conservative beliefs and practices and a potentially tyrannical insistence on conformism.

One feature of this debate that particularly struck me was the narrow and impoverished concept of community that was being employed on both sides. Some communitarian theorists – Alasdair MacIntyre (1984) and Michael Sandel (1982), in particular – talked about family and neighbourhood as primary attachments that served to locate individual selves within the community. But others, both liberals and communitarians, strongly objected to placing so much value on small group attachments that flaunt the banner of 'tradition'; these solidarities, they said, were more often than not the means through which socially conservative, patriarchal and illiberal practices were maintained and transmitted. There have also been movements, in political writing as well as in activism, for community-based participatory politics in local neighbourhoods, both urban and rural, in different countries of Europe and North America. These movements have been inspired by populist or anarchist ideologies of both left and right wing varieties. One of their principal characteristics, however, has been their marginality, often a preferred marginality, to the main institutions and practices of political life in those countries.

Looking back on the liberal-communitarian debate, the only form of the community that seems to have found a large measure of approval was the political community of the nation. Michael Walzer (1983) argued that the nation-state was the one community which could give every person within a certain territory the same status as citizen and also satisfy every person's need to participate in the social distribution of goods. This gave rise to charges that by emphasizing uniform citizenship, Walzer was implicitly arguing against immigration and cultural diversity within the nation. David Miller (1989), who has recently attempted to construct a theory of socialist politics in industrially advanced Western democracies, also argued that the aspirations of community were most feasibly satisfied in the citizens' membership of a nation.

It would appear then that Western political theory does not deny the empirical fact that most individuals, even in industrially advanced liberal democracies, lead their lives within an inherited network of social attachments that could be described as community. It also recognizes to a large extent that the community fulfils a certain moral condition for an effective and satisfying sense of participation by people in a social collective. Nevertheless, there is a strong feeling that not all communities are worthy of approval in modern political life. In particular, attachments that seem to emphasize the inherited, the primordial, the parochial or the traditional are regarded by most theorists as smacking of conservative and intolerant practices and hence as inimical to the values of modern citizenship. The political community that seems to find the largest measure of approval is the modern nation that grants equality and freedom to all citizens irrespective of biological or cultural difference. But in this respect too, there is a recent spate of criticism that attacks the idea of the nation as inherently intolerant, patriarchal and suspicious of diversity and argues that the time has come to develop post-national forms of political solidarity. This is an interesting development, but I will not have the opportunity to consider it in this chapter.

Community in the East

Turning to the idea of community in the non-Western parts of the world, one notices a similar opposition in most of the theoretical literature between community as the relic of pre-modern tradition and large, universalist and impersonal political identities as the hallmark of modernity. Guided by this modernizing propensity, much of the recent history of non-Western societies has been written as a progressivist narrative of the evolution from small, local and primordial community attachments to large secular solidarities such as that of the nation. In the era of colonial rule, colonial writings usually described these societies as a collection of backward *gemeinschaften* lacking the internal dynamic to transform themselves into modern industrial nations. Nationalist thinkers challenged the assumption of historical incapacity but agreed that their own project was to overcome the numerous community attachments and build up the nation as the most powerful and legitimate claimant for political loyalty.

There is, however, an interesting twist to the way in which this nationalist project of modernity was formulated as one that was different from Western modernity. While non-Western nationalists agreed that many of the traditional institutions and practices in their societies needed to be thoroughly changed for them to become modern, they also insisted that there were several elements in their tradition that were distinctively national, different from the Western, but nevertheless entirely consistent with the modern. Borrowing the categories of orientalist or colonial thought, they frequently posed this difference as one between Western materialism, individualism and disregard for traditional values and Eastern spiritualism, community solidarity and respect for tradition. In doing this, nationalist writers picked out the liberal individualist strand in modern social theory as the one that was most characteristic of the West and often exaggerated its features to the point of caricature. But in posing the contrast between individualism in the West and communitarian values in the East and insisting that the latter represented a better, or at least more appropriate, version of modernity for non-Western countries, nationalist thinking in effect played out the same arguments that we encountered in the liberal-communitarian debate. Indeed, one still hears these arguments as part of the official ideologies of many Asian and African states – arguments that are sometimes used with complete cynicism to defend authoritarian regimes and policies. It should be obvious, therefore, that having been born in an intellectual climate in which these arguments were the staple of everyday conversation, I found little in the debate of the 1980s that could hold my attention.

The nationalist posing of the question as one between Western individualism and Eastern communitarianism did not provide any new theoretical answers regarding the place of community in modern political life. On the contrary, just as there were, among non-Western nationalists, advocates of community attachments as the repository of social solidarity, moral value and national tradition, so were there critics who condemned those attachments as signs of parochial backwardness, feudal and patriarchal bondage and the failure of the nation to attain the true heights of modern political association. The theoretical terms had been set by the categories of Western social theory; apparently, all that non-Western thinkers could do was fill up those categories with a different cultural content and then play out the same arguments in a different national arena.

I could give many examples from the history of modern political thinking in India, a field with which I have some familiarity. The setting up of the contrast between individualism in the West and community in the East is as old as modern Indian nationalism. When Indian travelers visited England in the late nineteenth century, they marveled at the achievements of Western science and technology and fervently wished to emulate them in their own countries. But they were also appalled by the conditions in which the poor lived in the industrial cities and were convinced that this could never happen in India where community ties would ensure that not even the poorest were reduced to such a degraded state. The contrast was present in the more basic dichotomy between Western materialism and Eastern spiritualism which was central to the construction of non-Western nationalist ideology. Western materialism was easily connected to an individualist way of life and criticized for its lack of regard for social obligations, mutual dependence and the solidarity of the social whole. This limitation of Western modernity was sought to be rectified by what was claimed to be the spiritual aspect of culture in which the Eastern traditions of community life were said to hold out many lessons for the modern world.

In the history of Indian politics, Gandhi's intervention in the 1920s produced one of the most remarkable trends in both political thinking and activism that extended the possibilities of this argument to its limits. In recent years, Ashis Nandy has reworked the Gandhian position with much ingenuity. His principal argument is that for more than a hundred years, with the advance of nationalism and the institutions of the modern state, there has occurred in countries such as India a tussle between the forces of modern individualism and those of traditional primordialities. What is highlighted in liberal economic and political theory is the bright side of modern individualism with its emphasis on the rapid creation of wealth and general prosperity and the free flowering of the individual personality. What is ignored is the underside of modern individualism – the callous impersonality and massification of market-driven societies that destroy age-old institutions of sociability and community living without putting anything in their place. Contrary to the beliefs of the modernizers, traditional community structures are not simple and inflexible: primordialities are multilayered, the self is open-ended, adjustment and compromise are ethical norms. Left to themselves, Nandy argues, these traditional community structures have more effective civilizational resources than the institutions of the modern state to resolve disputes, tolerate difference and allow for the development of a better adjusted and more accommodative personality. The crucial institutions here are those that belong to the 'little traditions' of local community life which are the products of many centuries of coping with social change. The difficulty is that the ruling elites in non-Western countries have increasingly surrendered to the intellectual and procedural sway of the modern state and have used its capacity for the efficient deployment of force to break down the supposedly retrograde and parochial institutions of traditional community life. At this time, Nandy thinks, the odds are overwhelmingly stacked against the little traditions as the modem nation continues to be built 'on the ruins of one's civilizational selfhood' (Nandy et al. 1995: xi); the community, if not defeated, 'is certainly in decline' (ibid., 203).

The defence of community institutions in Gandhian thinking has had a fair degree of influence on movements of resistance by weak and marginalized sections of the people threatened by the onward march of modernization. In particular, its emphasis on indigenous cultural modes of collective action has encouraged the development of many innovative forms of campaign and mobilization even in the arena of modern political organizations. The mass movements of the Indian National Congress under the leadership of Gandhi in the last three decades of British colonial rule are well known examples (Rudolph and Rudolph 1967). But similar examples of political mobilization shaped by indigenous cultural forms that are quite different from those made familiar by the history of modern politics in the West can be found in many countries of Asia and Africa in both colonial and post-colonial periods. These examples constitute essential materials for a history of the domestication of the modern state in non-Western societies.

In theoretical terms, however, I am not persuaded that arguments of the Gandhian type, including their recent modified versions such as those proposed by Ashis Nandy (Nandy 1983, 1987, 1989, 1995), can make any contribution that could take the debate between individualism and communitarianism beyond the apparent impasse in which it has found itself in Western political theory. The identification of all modern institutions of state and politics with the ideology of Western individualism and their conflict with the traditional communities of the East collapses the opposition once more into the familiar terms of modernity versus traditionalism, with the exception that this time it is tradition and primordiality which are privileged over modernity. True, the Gandhian position has been able to gain considerable tactical leverage in its struggles against the depredations of the modernizing state by placing itself outside the intellectual and institutional arena of modernity. But since it refuses to acknowledge its own role as a constituent part of the politics engendered and ordered by the presence of the modern state in non-Western societies, it chooses to end every argument with a stubborn gesture of rejecting the modern state altogether. By doing this, it also refuses to make the unique experiences of modem politics in the non-Western world a constituent part of the task of rethinking modern political theory itself.

Capital and community

That is the task which, I think, faces the non-Western political theorist: to find an adequate conceptual language to describe the non-Western career of the modern state not as a distortion or lack, which is what inevitably happens in a modernization narrative, but as the history of different modernities shaped by practices and institutions that the universalist claims of Western political theory have failed to encompass. But before I come to the implications of this task, I need to dwell a little on that other lack – the incomplete universalism of modern political theory.

In an earlier work, I have attempted to state what I think is the main reason for the poor theorization of the concept of community in modern social thought (Chatterjee 1990, 1993: Chapter 11). Western political theory since the Enlightenment has been organised around the idea of the free and equal individual as the locus of productive energy, subjective rights and cultural creativity in modern society. The power of this abstract idea has been accompanied by the equally powerful historical process of the dismantling of feudal as well as absolutist institutions in Western Europe and the release of productive capital and productive labour on an unprecedented scale. The conceptual device of abstract liberty and equality which gave shape to the universal rights of the citizen was crucial not only for undermining precapitalist practices that restricted individual mobility and choice to traditional confines defined by birth and status but also, as the young Karl Marx noted 150 years ago, for separating the abstract domain of right from the actual domain of life in civil society (see especially Marx 1975). In legal-political theory, the rights of the citizen were unrestricted by race, religion, ethnicity or class (by the early twentieth century, the same rights would also be made available to women), but this did not mean the abolition of actual distinctions between men (and women) in civil society. Rather, the universalism of the theory of rights both presuppposed and enabled a new ordering of power relations in society based precisely on those distinctions of class, race, religion, gender, etc. At the same time, the emancipatory promise held out by the idea of universal equal rights has acted as a constant source of theoretical critique of actual civil society in the last two centuries and has propelled numerous struggles to change unequal and unjust social differences of race, religion, ethnicity, class or gender.

In these transactions between theory and actuality, community attachments have been seen as belonging to the mundane lives of actual civil societies – obdurate remnants of their precapitalist pasts or practical instruments for managing social differences on the ground. They have been regarded as objects of inquiry by empirical sociologists, not of philosophical speculation by political theorists. In the mirror of theory, community attachments have always appeared as restrictions on universal citizenship as well as on the universality of capital. To the extent that the universality of the state has been limited by the existence of nations (that is to say, the universality of the state and of capital has had to reveal itself in the existence of many nation-states and many national economies), the nation is the only form of community that has sometimes found a place, and that too a fairly marginal one, in the high theory of political obligation.

As a matter of fact, the emergence of mass democracies in the advanced industrial countries of the West in the twentieth century has produced a new distinction between the domain of theory built around the idea of the citizen and the domain of policy inhabited not by citizens but by populations. Unlike the concept of the citizen, the concept of population is wholly descriptive and empirical: it does not carry a normative burden. Populations are identifiable, classifiable and describable by empirical or behavioural criteria and are amenable to statistical techniques such as censuses and sample surveys. Unlike the concept of citizen which carries the ethical connotation of participation in the sovereignty of the state, the concept of population makes available to government functionaries a set of rationally manipulable instruments for reaching large sections of the inhabitants of a country as the targets of their 'policies' – economic policy, administrative policy, law and even political mobilization. Indeed, as Michel Foucault has pointed out, a major characteristic of the contemporary regime of power is a certain 'governmentalization of the state' (see, in particular, Foucault 1991). This regime secures legitimacy not by the participation of citizens in matters of state but by claiming to provide for the well-being of the population. Its mode of reasoning is not deliberative openness but rather an instrumental notion of costs and benefits. Its apparatus is not the republican assembly but an elaborate network of surveillance through which information is collected on every aspect of the life of the population that is to be looked after. It is not surprising that in the course of the present century, ideas of participatory citizenship that were so much a part of the Enlightenment notion of politics have fast retreated before the triumphant advance of governmental technologies that have promised to deliver more well-being to more people at less cost. Indeed, one might say that the actual political history of capital has long spilled over the normative confines of liberal political theory to go out and conquer the world through its governmental technologies.

In countries of Asia and Africa, where the career of the modern state has been foreshortened, ideas of republican citizenship have sometimes accompanied the politics of national liberation. But without exception, they have been overtaken by the developmental state which has promised to end poverty and backwardness by adopting appropriate policies of economic growth and social reform. With varying degrees of success, and in some cases with disastrous failure, the post-colonial states have deployed the latest governmental technologies to promote the well-being of their populations, often prompted and aided by international and non-governmental organizations. In adopting these technical strategies of modernization and development, communities have often entered the field of knowledge about populations – as convenient descriptive categories for classifying groups of people into suitable targets for administrative, legal, economic or electoral policy. In many cases, classificatory criteria used by colonial governmental regimes have continued into the post-colonial era, shaping the forms of both political demands and developmental policy. Thus, caste and religion in India, ethnic groups in South-east Asia and tribes in Africa have remained the dominant criteria for identifying communities among the population as objects of policy. So much so that a huge ethnographic survey recently undertaken by a government agency in India has actually identified and described a total of exactly 4,635 communities that are supposed to comprise the population of that country (Singh 1995).

I am convinced that the attempt by modern governmental technologies to classify populations into determinate and enumerable communities is a telling sign of the poverty of modern social theory. It is a commonplace in the descriptive ethnography of the non-Western world to find that the community is contextually defined, that its boundaries are fuzzy, that a particular community identification does not exhaust the various layers of selfhood of a person, that it makes little sense to ask a community member how many of them there are in the world (Kaviraj 1992). And yet, it is this contextuality and fuzziness that legal-administrative classifications and statistical techniques of enumeration must erase in order to make populations amenable to governmental policy. What is lost in the process is the richness of meaning and the strategic flexibility afforded by the cultural repertoire of a people to handle social differences. This is the loss that writers such as Ashis Nandy bemoan. As I have said before, contemporary technologies of government regard communities as so much demographic material, to be manipulated instrumentally. They are not objects of philosophical or moral inquiry. In theory – to put it, if I may, in a nutshell – capital and community are antithetical.

The contradiction has been highlighted in an interesting way in the recent discussions over the work of Robert Putnam and his associates on governmental performance in northern and southern Italy (Putnam, Leonardi and Nanetti 1993). Two concepts have been proposed by Putnam to explain why governments seem to work better in certain regions of northern Italy. These concepts are civic community and social capital. In a civic community, according to Putnam, citizens have equal rights and obligations, participate actively in public affairs as well as in a dense network of civic associations and bear feelings of respect, trust and tolerance towards their fellow citizens. Where civic community is strongly rooted, democratic government tends to perform better. Why? Because civic community fosters the creation of social capital. Social capital, says Putnam following a suggestion by James Coleman, consists of organizational features such as trust, norms of reciprocity and networks of civic engagement that facilitate co-ordinated social action (Coleman 1990). Unlike conventional capital which is ordinarily a private good, social capital is a public good. It is not the personal property of those who benefit from it. Indeed, social capital, unlike other forms of capital, is mainly produced as a by-product of other social activities. Thus, the more intensive the network of civic associations engaged in various collective activities and the stronger the norms of reciprocity between the members of these associations, the greater the stock of social capital. Indeed, social capital is inculcated above all through socialization and civic education as well as by collective sanctions.

The examples Putnam cites of the working of social capital are, however, drawn from studies of rotating credit arrangements among peasants or urban workers in Indonesia, Nigeria and Mexico. The chief characteristic of these institutions is that they are able to create credit mechanisms in situations where conventional credit markets based on capitalist calculations cannot work. This is done, Putnam says, by pledging social capital, i.e., the stock of mutual trust built up through other social interactions and networks. Thus, Javanese peasants operate local mechanisms of mutual help based on traditional but concrete practices of interdependence in the exchange of labour, capital and goods in a variety of social activities. The urban poor in Mexico City have developed a whole array of credit associations based on reciprocity and mutual trust. These institutions are much more than merely economic; they are mechanisms that strengthen the solidarity of the community.

It seems to me that the concept of community is being invoked here to supply what does not properly belong to the concept of capital. The examples of credit associations are particularly telling. Anyone familiar with the ethnographic literature on non-Western agrarian or nomadic-pastoral societies will immediately recognize how deeply these exchange practices are implicated in the entire structure of material interaction and symbolic meaning that characterizes those societies. Such practices would be integral elements of the 'traditional' lives of those communities and, more often than not, they are likely to be destroyed by the advance of 'modern' institutions of capitalist production and exchange. When they survive, they do so on the margins of the modernized sectors, among populations and in activities that have still not been fully absorbed into the network of capital. Why are these examples that belong to the older communitarian histories of non-Western societies being mobilized here in the cause of political institutions in modern Western democracies?

My answer is that by adding 'social' to capital and making that the motive force of 'civic' community, capital is being made to do what it has always failed to do, namely, ground the social institutions of a modern capitalist economy in community. The description of the civic community as presented by Putnam is a restatement of the manifold virtues of participatory citizenship to which the communitarian theorists still sing their praises. Putnam's attempt is to show that a culture of active citizenship of this kind is empirically associated with well-functioning democratic systems. But in trying to establish this connection in theoretical terms, he is led into the same impasse where the liberal-communitarian debate has been stuck. To explain why the civic community only exists in some regions of northern Italy and not in others, Putnam has to move into a historical investigation going back to the thirteenth century. He must then say that the civic community can only function where it already exists as a part of historical tradition. On the other hand, the examples he cites of the working of social capital come from traditions that belong to places – Indonesia, Nigeria or Mexico – which not even the most starry-eyed modernization theorist would name as havens of good democratic governance. In other words, while modern Western political institutions appear to need a grounding in community in order to be successful, the only contemporary examples through which community can be made sense of, have to be borrowed from non-modern and non-Western cultural traditions. It is not surprising, therefore, that Putnam's work has come under fire from critics who have found it unduly pessimistic, because it suggests that good democratic government cannot be established by institutional modernization unless civic community already exists as part of the historical tradition. He has also been criticized for being unduly romantic in his portrayal of the associational life of the community. And finally, it has been pointed out that, contrary to Putnam's rosy picture, community life is usually conservative and resistant to change (Margaret Levi 1996). Traditionalism, romanticism, conservatism: all of these, you will remember, were familiar epithets used by liberal individualists against the communitarians. Evidently, we have not moved one step ahead of that debate.

Community and new institutions of the state

To give a sense of what political theory must cope with in countries where the history of the modern state is short, let me present some findings of a study of community-formation among poor migrants in an Indian city (Sen 1992). These migrants form a group of about 1,500 people living in a row of shanties perilously close to a railway track on the south-eastern fringes of Calcutta, not far from where I live and work. The land on which they have built their shacks belongs to the state-owned railways. They are, therefore, illegal squatters on public land. The settlement has grown here since the early 1950s. The migrants have come from different rural areas of southern Bengal and some from Bangladesh. Since they migrated from different places at different times, the settlers had no prior network of attachments given to them as a collective. The community, such as it exists here, was built from scratch.

The overwhelming reason why they have acted as a collective is the very survival of their habitation. Ever since the emergence of the settlement some 40 years ago, there have been periodic attempts by the railway authorities to evict them. These attempts have been resisted, as the settlers will proudly tell a visitor, by the concerted efforts of the community as a whole. The most common metaphor by which the settlers speak about their community is that of a family. They do not talk of the shared interests of the members of an association, but of the more compelling bonds of a shared kinship. Nevertheless, there are concrete associational forms through which the collective functions. The most important of these is a welfare association which has its own office where it runs a small library and a medical clinic and which acts as the centre of community activity. It organizes sports and recreation activities and community festivals (including religious ones) and resolves disputes (even family disputes). It is also the body through which the community negotiates with the outside world – with government agencies such as the railways, the police or the municipal authorities, with voluntary agencies offering welfare and developmental services, with political parties and leaders.

But apart from this formal body, there are other networks of community support that are vital in securing work or financial help. Many men here work as unskilled labourers in the construction business and depend on mutual contacts to find work. Most women in the settlement work as domestic help in middle-class houses in the neighbourhood for which again mutual references are important. Caste and village networks are sometimes activated for negotiating marriages, but everyone agrees that these obligations are much less stringent here than in the village. Although all members of the settlement see themselves as poor labourers, some are less poor than others, and in fact some live as tenants in rooms let out by those who originally built the shacks. Most are unhappy with the conditions in which they live in the settlement and would love to move out. A few who have had the chance have indeed moved to other places in the city. But most stay on, struggling collectively 'as a single family' with their uncertain status as illegal squatters.

There are several conceptual problems raised by these findings. First, it is difficult to think of the collective form evolved by the settlers as a civic association. The association itself springs from a collective violation of property laws and civic regulations. The state cannot recognize the rationale for the association's existence as having the same validity as that of other economic and cultural associations of citizens pursuing more legitimate objectives. On the other hand, given the fact that this is only one of numerous other groups of population in Indian cities whose very livelihood or habitation is premised on violations of state law and civic regulations, the state cannot altogether ignore the collective claims of the association in making its own policies. Thus, state agencies such as the police or the railways and non-governmental development agencies deal with the collective body of squatters not as a body of citizens but as convenient instruments for the administration or welfare to marginal and underprivileged population groups.

Second, although the squatters accept that their occupation of public land is both illegal and contrary to the requirements of good civic life, they make a claim to a habitation and a livelihood as a matter of right. State agencies, on the other hand, are prepared to concede that this claim has a moral force that should be borne in mind when carrying out welfare policies but are strongly opposed to recognizing it as a justiciable right since, given the paucity of resources at the disposal of the state, it cannot be effectively delivered to the whole population of the country. Since places of residence and sources of livelihood are likely to remain in short supply in the foreseeable future, a general and principled recognition of the claim, as opposed to a contextual and instrumental one, say state officials, would only act as an invitation to further violations of public property and civic regulations.

Third, when the squatters demand the right to livelihood and habitation, they demand it as a collective right which they claim belongs to them as a community. This impinges upon a question that has vexed the modern state in post-colonial countries, especially those that have been modeled on Anglo-American constitutional procedures: can citizens have rights that belong to them by virtue of their membership of particular communities, defined by ethnic, religious, linguistic or other criteria? Many states have recognized such rights for specific purposes, creating numerous legal anomalies and a theoretical defence of the practice that is hesitant and shamefaced. That equal homogeneous citizenship ought to be the norm seems to be conceded; current practices that do not conform to this norm are seen as deviations produced by colonial legacy or social backwardness or cultural exceptionalism.

Finally, the site on which our community of squatters have managed to conduct their struggle for survival is not that of a civil society of citizens dealing with a state in whose sovereignty they participate but rather that of a political society where claims and benefits can be negotiated between governmental agencies responsible for administering welfare and groups of population that count according to calculations of political efficacy. The settlers, therefore, have to pick their way through a terrain where they have no standing as citizens; rather, their strategies must exploit, on the one hand, the political obligations that governments have of looking after poor and underprivileged sections of the population and, on the other, the moral rhetoric of a community striving to build a decent social life under extremely harsh conditions. These strategies, far from being inward-looking and isolationist, actually involve making a large array of connections outside the community – with other groups in similar situations, with more privileged and influential groups with whom the community has social or economic exchanges (such as employers or middle-class neighbours), with government functionaries, with political leaders and parties, and so on. These are the means through which the community has found a place in urban political society. It is by no means a secure place, for it is entirely dependent on the community's ability to operate within a field of strategic politics. Many of the connections it has established with other forces in political society seem to resemble the supposedly traditional forms of patronage and clientilism but – and this is my claim regarding the ineluctable modernity of this political experience – they are enmeshed in an entirely new set of governmental practices that are the functions only of the modern state in the late twentieth century. The most significant feature of the survival strategies adopted in the last few decades by thousands of marginal groups such as the one I have talked about is the way in which the imaginative power of a traditional structure of community, including its fuzziness and capacity to invent relations of kinship, has been wedded to the modern emancipatory rhetoric of autonomy and equal rights. These strategies, I am suggesting, are not available within the liberal space of the associations of civil society transacting business with a constitutional state. For the majority of people in postcolonial societies, the normative status of the virtuous citizen will remain infinitely deferred until such time as they can be provided with the basic material and cultural prerequisites of membership of civil society. Until the arrival of that liberal millennium, however, they can only deal with a governmental system with the resources they can muster in political society. As we have seen before, community has a very tenuous place in the Western liberal theory of civil society and state; in the new political societies of the East, communities are some of the most active agents of political practice.

Undoubtedly, the possibilities of strategic politics by numerous groups representing perhaps a majority of the population in India are greatly facilitated by the existence in that country of an electoral democracy and a liberal constitutional system. However,

I have little doubt that other groups of population in other Asian and African countries also adopt strategies of a similar sort to deal with governmental systems which, in this globalized age, tend to function largely through similar procedures and with similar technologies. The most significant feature of this strategic politics of the communities is the increasingly overriding importance of notions such as autonomy and representation for which reason, I think, it is entirely valid to see in this politics a desire for democratization. The important differences of this politics with the classical history of democracy in the West are, first, that autonomy and representation are being claimed on behalf not only of individuals but of communities and, second, that these democratic claims are being made in relation to a state whose governmental functions already encompass the bulk of the population well before the latter have been socialized into the institutions of civil society. The politics of democratization must therefore be carried out not in the classical transactions between state and civil society but in the much less well-defined, legally ambiguous, contextually and strategically demarcated terrain of political society.

Conclusion: the task for twenty-first century Indian political thought

This, I am suggesting, is one of the principal tasks of Indian political theory today: to provide a conceptual map of the emerging practices of the new political societies of the East. The normative models of Western political theory have, more often than not, only served to show the non-Western practices as backward or deviant. What we need is a different conceptualization of the subject of political practice – neither as abstract and un-encumbered individual selves nor as manipulable objects of governmental policy, but rather as concrete selves necessarily acting within multiple networks of collective obligations and solidarities to work out strategies of coping with, resisting or using to their advantage the vast array of technologies of power deployed by the modern state. In the received history of Western political theory, as I have said before, capital and community have been antithetical. When the new history of Eastern modernity gets written in the twenty-first century, perhaps capital will at last find a resting place in community. In the course of that journey, political theory as we have known it for so long will also get rewritten.

Note

1 This is an abridged and revised version of the article that appeared as 'Community in the East', *Economic and Political Weekly*, 33(6), 1998.

References

Avineri, Shlomo and de-Shalit, Avner (eds) (1992) *Communitarianism and Individualism*, Oxford: Oxford University Press.

Chatterjee, Partha (1990) 'A response to Taylor's Modes of civil society', *Public Culture*, 3(1): 119–32.

—— (1993) *The Nation and Its Fragments: Colonial and Postcolonial Histories*, Princeton, NJ: Princeton University Press.

Coleman, James S. (1990) *Foundations of Social Theory*, Cambridge, MA: Harvard University Press.

Foucault, Michel (1991) 'Governmentality', in Graham Burchell, Colin Gordon and Peter Miller (eds) *The Foucault Effect: Studies in Governmentality*, Chicago: University of Chicago Press, pp. 87–104.

Kaviraj, Sudipta (1992) 'The imaginary institution of India', in Partha Chatterjee and Gyanendra Pandey (eds) *Subaltern Studies VII*, Delhi: Oxford University Press, pp. 1–39.

Levi, Margaret (1996) 'Social and unsocial capital: a review essay of Robert Putnam's *Making Democracy Work'*, *Politics and Society*, 24(1): 45–55.

MacIntyre, Alasdair (1984) *After Virtue: A Study in Moral Theory*, Notre Dame, IN: University of Notre Dame Press.

Marx, Karl (1975) 'On the Jewish question' [1843], in Karl Marx and Frederick Engels, *Collected Works*, vol. 3, Moscow: Progress Publishers, pp. 146–74.

Miller, David (1989) *Market, State and Community*, Oxford: Oxford University Press.

Nandy, Ashis (1983) *The Intimate Enemy: Loss and Recovery of Self under Colonialism*, Delhi: Oxford University Press.

—— (1987) *Traditions, Tyranny and Utopias: Essays in the Politics of Awareness*, Delhi: Oxford University Press.

—— (1989) 'The political culture of the Indian state', *Daedalus*, 118(4): 1–26.

—— (1995) *The Savage Freud and Other Essays on Possible and Retrievable Selves*, Delhi: Oxford University Press.

Nandy, Ashis; Trivedy, Shikha; Mayaram, Shail and Yagnik, Achyut (1995) *Creating a Nationality: The Ramjanmabhumi Movement and Fear of the Self*, Delhi: Oxford University Press.

Putnam, Robert D.; Leonardi, Robert and Nanetti, Raffaella Y. (1993) *Making Democracy Work: Civic Traditions in Modern Italy*, Princeton, NJ: Princeton University Press.

Rudolph, Lloyd D. and Rudolph, Susanne H. (1967) *The Modernity of Tradition: Political Development in India*, Chicago: University of Chicago Press.

Sandel, Michael (ed.) (1984) *Liberalism and its Critics*, New York: New York University Press.

—— (1982) *Liberalism and the Limits of Justice*, Cambridge: Cambridge University Press.

Sen, Asok (1992) 'Life and labour in a squatters' colony', Occasional Paper 138, October, Centre for Studies in Social Sciences, Calcutta.

Singh, K. Suresh (ed.) (1995) *People of India*, 43 vols, Calcutta: Anthropological Survey of India.

Walzer, Michael (1983) *Spheres of Justice*, New York: Basic Books.

Index